Learning
to Be Modern

NEW PERSPECTIVES ON ASIAN HISTORY

Series Editors   Ainslie Embree and Edward Farmer

Learning to Be Modern: Japanese Political Discourse on Education,
Byron K. Marshall

Merchants and Faith: Muslim Commerce and Culture in the Indian Ocean,
Patricia Risso

LEARNING TO BE MODERN

Japanese Political Discourse on Education

BYRON K. MARSHALL

University of Minnesota

WESTVIEW PRESS
Boulder • San Francisco • Oxford

Copyright ©1994 by Westview Press, Inc.

Published in 1994 in the United States of America by Westview Press, Inc., 5500 Central Avenue, Boulder, Colorado 80301-2877, and in the United Kingdom by Westview Press, 12 Hid's Copse Road, Cumnor Hill, Oxford OX2 9JJ.

Library of Congress Cataloging-in-Publication Data
Marshall, Byron K.
Learning to be modern : Japanese political discourse on education /
Byron K. Marshall.
    p. cm. — (New perspectives on Asian history)
Includes bibliographical references and index.
    ISBN 0-8133-1891-2 (hardcover). — ISBN 0-8133-1892-0 (pbk.)
    1. Education—Japan—History. 2. Educational change—Japan.
3. Schools—Centralization—Japan. 4. Elite (Social sciences)—
Education—Japan. 5. Nationalism and education—Japan. I. Title.
II. Series.
LA1311.M29 1994
370'.952—dc20   95-5182
                                                                                          CIP

Printed and bound in the United States of America

⊗   The paper used in this publication meets the requirements
      of the American National Standard for Permanence of Paper
      for Printed Library Materials Z39.48-1984.

10   9   8   7   6   5   4   3   2   1

For Dorothy Munkberg and her extended family

Contents

Tables

Figures

Preface

Anyone who attempts to synthesize a great deal of scholarship by others faces the conundrum of acknowledging sources without overburdening the whole with more scholarly apparatus than is warranted by the modest end product. In the Notes section, therefore, I have most often listed only English secondary sources on the assumption that these best serve the great majority of my readers. Those others who read Japanese can consult the fuller list of sources in the Bibliography. Direct quotations, of course, are referenced in the conventional manner, but unless the translation is my own I usually have not cited the original Japanese source. The majority of the translations are not mine: As a rule it seems sounder procedure to rely upon the work of those who have greater expertise with an individual Japanese voice or a specific set of documents than to retranslate. In the case of the names of government offices, political societies, and the like, I have throughout used English translations (not necessarily official ones) and included the original Japanese in index entries.

In Japan, individual names are normally given with the family name first, and that practice is followed here except when individuals have indicated that they wish to follow Western order, as in English-language publications. The vowels in Japanese are pronounced roughly similar to those in Italian or Spanish, but in order to indicate elongated vowel sounds in romanization it is common to use ō, ū, Ō. This is done here except where it involves a well-known place name—for example, Tokyo or Osaka—or the original is romanized without the diacritics.

And a word on sexist language: There is little use of pronouns in Japanese, and equivalents for English pronouns and other gendered words frequently are neutral. Nevertheless, some translators have used "he" for "he or she" and "his" for "his or hers" and these are quoted as found.

Finally, I would like to express my gratitude to the following: the Graduate School at the University of Minnesota for financial aid; Ted Farmer and Peter Kracht for having early faith in the project; Deborah Lynes, Sarah Tomasek, and the production staff at Westview Press for their professionalism; my in-laws to whom the book is dedicated; and to my wife for everything else.

Byron K. Marshall

Introduction

Basic Premises

This study of Japanese educational history begins with two primary propositions. First, contrary to myth, Japan is not a single, monolithic culture persistently characterized by harmony and consensus—a misunderstanding that still forms one of the most pernicious obstacles to understanding both past and present. Rather, Japan is a nation of complex subcultures and has a plurality of traditions that have undergone considerable change over time.

Second, nowhere is this past better seen than in the repeated controversies about schooling over the past 150 years. One of the swiftest entrées to understanding any modern society is through listening to political discourse about education. Power struggles and ideological controversies about how to socialize and enculturate youth are at the heart of the processes by which a society is continually recreated, affording the historian some of the most audible record of those processes over time. Japanese commentators today often speak of three educational revolutions. The first refers to the late nineteenth century Meiji Restoration period, the second to the mid–twentieth century American Occupation period, and the third to the more recent efforts at yet another set of sweeping reforms. To comprehend these efforts at a third "revolution" it is essential to explore the history of the first two. Many if not most of the major participants in contemporary debates over educational issues have been quite conscious of the past and their discourse is often incomprehensible without knowing something of that history.[1]

Yet, despite this and the great international interest in the role of education in Japan's rise to a position of world influence, there is no satisfactory history of modern Japanese education presently available in English. The last major undertaking was three decades ago by the gifted sociologist Herbert Passin. But his *Society and Education in Japan* is now, unfortunately, both out of print and, inevitably, outdated. Since Passin wrote, there has been produced a considerable new body of scholarship in English as well as Japanese. I have mined some of that scholarship seeking to provide a synthesis more germane to the 1990s.

It should be clear at the outset, however, that my approach differs from Passin's. I have been less interested in such comparative educational topics as the internal organization of schools, innovations in pedagogy, or the professional training of teachers. These are featured only where they have become central issues in the national political debates. More important, whereas Passin was working within a modernization paradigm that conflated chronology with progress, I have structured my narrative around contention over three overarching characteristics identified by the reformers in the American Occupation as centralization, elitism, and nationalism.[2] *Centralization* refers to the role of the prewar government in limiting the popular control of school at the local level. *Elitism* is shorthand for privileging academic merit at the expense of egalitarianism as well as discriminating openly on the basis of gender. *Nationalism*—or at least an ultranationalism that asserts a Japanese cultural uniqueness—has been seen as the root cause of aggression abroad and suppression at home.

These were not issues limited to the immediate postwar period. They had been present in the first education "revolution" in the nineteenth century and they continue to be contested in the 1990s. *Politically* they involve fundamental questions about power: Where, how, and who is to make the critical decisions about what is taught by whom to whom? Are such decisions made by the members of an egalitarian community engaged in open dialogue? by local notables conferring only among themselves? by an authoritarian elite administering through a centralized hierarchy? or by an elected parliament representing regional and class interests? *Socially*, access to formal schooling and its outcomes has in Japan as elsewhere been closely correlated with social status derived from class, gender, region, and/or ethnic membership. To what extent is schooling to be accessible to all individuals and groups on an equal basis? Is social status to be dependent upon achievement in educational competition or is access to schooling to be determined by gender and family income? *Culturally*, it is in the contested discourse about "politically correct" values in the textbooks and classrooms that a society's normative assumptions and hegemonic ideals are most clearly revealed at any given moment in its history. Is priority to be given to the individual or the collectivity, and if the latter, which collectivity (family? community? race? the state?)? How are citizens to relate to one another? to the past? to the future? What gives this nation its cultural identity and distinguishes it from all others? Or are values universal among humankind? In *economic* terms, the role schools play in creating human capital is perhaps the least understood of the variables that make industrial development possible, although the Ministry of Education expressed what has long been the prevailing view in Japan when it stated, "One of the basic factors in achieving such national development has been the expansion and redirection of education."[3] But to what extent should schools be merely training grounds for future workers?

Viewed from these angles, then, the educational system can teach much about such competing polarities as equality versus merit, individual creativity versus team cooperation, uniformity versus innovation, cosmopolitan universalism versus cultural exceptionalism. Over the past 150 years, the Japanese have attempted in their national decisions to balance these competing polarities. Since their attempts have dealt with dilemmas endemic to all school systems, it is hoped that this account may find an audience not only among those concerned with Japan but those interested in the politics of education everywhere in industrialized societies.

Limits on Focus

In the quest to sharpen the focus, I have consciously limited the scope in a number of ways. First and foremost, this is a study concerned with formal education in schools for youth—public and private, including military and other vocational schools—but not such other forms of education as apprenticeships, company training programs, and private tutoring or the socialization that takes place in youth groups. Historians of education in Europe and North America have demonstrated that what is novel about the modern period is the emergence of institutionalized schooling as the dominant means of training and enculturating youth. Much emphasis has sometimes been placed on Japan as a late developer. As true as such a generalization may be for industrial technology or military weaponry, in the sphere of modern schooling it is important to remember just how new a phenomenon modern educational systems were in Western Europe and North America.[4] One of the most interesting aspects of this is the relative balance of vocational training in the public schools versus that in private firms. But the Japanese case is so complex that the reader seriously interested in this subject is advised to start with one of two specialized studies: Dore and Sako, *How the Japanese Learn to Work,* or Levine and Kawada, *Human Resources in Japanese Industrial Development.*

I have also consciously chosen here to privilege the conflicts *among* the dominant classes and *between* these elites and counterelites at the national level. The latter group includes political activists and intellectuals who have often claimed and sometimes have actually spoken for the populace but have almost always been distinctly separate from the common people. In other words, in focusing on relations between the state and the school, on the politics of schooling, and on the words and deeds at the national level, I have paid most attention to those who possessed sufficient power or status to play a leading role in the conflicts over the educational system. Of course, this is not to assign moral or even cultural superiority to these actors. But in the politics of schooling over the past 150 years in Japan the average rural cultivator and urban worker have articulated their priorities clearly only episodically and it is not until after World War II that the Japanese citizen was able to effectively influence national politics through the ballot box.

Among other shortcomings, there is also my failure here to treat schooling in the prewar Japanese colonies. Colonial policy did give rise to debate in Japan from time to time but it was never at the center of political discourse about education. For those interested, there is an excellent study in English of schooling in Taiwan by E. P. Tsurumi but nothing yet comparable on Korea.[5] I have touched on the plight of Korean residents in postwar Japan in Chapter 8.

1

Clarifying Loyalty and Filial Piety: 1800–1850s

The aim of education, elementary and advanced, is to clarify human relationships. In the elementary program of education the various human relationships are made clear.

—Yamazaki Ansai, 1650[1]

The [Confucian] teaching of Chu Hsi has had the full confidence of successive shoguns. . . . Lately, however, various new theories have been put forward, heterodox teachings have become popular, and social standards have been broken down.

—Lord Matsudaira Sadanobu, 1790[2]

The patterns of schooling in Japan of the early nineteenth century formed a richly textured mosaic, reflecting the patchwork political quilt and the multicolored social life of the late Tokugawa era. Politically, the country was divided into some 250 semiautonomous domains under the control of hereditary lords, or daimyo, and their retainers, or samurai. Legally, the population was sharply divided into three groups—nobles, peasants, and townspeople—which formed a steep pyramid with the nobles at the top. But in terms of economic income and social status, the shapes of Tokugawa life were much more complex and fluid than the official view would have it. Although much of both structure and ideals would be swept away in the civil war that accompanied the Meiji Restoration at the end of the 1860s, the revolutionary nature of the Meiji reforms cannot be appreciated without at least a brief overview of the educational policies and intellectual currents that formed the traditional background for modern Japan.

The Decentralized Tokugawa State

The political regime that gave its name to the early modern period in Japanese history was founded in 1600. In that year a coalition of daimyo led by the House of Tokugawa won a huge military victory and ended over a century of feudal warfare among the samurai class. The central government created over the next several decades is referred to as the Tokugawa shogunate, reflecting the decision by the head of the Tokugawa family to take shogun, or "generalissimo," as his formal title rather than to usurp the imperial throne. The result was a political system in which the Tokugawa shogun nominally recognized the ultimate sovereignty of the imperial house, which resided at the court in Kyoto, while the shogun actually exercised power from the Tokugawa castle in the city of Edo (modern-day Tokyo). The imperial court with its royal family and associated nobles was permitted to continue much as it had for the previous eight centuries, without political power and dependent upon the leaders of the samurai aristocracy for economic sustenance. In return the shogun could claim, as viceroy or military commander, a historical legitimacy and political authority derived from the myths about the imperial house.

Daimyo and Samurai

Beneath these dual peaks of court and shogunate, the rest of the political pyramid consisted of daimyo lords and their samurai retainers. The victory of the Tokugawa coalition had led not to the destruction of the autonomous domains of the daimyo but rather to a pragmatic compromise. The hereditary daimyo families were permitted to administer their domains as fiefs from the shogun, their liege lord. In these domains the daimyo each administered criminal and civil law, levied taxes, planned public works, and maintained their own corps of armed samurai. In law, daimyo were answerable only to the shogun, who held them to certain basic rules regarding such matters as arms limitations and who also issued vague abstract injunctions to the daimyo about benevolence in their treatment of the people.

What is important for our purposes is to note that the Tokugawa political tradition was one in which educational policy, like other matters of public policy, was left largely in the hands of these domain governments. This does not mean that there were over 250 separate styles of political rule or 250 educational philosophies. The daimyo houses had survived the civil wars of the sixteenth century by learning similar lessons about governing their territories. They were now participants in a national political culture that strongly influenced their administrations toward a common pattern. There was also the model of the shogun himself, the national hegemon who in his other role as a territorial lord governed the largest single domain in the country, a domain that included about one-third of all urban dwellers as well as a large percent of the nation's villagers. Nevertheless, it must be emphasized that the Tokugawa tradition of political control in early modern Japan was one of decentralization, not centralization.[3]

The higher echelons of both shogun and daimyo governments were staffed by samurai. The samurai class made up somewhere between 6 percent and 10 percent of the population. Each samurai head of household was separately linked by feudal ties of fealty and benevolence to his own daimyo. Although the Tokugawa had samurai of its own, the overwhelming majority of the samurai were not direct vassals of the shogun but rather were vassals of lords who were in their turn vassals to the Tokugawa. The aristocratic samurai of the nineteenth century were descendants of medieval military knights formerly based on agrarian land. By the early eighteenth century, however, all but a small minority of samurai had been moved into urban areas around daimyo castles and placed in quasi-bureaucratic chains of command.

The establishment of the Tokugawa regime resulted in over 200 years free from civil war and, since Tokugawa foreign policy aimed at limited contact with its neighbors, free from foreign wars. Thus, although the Bushido ideology of the samurai continued to stress their martial heritage, the samurai of the Tokugawa period filled the bureaucratic hierarchy of officialdom rather than riding to battle as swordsmen and archers, as had their forefathers. In their roles as civil servants, samurai were responsible for directing the collection of taxes, administering the cities, supervising village officials, overseeing the police courts, inspecting religious establishments, and regulating commerce and the other functions of early modern government. In short, in the course of two centuries between 1600 and 1800 the samurai were transformed into a civil administrative class. The corollary was that they were increasingly required to prepare for these roles through formal schooling.

Entry into samurai status and the rank of each samurai family was determined primarily by birth; therefore the crucial qualifications for office were inherited. The prolonged civil wars of the medieval period had culminated in the stable sociopolitical order of seventeenth-century Tokugawa Japan. The military's preoccupation with a bureaucratic chain of command and the feudal aristocracy's fastidious concern for genealogical propriety combined to produce an interlocking latticework of governmental posts and official ranks. In this hierarchy the relative income, power, and prestige of a samurai and his family were to a great degree determined by the quality of the service that had been rendered by his forefathers. Few formal mechanisms for either promoting the talented or demoting the mediocre were resorted to with any frequency in normal times.[4] The only routine way in which an individual male samurai could permanently move up in rank was to be adopted by another samurai family who needed an heir. This opportunity, of course, was very rarely available to the eldest son, who was needed to carry on his own family line.

Commoner Society

In law and social theory, Tokugawa was a hierarchically ordered society in which various functional classes, including townspeople, had different obligations and privileges. There was variation among daimyo domains but some generalizations seem accurate of all domains.

Commoners in urban communities, though not routinely taxed, were subject to special regulations. Nevertheless, the urban mercantile elites in their roles as commercial bankers, rice brokers, shippers, warehousers, and wholesalers acquired over time a great deal of economic power. Socially and culturally as well as economically, this class came to dominate the life of the city. Although municipal government was the prerogative of the samurai bureaucracy, neighborhood affairs were largely left to the leading citizens, who arranged such basic needs as fire fighting, rubbish removal, and what formal schooling that existed in the towns.

One of the most remarkable features of the cultural life of early nineteenth century Japan was how much of it assumed literacy, indeed depended upon it. Although there are no statistical measures of literacy per se, there is a wealth of indirect evidence to support the generalization that mid–nineteenth century Japan compared favorably with almost any country in the world.[5] It is estimated that some three-quarters of merchants in large cities and more than half elsewhere would have been literate in part because of the importance of keeping business accounts. Data on the number of bookstores, lending libraries, and publishing houses suggest a large urban audience for other printed materials.[6] Perhaps half of the wives and daughters in this merchant class would also be able to read. Literacy among male artisans would vary according to type of community and even region of the country, but a reasonable estimate would be between 40 and 60 percent. That there were libraries lending books for a small fee implies a reading public not exclusively in the upper-income brackets, since presumably the wealthier individuals could afford to purchase their own copies. In the 1830s, Edo, with a population of a million, had 800 such lending libraries, approximately 1 for every 1,250 inhabitants. Osaka, smaller at 400,000 people, had about the same number of libraries per capita.[7]

Despite the significant degree of urbanization in nineteenth-century Japan, over 80 percent of the population was rural. The most common livelihood was agriculture, which was sometimes accompanied by fishing in coastal villages and timbering in the mountains. Rice was the dominant crop wherever it could be cultivated efficiently. Other grains were grown in the colder season. By the early nineteenth century there was a wide variety of foodstuffs as well as commercial crops such as oilseed, cotton, and tobacco. The rural villages were also the main source of such highly valued handicraft products as pottery, lacquer, paper, sake wine, and raw silk.

The long process of commercialization in Tokugawa agriculture contributed to marked social stratification in most if not all Japanese villages with a considerable disparity in the distribution of wealth, power, and prestige. Since urban merchant enterprises were commonly restricted by law in their rural activities, affluent village families had opportunities to combine landholding with commercial operations such as marketing, handicraft industries, and moneylending. The patriarchs of these households filled the political roles of village headman and community elder and organized such communal affairs as the annual cycle of religious festivals.

At the bottom of village society were landless peasants, who tilled their landlords' fields as sharecroppers and provided the seasonal labor needed in such handicraft industries as rope making, textile weaving, and sake or soy sauce brewing. They had little direct say in village affairs. Instead, landless peasants' interests in community water rights and similar concerns were represented by their landlords, whose ancestors had often been the landlords of the peasants' ancestors. In between the very top and bottom of rural society were the small and medium-sized landholders who might or might not have direct inputs into village politics, depending in many cases upon their family relations with the village elite.

In rural areas the rate of literacy was doubtless considerably lower than in the towns and cities. Nevertheless, it would be erroneous to picture the nineteenth-century village as composed of nothing but unlettered peasants. Daimyo and their samurai depended a great deal on the written word in their attempts to control their subjects and thus rural Japan was thickly papered with government records of many kinds.

Census accounts, land registers, and tax files were just the beginning of the layers of records that accumulated. Added to these were the written pronouncements distributed by their lords to inspire and warn the people about immoral and criminal behavior. All of these writings imply that at least those male peasants who served as local officials had to be literate. Moreover, the agricultural almanacs that were published in large numbers as well as the discovery of storerooms well stocked with books in the homes of nineteenth-century villagers reveal that literacy was by no means limited to such official matters. Perhaps half of the middling peasant males and a third of the lower strata may have been able to read and write some simple Japanese, although there were no doubt isolated areas where less than a quarter would have had even this rudimentary skill.[8]

Nationalism and Tokugawa Ideology

Nationalism, as it came to be understood in Japan by the end of the nineteenth century, had only limited meaning or emotional appeal in the Tokugawa period. Although Japan already possessed many of the characteristics of a modern nation-state—an ethnically homogeneous populace with a common history and political sovereignty over a distinct area—the notion of nationhood was not necessarily a meaningful reference for identity or a sanction for behavior. The main foci for identity for the commoner were the village community and the extended family group; for the samurai, the feudal domain. Loyalty was owed by the samurai specifically to his feudal lord, who, in turn, owed allegiance to the Tokugawa house as hereditary liege lord. The imperial throne, later to become the premier focus for national identity, was a very shadowy institution in the early nineteenth century. Sanctioning political authority and underlying the norms of political behavior was a set of ethical assumptions stemming in large part from a neo-Confucian reading of human history and of natural principles that govern the larger world.

The focus of cultural loyalty formed when these originally Chinese views of the moral order of the universe became intermixed with Shinto and Buddhist precepts and adapted to the Bushido tradition of the Japanese samurai class. In the neo-Confucian intellectual tradition patronized by the shogun and most daimyo, cultural identity resided in an identification with the devotion to an ethical conception of what it meant to be civilized in general rather than what it meant to be Japanese in particular. But Confucianism was only one of the intellectual traditions of the Tokugawa era. By the early nineteenth century three distinct intellectual currents flowed through the educational field and affected the content of school curriculum as well as administrative policy: (1) that of the Confucians, who can be considered an intellectual elite under the Tokugawa regime by virtue of the subsidies received from the shogun and various lords; (2) that of scholars of Nativist Studies, who increasingly challenged the Confucians on the basis of an indigenous tradition they claimed predated Chinese influence; and (3) that of a small but increasing number of specialists in Western Learning, whose services came into greater demand after 1800.

Confucian Studies

Although Confucianism in the late Tokugawa period was not quite as fractured as nineteenth-century Christianity in the West, there were many rooms in its mansion. Originating in China, whose culture continued to be held in great esteem by Japanese Confucians in terms of institutional ties and even, to a significant extent, in doctrinal aspects, Tokugawa Confucianism developed largely independently from China. The single most important seat was the Shōheikō Academy. In addition to serving as the main facility for advanced schooling for Tokugawa housemen, it also produced teachers who were employed in the samurai academies of numerous daimyo domains. Politically, Shōheikō Confucians preached loyalty to the Tokugawa shogun as either himself the virtuous prince envisioned by Confucius or at least the viceroy of an emperor who reigned with the mandate of heaven but delegated governmental power to the shogun. Political stability, social harmony, and economic well-being were all deemed to depend upon a government that maintained a proper social hierarchy and induced correct moral attitudes among its people. Since different social classes had different social functions, they were appropriately entitled to differing shares of wealth, social prestige, and, especially, political power. Thus justice or righteousness did not entail political or social equality. Elitism was accepted as both inevitable and desirable.

Nor was there any doctrine of the separation of church and state. There were several major Buddhist churches in the nineteenth century, each with networks of monasteries, nunneries, and temples, but for two centuries all these had been subjugated to the political control of either the shogun at the national level or the daimyo at the regional level. This was true also of the main Shinto shrine organizations, although some of these were nominally linked to the imperial court. Religious beliefs and private morality were very much the business of the state in both the Chinese and Japanese political traditions—indeed, it could be said that the key function of the Confucian state was to assure the moral behavior of its subjects. If it did not, the balance between the cosmos and humankind would be disrupted and the mandate of heaven would eventually be withdrawn from the ruling dynasty. In a major departure from Chinese political doctrine, the Japanese imperial house possessed the mandate eternally. Dynasties of viceroys such as the shogun rose and fell over time because of immorality, not the ever-virtuous emperor.

The bedrock of a moral society in Confucian doctrine was the patriarchal family in which parents held authority over children, males took primacy over females, and the elder ranked above the younger.[9] This became the paradigm for all legitimate authority: the ruler as humane patriarch to his subjects, the daimyo as the benevolent father to his samurai, the teacher as wise mentor to his pupils. Schooling in the Confucian tradition was above all the inculcation and internalization of the right moral attitudes through the cultivation of such virtues as filial piety toward parents, loyalty toward superiors, and generosity toward inferiors. In Tokugawa Japan it also emphasized the acceptance of social hierarchy whereby social harmony and economic well-being were deemed possible only if all did their duty in keeping with their stations in life.

The beginnings of alienation from cultural orthodoxy in the Tokugawa period can be seen clearly in the eighteenth century, when groups of dissident intellectuals called into question the adequacy of neo-Confucianism as a means of comprehending and responding to the socioeconomic changes of their times. One current of this criticism originated from within the traditions of Chinese scholarship itself, as some scholars were disturbed at the failure of Tokugawa leaders and their Confucian advisers to formulate policies appropriate to the present. The orthodox preoccupation with fixed precedents was seen by some as a distortion of Confucianism. Although historical inquiry was indeed the path to understanding the present—a key tenet in neo-Confucianism—the true message to be learned, according to these critics, was that great leaders made history. Most significant about this approach to history for later

Tokugawa thought was the concept that reform was not a matter of readjusting society to bring it into accord with timeless principles of a traditional order but rather a matter of making creative responses to the conditions of the particular times in which people found themselves.

The hold of the orthodoxy on the minds of most Japanese Confucians proved extremely resistant against such attempts at reinterpretation during the eighteenth century. But the Confucian stress on the relevance of historical inquiry as a source of understanding basic truths about social life had ramifications in the Japanese context, which were to render the Confucian intellectual framework vulnerable. By the turn of the nineteenth century a small but vigorous reaction had developed in the form of what came to be known as "Nativist Studies," or "National Learning."

Nativist Learning

The common point of departure for these thinkers was their insistence that Japan had a history of its own—a past distinct and different from that of China. If so, was this Japanese past not as valid a subject matter as the history of China, studied in the Confucian academies? Were not the ancient Shinto religious texts and the early chronicles concerning the origins of the Japanese imperial house important sources of historical information? Did not ancient Japanese prose and poetry possess beauty?

Some Nativist scholars, such as Motoori Norinaga, who acquired a considerable reputation for his mastery of these ancient texts and the brilliance of his commentaries on classical poetry and prose, utilized the Japanese past to launch a biting attack on Chinese Confucianism. In his hands the ancient period prior to the importation of Chinese learning appeared as a Japanese golden age, a time when people's hearts were naturally sincere and, as a consequence, society was both harmonious and prosperous. The obvious question, then, was why present conditions in the land were so different. The answer they gave was that Chinese culture—the borrowing institutions and values foreign to Japan—had corrupted the purity of the Japanese soul and formed a layer of corrosion that had thus obscured the essential genius of Japanese culture.

These early Nativists were not, however, calling for a reorganization of contemporary society or a restructuring of the political system. They advocated a revitalization of native culture and thereby a restoration of morality. Nevertheless, two of their basic arguments were to have radical political implications: (1) that Japanese culture had an origin and a historical life separate from that of Chinese civilization and (2) that the historical manifestation of the uniqueness of Japan as a cultural entity was the uninterrupted reign of the imperial family.

As developed in the late eighteenth century, Nativist Studies came to be most closely associated with activists like Hirata Atsutane, who not only rejected the worldviews of both Confucianism and Buddhism but also advocated a return to the political institutions as well as the cultural values of the ancient past.

The political focus for these men was the emperor, as descendant of the gods and proper object of all patriotic devotion and religious reverence. Thus by the mid–nineteenth century, the fundamentalists in this movement had a political as well as religious message. Although by no means were all Shinto clergy adherents to this new ideology, many of its advocates were members of the Shinto priesthood. Others were lay advisers to political figures or were teachers in domain schools or proprietors of private academies. Still others were itinerant scholars patronized by villages and urban groups. By the end of the Tokugawa era, Nativist Studies had also found a place in about one-third of all domain schools and adherents were scattered throughout the country. One of the more important political strongholds for the movement was the Institute for Imperial Studies in Kyoto. Here scholars claiming Hirata's mantle of leadership had access to influential court nobles who were increasingly interested in justifications for their playing a larger role in the political affairs of the day.[10]

This emphasis on a past glory in Japan that might be recaptured and the unique position of the imperial institution in Japanese political culture was to become increasingly more salient as the threat of Western encroachment created a new sense of crisis in the decades between 1830 and 1860.

The first systematic consideration of the meaning of Western expansion for Japanese society came early in the nineteenth century. Many were originally orthodox both in their support of the Tokugawa regime and in their adherence to neo-Confucian principles as the ultimate source of truth. Barbarian intrusion was viewed as clear evidence that the internal crisis had reached serious proportions. The solution was revitalization along traditional lines—that is, a restoration of the ideal order as understood within the neo-Confucian paradigm. This restoration would assure that the barbarians would be turned back and Japan defended. In their analysis of what had gone wrong within the country and what it was that needed defending, however, some of these thinkers produced a description of Japan as a nation that incorporated key elements from the Nativists. A very strong emphasis was placed on the Japanese as a historical community and the imperial throne as a rallying point in the struggle against the outside threat. Their slogan was "revere the emperor and expel the barbarian," which was widely used in the 1850s and 1860s to exhort Japanese to patriotic effort.

Such ideas influenced a group of powerful domain leaders from various parts of the country, who in turn sought to persuade the Tokugawa to reorganize Japan's military defenses. By the 1850s many voices within the country were calling for extraordinary measures to drive off the Western barbarian, including the adoption of Western military technology and organization in an attempt to fight fire with fire.

Western Learning

The third major intellectual current in early nineteenth century Japan was typically referred to at the time as either "Dutch Studies" or "Western Studies."

Although most Europeans had been ordered out of the country in the early seventeenth century because they were perceived to be agents of subversion, the Dutch had been allowed to maintain a small permanent trading post at Nagasaki and to send a limited number of merchant vessels. Shogunate officials tightly controlled this interaction, but it nevertheless provided a conduit for information about the outside world. The Tokugawa shogunate had always maintained some interest in what could be learned from the Dutch about international developments and had long subsidized the study of such practical subjects as medical science and astronomy.[11]

In 1811, as foreign pressure on the Tokugawa seclusion policy intensified, an additional bureau for the translation of European writings was created, the Institute for the Investigation of Barbarian Books. By the end of the Tokugawa period, Western Studies had been incorporated into about one-fourth of all domain schools.

There were also small numbers of men outside such schools who pursued their curiosity about the Western world, often by traveling privately to Nagasaki to attempt to communicate with the Dutch there. The borrowing of foreign weapons or military techniques did not itself constitute a betrayal of traditional culture so long as the existing values and institutions were not jeopardized. For the traditionalist this was to be merely a grafting on of a useful branch, not a break with the cultural roots. In the eighteenth century the subjects of learning that drew upon Western knowledge were largely limited to such utilitarian fields as ballistics theory or the medical arts. Those who strayed too obviously into areas that might stimulate criticism of Tokugawa social, economic, or political policies risked investigation by the authorities. In one of the more famous cases, a number of members of a Dutch Studies circle were jailed in 1838.[12] As in most such instances of the persecution of private scholars in Tokugawa times, this seems to be a case in which the victims had been politically active, not merely teaching heresy. The group was charged with conspiring with foreigners. These events help explain why Dutch medicine was particularly well developed: It could remain politically neutral yet command high fees and even official patronage.

For some, however, the recognition of Western superiority in military science led to consideration of whether the West did not have other things to offer. If Western astronomy, medicine, metallurgy, and ballistics were demonstrably superior to what existed in Japan, could it be that the foreigner understood some underlying principles within the natural world not comprehended by the neo-Confucian orthodoxy? By the end of the 1860s the number of activists and thinkers who had lost faith in the ability of the traditional order to cope with the crises of internal decline and external pressure had greatly swollen, and many of them were prepared to look outside for new solutions. At the same time, this intense concern about the threat from outside stimulated a new sense of nation.

Elitism and Schooling

Domain Schools

Schooling was an integral element in the transformation of samurai from medieval knights to early modern bureaucrats. By the nineteenth century it was generally expected of all samurai that they have an education adequate to their governmental roles. Moreover, in early nineteenth century cities and—to a much lesser but nevertheless significant degree—in rural Japan as well, literacy was a valued skill for taking part in commercial and cultural life. Thus schooling increased. Nevertheless, to speak of an educational "system" or "state policy" in Tokugawa Japan is misleading. There was no nationwide system or state policy as such. Most aspects of schooling varied not only from domain to domain but also from one social stratum to another. When the Tokugawa shogun or one of his 250-odd daimyo concerned himself with schooling, it was almost entirely within the domains he directly administered. Moreover, when there was government funding, it was usually only for his samurai. Thus it is necessary not only to distinguish between the various levels of schooling—primary, secondary, tertiary—but also to describe separately the various categories of schools.

In the early nineteenth century, schooling was most generally associated with one of three traditions: private teachers, domain academies, and local community schools. The most common and perhaps oldest form of instruction outside the family for Japanese youth was privately arranged study with a master willing to accept a pupil even if not necessarily as a disciple or apprentice. If we exclude one-on-one tutoring and on-the-job apprenticeships from our discussion of formal schooling, the most deeply ingrained tradition was that of a master passing on knowledge and skills to individuals or to small groups. Thus such diverse subjects as calligraphy, Chinese classics, martial arts, Japanese poetry, or the tea ceremony might be studied with a master teacher either in the teacher's home or in a more specialized facility—a *shijuku,* which was a "personal school," or "private academy."[13]

Almost 500 private academies have been identified as opened prior to 1830, and three times that many new ones were established between 1830 and the end of the era in 1867. Most were small establishments with a single male teacher, who was very often born into the samurai class, instructing local youth in his own home. Some teaching was done by women in this same manner but the majority of all professional teachers seem to have been male. Nor were private academies normally coeducational.[14]

Some private schools were quite large and might have dormitory space for a hundred students or more. Often a son or disciple of a successful teacher might inherit the school, which gave it institutional continuity. In most cases these instructors were not licensed or otherwise credentialed by any political authority.

Expenses were defrayed by gifts upon admission and by periodic tuition fees that were paid in cash or commodities. Such fees would have precluded poor families from sending their children to these schools. Nor would a poor or isolated village commonly have had an academy. But for samurai sons and the males from commoner families with at least moderate means living in urban areas or villages of medium affluence, there were abundant opportunities to pursue an education in *shijuku*.

Private academies were not ordinarily licensed or otherwise subject to regular official supervision, but they sometimes provided the original institutional base for the development of other types of educational institutions that did directly involve government at one level or another. Many domain schools traced their origins to private establishments.[15] By the early decades of the nineteenth century, about half of all domains had a daimyo-supported school, and by the 1860s the total reached three-quarters.

Most samurai youth were being educated this way by 1800. Herbert Passin estimated domain school average attendance in the first quarter of the nineteenth century at over 51,000, rising to almost 64,000 by the 1860s.[16] Samurai sons of all but the very highest and lowest ranks—who would be taught by tutors or members of the family—began attending these schools as early as the age of six or seven and were expected to continue until at least thirteen or fourteen, the age at which males ritually left childhood.[17] Most samurai resided in their lords' castle town unless on official duty elsewhere and their young sons attended the domain school as day students, if not necessarily every day. By the early nineteenth century, such official domain schools were enrolling, tuition free, hundreds of samurai boys at a time, although attendance in most domains was not necessarily compulsory. The very lowest ranks of the samurai were sometimes excluded, either because of domain policy or because their families chose not to send them. Although tuition in such schools was generally free, there were the costs of books, supplies, and, in some cases, dormitory fees. Older boys were more likely than younger ones to be housed in a school dormitory. Most samurai children had homes nearby, but there was a belief, apparently widespread, that their education benefited from the close supervision made possible by dormitories. Some domains provided subsidies for those whose family stipends were so low as to make schools expenses a burden.

Originally, many such schools, including the shogun's own Shōheikō, had grown out of private academies that only later came to be subsidized from official funds. By the late Tokugawa period, however, the head teachers and staff were commonly responsible directly to the domain bureaucracy, which paid their stipends as official retainers as well as paid expenses of the school as an official agency. Most teachers would have been samurai of the lord in whose domain they taught, but lords also employed famed teachers from outside their borders. Administrators were not necessarily scholars themselves, and scholars did not usually enjoy high ranks within the samurai hierarchy. There is even evidence to suggest that the income of teachers actually fell in the last half century before the collapse of the Tokugawa regime. Perhaps this took place because the number entering the profession increased even more rapidly than the demand while at the same time the profession may have attracted a disproportionate number of low-ranking samurai or second sons for whom even a lowly teaching post was a financial improvement.[18]

As with other aspects of Tokugawa educational history, there is much more material available on the curriculum and pedagogy in domain schools than in other types of schooling. From this material emerges a picture of paramount emphasis on moral cultivation with lessons taught through pedagogic formalism. The main texts at most schools for samurai were the Sino-Japanese classics. Ronald Dore put the matter in comparative perspective:

> [Samurai] schools had a remarkable similarity to the grammar schools of Europe.
> . . . Education centered on learning to read a classical language—ancient Chinese
> rather than Latin and Greek. The purpose of mastering that language was to read
> the Chinese classics, for the historical, literary and philosophical writing of the
> Chinese sages, like Greek and Latin classics, were seen as the chief repository of ex-
> perienced wisdom, of aesthetic values, of philosophical sophistication and nobil-
> ity, and even of ontology and morality (much more so than in England, since
> Buddhism was much less effective than Christianity in claiming parity of esteem
> with the classical tradition).[19]

By the end of the era there were innovations in curriculum, as many domain schools had become increasingly more oriented toward the practical affairs of government. Mathematics, for one, had not been traditionally part of the core curriculum of the typical domain schools, but attention to it increased steadily after 1830, and by the 1850s forty-five schools did have courses on the subject.[20] Where medical training was funded by the lord, it usually took place in separate facilities, but from the turn of the nineteenth century other Western Studies were gradually introduced into the curriculum of domain schools.

Domain schools were for the most part located in the lord's castle town. In some cases, however, the domain also funded branch schools in the countryside where there were rural samurai. These were not, however, widespread.[21] Nor did most domains admit non-samurai into their schools prior to 1868, although there were some notable exceptions. It is estimated that at most only about a third of the domains may have allowed commoners, and this number is probably inflated. At the local level of villages, domain governments, though quite concerned with tax revenues and social order at the local levels, were remarkably laissez-faire about schooling. Fewer than fourteen are reported as having established schools for commoners and only approximately 10 percent of the daimyo governments can be said to have routinely inspected or even licensed schools at the local level. Somewhat more prevalent was the funding of occasional public lectures or other measures aimed at promoting social morality.

Still, fully 30 percent of the domains reported no involvement at all in education for commoners.[22] This was left either to private initiative or to communities of commoners.

Community Schools

Although not every domain school excluded all commoners, the Tokugawa roots of "public" schooling for ordinary people in modern Japan lie elsewhere, especially in what have most often been termed *terakoya*—"temple schools," or "parish schools."[23] They were so named because their teachers had inherited functions once filled by the Buddhist priesthood. But during the Tokugawa period, most of the 10,000 or so *terakoya* were secular establishments and far more likely to be Confucian than Buddhist in orientation (although the distinction is problematic). In the eastern regions of Japan they were usually called more accurately "writing schools" (*tenari-sho*). Perhaps the least misleading English label might be "community schools" because of the nature of their funding and oversight. By the 1860s the country as a whole is estimated to have had 15,500 such schools.[24] Although they enrolled probably fewer than half of even the male youth of late Tokugawa Japan, they were particularly well attended in the cities, where in some cases commoners and samurai might have enrolled together.

Since the shogun and daimyo paid little if any attention to such arrangements, it was left to the elders of the villages or prominent merchants in the urban neighborhoods to recruit teachers, sanction curriculum, determine attendance policies, and provide funding. Thus the variation in such schools was so great as to make one hesitate to hazard generalizations; similarities among them resulted more from common cultural predilections than any governmental design. It is reasonable to believe, however, that the usual age for the beginner was about six and that most children would not have attended for more than three or four years. The teachers included women but the majority were men drawn from the samurai class, retired doctors, and other literate persons, including some Buddhist priests.[25] In rural areas there might not be more than a single teacher with a dozen pupils, whereas in urban schools both staff and student body would be much larger, perhaps numbering as many as 300 pupils. Usually, these schools focused on basic skills deemed necessary to prepare a child for the vocational training he or she would receive in the family or workplace. But, as has been pointed out, "Reading and writing, however, went beyond mere rudimentary levels. In the process of learning these skills, children studied what are now called social studies, vocational arts, and moral values."[26]

For most Japanese males in the nineteenth century, then, primary instruction other than that from family or tutors took place at schools that were supported by tuition and/or donations from the community. In the agricultural and fishing villages, where the overwhelming majority resided, we can speak of "public" schools only in the sense of institutions open to the children of most if not necessarily all inhabitants and funded mostly by the community itself. They were particularly popular in the cities. Edo is estimated to have had approximately 1,200 by the 1860s.[27] Altogether these various types of facilities for primary education are estimated to have enrolled more than 40 percent of all males for at least some formal schooling.[28]

Far fewer females—perhaps only 10 percent—would have had comparable experiences. Females were admitted to some private academies, and daughters of families in the highest classes might also have had tutors in such "feminine arts" as calligraphy, poetry, and sewing in addition to etiquette and morals.[29] More practical training in housewifery for these social classes as well as the underclasses would be imparted in the home by female relatives. The daughters of middle-stratum peasants did sometimes attend community schools although not in the numbers that male children did.[30] In the cities, however, middle-class families may have sent their daughters almost as often as their sons to community schools at least long enough to acquire some basic literacy.[31]

Higher Education

Commoners of either gender would be much less likely than samurai males to receive formal schooling beyond the basics. Samurai sons who reached the age of thirteen or fourteen were usually treated separately from younger boys in a number of ways analogous to separation between primary and secondary schooling in modern societies. In some of the domains where further schooling was provided these youth were required to take an exam to move on to the next levels. In addition, formal military practice was usually added at this level, although not necessarily in the same school facilities.[32] That there had been nothing resembling a true war since the late sixteenth century, indeed almost no civil strife serious enough to muster any large number of samurai since the early seventeenth century, did not change the tradition that samurai were first and foremost military aristocracy. The bow, the horse, the lance, the sword, the musket, and other such military equipment were the tools of a samurai's trade, although weaponry varied with different ranks: Musketry was appropriate only for the lower samurai, and horsemanship was appropriate only for the officers whose rank meant they would be expected to engage in mounted combat. Judo and similar martial arts were likewise part of a gentleman's training. Interestingly enough, however, dueling was strictly forbidden and competition was usually limited to the confines of the practice arena or ceremonial exhibitions of skills.

Some samurai students might continue their formal schooling into their midtwenties, and of these a select few prepared for a scholarly career.[33] Those judged most suitable for advanced training were often sent at domain expense to schools in Edo or other places for further study. By the end of the Tokugawa era over 90 percent of the domains had such travel study programs to provide for bright students to continue their education outside of the domains. Most attended private academies, which, as Richard Rubinger stresses, collectively provided a national network that transcended geography and domain ties.[34]

The shogun's central government also maintained several institutes of higher learning. The Tokugawa facility for Western Studies has already been mentioned, as has the Confucian college, the Shōheikō (or Shōheisho). Founded as a private academy in the seventeenth century, the latter received increasing subsidies from the Tokugawa shogunate and eventually became the equivalent of a domain school for advanced training in the Confucian classics. This school was also the closest approximation to a seat of national orthodoxy existing in Tokugawa Japan, for it both enjoyed a unique official status and provided advanced training to promising scholars from throughout the country. At the heart of its curriculum were classical Chinese Studies, particularly in the tradition of Chu Hsi neo-Confucianism.[35] In Kyoto the shogunate also subsidized the Confucian-oriented Gakushūin (or Kangakusho, as it eventually came to be called).

There was one other noteworthy type of advanced institute subsidized by the shogunate. In the 1790s, under pressure from those who believed that Japanese history was being neglected because of the attention paid to Chinese classics, the shogunate agreed to subsidize an Institute for Japanese Studies. Nativist scholars also dominated the Institute for Imperial Studies in Kyoto. For the most part these facilities were limited to a small body of advanced students and therefore analogous to the relatively small graduate schools and research institutes of today's Japan.

One of the most interesting "public" academies for advanced study funded by a local community was the Kaitokudō in Osaka. It had begun in the 1720s as a private academy identified with a particular Confucian scholar but soon drew support from the merchants of the city. Although its funding and administration were local, it attracted teachers and visitors from throughout Japan and it even received from the shogunate some gifts and a "charter" that granted it rare legal privileges within the administrative framework of Osaka. Most of the students were commoners, although samurai were also in attendance.[36]

Other opportunities for postprimary education open to commoners could be found in the 180 private academies supported by the Shingaku movement, which synthesized certain Confucian, Buddhist, and Shinto elements. These offered lectures to females, both children and adults, as well as to males. Some of the movement's most famous lecturers were themselves women. These women lecturers can be traced back to the eighteenth century, starting with Jion-ni Kenka, a Buddhist nun and professional lecturer on her own before becoming a disciple of Ishida Baigan, a philosopher from the merchant class who founded Shingaku. His followers were particularly keen on education for the common people. But they also stressed the subordinate and separate role of women as wives and mothers, despite the fact that Kenka and some of the other women involved were quite strong-minded and learned people who hardly fitted that stereotype.[37]

The Tokugawa Legacy for the Modern Era

Although there were alarming signs of internal stresses in Tokugawa Japan as early as the eighteenth century, the single most shocking stimulus to change in education came with the arrival of Commodore Matthew Perry's U.S. flotilla in 1853. The goal of U.S. as well as British and French policy at this time was to coerce Japanese leaders into opening the country to Western economic and cultural penetration. The inability of the shogunate to protect the nation against this foreign threat combined with a long decline in confidence in Tokugawa domestic policies to produce an explosion of political activity in the late 1850s and 1860s. This activity originated in attempts by leading daimyo domains to pressure the shogunate into certain political and economic as well as military reforms. But soon leadership of the various reform movements increasingly passed into the hands of lower samurai who had become convinced that the shogunate itself had to be destroyed in order to save the nation as a whole. At the end of 1867 a "restoration" of government based on the imperial throne was proclaimed and in less than two years the supporters of the Tokugawa regime had been overcome.

This was a critical juncture for the development of Japanese nationalism, for it was here that the imperial throne once again moved unequivocally into the center of political thought. The concept of the imperial will, which took precedent over and was the only legitimate authority for government policy—a principle long paid lip service to by the Tokugawa shogunate—was now used to justify anti-Tokugawa acts. Anti-Tokugawa forces marched to battle as "loyalists" protecting the throne against Tokugawa "rebels." The throne as an overriding focus for ultimate loyalty also justified the insubordination of those samurai activists whose domain leaders were slow in acting or who supported the status quo. True, domain loyalties were quite strong and were to remain so through the early years of the new era after 1868. True also, the domains served as the primary vehicles for the movement against the Tokugawa regime. But the ideological sanction for this radical break with the political tradition was neither individual freedom nor domain rights. It was an appeal to patriotic devotion to the nation as a whole and to the imperial throne that symbolized that unity.

Ironically, in its death throes the shogunate did attempt a number of reforms, some of which laid more groundwork for later Meiji innovations. It is noteworthy, for example, that in 1863 the shogunate ordered new elementary schools to be opened with central funds in Edo.[38] Even more consequential was the creation or expansion of schools focused on Western learning. Some of these specialized in military techniques to bolster national defense. After Perry's second visit in 1854 the Tokugawa asked the Dutch to provide instructors for some 200 students in its Naval Institute built in Nagasaki to introduce steam technology. Within three years a second academy was created in Edo, which eventually employed first French and then British advisers. In 1862 the shogunate sent five naval cadets and six seamen to study in Holland.[39] The next year another training facility was opened in Hyogo, although this one was soon closed.

Shogunate patronage of Western Studies in this period was not limited to military training. In 1857 it added a Medical Institute, also with help from the Dutch. In 1861, a Western medical school run by private Japanese specialists in Edo was placed under the shogunate's control and expanded.[40] One thing soon lead to another: Both medicine and explosives called for some knowledge of modern chemistry, and warships required mathematics for navigation and ballistics, metallurgy for boilers, and coal mining techniques for fuel. In 1855 and 1856 the shogunate expanded its old Institute of Western Studies, carefully attempting to divert anti-Western feelings among Tokugawa's critics with the name Bansho Shirabesho—Institute for the Investigation of Barbarian Books. Its focus was now on producing a new generation of Western area specialists. Those subjects most closely related to military and coastal defense were given special priority, but by 1861 and 1862 this study was seen as also requiring courses in English, French, and German in addition to the original Dutch language classes. Texts for these courses included political and social material as well as more narrow technological topics. To train Japanese as instructors in these fields, the Tokugawa launched a program to send promising trainees to England, France, and Russia. Other domain governments initiated their own programs but more than half of all those Japanese who are identified as having studied abroad with official support prior to the 1868 Restoration went under the auspices of the shogunate's program.

It is to the credit of the Tokugawa government that it gradually but steadily accepted trainees from outside its own retinue even though this policy was to jeopardize the delicate domestic balance of power. Even some commoners were recruited on the basis of merit. But however modern the curriculum, within this new educational system the government still strove to maintain a proper respect for aristocratic rank.[41]

Many of the outsiders in these programs would remain loyal to the shogun or at least neutral in the politics of the 1860s, but others would eventually help overthrow the shogunate. Among the more notable of the latter was Ōmura Masujirō, who would become head of the new Meiji army.

The shogunate had also planted other seeds of its own destruction when it adopted a more favorable attitude toward both domain and private schools of Western Studies. The domains of Satsuma and Saga were quick to add Western technology to the curricula of their domain schools and trained cadets to staff the naval vessels they purchased abroad. Schooling in infantry and artillery became common in these and a number of other domains in the 1860s. Teachers with knowledge of such subjects were in demand by private students. It was in these schools outside of the shogun's control that some of the best-known heroes of the Restoration first encountered Western culture.

Two major generalizations can be made about these future leaders. First, they usually began their education in the Chinese classics before they were exposed to Western Studies. Second, for most it would seem that Western languages were initially a means to acquire practical knowledge of the technology that would serve the immediate needs of national defense. Indeed, the typical approach to reconciling assumptions about the completeness of East Asian civilization with the seductiveness of the "barbarian" knowledge was to view the latter as merely external "branches" that could be grafted onto the indigenous "roots" without violating the integrity of traditional learning. Only gradually did many of them come to the view that the Western law, history, and contemporary institutions were worth knowing in greater depth. But, as we shall see in the following chapter, only a small minority of this generation would ever turn their backs on their Tokugawa intellectual heritage with the disdainful irreverence of a man like Fukuzawa Yukichi. Most would settle for an eclecticism that, though pragmatic enough, would be vulnerable to tensions generated by internal contradictions.

Conclusion

All modern school systems owe something to past traditions, but in few industrial societies is the tradition of ascribing traditional origins to modern phenomena more ingrained than in Japan. Perhaps the most crucial legacy from the Tokugawa period to modern Japanese schooling was stated concisely by Herbert Passin: "The notion of spending several hours a day for part of the year away from home, associating with non-kin age-mates, entering relations with a special kind of adult, and following a sequence of study, was already a familiar one to a good part of the population."[42]

However, there was much about the Tokugawa period that would have to change dramatically as the Japanese modernized their educational system. The Tokugawa held no real precedents for the national system of integrated and articulated levels of schooling that were to be developed with central government leadership in late nineteenth century Japan. This is not to say that a state-supported and centrally organized school system was an entirely new notion in post-Tokugawa times. In 1789 and again in 1791 an Osaka scholar of Confucianism sent memorials to the shogunate recommending an expansion of central government institutes of higher learning for meritorious scholars of all classes as well as transforming *terakoya* into government schools.[43] Nothing came of the proposal before the 1860s. The decentralized character of the Tokugawa state was too great an obstacle to such radical reform.

Second, elitism in Tokugawa society also remained strong. But the Tokugawa samurai elite were fundamentally different from modern Japanese business or governmental elites in the way they were recruited, promoted, and rewarded. Although new knowledge and skills became rapidly more important to ambitious samurai during the crises of the mid–nineteenth century, nevertheless family membership and domain ties—that is, ascribed, not achieved, status —still determined much of the opportunity for them until the Tokugawa system crumbled entirely. The same was true of commoners, including even the most wealthy.

Third, the seeds of modern Japanese nationalism had only begun to bear fruit by the time of the arrival of Perry's gunboats and for many of the anti-Tokugawa activists the cause of patriotism did not entail a vision of a modern future. For every Fukuzawa Yukichi, Itō Hirobumi, or Mori Arinori, there were numerous others whose goals were culturally reactionary—to drive off the West in order to preserve traditional institutions and values.

In short, the modern Japanese school system as it exists today at the end of twentieth century was largely built on foundations and frameworks constructed only after the collapse of the Tokugawa. Although there are certainly cultural and even institutional underpinnings that reach back into the Tokugawa period and beyond, the overthrow of the shogunate and the establishment of the new centralized state in the Meiji Restoration of 1868 brought about changes in schooling so extensive as to warrant the label "revolutionary."[44] Over the next decade the institutional organization and ideological orientations of formal education were almost entirely reshaped as part of an attempt to transform political, economic, and social life in Japan.

2

Knowledge from Throughout the World: The Reforms of the 1870s

Evil practices of the past shall be abandoned, and actions shall be based on international usage.

Knowledge shall be sought from throughout the world, and the foundations of Imperial rule shall be strengthened.

—From the Charter Oath of 1868[1]

Behind the wealth, power, security and well-being of a nation there lies invariably an advance in the talents of a civilized people. Therefore, it is necessary to build schools and establish educational methods which enable us to attain similar goals.

—Ōki Takatō, Minister of Education, 1872[2]

The transition from Tokugawa to Meiji was no smoother in education than it was in other important spheres.[3] True, there does seem to have been a consensus among the majority of Meiji leaders from the outset in favor of radical educational reforms. Nevertheless, more than three decades passed before there was anything resembling closure on such crucial issues as where administrative power should lay, what should be taught, who should attend, how to articulate the various levels, or how to fund it all. Over those three decades government policy zigged and zagged, at times with bewildering suddenness. Some of these shifts resulted from vicissitudes of political struggles as conflicting views gained supremacy within the government. Others turned out to be temporary deviations from an earlier blueprint attributable primarily to a lack of resources to carry out an agreed-upon policy. The problem for the historian is to sort out one from the other.

The new Meiji leaders were initially preoccupied with a wide range of crises, including campaigning militarily against the diehard Tokugawa supporters, appealing diplomatically for Western recognition, building an acceptable administrative structure, and seeking funding for all of this. Yet the new government also found time from the very beginning to address educational issues. Among the new leaders were such strong advocates of radical education reform as Kido Takayoshi (Kōin) and Itō Hirobumi. Early in 1868 a government office for education was created and in April the so-called Charter Oath issued over the seal of the emperor included the injunction "Knowledge shall be sought throughout the world." Early Meiji government instructions to the new provincial units included the more specific injunction "Elementary schools shall be established," and within the city of Kyoto, the original seat of the new government, a scheme for both elementary and secondary schools was actually put into place very soon after the Restoration.[4] Although policy questions were yet to be systematically addressed, the central government was clearly asserting its leadership in educational matters even if implementation was being left to the regional and local political units at least for the time being.

One of the earliest important steps toward a centrally administered school system actually came in the form of military academies for national defense. In 1868 a military training institute was opened in Kyoto. This was moved to the new capital in Tokyo in 1871 and then temporarily shut down in the political tumult of governmental reorganization, but in 1875 a modern Military Academy for army cadets was created.

The new government soon also formulated policies regarding advanced training for civilian occupations. In July 1869 the three Tokugawa academies in Edo—the Confucian Shōhei Gakkō and the schools for Western Studies and modern medicine—were amalgamated into a single school with the title "Daigakkō," the University. It was then reorganized in January 1870 and renamed "Daigaku," also translatable as "University" but a term with explicit allusions to the only official seat of higher learning in the ancient Japanese court. In addition to teaching and research responsibilities, this university was charged with officially overseeing "middle and elementary schools in the provinces."[5] Thus the central government was drawing upon a historical precedent, albeit a very distant one, for asserting its jurisdiction over a national school system.

The first comprehensive plan for all levels of education, "Rules for the University and for Elementary and Middle Schools," was submitted to the Council of State in spring 1870. The proposal was tabled pending a resolution to the growing ideological disputes about the direction for education in a new era.

Early Ideological Conflict

The Struggle for the University

As might be expected, some of the first open clashes over political ideology following the Restoration were fought over control of the university. At stake was its potential for leading the nation not just in terms of schooling but also in terms of political philosophy, and the chief adversaries in the struggle to control the university were advocates of the same intellectual movements that had vied for primacy in the late Tokugawa period—the specialists in Nativist, Confucian, and Western Studies.

At this point the Institute for Imperial Studies in Kyoto emerged suddenly into the foreground of the strife over educational policy. Because of the access its faculty enjoyed to such influential imperial court nobles as Iwakura Tomomi, the school immediately became one of the more important political strongholds for the Nativist movement. Hirata Kanetane, the heir to one of the most renowned of early nineteenth century propagandists, moved swiftly to lay claim to the Restoration on the basis of the Nativists' long championship of the centrality of the imperial throne. For Hirata and his fellow ideologues, the meaning of the Restoration lay in the repository of ideals contained within the indigenous tradition. Their form of nationalism had considerable appeal at court, and within a month of the formal proclamation of the establishment of the new government, Iwakura Tomomi had three Nativist scholars appointed to the Bureau of Internal Affairs with the charge to draft an educational policy for the new government.

The faculty at the Institute for Imperial Studies was not the only group of academic intellectuals seeking to exploit connections to the court. Also in Kyoto was the Institute for Chinese Studies, soon to be known again by its older name, the Gakushūin. These scholars of Chinese classics hoped to inherit the patronage formerly bestowed on the Tokugawa college. As a preliminary step, they obtained permission to rename their institute "Daigaku," the name taken from the official school created at the ancient Heian court a thousand years earlier. The symbolic significance of the title was clear: It would signify the supremacy of the imperial throne as the source of legitimacy for the nation's intellectual life.

Iwakura Tomomi's Nativist advisers were equally sensitive to the symbolic significance of the resurrection of such an imperial seat for higher learning and also sought an academic base within the new central government. Their original proposal, however, did not insist upon a monopoly in the new university. Rather, Nativist learning was to constitute the "central main body" whereas both Confucianism and Western learning were to be represented in "wings."

With the transfer of the government to Tokyo, its leaders sought to deal with the question of what to do with existing Tokugawa schools and the competing claims for official patronage. At first they established a multifaculty facility in an attempt to accommodate all three of the major claimants. Adopting the proposal of the Nativists, they appointed specialists from the Kyoto Institute for Imperial Studies to the main school within the university and charged them with elucidating the national polity and exalting what they referred to as the Imperial Way, that is, a nationalism centered on the history of the imperial throne.[6] But also appointed to the main school were scholars of the Chinese classics drawn from among the Kyoto Confucians as well as from various loyal daimyo domains. Flanking this on the organizational charts were the two lesser divisions: the East Campus, which housed the faculty of Western medicine, and the South Campus, which dealt with the other aspects of Western learning.

This attempt at compromise was fated to fail. Internal tensions between the Nativists and the Confucians surfaced from the very outset. The two sides chose to do battle over both form and substance. The more substantial intellectual dispute concerned the proper reading of ancient Japanese texts written in classical Chinese. These included some scholarly points that doubtless were lost on many if not most of the Meiji leaders. The question of school ceremonies was more easily grasped. It had been the practice through much of the Tokugawa period for faculty and students at the Shōheisho as well as at many domain schools to perform at specified times in the school calendar public ceremonies and formal observances in honor of the Confucian sages. Schools of Nativist learning, by contrast, had developed their own distinguishing sets of prescribed rituals devoted to indigenous Shinto deities. Their spokesmen persistently expressed indignation that the Tokugawa regime had permitted Shinto deities to be ignored in favor of Chinese figures by the Confucians at the Shōheisho. They argued that this was another instance of the manner in which Chinese "habits had perverted the national essence."[7]

In autumn 1869, the Nativists enjoyed a sweet if all too brief triumph. The university rector ruled that "the gods of learning of the Imperial nation shall be celebrated and the shrine of Confucius shall be abandoned." The Nativist style of reciting the ancient texts was also recognized as orthodox and some works in classical Chinese "not in keeping with the national polity shall not be permitted in the curriculum, although it is not prohibited to study them on one's own."[8]

Thus having vanquished their old foes, the Nativist scholars had reason to celebrate. But any celebration was to be short-lived. They soon became painfully aware of the growing official patronage being given to the faculty of Western learning. In reaction, members of the faculty and students of Nativist learning again petitioned the rector to support their claims to preeminence. The teachers of European sciences and culture had sometimes in the past served as useful allies to Nativists in their struggle against the advocates of

Confucianism, but with the Confucians defeated, Western Studies at the university were now perceived to be the main threat. By 1870 the South Campus already had some 300 pupils enrolled in courses on Western Studies. Another 310 more were being recruited as "tributary students" from the daimyo domains. Each domain was invited to send at its own expense one or two students, depending upon its size, with the thirteen largest domains being permitted three each. This and other government actions gave clear warning that "barbarian" learning was being favored.

These ideological issues were by no means merely academic. Reactionary feelings against Western culture ran high in these early years following the Restoration, as testified to in February 1869 by the assassination of Councillor Yokoi Shōnan. His offense, his assassin alleged, was being "of one mind with barbarian teachings."[9] The situation was so dangerous in Tokyo that bodyguards were assigned to foreign teachers whenever they left the campus. Despite the guards, two teachers were severely wounded by swordsmen. Another, serving in the provincial city of Shizuoka, was fired upon while out duck hunting.

In September 1871, the Meiji government, unable to find an acceptable compromise to the struggles within the university, ordered it closed. Its supervisory functions were transferred to the new Monbushō, or Ministry of Education.[10] The experts in Western Studies continued to be housed in the former South and East Campuses while the government groped for a resolution to the political impasse on educational policy. Senior Confucian and Nativist scholars were dispersed, some to minor posts as archivists, some employed as ritualists in the imperial court or in the Shinto shrines system. Others became teachers at private schools. Some combined these positions with a role in the Great Promulgation Campaign.

The Great Promulgation Campaign

While the dispute over higher education was still raging at the university, closely related ideological campaigns were being waged elsewhere. In February 1870 the government had announced the Great Promulgation Campaign, a Ministry of Divinity program to unify and uplift the general populace through spiritual propaganda.[11] In this the Nativists, thanks to the initial support of friends at court, were allowed to take the lead.

As developed in its first years, the campaign aimed at popularizing a new nationalism to counter the old threat of Christianity on the one hand and justify the new radical reforms on the other. Based on a synthesis of Japanese religious values, its Three Great Teachings combined patriotism, piety, and reverence for the imperial house. Elaborate plans were laid for a huge corps of "evangelicals" to preach to the people in official gatherings arranged by local authorities. They were to be trained in a network of facilities coordinated by a central Great Teaching Institute. The texts of their sermons were structured around the government's call for measures to construct a "rich country and strong defense" through the adoption of "civilization and enlightenment" from abroad. Thus the people would be asked to bear the burden of national taxes, military conscription, and compulsory education as part of their religious obligations.

From the outset, the Great Promulgation Campaign faced several sets of intractable problems, in part because there were inherent contradictions in the Three Great Teachings. By 1875 control over the campaign had been seized by Nativists among the Shinto priests at the Ise Grand Shrine, the most important place of worship for the mythical progenitor of the imperial line, the Sun Goddess. Not surprisingly, these men soon turned the campaign as much against Buddhism as against Christianity. They proposed such things as replacing traditional Buddhist rites at funerals with the less common Shinto rituals. Much was made of the fact that Buddhism was in origin an alien religion that came to Japan, as did Confucianism, from China.

A second set of problems for the Great Promulgation Campaign stemmed from the indifference and even hostility generated by its religious complexion. Helen Hardacre described the reaction of at least the more literate public:

> [Letters to the editor] lampooned the Campaign mercilessly, opining that the Evangelists' internal rivalries were more likely to drive the populace to Christianity than to prevent its advance. No one likes Shinto funerals, they complain; the Teachings are not believable; the sermons are boring; the Evangelists are ridiculous jackasses unfit to serve the nation; Shinto priests are ritualists—it is absurd to think of them reaching a creed; Shinto has nothing to contribute to ethical thought.[12]

Despite this cold reception, the campaign continued on until the mid-1880s and was a prologue to later governmental policies that made Shinto the state religion in fact if not in name. Long before the demise of the Great Promulgation Campaign, however, the Nativists suffered another blow, when in April 1872 the separate agency for religious affairs within the central bureaucracy was closed and many of its functions transferred to the Ministry of Education. Over the next two decades, this ministry was dominated by reformers with an agenda that stressed Western learning.

Moral Values in Schools

Although much that Meiji reformers had to say about education stressed cognitive and utilitarian outcomes, there was also clearly the assumption that those outcomes were dependent upon right attitudes. Schooling for these Meiji reformers was about inculcating morality, especially those civic virtues that would mobilize support for the new government in its efforts to save the nation from decline and perhaps conquest. This was not just true for the more traditional-minded; it was equally so for early Westernizers such as Fukuzawa

Yukichi or Nishi Amane, prominent intellectuals who were to serve as presidents of Tokyo Academy, which was sponsored by the Education Ministry.

Nishi, who did not systematically expound on morals in his private academy, nevertheless told the students in 1870, "Since morals are the principles practiced by individuals in daily life, you should neither neglect them nor stray from them for a moment." Fukuzawa was also deeply concerned with moral education—his complaints about Confucianism were not just that it did not teach useful science but that it taught the wrong morals: "In the education of the East, so often saturated with Confucian teaching, I find two things lacking; . . . a lack of studies in number and reason in material culture, and a lack of the idea of independence in spiritual culture."[13]

This Meiji consensus on the importance of "spiritual culture" was in no way less significant because of the lack of agreement about which moral principles were to be used as the foundation. On the one hand, the new curriculum and textbooks in the 1870s leaned heavily upon Western models. Indeed, all the textbooks recommended in 1873 by the Education Ministry for teaching morals were based on Western texts. The most widely used was directly translated from the French and laid heavy emphasis on respect for the Christian God and the Second Republic.

On the other hand, the Education Ministry in 1874 did add to its textbook list two Tokugawa-period works on ethics, and closer inspection indicates that actual lessons in classrooms were not necessarily so sharp a departure from previously nor so Western as some reformers may have wished. As yet only a small minority of the teachers had been trained in the new normal schools. Since the teachers most often gave ethics lessons orally rather than relying primarily on textbooks, there must have been a good deal of carryover from the Tokugawa period, with its concern for loyalty to superiors, filial piety, diligence in overcoming obstacles, and praise of traditional heroes from the Chinese classics as well as from Japanese history.[14]

This Meiji Japanese faith in education as morally uplifting as well as of utilitarian value had its roots in earlier times, but it should be remembered that emphasis on morality and ethics was also an integral part of contemporary Western educational systems and was thus "modern."[15] For example, Theodore Woolsey, erstwhile president of Yale and one of those prominent U.S. educators from whom the future minister of education Mori Arinori sought advice on how best to modernize Japanese schools, responded in part: "Morality, then, including the duties of the family, of society, toward the state, and toward God, cannot be left out of education."[16] An influential U.S. treatise, *Theory and Practice of Teaching,* translated into Japanese for use by the Ministry of Education in 1876, included the following precept: "The teacher is in a degree responsible for the moral training of the child. . . . It is all-important that our youth should early receive such moral training as shall make it safe to give them knowledge."[17]

The rationale behind the expansion of schooling in modern France and Germany was described by the historian M. J. Maynes in the terms that might well apply to Meiji Japan:

> Schooling proponents [in late eighteenth and early nineteenth century Europe] saw education both as a solution to the structural disruptions generated by social and economic change, and a political necessity in an age of ascendant mass politics. . . . And if there was talk, toward the end of the eighteenth century, of the need for places for these people to learn skills, educational writers as often as not simply emphasized the moral and intellectual traits demanded of a modern people. Schooling campaigns spawned in this era bear the mark of fear, of the need to moralize and manage the poor.[18]

Schools could also, of course, play a role in political resistance to the government. When Saigō Takamori and others left the government in 1873 because of disagreements over policy and patronage, Saigō returned to his home in Kagoshima in southern Kyushu, the castle town of the Satsuma domain. There his lieutenants organized an educational system with heavy political overtones. Their instructors and administrators included some of the most vehement critics of the Tokyo leaders, condemning them for having betrayed the Meiji Restoration. Funded by local taxes as well as private donations, many of these schools stressed instruction in military weaponry and tactics. The prefectural governor, although appointed by Tokyo, not only approved funds for these military academies but also provided jobs in the local bureaucracy and police for their graduates. In 1877 Satsuma exploded into open rebellion, and it took the Tokyo government nine months to end this particular political threat. Clearly the new nationalism had not yet eradicated class or regional loyalties.

Centralized Government Planning

The closing of the government-sponsored university and the creation of the new Ministry of Education opened the way for a clearer emphasis on Western learning. Ministry leaders were drawn from among those who believed that knowledge had to be acquired wholesale from the West. In charge of the ministry in 1871 was Ōki Takatō, a Saga samurai who had once studied English with a Christian missionary in Nagasaki. One of his key assistants, Tanaka Fujimaro, was immediately dispatched with the Iwakura Mission to inspect educational systems in the United States and Europe. A year later, in September 1872, the Supreme Council of State endorsed a ministry proposal entitled "Gakusei" (the School System)—the first detailed plan for a national school system.[19] This plan reflected clearly three major assumptions that, if not universally held by all the decisionmakers, certainly underlay the views of those who had the greatest influence on early educational policy.

One major theme was the widely held axiom that a primary goal of schooling was to build character or, in the words of the 1872 Plan: "It is only by building character, developing wisdom and cultivating their talents that people may prosper in their occupation, manage their property, and thereby achieve their goals in life. But people cannot build character, develop wisdom, or cultivate their talents without education. This is the reason for establishing schools."[20] A second crucial premise was that the making of national educational policy, including decisions on moral education, was the proper function of the central government and no longer to be left to local communities. The third axiom upon which there was broad consensus among the leaders was that schooling, at least at the primary level, was essential for all Japanese regardless of class or gender. We have already seen something of the struggle over what moral principles should form the basis for such "character" building; let us examine each of the other two themes in turn.

Plans for a National System

The blueprint laid out in the 1872 Gakusei Plan consisted of an initial 109 articles followed in 1873 by an additional 104 items. The intent was obviously to provide detailed guidance for local officials on a wide range of organizational, fiscal, and curricular matters. The document is less important for what was immediately accomplished than for what it reveals about the ambitions of the architects.

Their idealistic proposals were based on an extraordinarily systematic design—a huge pyramid with a state-supported university at the apex. The country was to be divided into eight school districts, each including at least one large city—for instance, Tokyo with its thirteen surrounding prefectures constituted District 1; Nagoya was in District 2, Osaka and Kyoto, District 4, Nagasaki, District 6. The districts were to be symmetrical, each to have 1 university, 32 secondary schools, and 6,400 primary schools. Each primary school was to be under the administration of local government authorities, who were in turn to select people from the communities to serve as school officials. The salaries of such officials were to be paid from local funding, but the teachers and the system as a whole would be under the ultimate supervision of the central government.

Although the role of the Education Ministry set forth in the 1872 Gakusei Plan resembled the centralized control in a European country such as France, the early foreign influences on Meiji curriculum and pedagogy were actually predominantly U.S.[21] The head of the Education Ministry, Ōki Takatō, turned for advice to his former teacher, Guido Verbeck, a U.S. (albeit Dutch-born) missionary. Meanwhile, Mori Arinori, then chargé d'affaires in Washington, was collecting written opinions from prominent U.S. educators. In 1873, one of these, Professor David Murray of Rutgers University, was invited to advise the government at the highest level with the title of "National Superintendent of Education." In 1876 the Education Ministry sent sixteen educators to study at the State Normal School at Bridgewater, Massachusetts. One of these, Izawa Shūji, would become head of the Tokyo Normal School upon his return in 1878.[22]

As the Ministry of Education planned for a primary school system, different educational programs were created by other government bureaus also concerned with reforming Japanese institutions with the aid of Western models. The army and navy officer training schools have already been mentioned. In 1871 the civilian Ministry of Industrial Works opened a school of engineering; in 1872 a law school was established by the Ministry of Justice; in 1873 a foreign languages institute was attached to the Ministry of Foreign Affairs; in 1874 the Finance Ministry began offering courses in Western economics. There were also a government school of Western art (1876) and one devoted to music (1880).

On the surface, the proliferation of these specialized institutions for advanced training resembled the French pattern of *grande écoles,* but it also reflected the fact that there was still too little ideological consensus within the central government to permit a truly integrated system of higher education. Each ministry, therefore, tended to pursue its own separate agenda for advanced training.

This pattern meant that these institutions faced the problem of preparatory study. So long as there was a shortage of competent Japanese experts to teach law, engineering, medicine, agriculture, and the other branches of the new learning, foreigners would have to serve as core faculty. Collectively, these government schools employed a large number of foreigner advisers and teachers. But this in turn created linguistic as well as other problems. The foreigners could very rarely communicate in Japanese and too few young Japanese had the requisite foreign languages to understand either foreign lecturers or foreign textbooks. The Justice Ministry utilized its legal advisers from France as lecturers in its law school, but because it was unable to recruit students with adequate language skills, it had to establish a four-year preparatory course in French. The engineering college of the Industrial Ministry, which relied upon a British staff, likewise soon came to the realization that it would be necessary to offer basic English to prepare students for the four-year curriculum. It therefore established a two-year course at the post–primary school level. The Sapporo School of Agriculture in Hokkaido, operating on U.S. models, also used English as the main medium of instruction in these early years and found it necessary to create a preparatory division to impart basic language skills. Three years of instruction was deemed essential before continuing on into the four-year regular curriculum.

The very same difficulties had to be faced at three institutes of advanced training under the direct control of the Ministry of Education. With the collapse of the central university, the ministry had inherited the two nontraditional faculties, the school for general Western Studies, which was the Kaisei Institute on the South Campus, and the more specialized Medical School on the East Campus. Both used Western languages as the media of instruction, German for the Medical School and English for the other. William Elliot Griffis, a Rutgers University graduate who visited the South Campus in January 1871, expressed shock at the rudimentary level of the curriculum and the character of the faculty:

> It was called a "university," but its proper name was a school of languages. The Japanese had very primitive ideas concerning the fitness of men to teach. . . . Anyone who could speak English could evidently teach it. The idea of a trained professional foreign teacher was never entertained by them. . . . The "Professors" at first obtained were often ex-bartenders, soldiers, sailors, clerks, etc. When teaching, with pipe in mouth, and punctuating their instructions with oaths, or appearing in the classroom top-heavy, the Japanese concluded that such eccentricities were merely national peculiarities.[23]

As in the case of the other government schools, preparatory courses had to be created: a three-year course in German and basic sciences for the Medical Department and a four-year (later shortened to a three-year) curriculum in English and other Western Studies for the Kaisei Institute.

These preparatory courses constituted the first "secondary" schooling in the new educational system—curricula intended to bridge the gap between primary schools and advanced education. The 1872 Gakusei Plan had envisioned some type of secondary schools from the beginning, and in November 1872 the Ministry of Education issued the "Rules for Instruction for Middle Schools."[24] But the complications were so great that revised plans for this middle level had to be issued almost immediately and further revisions continued over the next dozen years.

Indeed, from the beginning, educational reformers exhibited considerable ambivalence about postelementary schooling. On the one hand, secondary schools seem to have been conceived of as an intermediary or middle level of comprehensive instruction that would prepare at least a small percentage of students for higher education at the university, thus giving "middle schooling" a role more similar to that of the nineteenth-century French *lycée* or German *gymnasium* than the late twentieth century U.S. high school.[25] For those who successfully navigated the primary courses, the 1872 Plan called for public secondary schools that would both charge tuition and be selective in admissions.

On the other hand, the reformers recognized a need for a secondary level of comprehensive instruction even for those not going on to the university. The 1872 Gakusei thus called for 256 schools to be established at this level—32 for each university in a district but only 1 to each 600 primary schools (or less than 1 for every 120,000 inhabitants). The course of study was further divided into a three-year lower secondary level for fourteen- to sixteen-year-olds and a three-year upper secondary level for seventeen- to nineteen-year-olds. Both levels would teach foreign languages, classics, mathematics, science, and ethics, although political economics was deemed an upper-level subject and apparently three years would suffice for history and geography.[26] A diploma from the upper level was a requirement for entering the university.

The necessity of Western language skills at the tertiary level caused the Ministry of Education to refocus on foreign languages at the secondary level, especially on the English language.[27] In 1873 it issued a new plan, "Rules on Foreign Language Schools," under which each of the now seven university districts were to have a Foreign Language School with foreign instructors on the staff. By 1876 the first seventy-five products of the schools in Aichi, Hiroshima, Nagasaki, Osaka, and Tokyo qualified for admission to advanced studies at the Kaisei Institute. Eleven more graduates simultaneously entered the Sapporo School of Agriculture. Despite these signs of success, the network of language preparatory schools was closed down in 1877, apparently because the expense was simply too great for the government to bear. The Tokyo Foreign Language School survived but only as a four-year preparatory division of a new Tokyo University, admitting primary school graduates seeking eventually to pass through to the university departments of natural sciences, letters, or law.

Thus, a decade after the beginning of the Meiji era, there was still no systematic solution to the question of secondary education. The challenge of how to bridge the gap between mass primary schooling and advanced specialized training remained. Moreover, there was still a demand for middle-echelon technicians, schoolteachers, and other vocational training. The result was a very untidy set of multiple tracks for postprimary schools. By the early 1880s an array of special schools were attached directly to the new public institutions of higher education (see Figure 2.1).

The solution to the language problem and the ultimate goal in the educational system, no less than in the military and economic spheres, was always indigenization—the filling of these new roles with native Japanese. But advanced study for most fields of the new Western knowledge in the 1870s could be acquired only by study abroad. The modernizers within the new government recognized this from the outset, and almost immediately after coming to power they had reinstated the overseas scholarship program inherited from the Tokugawa regime.[28] All government-sponsored students were initially placed under the jurisdiction of the Ministry of Foreign Affairs, which then ordered all Tokugawa selected students to return home while new policies were being formulated. Over the next three years, 1868 through 1870, a total of 174 new students were sent abroad at government expense.

But the program also had heavy opposition. The main issues facing the proponents of a large-scale overseas program mirrored those in higher education policy as a whole: (1) ensuring quality, (2) fending off critics who saw such programs as blatant Westernization, and (3) finding adequate funds. The first

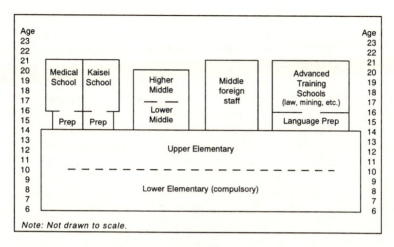

FIGURE 2.1
Main Tracks in Public School System, 1873.
Source: Adapted from chart in Monbushō, *Gakusei 80 nenshi*, p. 1026.

new regulations, announced in spring 1868, included a specific prohibition against conversion to foreign religions, doubtless an effort to reassure the traditionalists about the dangers of being infected with Christianity. Subsequently, the comprehensive "Rules for Overseas Study" promulgated in February 1871 ordered government-sponsored students to visit their local Shinto shrine prior to departure to reassure the deities that they would conduct themselves properly while away. Under these regulations, legal jurisdiction came to be shared with the Education Ministry and included private students as well as those on government funds. The following year, when the Education Ministry set forth the enormously ambitious Gakusei Plan of 1872, it envisioned annually sending as many as eighty students for periods of between three and five years at a cost of the equivalent of $900 to $1,800 each per annum—over 10 percent of the total projected ministry budget. This program fell victim to the cost-cutters in the Finance Ministry, who sliced the total Education Ministry request in half. A report drawn up within the Finance Ministry spelled out some of the difficulties with the existing program:

> What the students are actually studying differs tremendously from what they should be studying. There are those who go on to specialized study without finishing their preparatory work or those who hire private tutors and do not attend a school or those who are constantly changing their teachers and their schools. . . . In general, seven or eight out of every ten students now overseas are doing this kind of poor work.[29]

Tests given to returning students substantiated the charge that few could demonstrate that their studies had resulted in usable skills even in foreign languages.

Faced with such justifiable criticism and a woefully inadequate budget, Ministry of Education officials saw little choice but to radically overhaul the program. A number of students were recalled, and procedures for recruitment within Japan as well as supervision while abroad were tightened. When it still proved impossible to balance its budget at the end of 1873, the Education Ministry shut the government subsidy program down for two years. In 1875 it came up with a new scheme, substituting long-term loans for scholarships. To ensure proper language and other preparation, qualifying examinations were made more rigorous. In practice, these policy changes meant that only those who had studied at the Tokyo Kaisei Institute proved eligible for the first two years under the new procedures. Nevertheless, by 1880 these renewed efforts to promote overseas studies had helped to raise the number of Japanese youth with experience studying abroad to over 900: There were 407 under government sponsorship, and 519 on private funds.[30]

From these ranks came the Japanese who would staff Tokyo University and other institutions of advanced training in the 1880s. With a few notable exceptions in the early years, they had studied at Tokyo University or its predecessor institutions—entering at an early age, acquiring a basic knowledge of foreign languages and Western learning, and then being selected among the very few sponsored by the government for study abroad.[31] One of these students recalled vividly the excitement that sustained them during the twenty-five day ocean voyage from Yokohama to San Francisco, the long transcontinental rail trip to the Atlantic coast in order to sail for London, and the five-year stay in England:

> It was, however, not the scientific training alone that I received in England. [It] was a period in which some of the greatest and most illustrious men and, also, of women were to be met with in almost every field of human activity. . . . Having had the rare fortune of being in England at such a glorious time, I could not and would not confine myself to scientific sciences studies alone, but wishing to look upon England with more widely opened eyes, I studied something of English History, of English Literature, of English Art, and even, of English Drama.[32]

Typically such early government-sponsored students would be assigned a post in the civil bureaucracy upon their return to Japan and many eventually joined the faculty at Tokyo Imperial University. This service was mandatory at that time for those who had received government support abroad. The student quoted above was appointed both full professor and head of the law faculty at Tokyo University. Many of his colleagues had similar career paths.[33]

The Place for Private Schools

Although the 1872 Gakusei Plan had clearly projected a role for the state in providing secondary education, it was neither compulsory nor subsidized to the extent that primary schooling was. As the preamble to the plan had explicitly proclaimed, "Higher [than primary] education is left to the ability and the means of the individual."[34] But there was considerable demand for postprimary schooling, and when the government did not fill this vacuum, the private sector rushed in.

To some extent the government expected and may even have welcomed the private-sector involvement, although if so this was not evident at the beginning. In early 1871 the Council of State had promulgated a regulation that stipulated registration and record-keeping procedures for private academies. These rules were tightened up the next year, and the following year those students receiving government aid were prohibited from using it at private schools. Private middle schools were also affected by the economic problems of the samurai class, which grew worse after their guaranteed stipends were ended in 1876, since it was from these families that many of the pupils came. However, the government did indirectly subsidize these private schools to the extent that faculty at government facilities were permitted to moonlight part-time as teachers in the private sector.[35]

It is possible that the government was more concerned with competition at the primary school level than with postprimary levels. Certainly its policies were not a serious effort to stop a proliferation of private middle schools. Continuing a tradition from the Tokugawa period, Tokyo and other major cities continued to have numerous private academies of one sort or another. Where there had been a total of 20 both public and private academies in 1873, there were 201 in 1876 and 784 in 1879; of the 784 schools, 86 percent were private.[36] Many of these private academies were quite small, with only one or two teachers, and some were run by women as a family enterprise.[37]

Among the best known of the larger private academies was Fukuzawa Yukichi's Keiō. Founded in the last days of the Tokugawa regime, it flourished in the first years after the Restoration as Fukuzawa's writings gained him a sizable reputation. It had 325 students in 1870, stimulating Fukuzawa to use his contacts within the government to lease land for a new facility.[38] By 1875 it had a total of over 370 students studying the English language and Western learning.

Yet another type of private institution was built with funds from the new business community, organized by modern entrepreneurs such as Shibusawa Eiichi. Shibusawa had led the effort to create the Tokyo Chamber of Commerce and then helped Mori Arinori gain the backing of businessmen to create in 1875 the forerunner of the prestigious Tokyo School of Commerce. This school began as a private institution; later it was transformed into a government-supported facility. Still other private schools were devoted to more traditional studies, especially the Chinese classics that so long dominated Japanese views of serious education. Some Buddhist churches also expanded existing schools or opened new ones.

One of the actions by the new government that most upset conservatives was its permissive policy toward Christianity. The 250-year-old ban on the religion was lifted in 1873, and by the end of the 1870s there were over fifty Christian churches functioning in the country with some 5,000 converts. Education in Western Studies was one of the chief attractions offered by the Protestant missionaries and a number of schools of various levels sprang up in Yokohama and Tokyo in the 1870s. Nor was it long before Japanese converts themselves began to be involved in teaching. In Kyoto a young graduate of Amherst College and Andover Seminary, Niishima Jo, was given permission in 1874 to open Dōshisha Academy. Niishima (or Joseph Harding Neeshima, as he was known to foreigners) had good connections with some in the central government because he had served as a translator to the Iwakura Mission during its stay in the United States. It is also said that the Kyoto prefectural governor favored the opening of Dōshisha Academy because he was grateful for treatment received from a medical missionary.[39] But others among the Kyoto populace were less congenial and some even attempted to drive the Christian academy out of town.

Many more young Japanese were being exposed to Christianity through contact with foreigners hired to teach in the public schools. A well-publicized incident took place at the Kumamoto Academy in 1872 when three dozen young samurai ignored family pressures and disobeyed domain regulations to convert to the new religion. The local authorities retaliated by not renewing the contract of their teacher, L. L. Janes, who had been prohibited from proselytizing.[40] The central government was far more lenient: William S. Clark, the director of the government's new Sapporo School of Agriculture, was permitted to use the Bible in teaching morality.

Access to Educational Opportunity

Another major premise evident in the 1872 Gakusei Plan was also quite radical. All of the nation's youth, regardless of former social rank, geographic region, or even gender, were to receive an elementary education; moreover, admission to postprimary schools was also to be based upon ability, not socioeconomic class. This principle was firmly held by the dominant faction within the new leadership. The preamble of the 1872 Gakusei Plan explicitly and emphatically rejected the view that "learning was something only samurai and above" did; rather, all Japanese were equal in the need to receive schooling. Moreover, this principle was explicitly extended to females as well as males:

> Henceforth, in the future, there shall be no community among the people as a whole—whether they be noble, samurai, farmer, artisan, merchant, or woman—where there is an uneducated household nor a family with an uneducated person.

... Parents and guardians should be held at fault if they fail to have a child—whether boy or girl—attend primary school.[41]

Nowhere were the revolutionary intentions of Meiji reforms more evident than here. In the Meiji period, as in the Tokugawa period, the purposes of schools were to teach basic skills appropriate to expected socioeconomic roles and political loyalty. But the definitions of expected roles and political loyalty were now in flux. Under the Tokugawa regime, roles in society had ideally been allocated on the basis of inherited social rank, and at least among the samurai political elite this was to a considerable extent carried out in practice. Formal education, though increasing in importance during the early nineteenth century, was still viewed by the Tokugawa governing elite primarily as a means to prepare samurai youth for roles already reserved for them. Schooling for others was not routinely a concern of either the central government or the domain lords.

The Meiji period witnessed the reversal of this—ideally roles were now to be allotted according to merit. Of course, there is no question that inherited family status and wealth would in practice continue to mean a great deal. Nonetheless, it is also true that wealth and status were not sufficient credentials for those seeking entrée into the new bureaucracies and professions.

Equal opportunity and egalitarian outcomes are, of course, different matters, and there were divergent views of how much equality there should be once the competition had run its course. Fukuzawa gained fame for such pronouncements as "When men were created by heaven, there were attached to them certain fixed, inalienable rights, and these rights, having been bestowed upon men equally by heaven, cannot be usurped by human power." He expressed great optimism about the potential of commoners if only given the opportunity: "If you ask why these commoners are now without spirit and power, it is because they have had to live in servitude under an oppressive government. . . . Commoners were not born without spirit or power; they are merely oppressed by what you call the [samurai's] spirit and power and thus have been unable to exhibit their vitality."[42]

But Nishi Amane stated the more accepted view when he said, "People generally have the same heaven-bestowed intellect, but some are naturally able and some are dull. . . . No matter how much you teach those who are naturally dull or force them to learn, they cannot be superior to others or become men of talent. Thus what is needed is to teach them right away some other trade which they can do."[43]

Commoners Versus Samurai

Early Meiji educational reforms were closely related to the decisions to remove the variety of legal restrictions on the different social classes that had previously characterized Tokugawa social policy. In late 1871 the government announced that members of the samurai class were legally permitted to "perform duties in agriculture, industry, and commerce" without losing their official status as samurai.[44] Recipients of larger annual stipends were offered, on a sliding scale, lump-sum payments of cash and/or government bonds in lieu of a guaranteed annual income. These arrangements for what amounted to a severance pay or a buyout were initially offered on a voluntary basis, as was the government decree that samurai swords need no longer be worn except on official duty. But the message was unmistakable: The legal as well as economic distinctions that had separated samurai from commoners were being systematically abolished.

In a parallel series of government decrees between 1871 and 1873 the ordinary peasants were emancipated legally from feudal restrictions of the past although simultaneously burdened with new obligations. Commoners were now permitted to plant whatever crops they wished, travel freely, ride horseback, adopt formal surnames, and marry into samurai families—actions previously restricted under shogunate and domain laws. Equality in civil and criminal law courts was also promised and even the outcast groups—the hereditary Burakumin, who had been traditionally limited to certain residential areas and occupations having to do with butchering animals, tanning leather, and disposing of the dead—were now legally emancipated, although social discrimination against them certainly did not cease. Accompanying the removal of these restrictions were a new type of land tax and a conscription law that made each able-bodied male subject to military service. Moreover, in 1869 the Kōgisho, primarily an assembly of samurai from the various domains, debated a proposal to introduce an examination system to decide recruitment into government service. Three-quarters of the almost 200 members voted in favor, but the issue was then left unresolved for some time.

Meanwhile, admissions to the first university had initially been based on what has been labeled a "tribute system of selecting students": Each daimyo sent students and paid their expenses, and the number of students was based on the size of the domain.[45] This same system was used when the new naval training facility was inaugurated in October 1869. But the contradictions inherent in recruiting samurai from the daimyo domains in order to build a central military force led, by the end of 1870, to abandoning this "tribute system" at the military academy. It was replaced by admission based on the ideal, if not necessarily always the practice, of merit. In the words of the January 1871 announcement, the navy was accepting applications "whatever their social class and geographical origins."[46] It was not long before government civilian schools followed suit. Students at Tokyo University, like those at its predecessor, the Kaisei Institute, continued to be drawn primarily from among the sons of samurai families as late as the early 1880s. Nevertheless, by the mid-1870s admission policies had shifted away from nomination by local officials in favor of demonstrable merit.

The government commitment in principle to equal opportunity for all to serve their nation in these areas was paralleled by its concern for breaking down inherited social class distinctions within the schools. Schooling came to be viewed ideally as the primary mechanism both to prepare youth for their futures and to certify meritorious achievement. This momentous shift in perceptions of what schools were for came about only through massive changes in state policy as the Meiji government destroyed the notion of "reserved" slots and relied increasingly upon a state-sponsored school system not only in mobilizing the masses of the populace for new tasks in an industrializing society but also in recruiting commoner and samurai youth into new elite roles.

The 1872 Gakusei Plan was quite detailed. At the coeducational primary level it called for a fixed national curriculum for all children beginning at the age of six. In the first four grades—named the "ordinary" course—they would study Japanese language skills, elementary arithmetic, the principles of natural science and geography, ethics, singing, and physical education. Promotion would depend upon semiannual examinations. After the initial four-year curriculum, they would advance to an upper elementary level, ideally completing a total of eight years by the age of fourteen. The upper elementary curriculum would include, among other subjects, history, foreign languages, drawing, geometry, chemistry, and biology.

The regular use of examinations constituted an important innovation in Japanese schools and had several purposes. The reformers within the central government were intent upon establishing a set of national standards to replace the decentralized anarchy of Tokugawa education. At the same time they were also interested in objective, impersonal criteria to select those who would go on to more advanced schooling. Evidence that these examinations were taken seriously can be found in accounts of local officials and district school chiefs in attendance during the oral testing. Some prefectures held intramural competitions, which presumably helped motivate students and teachers alike. Such emphasis on competition worried some observers that teachers would care only about the best and brightest: "[It was] as if the teachers were bringing their students to a horse race or cockfight. It seemed that the teachers devoted all their energies to 'choosing and training good horses and cocks, while they didn't care for the rest of the animals, whether they died or not.'"[47]

How well grounded such fears were is difficult to ascertain. The exams themselves are said not to have been unduly difficult. Nationwide statistics from these early years are not available, but in 1877 in Tokyo 96 percent passed the first-term tests and 92 percent passed the graduation exam.

Females Versus Males

For some, the more shocking aspect of these changes was the inclusion of females in compulsory primary education. This policy had surprisingly strong support among Meiji leaders. One of the earliest indications of elite attitudes toward the education of females can be found in an 1871 memorial by the influential Satsuma samurai Kuroda Kiyotaka. He advocated sending numbers of young girls abroad for an education, and in October 1871 the imperial court proclaimed that those males receiving government funds to study abroad should take their wives along since "the upbringing of children is closely related to the training they receive from their mothers."[48] Since the proclamation also stressed giving priority for foreign study to nobles over commoners—something that was clearly not settled policy—the document cannot be taken to represent a firm consensus within the government even at that time. But it is true that the official mission led abroad by Prince Iwakura in November 1871 took with it five young females: two aged fifteen, one twelve, one ten, and one seven. The youngest was Tsuda Umeko, who after graduation from Bryn Mawr was to become one of the most famous female educators of her generation.[49]

Mori Arinori, then chargé d'affaires in Washington, took the girls under his wing and arranged for them to be tutored in English in preparation for entering U.S. schools. Mori had already formed a conviction about educating females that he would zealously advocate upon his return to Japan in 1873: "If [mothers] have not studied in their younger years . . . they often drown their children in love without understanding the means for employing their loving power in rearing their offspring. Women, therefore, should first receive a broad general education, expand their intellectual horizons and learn how to use their wealth of love."[50]

This stress on utility of education for women's domesticity was, of course, not at odds with views of educators in the United States at the time. In fact Mori Arinori had previously sought advice from, among others, David Murray, then a professor of mathematics at Rutgers University. Murray, who would be invited to become a key educational adviser to the government in 1873, expressed a strong opinion about the purposes of female education in his reply to Mori:

> Female education is equally important with male education. The employments of woman do not carry her into the same . . . [spheres], but in her [own] . . . she is equally important. . . . She must receive that culture which will make her the acceptable and equal companion of man. The comfort and happiness of home depend largely upon her, and it is the part of wisdom to give her the means of making it refined and cultivated. The care and supervision of children naturally fall into her hands during their most impressionable years, and the guardians of the future men and women of a nation ought, in common prudence, to be well educated.[51]

Mori and his fellow reformers were certainly not advocating full equality for women. This was made clear by Katō Hiroyuki, who would soon be appointed president of Tokyo University. In an essay entitled "Abuses of Equal Rights for

Men and Women," Katō condemned "the ugly custom of keeping concubines promiscuously and the bad practice by which the husband holds the wife in contempt." But he also attacked Western social practices, such as allowing the lady to pass through a door first. To him, this seemed to verge on veneration because "the rights of the wife seem rather to surpass those of the husband."[52] The founder of Keiō Academy, Fukuzawa Yukichi, was less equivocal in his condemnation of men taking concubines or mistresses:

> Rather than become embroiled in a noisy discussion of the merits of equal rights, I would direct attention only to an aspect that anyone can easily understand. . . . This simple point is neither religious nor theoretical but rather a mathematical computation . . . since the number of men and women in the world are roughly equal, the calculation will show that one man should marry one woman.[53]

Although Fukuzawa did not open his own Keiō Academy to females, he professed to believe that "in matters of learning, there should be no difference between men and women."[54]

Nakamura Masanao, the noted translator of Samuel Smiles's famous book *Self Help,* who would become the first president of the Tokyo Women's Higher Normal School, is usually credited with popularizing the phrase "good wife, wise mother" to describe the goals of female education. In 1875 he wrote that "we must invariably have fine mothers if we want effectively to advance the people to the area of enlightenment and to alter their customs and conditions for the good. . . . To develop fine mothers, there is nothing better than to educate the daughters." A Christian convert, Nakamura went so far as to assert that the behavior of the mother during pregnancy would determine the physical strength of the newborn and also that "prenatal education is essential in moral and religious training." In 1877, when the new Gakushūin was opened for the children of the nobility, it admitted girls as well as boys.[55]

Since the first institutions of higher learning were limited to men, government-sponsored college preparatory schools also admitted males alone. Therefore, private schools, especially those run by Protestant Christian missionaries, had an opportunity to play a special role in offering schooling for females in this early period. In 1870 the American Mary Kidder opened the first such school for girls in Yokohama, which later became known as the Ferris Girls School. The following year the forerunner of Kyōritsu School for Girls also opened in Yokohama, and in 1873 the forerunner of the Women's Gakuin became the first girls' school in Tokyo run by Christians. By the end of the decade there were two more schools in the capital, two in Kyoto, and one each in Kobe and Nagasaki.

None of this is to say, as some general histories imply, that the early Meiji government was opposed to females going beyond elementary schooling. The 1872 Gakusei Plan included provisions regulating secondary schooling for women as well as men, and the Tokyo Girls' School was created that same year.

Moreover, until 1880 coeducation was actually permitted in public middle schools. In 1882 the government set forth regulations for a different type of secondary school—the *joshi kōtō gakkō,* or "girls' high(er) school." From even earlier, government reformers also included women in their plans for teacher training.

From its beginning the Education Ministry was also aware of the critical need to staff the new educational system with modernly trained teachers. In July 1872 it established the Normal School in Tokyo under the supervision of an American, Marion M. Scott. Only twenty-eight years old when he had arrived in Japan in 1871, Scott was nevertheless one of the key men in advising on the production of textbooks and training of teachers over the next three years. The Normal School enrolled just over fifty males in its first class. Two other normal schools were added in the following year, four more in 1874, and by 1879 there were ninety government teachers' schools and training institutes with over 6,500 students.[56] Two of these were designated "higher normal schools" for preparing instructors in the middle schools.

The first concrete step toward providing postprimary schooling to females came in January 1874 when the government approved Education Ministry plans for the creation of women's normal schools. The Education Ministry proclaimed that "for the people to be enlightened . . . it is very necessary to create a women's normal school. . . . It is necessary not merely because the gentle graces in woman's nature enable them to teach classes well but because they are suited to the nurture of children."[57]

There is an important point that should not be overlooked amidst the obvious sexism here. Although the role of nurturing children was of course a traditional one in Japanese society, the Meiji reformers did not intend that childrearing simply follow the customs handed down from pre-Restoration times. Here, as in so many other spheres, new attitudes and practices were to be taught in the public school system.[58] They further believed that the need for women teachers in this process was one of the important reasons for state-supported schooling for females beyond the primary level. The first Women's Normal School opened in Tokyo in 1875. The empress graced the ceremony with her presence and contributed ¥5,000 from imperial household funds. In that year there were only 662 females teaching at the primary school level—less than 2 percent of the national total of 36,866. Over the next five years other facilities to increase that number were created here and there in the country, and by 1880 the number of women teaching in elementary schools rose to 2,350. This effort almost doubled the percentage of women on primary school teaching staffs but still left 96 percent of the staff male.

Some of these early Meiji female teachers were holdovers from the Tokugawa period, and a number of these women were eventually retrained. Even though there were women teachers prior to Meiji reforms, some local communities did not welcome them. Not only did students in such places heckle them verbally, but there are even stories of women teachers being targets for rock throwers.[59] Nevertheless, there was no shortage of female applicants for admission to the normal schools and by 1900 they would make up 15 percent of the public elementary school teaching staffs.

The Failure of the First Central Plan

Despite, or perhaps in part because of, the ambitious goals, these early efforts at centralized planning were not very successful in the short run. The 1872 Gakusei proved to be an architectural blueprint without sufficient willing builders or adequate building materials. For the first few years following the 1872 commitment to a centralized structure of mass education, the government made great progress. By 1875 some 3,600 new primary school buildings had been built and there were an additional 17,600 other public schools in operation. Another 1,300 schools opened by the end of 1876. But momentum then ebbed. In 1879 the nation could still count only 27,000 public elementary schools and 107 public middle schools, half of what had been envisaged, and many of these housed in makeshift facilities inherited from the Tokugawa era.[60]

Enrollment and attendance figures are even more indicative of the problem. Of the primary school–aged children (six to thirteen years old) in 1875, only 50 percent of males and 19 percent of females were enrolled. The rate of enrollment had improved by 1879, but only to 58 percent and 23 percent respectively (see Figure 2.2).

Figures for the city of Kyoto in 1874 and 1879, for instance, list only a bit over half of the children as actually being enrolled in elementary school. Tokyo was somewhat closer to 60 percent. These percentages were high compared to the country as a whole. Kagoshima City, the castle town of the former Satsuma domain, had only a third of its children enrolled in elementary schools in 1879, and the figure for Aomori City in the far north of the island of Honshu was only a little more than one-fourth.[61]

Moreover, the enrollment figures alone did not tell the whole story. Rates of actual attendance were even lower. Even in the capital city, only a little more than half of all primary school–aged children were actually attending school in 1877. An 1882 Education Ministry survey estimated that nationwide, 56 percent were enrolled in elementary school and no more than 65 percent of those attended regularly. In other words, just barely over one-third of the age group was in the classroom regularly.[62]

Much of the problem was caused simply by a lack of central funds available to subsidize the plan. There is little question that the early reformers badly overestimated the central government's funding capacity and/or the willingness at the local level to bear the multiple burdens of such a system. Funding for the primary system had to depend almost entirely upon local sources—tax revenues

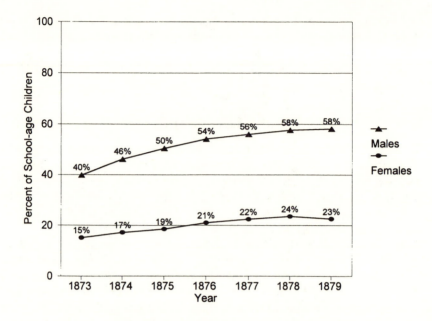

FIGURE 2.2
Primary School Enrollments by Gender, 1873–1879.
Source: Data from Monbushō, *Gakusei 80 nenshi,* table 1, p. 1036.

and private donations. In the first decade, central government funding exceeded 10 percent only in the year 1873 and then declined to half of that by 1879.

The reformer Kido Takayoshi, serving as minister of education in 1874, was furious at the failure of his colleagues to give higher priority to education. He particularly condemned the decision to mount a punitive expedition against aborigines in Taiwan (who had slain a number of Japanese seamen) as a diversion of funds from the school system: "The Court's conduct of education," he wrote, "is in some respects inferior to that of feudal days." The domestic agenda rather than foreign issues should command government's full attention: "When one imagines the plight of our thirty million poverty-stricken people, the controversy over which is more urgent, internal or external affairs, resolves itself."[63]

Although certain school districts—perhaps as many as half nationwide—did operate without charging elementary school tuition, in many other districts families too poor even to owe direct taxes were nevertheless required to pay tuition for their child to attend school.[64] The 1872 Plan referred to scholarship funds being made available at the local level for needy students of merit, but apparently the government intended that the affluent village landlords provide these funds, as many in fact did.[65]

But even when there were no direct fees required, poor families often needed the labor of children either to work alongside of adults or to tend to infants in order to free others to work. Thus, although attendance was legally mandatory and there was a long-standing tradition for well over a third of the male population to have some schooling outside the home, many parents were slow to see the benefits of sending off a child—particularly a female—who might be of some use helping on the farm, in the shop, or in the household.

Coming as this did simultaneously with new forms of land taxes and universal military obligations, it is not surprising that local sentiments were often both negative and heated. As the leaders of the political opposition asserted in their 1877 memorial "Advocating the Establishment of a Representative Assembly," "The establishment of schools and the promotion of agricultural industries are no doubt necessary and excellent, but when the ideas are carried out to an extravagant extent at the expense of the people, the only effect is to create a great deal of bitter feeling among the people, who complain that they are not profited by these new measures."[66] That the Western-style schoolhouse was often the finest building in the village was also a reminder that it was the most expensive. There were hundreds of instances in which the schoolhouses were damaged or even destroyed to make the point.[67]

Nor did attendance at school in these years mean that students were necessarily receiving a rigorous education. Richard Rubinger cited the memoirs of one Japanese growing up in the early years of the Meiji period whose class was held in a Buddhist temple building with a teacher less than rigorous: "Although we were supposed to be doing penmanship, we mostly just fooled around—painting each others' faces with ink and playing ghost behind the Buddhist altar."[68] Not only had most of the school facilities been inherited from the old Tokugawa community schools, but also, worse, the teachers were too often holdovers from the previous era. The most optimistic estimate was that only one out of six of these instructors in the first years had received training in the new institutes. An 1882 Education Ministry survey estimated one properly qualified teacher per primary school, or one to each 100 students. Hence, regardless of what curriculum and textbooks the Ministry of Education sanctioned, much of what went on in the classroom was mediated through teachers practiced only in the older methods.[69] Circumstances were even worse at the secondary level. The domain schools, which had at least provided samurai with postprimary schooling, closed in 1872 when the domains were abolished, and there were few government-sponsored replacements.

Some of the resistance to the centrally mandated compulsory schooling was doubtless less economic and more ideological in nature. Parents who did not find the tuition and tax burdens very great might still resist the new curricula being dictated from the center. Schooling involved not just new skills but also new attitudes and there were many who objected to alien values infecting their communities.[70] As we shall see, their complaints received a sympathetic hearing among the traditionalists in the Tokyo government.

Conclusion

The initial efforts at educational reform in the early Meiji period were bold in concept but haphazard in implementation. The early reformers placed a very high value on schooling, only to have other priorities drain away needed funds and energies, making the grand scheme enunciated in the 1872 Gakusei Plan impossible. Moreover, as long as the spotlight was diverted elsewhere, the radical Westernizers could dominate educational planning. But once implementation picked up momentum at the end of the first decade, a powerful political backlash developed.

Izawa Shūji, head of the Tokyo Normal School, provided us with a concise summary of the polarization of opinion in an 1879 report on the introduction of Western music into Japanese primary schools:

> The prevailing opinions . . . can be summed up essentially into three [theories]. The first says that, as music is the chief means which excites and stimulates our emotions, and as human passions are naturally expressed in musical notes, the same music might be universally used by all mankind . . . in spite of the differences of country or of race. . . .
>
> The second says that there are in every country and nation their own languages, customs, and usages, which being the natural outgrowth of the character of the people and the conditions of the land cannot be changed by human efforts. So the same is true with music which has its first origins in the inclinations of the human mind, and [existing national music] has since been preserved by each nation. . . . Therefore it will be a far wiser plan to take measures towards the cultivation and improvement of our own music.

Izawa attempted to escape from this polarization by "taking a middle course." "The proper measure would be to secure a new and suitable music for our country [today], by working out a compromise between European and oriental music."[71]

Although an early compromise might be effected over music in the schools, issues of moral instruction were not as easily settled. By the end of the first decade of reforms, the ideological struggle over what ethical values should be taught in the compulsory education was to burst into political fire.

3

Assimilating the Elements: 1879–1905

The pieces imported from foreign lands must more or less [be] naturalized. . . . Our aim is not entire adoption of European Musics, but the making or refining of Japanese Music by assimilating the elements of both Native and European Musics.

—Izawa Shūji, Head of Tokyo Normal School[1]

The administrators of our various schools . . . should at all times be mindful of the fact that the undertaking is on behalf of the state, not on behalf of the individual student.

—Mori Arinori, Minister of Education[2]

The first decade of the new Meiji regime had been one of confusion and even chaos in education. Progress in implementing the 1872 scheme had almost come to a halt despite the fact that in 1879 the nation could count only about half the public elementary schools or public middle schools that had been envisioned. Nor did the next decade see the end to the problems. Government budgetary problems, chronic throughout the 1870s, reached crisis proportions by 1880, leading to a drastic retrenchment in government expenditures that lasted into the mid-1880s, during which time there was little money for the Education Ministry to implement its plans.[3]

Moreover, conflicts over education within the central government erupted into the open more frequently at the end of the 1870s as the failures of the state to bring uniformity to the public education system became increasingly evident. But the tricornered policy struggle between Confucians, Nativists, and Westernizers that had characterized Japanese intellectual debates since mid-century now gave way to a new triangle of would-be reformist factions. Radical

Westernization continued to be advocated by Education Ministry officials inside the government and by some polemicists outside. Others persevered in their attempt at a Confucian revival. But the older forms of Shinto-centered Nativism had suffered devastating blows with the loss of the first university in 1870 and a subsequent bureaucratic reorganization that marginalized religious affairs within government.

The most effective factions among those vying to set educational policy were now led by men who proposed a syncretic version of modernization. They rejected rigid adherence to either Confucianism or Western liberalism while seeking to assimilate elements from both. These reformists had to cope with an increasingly fierce backlash from conservatives who, distressed by the enormous social and political changes taking place in the country, expressed particular horror at what was happening in the schools. The modernizing approach to schooling adopted by Itō Hirobumi and Mori Arinori generated such great resentment in some quarters that Mori was assassinated in 1889. Thus it fell to Mori's immediate successors at the Education Ministry to put the last of the framework for a state system of public schooling into place. By 1905 they would complete the foundations begun with the Gakusei Plan of 1872 and erect much of an educational structure that would remain in place into World War II and beyond. Throughout this building process, the key issues in the battles over how to educate the nation's youth remained (1) new values versus the old morality and (2) central government versus local control.

These battles were intensified after the adoption of the 1889 constitution, which created a parliament that served as a new central area for local elites as well as urban intellectuals to voice their views. Between 1875 and 1885 both the legislative and executive functions of the central government had been performed by the Council of State, a committee of imperial advisers and ministers nominally appointed by the imperial throne. Although there was also a consultative body, the "Senate," or Chamber of Elders, its members were also imperial appointees and exercised only what influence the council permitted. In 1885 the council was replaced by a smaller cabinet, made up of the heads of the various civil and military ministries. With the promulgation of the 1889 Meiji constitution, the Chamber of Elders was replaced with a bicameral legislature. This new parliament was composed in part of elected members who were often all too eager to enter the ideological fray and to represent the interests of their local constituents.

Renewed Ideological Struggles

The ideological content of education had begun to vacillate sharply at the end of the 1870s.[4] Although the Education Ministry continued to espouse a version of modernization virtually synonymous with the "civilization and enlightenment" of the West, there was now an argument over whether the wrong Western nations had been taken as models. Whereas the administrative framework in the 1872 Plan had been heavily influenced by France and the chief advisers to the early Ministry of Education had been American, there were now powerful voices advocating Germany as a better model on the grounds that its political culture was more appropriate to the new Japan.[5]

The ministry issued a new Education Ordinance in 1879 to supersede all previous ordinances, but almost simultaneously the imperial household issued another pronouncement in the name of the emperor. These "Great Principles of Education," written by Motoda Eifu, were in direct contradiction to the modernizing spirit of the 1879 ordinance:

> The essence of education—to pursue the way of man by mastering knowledge and skills, righteousness, loyalty and filial piety—lies in the great principles explained in our ancestral precepts and native classics. Yet in recent times there are not a few who ignore good conduct and violate our customs in their gallop toward civilization and enlightenment by pursuing only knowledge and skills. . . . In their racing after Western strong points they downgrade humaneness, righteousness, loyalty and filial piety. . . . People will cultivate sincerity and practice good conduct if ethical teachings are based on Confucius.[6]

The dominant faction within the ministry responded to its critics by seeking an even closer alliance with Westernizers among leading intellectuals. In January 1879 the ministry sanctioned the creation of the Tokyo Academy, a scholarly society to advise on policy issues.[7] All of its founding members had been pioneer reformers in the Meirokusha (The 1873 Society) and were among the most distinguished thinkers of their day. Fukuzawa Yukichi (founder of Keiō University) was elected chair of that society. The other founding members were Kanda Kōhei (author of the 1869 reform proposal on civil service examinations), Katō Hiroyuki (president of Tokyo University), Mitsukuri Shūhei (pioneer in Dutch Studies), Nakamura Masanao (headmaster of the Women's Normal School), Nishi Amane, and Tsuda Masamichi (both experts on Western legal systems). Mori Arinori also became a member in May before leaving to serve as envoy to London.

Fukuzawa, in particular, was an ardent foe of Confucianism and all traditional religious values, often attacking them with the rhetorical equivalent of an ax. Mori used a more honed style, as in the following remarks to the Tokyo Academy in a speech on the importance of physical education:

> All excellence or profundity of Confucian doctrine aside . . . those who study it generally ruin their health with long hours of passive sitting and end up by being, I regret to say, utterly enfeebled bookworms. . . . [Moreover], its pedagogical approach as such is mistaken. By luring its devotees into a life of unproductive study . . . [Confucian scholarship] has been the major source of effeteness in today's world.[8]

The Education Ministry also attempted to meet criticism by cutting costs, streamlining administration, and perhaps in the search for more political support, allowing greater autonomy to local communities. This last strategy was part of a new blueprint, the September 1879 Education Ordinance. If the blueprint in this 1879 ordinance had remained policy, it would have shifted much more of the responsibility for schooling down to the local levels of government. The ordinance did not, however, entail a complete reversal in philosophy, since it continued to espouse Westernization as synonymous with modernization. Indeed, the devolution of authority over educational matters to the local levels has been seen by some as simply favoring the U.S. model of Westernization over that of the French.[9] In any case, neither this plan nor Minister Tanaka were to survive long.

Motoda Eifu and Confucian Traditionalists

As Fukuzawa Yukichi had noted much earlier, "There are extremely few who can still be called conservatives of the old school. . . . Half of the old-style Chinese and Japanese Learning scholars have changed their persuasions. But they still fabricate farfetched theories that serve to cover their original positions; they seek to save face thereby and to appear in the ranks of the reformists."[10] It is thus perhaps more accurate to use the term "traditionalists" rather than "conservatives" to label the camp most opposed to Western-inspired reforms.

The chief spokesman for these Confucian traditionalists in 1879 was Motoda Eifu. His official post was that of imperial tutor on the Chinese classics, but from as early as 1871 Motoda had acquired considerable influence at court by combining unquestioned erudition, excellent rhetorical skills, and privileged access to the young emperor.[11] Education policy was central to Motoda's concerns and he expressed great scorn for the products of the new schools: "Outstanding in imagination and technical accomplishments, they are deficient in the spirit and soul of our country, their foundation in morals and courage for righteous causes is shallow." To reverse this trend and eliminate the "confusion between the root of education and its branches," he urged that an end be put to the "efforts . . . to convert Japanese into facsimiles of Europeans and Americans."[12]

In summer 1879 Motoda drew up a formal indictment of the Western-inspired educational reforms, which he now alleged were the main causes of the political turmoil that was endangering the government's stability. He asserted that this menace was directly attributable to the erosion of loyalty caused by "high-sounding ideas and empty theory" imported from abroad: "Although we set out to take in the best features of the West and bring in new things in order to achieve the high aims of the Meiji Restoration—abandonment of the undesirable practices of the past and learning from the outside world—this procedure had a serious defect: it reduced benevolence, justice, loyalty, and filial piety to a subordinate position."[13]

These traditionalists viewed the teachings of the West as inciting "freedom without restraint"—"doing what one pleases."[14] The remedy was to restore old values to their properly privileged place: "People should cultivate sincerity and moral conduct, and after that they should turn to the cultivation of the various subjects of learning in accordance with their ability." The wrong values were being taught: "For morality, the study of Confucius is the best guide."[15]

Often this dispute was at an even more basic level. Motoda charged that Western knowledge could never substitute for tradition because it was devoid of ethical principles, for the West was a "foreign civilization whose only values are fact-gathering and technique." What was being asserted is very close to the older position that Western learning was only supposed to provide "useful" knowledge as means to an end—not "essential" truth to evaluate end goals. The problem in this view was that the "useful" had come to preempt the "essential."[16]

Itō and Statist Modernizers

These traditionalists were not the only ones who criticized the Education Ministry for excessive Westernizing. Itō Hirobumi was also anxious to stem the "radical political party theories from Europe." He too saw the need for reasserting central government leadership over the school system, but he vigorously resisted Motoda's call for traditional Confucian solutions. In fact, Itō suggested that some of the blame for the political turmoil was due to too much study of Chinese classics:

> To have too many political disputants is no blessing for the nation. The root of present conditions can be ascribed to samurai youths of very little talent who compete among themselves as political disputants. The students of today are generally from academies of Chinese studies, and whenever these students of Chinese classics open their mouths it is to debate on world affairs, elbowing each other aside to expound on political theory.

For Itō, the main source of the problem was simply the rapid pace of the inevitable changes brought about by the Meiji Restoration. He therefore rejected singling out the schools as the cause: "Educational policy is only one of the remedies for the situation. Since education is not the principal cause . . . , it can be no more than an indirect cure." There was no choice but to be patient and continue to hold course:

> Some people, alarmed at the present ailments, impatiently leap to untried remedies; they go to extremes and thus bring about yet other evils. . . . At the beginning of the Restoration, our government looked far and reflected deeply on ways to eliminate stubborn evil customs. This was difficult, like tearing up twisted roots, and for all their effort they could expect only small success. Nor will it further our long range plans if in our impatience to remedy minor evils, we end up altering

the foreordained path of the Imperial polity and give protection to the undesirable customs of the past.

One of the most surprising aspects of Itō's statement was his explicit and even sarcastic rejection of the attempt to "establish a single national doctrine" to be taught in the schools. That, he asserted, "would definitely not be proper for government to administer; for this we must await he who is a sage"—a status that Itō was clearly not ready to grant to Motoda.[17]

Despite the obvious antagonism between these two points of view, Itō and Motoda were nonetheless united against the liberals in the Education Ministry and as a result the more radical Westernizers were ousted in March 1880. A new minister was appointed with a mandate to regain central control over the schools and the teachers within them. In April the government announced a new set of rules, the Regulations for Public Meetings and Associations, Article 7 of which prohibited teachers as well as students from participating in politics:

> All those now on active duty in the army or the navy or in either the first or second reserves, police officers, teachers and students of government, public, or private schools, and apprentices in agricultural or industrial arts must not attend any meeting where politics form the subject of address or deliberation. Neither may they become members of any political association.[18]

That same month, Motoda's sometime ally, Nishimura Shigeki, was appointed director of the Textbook Compilation Bureau in the Education Ministry and a survey was ordered to scrutinize the textbooks being used in private as well as public schools.

Nishimura was a particularly complex figure.[19] Like Motoda, his early training in Confucianism had been followed in the 1850s by study with the famed specialist in Western military science, Sakuma Shōzan. But in the 1870s Nishimura had been very closely identified with the radical reformers in such groups as the Meirokusha. In 1875 he was chosen as lecturer to the emperor as an expert on Western knowledge.

Nishimura was never committed, however, to such Western political ideas as egalitarianism or liberalism, and over the years he seemed to move steadily toward the right in his criticism of what he saw as the superficial imitation of the West. He advocated a synthesis of the best of East and West, although in his hands this usually meant a core of Confucianism. Like Motoda, Nishimura was particularly concerned about the failure of the government in promoting public morality. In 1880 he wrote, "Since the Restoration of the Imperial Government, there has been advance in all of the hundred matters and daily we are progressing toward enlightenment. Only in the one matter of morality we seem, in comparison to the feudal period, to be losing ground."[20] That same year, Nishimura had completed an official textbook intended to remedy this malady by substituting more traditional ideas for some of those imported from the West.[21] In May 1880 the Education Ministry created the post of "investigator" to check on the materials being used in the school system. Translations from Western works were ordered replaced, as were some other texts deemed too liberal.

Predictably, this brought down the wrath of one well-known textbook author, Fukuzawa Yukichi:

> Around 1881–1882, the government began to advocate in education the queer policy of Confucianism. For the alleged purpose of examining school texts, the Ministry of Education . . . officials met and decided whether to approve or reject them. It also brought together old-fashioned Confucianists to compile readers, and otherwise staged the farce of trying to restore past customs in a civilized world.[22]

In December 1885 Itō Hirobumi was named to the new post of prime minister. Determined to seize the initiative in educational policy away from the traditionalists, Itō insisted on Mori Arinori as the new minister of education. Mori's efforts during his four-year tenure earned him the sobriquet "the father of Meiji education."[23]

Mori's early years as a student and diplomat in England and the United States had made him a committed modernizer. But he was by no means a liberal Westernizer in the mold of a Fukuzawa Yukichi. Whereas Fukuzawa had viewed national strength as an *indirect* result of the pursuit of individual independence, Mori's educational philosophy had always stressed collective virtues and loyalty to the state in order for schools to contribute *directly* to the goal of national independence. As he expressed it in an 1889 speech to higher education administrators,

> [Public schools] serve, after all, the purposes of the state. . . . In the case of the Imperial University, for instance, the question may arise as to whether learning is to be pursued for its own sake or for the sake of the state. It is the state which must come first and receive top priority. The administrators of our various schools, therefore, should at all times be mindful of the fact that the undertaking is on behalf of the state, not on behalf of the individual student.[24]

Two years earlier he had told a group of local officials that "reading, writing and arithmetic are not our major concerns in education. . . . Education is entirely a matter of bringing up men of character . . . those persons who live up fully to their responsibilities as Imperial subjects." He was particularly concerned that prospective teachers in the normal schools have their moral character perfected through what he called "military-style physical training."[25]

Nevertheless, Mori was neither a Confucian nor a traditionalist. Like Fukuzawa, he forcefully rejected much of the traditional worldview. Upon entering the Education Ministry he ousted Motoda's ally, Nishimura Shigeki, from the Textbook Compilation Bureau. Nishimura later wrote about his indignation over how Mori, Itō, and their associates not only "imitated Europe and America in every detail in the legal system, customs, and ceremonial, and decked itself completely with foreign civilization" but even "gave special hospitality to foreigners, presenting such foreign amusements as balls, masquerades, and tableaux vivants, assiduously sought to win their favor." This kind of behavior, to men of Nishimura's leanings, "seemed to disregard and abandon the spirit of loyalty, filial piety, honor, duty, valor, and shame, which had been the traditional foundation of our country since ancient times." It was no wonder that "people became increasingly rash and flippant and frivolous in their manners and customs."[26]

Mori's disdain for tradition eventually cost him his life. In 1889 he was stabbed to death by an assassin who cited as his rationale Mori's alleged iconoclastic behavior toward the most important of all Shinto shrines, the shrine of the Sun Goddess at Ise.[27]

Nishimura and Motoda saw Mori's death as an opportunity to renew their efforts to gain control over the ethical content of school curricula. To bypass their foes in the Education Ministry, they proposed to have moral education come under the jurisdiction of a new institute within the imperial household itself. Failing that, they persuaded Prime Minister Yamagata Aritomo, Itō's main political rival within the inner circle of government, that a statement to define an orthodox view of morality was needed if only to preempt the newly elected parliament from too free a debate on educational policy. The result was the Imperial Rescript on Education of 1890, considered by many historians to be the single most important document on educational policy between the original 1872 Gakusei Plan and the 1947 Fundamental Law of Education passed under the American Occupation.[28]

The Imperial Rescript on Education

In its final form, the 1890 rescript, like many educational policy statements in the first quarter century after the Restoration, was a compromise aimed at bridging the gap between traditionalists and modernizers. As the following official government translation into English clearly reflects, the flavor of the text is quite archaic. The list of virtues is couched in traditional Confucian language but the whole reads like the work of several hands and the result is vague enough to permit more than the usual variety of textual interpretations.

Know Ye, Our Subjects:

Our Imperial Ancestors have founded Our Empire on a basis broad and everlasting and have deeply and firmly implanted virtue. Our subjects ever united in loyalty and filial piety have from generation to generation illustrated the beauty thereof. This is the glory of the fundamental character of Our Empire, and herein also lies the source of Our education. Ye, Our subjects, be filial to your parents, affectionate to your brothers and sisters; as husbands and wives be harmonious, as friends be true; bear yourself in modesty and moderation; extend your benevolence to all; pursue learning and cultivate arts, and thereby develop intellectual faculties and perfect moral powers; furthermore advance public good and promote common interests; always respect the Constitution and observe the laws; should an emergency arise, offer yourself courageously to the State; and thus guard and maintain the prosperity of Our Imperial Throne coeval with heaven and earth. So shall ye not only be Our good and faithful subjects, but render illustrious the best traditions of your forefathers.

The Way here set forth is indeed the teaching bequeathed by Our Imperial Ancestors, to be observed alike by Their Descendants and the subjects, infallible for all ages and true in all places. It is Our wish to lay it to heart in all reverence, in common with you, Our subjects, that we may all attain to the same virtue.[29]

The ambiguities in this final version were in large part due to the careful hand of Itō's associate, Inoue Kowashi.[30] Inoue had worked with Itō since 1875, and after Itō returned to the prime ministership in August 1892 he gave Inoue the education portfolio in his cabinet. Inoue apparently did not become involved in the process of writing the 1890 rescript until several drafts had already been attempted. He then made a successful effort to block an earlier version because he deemed it overly specific and with too many Western as well as explicitly Confucian elements. He and Itō were particularly keen on thwarting Motoda's renewed efforts to establish Confucianism as a moral orthodoxy or "national doctrine." Inoue's approach was to ground the national morality in the imperial institution, the throne being a concrete symbol of uniquely Japanese customs and mores.

Inoue differed from earlier Nativists who attempted to appropriate the imperial throne to their own cause in that he rejected any single set of religious rituals associated with education. In that sense, he was siding with those Westernizers within Japan as well as foreign observers who vehemently opposed the imposition of Shinto as a state religion. However, copies of the rescript would take their place alongside the imperial portraits in regular school ceremonies honoring the throne as the central focus of patriotism and national morality.

Just how successful Inoue was in walking the line dividing the traditionalists from the Westernizers on these points can be measured in part by reaction of commentators from the warring camps. Motoda professed himself satisfied that the rescript served his original purposes, whereas journalists in the opposite camp were pleased that it rejected classical Chinese values, privileging instead "the ordinary morality of the Japanese that has been transmitted from earliest times, even before there was Confucianism or Buddhism." Kuga Katsunan, one of the new young Japanist writers who rejected Western values as well as Confucianism and Buddhism, also supported the rescript: "Filial piety, brotherly affection, marital harmony, and the loyalty of all to the Imperial Throne . . . are Japan's distinctive national ethics. They are the historical customs of the Japanese people, the basic elements that support her society."[31]

The question of the compatibility of the rescript with Christian doctrine was raised most dramatically at First Higher Middle School in 1891. Two years earlier, the Education Ministry had ordered that all school ceremonies include a demonstration of respect toward the reigning emperor and empress as symbolized by their imperial portraits and that the Imperial Rescript on Education should be read aloud by the principal or appropriate staff member.[32] When Uchimura Kanzō, a thirty-year-old Christian teacher who had recently returned from Amherst College in the United States, failed to make the proscribed deep bow in front of the school copy of the rescript, he was fired from his post.[33]

This behavior was seized upon by some as proof that Christianity was incompatible with Japanese patriotism. But the reactions to the rescript by other Japanese Christians were surprisingly positive, perhaps because of their relief that the document did not proclaim a state religion. Yokoi Tokio, a leading Christian, characterized it as a cosmopolitan document that in no way conflicted with his own religious views.[34] Ōnishi Hajime, an influential Christian academic who lectured on neo-Kantism in the state higher normal schools, was somewhat more negative: "Since in terms of ethical theory, the Imperial Rescript does not point out the basis of morality, the various virtues proclaimed in it cannot be construed as an absolute in ethical theory." But Ōnishi also agreed that Christians could live within the banal principles articulated in the rescript: "Loyalty and filial piety! In what state, in what society are they not necessary?" In contrast, Inoue Tetsujirō, the well-known professor of philosophy at Tokyo University and longtime foe of Christianity, was invited by the Education Ministry to write a commentary on the rescript. He interpreted it as proscribing Western values in general and the Christian religion in particular.[35]

Over the years that followed there were to be numerous attempts at explaining to schoolteachers how the 1890 rescript should be implemented, but at least until the ultranationalist dominance in the 1930s, most explanations tended to resemble the "Explanation of School Matters" issued by the Education Ministry in 1891:

> The materials for regular education are provided by our national spirit, customs, prosperity, and strength, and all those who desire the strengthening of the eternal foundation of the nation must be careful to understand correctly our hundred-year national plan.
>
> In the elementary schools, the first objective—namely the spirit of reverence of the Emperor and patriotism—will be achieved through cultivating morality and practicing the Way of Humanity. Children must be encouraged in practical work, disciplined in simplicity, and developed into good and loyal subjects.

Such explanations also tended to straddle the divide between old traditions and the new knowledge: "The elementary school morals course must be based upon the Imperial Rescript on Education. It is also expected that it will be based on Japan's distinctive ways and *on full knowledge of the rest of the world*" [italics added].[36] Of course, most young pupils were little concerned about such lofty ideals. When in 1893 one girl in a third-grade class was confronted with the necessity of explaining loyalty and filial piety she responded simply, "Not being a thief."[37] However, even young children could presumably understand the simple message that they were to view the nation as a single family with the relationship between the emperor and the people being absolutely the same as "the intimacy between father and child."[38]

This effort to find a synthesis in which the old and new could be embraced simultaneously was not aided by developments in the intellectual world of the mid–Meiji period. The death of Motoda Eifu in 1891 symbolized the passing of the last generation of influential Confucians raised in the pre-Restoration milieu.[39]

The ranks of the Restoration generation of optimistic Westernizers were also slowly thinned, not only because of their advancing age but also because events of the 1890s would discredit the more naive forms of trust in European or American solutions. The Sino-Japanese War of 1894–1895 fought over Korea was something of a watershed in this regard. Victory over the Chinese gave credibility to the Meiji oligarchs' approach to reforms while at the same time threats by the Russians, Germans, and French—fearful of Japanese commercial and diplomatic rivalry in East Asia—snatched much of the prize of victory away from Japan. Popular sentiment against the Chinese resulted in, to quote the Waseda University literary and opinion magazine *Waseda Bungaku,* "an awareness of what it means to be a Japanese, and a sense of the fairness and justice of our heroic undertaking in Korea."[40] By the same token, the Triple Intervention by Western powers, which forced Japan to give up some valuable concessions won from the Chinese, was a shock to some influential Japanese who professed now for the first time to realize that the actions of Western powers did not match their pious rhetoric. In the words of Tokutomi Sohō, a widely read proponent of emulating Western models who had in the 1880s operated a private school devoted to "pure Western education": "Say what you will. . . . What it comes down to [in dealing with the West] was that sincerity or justice did not amount to a thing if you were not strong enough." What was necessary now was to "break the worldwide monopoly and destroy the special rights of the white races, eliminate the special sphere of influence and the worldwide tyranny of the white races, [and thereby] create true universal equality and progress in humanity, brotherhood, and civilization for the world."[41]

In this atmosphere, Nativism enjoyed something of a resurgence but only after undergoing a transformation in the hands of a new generation of intellectuals such as Kuga Katsunan and Miyake Setsurei. The emphasis of these "Japanists" was less on the study of ancient texts and religious doctrines than it was on the identification of the "essential character" of the nation. They sought to protect the country's cultural as well as political independence, but unlike the Nativists of the early Meiji period, they generally had a good knowledge of European culture and, indeed, seem to have been heavily influenced by Western notions of national character and cultural nationalism.

Sugiura Jūgō, for instance, explicitly rejected the old-fashioned Nativism: "I might be taken for a commonplace *kokugakusha* [Nativist scholar] type. I am nothing of the kind. The more one is acquainted with the customs, civilization, and political system of foreign countries, the more one feels the need [for knowing the Japanese spirit]." Kuga wrote, "We recognize the excellence of Western civilization. We value the Western theories of rights, liberty, equality. . . . In some things we have affection for Western customs. Above all, we esteem Western science, economics and industry. These things, however, ought not be adopted because they are Western, but only if they can contribute to Japan's welfare."

Although these Japanist writers varied in their individual concerns, they all shared a commitment to the premise that "each of the countries of the world which maintains its honor has its own special style. The style of course exists spontaneously, but it is an indisputable fact that all the people will put great effort into cultivating and preserving it." It followed that education required special attention and that the schools needed to ensure that "children should be thoroughly acquainted with the history and geography and literature of our country. The most vital point for Japanese education is that . . . [the Japanese spirit] should always be included in maxims, . . . elementary school readers, and other textbooks used in elementary schools."[42]

Elitism and Multitracking

When Mori Arinori entered the Education Ministry in 1885 he had sought to implement the original 1872 vision of an eight-year elementary curriculum broken into a four-year "ordinary" course and a four-year "upper" course. But he acknowledged the obstacles: the lack of school facilities, the shortage of funding, and parental resistance to a system being imposed from outside. Mori thus temporarily continued the 1880 provisions that recognized three years of only thirty-two weeks each as fulfilling the minimum requirement for each division. Public elementary education continued to be divided into the regular primary schools offering the lower four grades for all children and the higher elementary schools with two- to four-year courses of study for those seeking to go beyond. Under Mori, promotion from grade to grade was to be contingent upon passing regular examinations, a provision that remained in effect until the mid-1890s. Thus the 1886 Education Ordinance continued the compromise by which three years would fulfill the compulsory requirement while working toward the ideal of six years. (See Figure 3.1.)

The proportion of school-aged children enrolling in compulsory education did continue to climb in the 1880s and 1890s: The number of males rose from about 59 percent in 1880 to 91 percent by 1900, females from 22 percent to 72 percent. Perhaps more impressive was the increase in actual attendance as opposed to enrollments—up from 49 percent in 1890 to 81 percent in 1900.[43]

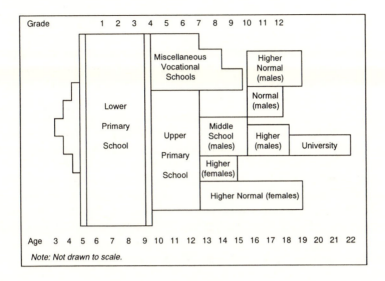

FIGURE 3.1
Main Tracks in Public School System, 1900.
Source: Adapted from Monbushō, *Gakusei 90 nenshi,* p. 586.

The bottleneck came just beyond compulsory education when it was time to move upward to the higher elementary schools level. As late as the beginning of the twentieth century, only a fourth of regular primary school graduates completed the higher elementary stage. One contemporary survey indicates that the odds of a boy who entered primary school in 1887 ever going on to complete higher elementary school were only one in ten.[44] There was, however, some improvement in this ratio in the next decade: One in four of the cohort entering in 1895 would complete both levels of primary education.

The problem was in large part economic. Sending children to higher elementary schools was more of a burden for poorer rural families for at least two reasons. First, the older the child the more likely he or she could contribute productively to the family. Second, by contrast with ordinary primary schools, higher elementary facilities in this period were lacking in many communities, meaning that students were often forced to find lodging away from home. There are no nationwide statistics available on the family income of higher elementary school students, but it can be assumed to have been somewhere in the middle ranges.

Postelementary Education

Beyond the primary level the Meiji state made no explicit commitment to provide public education for all. Rather, the basic philosophy underlying policies implemented under such ministers of education as Mori Arinori and Inoue

Kowashi was to create a variety of state-supported tracks to match the abilities and potential of youth. Although based on the principle of recognizing merit, this system was elitist in three senses. First, sexist assumptions about adult roles divided males and females into distinct categories, each with a separate track beyond the primary level. Second, to the extent that tuition and other fees at the secondary and tertiary levels were not offset by student aid, the poorer classes were for the most part denied the opportunities open to the offspring of the middle and upper classes. Third, the policies envisioned a society in which the structure of schooling should match the occupational pyramid. In this view, male industrial workers, farmers, craftsmen, and the like did not require academic schooling beyond the primary level, although some vocational training would be made available. By contrast, those destined for lower management or technical positions were to compete for admission to the middle school and eventually higher school levels. Ultimately, those males who would, in Mori's phrase, "wield the power of future Japan" needed to occupy one of the relatively few seats in the university. Higher education was deemed unnecessary for those not destined to fill such leadership roles at the apex of the system. In this view the elite was to be a meritocracy chosen on the basis of performance in educational competition rather than on the basis of the family's social rank or wealth. The test of Mori's success, then, lies in the extent to which the competition was open at least to all males if not to both genders.

Secondary schooling came under special scrutiny during Mori's tenure. With the 1880 Middle School Teaching Regulations, the first step had already been taken toward creating a two-tiered secondary system for males: a four-year lower-level curriculum and an upper-level course of two or more years to prepare males going on to higher education. When Mori came into office, however, the average middle school had a faculty of only eight teachers with just over 100 students, and the abilities of both varied greatly. Mori moved quickly to overhaul the system. He cut back on the number of middle schools to increase their quality and instituted rigorous entrance examinations. Under the 1886 regulations, any male twelve years or older who could pass the test was eligible for admission. Attendance at a higher elementary school was technically not a prerequisite. Nevertheless, an estimated three-quarters of those entering middle school in 1892 had attended higher elementary school for at least three years, with most of these having completed four.[45] Under Minister of Education Inoue in 1894 the minimum was raised to at least six years of primary school—four years in lower and two in higher elementary courses. But public middle school entrance examinations were so competitive that 80 percent of all incoming students in 1898 and 1908 continued to have more than the minimum time in school required (see Table 3.1).

Whatever their preparation, only 8 percent of males were advancing to this level in 1890. In 1900, middle schools admitted about 28,000 males, turning down another 18,000 (39 percent) and as late as 1905 only 13 percent of males

TABLE 3.1
Entrance to Public Middle Schools: Years of Study in Primary Schools

Years	1892 (%)	1898 (%)	1908 (%)
Eight	59	47	42
Seven	17	33	38
Six	4	14	18

SOURCE: Calculated from Amano, *Education and Examination*, pp. 146–147.

were entering middle school. Moreover, in the first years after Mori's tightening of standards, promotion was based strictly on test scores and only one out of ten who entered actually finished the three-year course. Under Inoue in the mid-1890s the rate of graduation reached 50 percent but it stopped improving after 60 percent.[46]

For the ambitious male, however, the elite track lay beyond middle school into "higher" school. In April 1886 Mori created a new type of institution that was to become the royal road to success: an elite "higher middle school" (*kōtō chūgakkō*). The name would be shortened in 1894 to simply "higher school" (*kōtō gakkō*). The first model was built around the existing Tokyo University Preparatory School, which had been separated off to become No. 1 Higher Middle School. Mori's initial plan called for at least five such schools located throughout the country and the existing Osaka Middle School became No. 3 Higher Middle School. The following year, 1887, the central government opened No. 2 Higher Middle School in Sendai. Four more were added by 1900.

Unlike the ordinary public middle schools, which were under the jurisdiction of the prefectures, the higher schools were funded and supervised directly by the central government. The three-year comprehensive curriculum of all these secondary institutions was devoted to preparing students for the university or other advanced training, although originally it was expected that many graduates would go immediately into the working world. In either case, Mori intended these schools to serve a very special purpose as "the wellspring for those who wield the power of future Japan." On this he was quite clear:

> Those who [graduate from] the higher school may . . . move immediately into business or pursue a specialized course of study [in higher education]. In either case, they will enter society's upper crust. . . . Men worthy of directing the thoughts of the masses: be they bureaucrats, then those of the highest echelon, be they businessmen, then those for the top management, be they scholars, then true experts in the various arts and sciences.[47]

In principle, these institutions were to be open to all males seventeen to twenty years old who had a lower middle school education or its equivalent. But so few applicants in the first years had adequate preparation that entrance examinations per se were not much used. Instead, the four higher schools out-side of Tokyo were ordered to create their own supplementary courses, open to those at least fourteen years of age. Students of various ages were then assigned to the supplementary or regular classes on the basis of regular testing rather than by age.[48] At the No. 1 Higher Middle School in Tokyo, in contrast with the other schools, there were many applicants who had attended the private mid-dle schools in the capital and almost 90 percent were admitted by examination directly to the regular course.

By the end of the 1890s changes in the system made it increasingly difficult to gain entrance, with over half of all higher school applicants failing in 1899 and over two-thirds unsuccessful in 1900. Some of these changes resulted from the increasing number of middle school graduates. In 1894, during Inoue Kowashi's tenure in the Education Ministry, the increased number of appli-cants with a middle school education permitted these higher schools to drop their supplementary curriculum and routinize their course of study at three years, entrance to which depended upon test scores.

The annual tuition plus fees for dormitory room and board were well within the means of the Japanese middle class, but since there was no public aid, working-class students were either effectively barred or had to find private sub-sidies.[49] Moreover, applicants could theoretically be denied entry if they did not have "acceptable manners, health, demeanor." But mere wealth or high so-cial status were not in themselves sufficient to get students into the regular course or graduate if they could not pass the examinations. In 1900 two out of three applicants were not able to do so. Information on the family income of those who were successful is not readily available for the Meiji period. The Ed-ucation Ministry did survey the higher school student bodies in 1890, 1891, and 1892. It found that ex-samurai, who would have constituted at most 8 per-cent to 10 percent of the population, did far better in achieving entry to these elite schools than their numbers would predict. Of course, the income of samurai families varied enormously and they may have been marked off from other families of similar economic status by cultural expectations and family ambitions rather than economic status. There were approximately 4,000 stu-dents enrolled in any given term in these early years and they were divided about equally between commoners and those whose families had belonged to either the court nobility or samurai class.[50]

In contrast to other secondary and tertiary tracks, the state-supported teach-ers' normal schools offered even the poorest Japanese a free education, pro-vided he or she could get through the primary levels and pass the entrance examinations. But the number of ordinary normal schools supplying teachers for primary schools was cut back to one per prefecture—from a total of sev-enty-two down to forty-six.[51] This reduction was made not only because of budgetary pressures but apparently also because Mori intended, as with the middle schools, to bring them under closer scrutiny. These government-supported normal schools were crucial to his overall blueprint because they were to produce the homogeneous teaching staff that would permit the standardization of curriculum and setting of uniform criteria for student achievement.

In addition to not charging tuition or for room and board, the government provided uniforms and even pocket money to those enrolled. In 1885 faculty and advanced students at higher normal schools were added to the expanded list of those eligible for fellowships to study abroad, a privilege until then largely dominated by the esteemed Tokyo University. Moreover, in the Meiji period, teachers' salaries and social prestige were relatively high and normal school students were virtually assured of a teaching position upon graduation. Free training for such a desirable vocation especially attracted youth who might not be able to hope for a university degree to get into other professions. It was not until the latter part of the Meiji period that salaries failed to keep up with living costs and teaching lost some of its attractiveness.

There is no available nationwide statistical evidence on the family income of those going into teaching, but some data on the family background do exist. Records from the Kumamoto Normal School and Training School between 1878 and 1917 show a steady increase in the ratio of commoners to samurai. In the decade from 1878 through 1887, four out of five are listed as samurai; in the period from 1898 through 1907 the ratio was one to one and the percentage of commoners was continuing to increase.[52] At Aoyama Normal School, samurai students made up 15 percent in 1900 and 11 percent in 1906; at Miyazaki Normal School, they constituted 19 percent in 1899 but fell to 8 percent by 1903. Beginning in 1904 there were records kept of the occupations of fathers of students admitted to the normal schools. In 1904, 61 percent of the 4,183 were identified as being in "farming," 11 percent in "commerce," and 2 percent as "workers"—the remainder falling into a miscellaneous category. Over the next twenty years farmers' sons and daughters would continue to make up the largest single bloc.[53]

Of course, these data do not necessarily indicate anything for certain about economic strata. Many commoner families were in better financial circumstances than samurai families were, particularly after the end of samurai stipends in 1876, and "farming" could indicate anything from a landless sharecropper to an affluent rural landlord. More of a social change was involved in the state support of women's normal schools as part of the reforms of schooling affecting females, as we shall see below.

As minister of education, Mori Arinori also presided over the recentralization of state-sponsored higher education. In 1886, almost two decades after the original plan for a central university, the vision of an imperial university was finally realized. The old South Campus of the original university had actually been designated Tokyo University in 1877, but foreigners had continued to constitute approximately two-thirds of the faculty and the level of instruction was quite low. Except in the semiautonomous College of Medicine, the curriculum was still limited to foreign languages, natural sciences, and some humanities. Moreover, the various government ministries had continued to run their own advanced training institutes apart from the Education Ministry. By the end of the 1880s, however, most of these competing institutes were shut down and Tokyo University became the premier institution for state-supported higher education. The Justice Ministry closed its law school in 1884 and Tokyo University thus became the main public institution for the study of *hōgaku*. Although translatable as "law studies," *hōgaku* was never merely the narrow study of jurisprudence for prospective lawyers. A survey of the 1,200 living graduates from the Tokyo University "law" college listed only 112 (9 percent) as lawyers, the same percentage that appeared in a 1926 survey. Legal studies actually entailed the broad study of comparative government, economic systems, and social thought—what might be termed, somewhat anachronistically, the "policy sciences" or "public administration."[54]

Also incorporated into the new Imperial University were other formerly separate facilities. The Engineering School, first opened under the jurisdiction of the Ministry of Industrial Works, was added to the university in 1886. That same year the government's Bureau of Historical Compilation, with its Nativist specialists on traditional texts and other such potentially sensitive subjects as the history of the imperial throne, was brought under the central control of the Education Ministry and attached to the new university. In 1890 a College of Agriculture was created within the school to replace the Agriculture Ministry's school at Komaba. Thus law, letters, science, medicine, and engineering had all finally been physically relocated onto a single campus and collectively raised to the level of a centrally controlled university.

In 1897 a second imperial university was created in Kyoto. Both elite schools were kept small: In 1900 the two together took in only 564 applicants. Graduation from a higher school did not guarantee entry into either of the two state-supported universities. Once students were admitted to Tokyo Imperial or Kyoto Imperial, however, they rarely flunked out.[55]

But the route from higher school to imperial university was not taken by most males who went beyond middle school in the Meiji period. Much more common was attendance at one of the bewildering array of public and private institutions known in Japanese as *senmon* schools, a term for which there is no agreed-upon equivalent in English. English words that have been used to describe the *senmon* school include "college," "professional school," "specialty school," "specialist school," "special school," "school of special studies," "specialized school," "technical school," and "vocational school." A given *senmon* school may fit any one of these descriptions. But each of these English terms has its own disparate connotations of analogous institutions in the United States or Britain, which do not always apply to the Japanese school.

A *senmon* school is, to be sure, literally a "specialty" school, but the term was initially used by the Meiji government to refer to a miscellaneous grouping of post–elementary level schools that did not fit into any of the other categories covered in the 1872 Gakusei Plan.[56] The 1879 Education Ordinance had differentiated them from universities on the grounds that they were specialized in only one discipline whereas the university was defined as teaching numerous subjects.[57] Thus the classification initially included a dozen or so state-supported schools—for example, the Tokyo School of Commerce—as well as "private" *senmon* schools, which took students more advanced than ordinary middle school—for example, Keiō and Dōshisha. Whereas the public *senmon* institutions did tend to be tightly focused on a single specialty, the private *senmon* schools often taught a broader range of subjects, especially in what we may call somewhat loosely the humanities and social sciences.

Hence by the mid–Meiji period, "*senmon* school" became an official government category that included public institutions at the post–middle school level that were not officially designated either higher schools or universities. It also included private schools. The English translation "college" is appropriate for some of these schools, such as Keiō and Waseda, which were intended from the beginning to offer a broad liberal arts curriculum. Other private schools were initially intended to prepare men specifically for the civil service or bar examinations and only gradually widened their scope. But legal studies in the private schools were always broadly conceived and private "law schools" in fact mostly produced graduates who went into teaching, commerce, or other occupations not directly concerned with jurisprudence.

In the natural sciences or technology, none of these private schools could rival the state-supported schools in the Meiji period.[58] Keiō had opened a medical school in 1872 but it was closed after a few years and Keiō did not try again until 1917. Waseda had planned an engineering school but closed it in 1884 and did not reopen it until 1907. Dōshisha closed its School of Science in 1892 after ten years of operation.

Until 1903 the government refused to allow any school, public or private, to use the designation "university" unless it had faculties in a wide range of specified disciplines. But thereafter those private schools with university preparatory divisions were allowed to call themselves "university" even if in other regulatory contexts they remained officially in the *senmon* school category until after the reforms of 1918.[59]

Two points regarding higher education need to be stressed here. First, acquiring higher education of some sort was remarkably important to upward mobility in both the political and business worlds of late Meiji Japan. Although the senior members of the elite were for the most part born too early to attend post-Restoration schools, by the end of the First World War a generation who had been of school age in the Meiji era were taking their places among government and business elites. And for these men, schooling was closely correlated with success. For example, one study of cabinet ministers between 1885 and 1918 showed that 45 percent had no modern formal schooling, but this figure would drop to 9 percent for those serving between 1918 and 1932.[60] Around the year 1920, 59 percent of those in the political elite (331 individuals including cabinet ministers, top civil bureaucrats, and others) had studied at a Japanese university and/or abroad and another 21 percent had gone to a secondary school or *senmon* school if not to a university.[61] What makes these figures even more telling is that the 1920 sample still included 25 percent born before 1860 and therefore many were already in their teens or older by the time of the 1868 Restoration. Thus the overwhelming majority of the Meiji-era cohort among this 1920 political elite had experienced formal higher schooling.

Higher education was only slightly less important for the business elite. The large corporations such as Mitsui, Mitsubishi, and Sumitomo stressed formal schooling in their recruitment almost from their beginnings as modern enterprises. Two-thirds of a sample of 1,000 business executives in 1928 had attended some institution of higher education.[62]

The second point that must not be overlooked is that not all college diplomas were equal; rather, the Meiji reforms constructed, as Edward Beauchamp has succinctly put it, "the so-called 'Mount Fuji' system of higher education, in which a handful of elite schools, led by Tokyo University, produce nearly all of the society's leaders."[63] Tokyo University graduates made up a disproportionately large percentage of the political elite, not only in the higher echelons of the administrative elite but also in cabinet positions, judgeships, and as advisers to the imperial throne. The top post in the career civil service was that of vice minister: Ninety-two percent of all who served in that position between 1894 and 1926 had attended Tokyo University or its predecessor. The most powerful ministries are generally agreed to have included finance, home, justice, commerce and agriculture, and foreign affairs: Seventy-one percent of all the vice ministers and bureau chiefs from these five ministries between 1894 and 1926 were from Tokyo University or its predecessors.[64]

Cabinet ministers in this same period included military men, parliamentary politicians, as well as civil bureaucrats and other technocrats. Nevertheless, of the seventy-eight men who held a cabinet post between 1918 and 1932, 91 percent had some college-level school: Forty-six percent had graduated from Tokyo University (another 4 percent studied at it or Kyoto), 19 percent from military academies, and only 5 percent from Keiō, Waseda, or other private colleges.[65] Those elected to parliamentary positions often included rural political bosses who had far less education than their bureaucratic counterparts. Yet three-quarters of the leaders in the House of Representatives during the period from 1918 through 1932 were college-educated men: graduates of Tokyo (15 percent), Kyoto Imperial (2 percent), a foreign university (6 percent), and Waseda or Keiō (5 percent combined). Another 31 percent had a diploma from a *senmon* school.

The dominance of Tokyo University alumni was also evident among business executives. A sample in 1928 listed almost a fourth as having attended

Tokyo University or its predecessors. This group was followed by alumni of Keiō, with 11 percent, and Tokyo Higher School of Commerce, with 10 percent. Other schools produced a sprinkling at most.

The other important type of secondary schooling developed in the Meiji period was technical training.[66] In the 1870s the government had launched a variety of technical training programs, most originally attached to government-run industrial enterprises. The first modern silk filature built in Japan had been conceived as a model factory for training workers as well as demonstrating new technology to potential private investors. In the same spirit, government arsenal and shipyards had included programs to train skilled workers. When many of these enterprises were sold off to the private sector in the 1880s, the government set up vocational schools to take over some of their training functions.

There was also early government interest in more advanced programs for technicians. Itō Hirobumi even expressed the opinion that it would be better politically to have more students in industrial arts than so many in legal studies.[67] Advanced secondary schools created by Minister of Education Mori in the 1880s offered specialized curricula in vocational training. One is particularly noteworthy because it would develop as an important school for advanced training for government and private business careers: the Tokyo School of Commerce (forerunner of today's Hitotsubashi University). Originally founded in 1875 by Mori and his friends as a private school, it was transformed into a public school in 1885 and then given the status of a higher school. Other institutions were redesignated higher schools of agriculture, medicine, or technology and given the same legal status as the higher middle schools, admitting those graduates of ordinary middle schools who could pass the entrance tests. Thus, for example, the Tokyo Worker Training Institute became the Tokyo School of Technology in 1890.

When Inoue Kowashi assumed office as minister of education in 1893, he was especially forceful in his efforts to focus more attention on technical training. Elsewhere in the world, he asserted, "production is greatly increased by their insistent effort in improving technical schools"; in Japan, however, "education and labor have no influence upon each other."[68] In early 1893 a new type of supplementary, or continuation, vocational school, parallel to the ordinary middle school, was authorized for males who had completed primary school. In 1901 the Tokyo College of Technology became a higher school of technology, as did a similar institution in Osaka.

Enrollments in these technical and vocational schools at the secondary level were only about one-third those in the academic secondary schools. Some of the technical schools also had annexes that offered apprentice programs for workers. These programs were officially classified at the primary level, whereas secondary-level practical courses were created at some middle schools and higher schools. Inspired by German models, the 1890 revision of the Elementary

School Ordinance and the 1893 Regulations for Vocational Continuation created new types of training programs at the primary level.[69]

Thus, by 1905 there had been developed a complex pyramid of vocational and technical training programs that paralleled the academic track at the primary, secondary, and advanced levels. Since these were intended to mirror the occupational structure, they clearly reflected a hierarchy of strata with quite distinct prospects for income, power, and prestige. In this sense the system was conceived of from the beginning as elitist for males as well as females. The question, therefore, is not merely how egalitarian the resulting hierarchy was but rather how meritocratic or open the system was to upward mobility. When the hierarchy is seen in this light, the nation's girls and women constituted the largest and most obvious category for whom the system was neither egalitarian nor meritocratic.

Schooling for Females

Consistent throughout the twists and turns of state policies in the decades after the Restoration was a commitment to compulsory, tax-supported public education at the primary level for all social classes and both genders. Minister of Education Ōki Takatō reaffirmed this commitment in 1891: "At the present time less than one-half of the school-age children are attending school. Most of the remainder are from poor families, and it is our urgent task to find ways to make them come to school."[70] In 1893, Minister of Education Inoue Kowashi expressed serious concern about the gender gap in primary school attendance:

> There is no distinction between male and female in the requirement for general [primary] education. Moreover, there is an exceedingly close connection between the education of girls and the future education of the [children in a] family. [Nonetheless,] presently, out of every 100 school-age children at most 50 are pupils [actually in attendance], and among those no more than 15 are girls. We must relentlessly stimulate those parents and guardians who are not now sending their girls to school to do so, and at the same time make the curriculum for girls more and more of practical use in their daily lives.[71]

The only concrete measure mentioned in this memorandum was the expansion of instruction in sewing. Yet the ministry did take other measures. The single most important step toward increasing the attendance rate for females was the removal of all tuition charges for compulsory schooling, which was accomplished by 1900. By 1905 the enrollment rates had soared for females—up from 70 percent to 90 percent—while reaching 97 percent for males (see Figure 3.2).

By contrast, government policy on postprimary schooling was self-consciously sexist. The Education Ministry had often reiterated the principle that coeducational schooling should cease after the elementary level. For example, the 1882 annual report stated, "Girls' high school education should not have

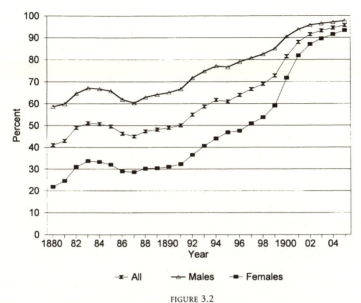

FIGURE 3.2
Primary School Enrollments by Percent of Age Group, 1880–1905.
Source: Data from Monbushō, *Gakusei 80 nenshi,* table 1.

the same curriculum as that of the boys. The most important aspect of education for girls is moral education. . . . In addition to teaching the principles of correct behavior, household economy, the nursing of infants, sewing and handicrafts should be part of the curriculum."[72]

Influential voices challenged such conservative biases. Fukuzawa Yukichi, the founder of Keiō University, was particularly incensed by the continued strength of Confucian and Buddhist ideas about education for women: "Such education is less than useless, for it serves only to oppress women and to beat them into a kind of 'modesty' and 'reticence' . . . some educators . . . have veritably been doing nothing but hindering the healthy development of women's minds and bodies."[73]

But there were many more among the political elite who agreed with the influential headmaster of the Peeress School in 1889, Nishimura Shigeki:

Frivolous people are inclined to say that the old Eastern education of women is extremely subservient and bigoted and should be abolished quickly. This opinion is greatly mistaken. As is well known, the Eastern education of women emphasizes submissiveness and faithfulness. . . . In recent years, many foreigners who have stayed in this country a long time have admired the submissiveness and virtuousness of Japanese women.[74]

In addition to authoring an influential book on women's education, Nishimura reorganized a small group into the Japan Society for the Expansion of the Way, which grew to some 10,000 members by 1900. It included a women's section and one of the more influential members was Tanahashi Ayako, a prominent female educator who became principal of the Nagoya Higher School for Girls in this period. Tanahashi had previously helped found the Greater Japan Women's Educational Society, which, like Nishimura, stressed the need to preserve Japanese virtues in the face of the influx of Western values.[75]

Minister of Education Ōki Takatō's official instructions to the nation's schoolteachers in 1891 echoed these convictions: "We must be careful that education does not bring about harmful effects, that girls, for example, do not lose their chastity and beautiful manners."[76] No essential change occurred in this official outlook during the remainder of the Meiji period.

Nevertheless, this lack of change should not be construed to mean (as is sometimes misleadingly implied in general histories) that the state had no concern with secondary schooling for females. In fact, the 1890s saw an expansion of two postelementary tracks for women that were subsidized with public funds: a growth, on the one hand, of teachers' training facilities for females and, on the other, what were somewhat misleadingly called women's high(er) schools. By the mid-1890s there were seven women's higher schools, with just under 2,000 students. The 1899 Higher Girls' School Law mandated there be at least one women's higher school in each prefecture, and by 1900 there were forty-five schools, enrolling almost 10,000 young women. By 1905 the numbers were still climbing, with eighty-nine schools and over 28,000 enrolled.[77] In addition, the state legally recognized a number of private schools, which in 1905 had a total of another 3,400 female students (see Figure 3.3).

The 1893 regulations for these schools set the entrance requirements at six years of elementary school. The course of study was ideally to be four years, but, as in the past, the government was flexible at the outset, recognizing a range of three to five years. Although designated as secondary schools, they were never intended to match the male middle schools much less the higher schools. Whereas the male schools provided preparatory courses for those who might attempt the entrance examinations for higher education, women's higher schools were conceived as terminal institutions except for those relatively few female graduates who might then enter advanced teachers' training. The curriculum therefore was practical, stressing home economics or the domestic sciences at the expense of physical science, advanced mathematics, or foreign languages, although the 1895 regulations did specify that languages and science could be included along with such subjects as history, Japanese, sewing, and physical education.[78]

The majority of the faculty at these women's higher schools was female but there was also a large number of men (see Table 3.2).

The steady growth of primary schooling, when coupled with the commitment to staffing public schools at the coeducational level with a mix of females and males, meant that there was a need for more trained women teachers. The

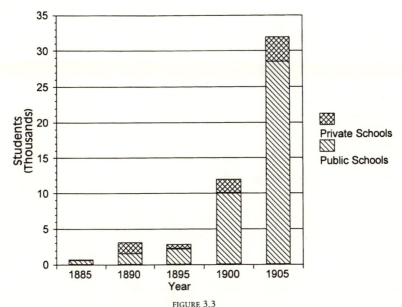

FIGURE 3.3
Women's Higher Education: Number of Students, 1885–1905.
Source: From Monbushō, *Gakusei 90 nenshi,* pp. 606–607.

percentage of women teachers in the nation's coeducational primary schools was only 1 percent in 1875. From this low base, however, it did rise steadily, to 5 percent in 1890 and then to 20 percent by 1905 (see Table 3.3). Teacher training programs for women were expanded accordingly, but the percentage of women on the faculty at ordinary women's normal schools never exceeded 13 percent in the Meiji period (see Table 3.4).

The opening of women's secondary schools led to a decision to provide facilities to train female teachers for that level as well. Thus, in 1890 the government

TABLE 3.2
Women's Higher Schools: Faculty by Gender, 1885–1905

	Total Number	Number of Males	Number of Females	
1885	72	22	50	(69%)
1890	97	49	48	(49%)
1895	112	38	74	(66%)
1900	544	170	374	(69%)
1905	1,395	508	887	(64%)

SOURCE: Calculated from Monbushō, *Gakusei 90 nenshi,* table 5, p. 607.

TABLE 3.3
Public Elementary Schools: Faculty by Gender, 1875–1905

	Total Number	Number of Males	Number of Females	
1875	41,113	40,571	572	(1%)
1880	70,835	68,940	1,895	(3%)
1885	98,500	93,821	4,679	(5%)
1890	66,494	62,879	3,625	(5%)
1895	71,979	93,821	4,679	(9%)
1900	91,798	79,888	11,910	(13%)
1905	109,016	87,083	21,933	(20%)

SOURCE: Calculated from Monbushō, *Gakusei 90 nenshi*, table 3, p. 600.

TABLE 3.4
Women's Ordinary Normal Schools: Faculty by Gender, 1875–1905

	Total Number	Number of Males	Number of Females	
1875	527	527	0	(0%)
1885	632	571	61	(10%)
1890	701	653	48	(7%)
1895	678	633	45	(7%)
1900	958	891	67	(7%)
1905	1,091	960	131	(12%)

SOURCE: Calculated from Monbushō, *Gakusei 90 nenshi*, table 12, pp. 629–630.

created the Women's Higher Normal School. Its first headmaster was the well-known male intellectual, Nakamura Masanao, and women made up an even smaller proportion of the faculty at this level than at the ordinary normal schools.

Private schools also produced some female teachers as well as providing opportunity for a general secondary education for women. Most of such education was of the finishing school variety. Lower-class women who worked in large numbers in the textile factories had no economic need of secondary schooling and there were few occupations other than teaching for middle- or upper-class women in Meiji Japan. Hence the schooling of those sent beyond the elementary level usually stressed home economics, sewing, and other subjects related to running a household.

Medicine was an important exception, although less significant for the numbers actually involved than as an opportunity for entry into a profession dominated by males. In 1884 the state first permitted women to take the medical licensing examinations and in 1887 the first female qualified. In 1900 Yoshioka

Yayoi opened the first medical school specifically for women, although she was not successful in getting her graduates permission to take the licensing examination until 1912.[79] The state itself provided training for midwives and nurses, who were granted licenses upon completing a prescribed course of study.

Other private schools offered a more general education. For example, Miwata Masako was an expert in the Chinese classics who served on the staffs of several public schools, eventually joining the faculty of Japan Women's College. In the course of her earlier career she had operated several private academies where girls and boys studied Chinese and English as well as mathematics and other subjects.[80]

The most numerous private schools for women in this period were those supported by the Christians. Among foreign Christian missionaries, Protestants from North American denominations predominated but there were also girls' schools run by Roman Catholic nuns.[81] Among those schools opened by Japanese Christians in the Meiji era were two that were destined to enjoy particular respect: the predecessor of Tsuda University, the Girls' English Institute, founded in 1901 by Tsuda Umeko; and Japan Women's College, founded in 1901 by Naruse Jinzō. Both educators were Christian converts and both had studied in the United States: Tsuda first as a small child and then as a young woman at Bryn Mawr; Naruse as a young man already focusing on women's education before traveling abroad. Neither was a feminist in the sense of the late twentieth century but both sought greater respect and greater independence for their female students. Tsuda's school trained women for posts as teachers in girls' higher schools.

Naruse was a graduate of an early Meiji teachers' training institute and had served as a principal of a public elementary school before converting to Christianity. Upon conversion he was appointed head teacher in 1878 of the first Christian school for girls in Osaka—a school he described as "a girls' school for the glory of God; . . . we must educate women and suit them for the Bible." After serving as a clergyman in Niigata, where he founded another school for girls, Naruse spent several years in the United States studying at the Andover Theological Seminary and Clark University. Naruse's convictions about female education had two major premises. First, since "the main purpose of education is not to teach students how to get on in life, but to develop them as complete human beings," it followed that it was wrong to think that either vocation or gender should determine the content: "One's vocation . . . is irrelevant. There should be no distinction between the sexes." Second, "the principles of education are not determined by race or by nation but by humankind and universal ideals." Nevertheless, he also refused to merely imitate foreign missionaries' practices because even Christian education "should be thoroughly compatible with each country's history and conditions." Therefore "it is inappropriate to provide for Japanese women, who are less educated than western women, an education designed specifically for women in the West." It is worth noting that

Naruse's schools were helped by support from members of the Meiji elite, including Itō Hirobumi as well as the Mitsui and Sumitomo families.[82]

Tsuda Umeko had also enjoyed the personal support of Itō Hirobumi, who had employed her as a tutor for his family and recommended her to a post at the government Peeresses' School in 1885. In addition to teaching the daughters of the elite there, Tsuda also taught part-time at the Women's Higher Normal School in Tokyo. In 1900, at the age of thirty-six, she resigned from both to open her own school, giving up her civil service rank "to get away from all the conservatism and conventions." Although Tsuda was a devout Christian throughout her life, the curriculum at her girls' school did not stress religion. It was initially aimed at preparing women for the teachers' certificate in English. But from the beginning Tsuda planned for a broader educational mission: "At the moment, our school is so insignificant that it barely casts a shadow, but in the future, as a place which gives women the opportunity of work worthy of their abilities, it will be an absolutely indispensable institution."[83]

The biography of Yosano Akiko, Meiji Japan's foremost female poet, illustrates something of the educational experiences of women in this era. Akiko was the daughter of a successful shop owner in Sakai City, a medium-sized town near Osaka. Her father's third daughter but the first by his second wife, Akiko was so precocious that her parents actually entered her in primary school when she was only four years old. They soon withdrew her when she had difficulties in the new environment. She was readmitted at the customary age of six and finished the mandatory four years of lower elementary schooling.

At this point Akiko's coeducation ended and when she continued it was at the Sakai City Girls' School. There she received six more years of formal education in a curriculum deemed appropriate for a middle-class female. It stressed Japanese literature, home economics, and sewing. Earlier she had also studied Japanese dance, music, and some Chinese classics with tutors. Somewhere along the way, however, she had learned enough practical arithmetic to help keep the books at her family's shop. Graduating from four years of secondary school at the age of fourteen in 1892, Akiko stayed on in a two-year supplementary program that involved more courses on home economics. These schools were the extent of public education available to young women in Sakai City in the 1890s. But when Akiko's younger sister reached this level five years later, the family sent her to the nearby city of Kyoto, where more advanced schooling was available.[84]

One Meiji woman who had already been able to take advantage of such educational opportunities was Yamawaki Fusako. A samurai daughter born in rural Shimane Prefecture at the time of the Meiji Restoration, Yamawaki was fortunate enough to have a scholarly grandfather willing to teach her classical Chinese at a young age. She graduated from the Shimane prefectural Women's Normal School in 1881. Her first marriage ended with the death of her husband but Yamawaki busied herself by studying with foreign tutors to add English to her repertoire. A second marriage to a member of the parliament gained her entrée to high society and in 1903 she became a founding director of the Patriotic Women's Society. Prior to her directorship she used her social connections in combination with her traditional learning and modern language skills to open a girls' higher school and soon became an influential woman educator. Like her fellow educator, Tanahashi Ayako, Yamawaki was a conservative in her views of how education of girls should differ from that of boys.[85]

Something more of the Meiji milieu for women can be glimpsed in the girlhood experiences of Hani Motoko, who became a much more innovative educator than either Tanahashi or Yamawaki. Born in 1873 the granddaughter of an ex-samurai, Motoko finished eight years of elementary school in a small community in Aomori Prefecture, the only remaining girl in a graduating class of less than thirty. She then spent a year at home in further study of English. Although her mother and grandmother were both illiterate, her grandfather owned farmland and there was enough money to send Motoko to Tokyo in 1889. In two years there she completed a course of study that qualified her to apply to the Women's Higher Normal School, where her tuition would have been free. But she failed the entrance examinations.

When no further financial support was available from her family, Motoko prevailed upon the principal of Meiji Women's School, a private Christian school, not only to waive tuition but to give her a job on its *Women's School Magazine* so that she could earn her living expenses. In the course of these journalistic duties, she met some of the leading Japanese intellectuals of the day. Three years later she emerged as one of the first few hundred women in her generation to have completed thirteen years of formal schooling. Upon graduation Hani Motoko took one of the few positions open to her gender: teacher at the same rural elementary school from which she had graduated. A failed first marriage led her back to journalism and eventually a career as an educator, which she shared with her second husband, Hani Yoshikazu.

Although Hani Motoko was female, her early life in many ways reflected something of the experiences of a whole generation of rural youth of both genders. In addition to being influenced by a foreign religion legally banned in her grandparents' era, she was exposed to many novel customs in the dormitories of the new schools, which were, as Hani reminds us, much more mundane but not necessarily insignificant: "For a country girl like myself, it was not easy at first to get up early in the morning, to wash in a crowded washroom, and to eat and bathe expeditiously. . . . I was cured, moreover, of the bad habit of snacking ingrained as a child growing up in the countryside, where constant nibbling was a way of life."[86]

Despite the social and cultural changes taking place in these women's lives, the official view of the need for separate and unequal educational opportunities for the genders remained essentially unchanged during the Meiji period. In 1906 the prominent bureaucrat Makino Nobuaki, then serving as minister of education, summed it up once more with the widely used phrase "good wife and wise mother" (*ryōsai kenbo*): "As the male and female sexes differ, so do their duties differ. The purpose of girls' education is to make good wives and wise mothers. Recently some girls have received specialized education and wish to engage in vocations, but they are exceptional. In the end, a girl's duty is to become someone's wife and someone's mother; to manage the household; and to educate children."[87]

Central Government Control

The views of Education Ministry officials were particularly crucial because of the highly centralized nature of control of public schooling achieved by the mid-Meiji period. The original 1872 Plan, it is true, had been amended with the 1879 Education Ordinance, and if fully implemented, this ordinance would have shifted much more of the responsibility for schooling down to the local levels of government. Under its provisions, not only were prefectural education officials to operate more independently of the central government but also school boards were to be elected to manage local primary schools. But by the end of 1880 the Revised Education Ordinance had been drawn up, reversing much of what had been basic to the ordinance of the previous year. In the case of the local school boards, the provision for election was changed to give the governor or other administrative head of the unit the power to select their membership. In this and other ways over the next decade, educational policy veered sharply away from the decentralized administrative patterns and liberal values of the late 1870s. It is not coincidental that during these years the Americans who had been hired in key roles as advisers in the Education Ministry and at other levels began to leave: David Murray in 1879, Marion Scott in 1881, Luther W. Mason in 1882.

Mori Arinori came to the post of minister of education in the mid-1880s believing, as did Prime Minister Itō, that national school reform would continue to flounder without standards imposed from above. They may also have been stimulated to press forward as quickly as possible by the impending creation of an elected parliament. Mori, at least, did not have "very much faith in Parliaments . . . I doubt whether parliamentarianism can be successfully grafted on Japanese habits of thought."[88] In matters of importance, including education, Mori preferred decisionmaking by a technocratic elite. He thus set out to use the power still concentrated in the executive Council of State and the Education Ministry to create order and uniformity out of the chaotic system of schools that had grown up over the previous two decades.

As one step in recentralizing control, Mori dismantled the system of local school boards in 1885. However, he also attempted to convince local officials, somewhat paradoxically if not hypocritically, that he respected their expertise on local conditions and would encourage their independence from central government dictates.[89] His successors in the Education Ministry were not unequivocally opposed to leaving some nominal authority in the hands of local officials. These attitudes seem less inconsistent when one examines the configuration of local government that was taking shape in the 1880s.

The first Meiji attempt at systematizing local government had come in 1878 when the Council of State promulgated a set of laws defining the powers and responsibilities of units below the central level. It was a system of considerable complexity with a three-tiered administrative hierarchy of (1) prefecture-level units (*ken, fu,* and *dō*), including large metropolises (*fu*), (2) county districts, and (3) municipalities and villages. Governors and district chiefs were appointed by the central government but the new 1878 laws provided for the elections of town and village heads as well as legislative assemblies for prefectural units and towns/villages. In 1879 elected school boards had been added. But by the time the first nationally elected parliament met in 1890, these provisions for local government had been thoroughly revamped and the 72 prefectural units and almost 63,000 villages and towns that had existed in the early 1870s had been reduced to 47 and 15,820 to make it easier to bring them under central control.

The key figure here was Yamagata Aritomo, who became known as the father of both the modern Japanese military and of modern local government.[90] His role in the creation of the local government began in 1882 when he became chairman of the commission set up to prepare for the new constitution. During his tenure there, Yamagata proved intent on fixing the shape of local government prior to the advent of an elected national parliament lest liberals legislate a more radical system. As he put it later, "Without the establishment of the local system, the central government system will not work. . . . Now, one year before the constitution and two years before the Diet opens, we cannot lose a single day in setting up the local system."[91]

The system crafted under Yamagata's lead retained the original three-tiered structure. All levels now had legislative assemblies elected by limited franchise, but all levels tended in practice to be dominated by the executives—governors, district chiefs, and mayors or town/village heads. All these administrative heads were appointed. The relevant local assemblies submitted a list of several nominees, and then a finalist was selected by the governor in the case of mayors and by the Home Ministry in other cases. The executives sat as president of the local assemblies and all legislative acts had to be approved by an appointed executive council and, ultimately, the Home Ministry. Action at all levels of local government was, as clearly stated in the 1888 law, "subject to the supreme control of the central government,"[92] which could both impose its will upon the local units as well as veto their initiatives. This was particularly true in such politically sensitive areas as "the management of police affairs, public works, hygiene, education."[93] In education, school boards were reintroduced in the 1890

Elementary School Ordinance as committees within the local government unit. The membership was appointed by the governor, mayor, district chief, or headman and served only in an advisory capacity. The ninety-seven detailed articles in this ordinance were typical of such ministry regulations in that they left little discretion to local units.[94]

Despite the centralized character of power within this system, it must not be forgotten that the central government could operate smoothly only if it gave some measure of recognition to the needs and desires of local elites. Thus there was always room for a certain degree of compromise or at least flexibility in the implementation stage—"in accordance with the needs of the region," as it was sometimes phrased in official regulations. This was also true in policy formulation once the House of Representatives came into being. Its members were elected in political campaigns for which the support of local elites was crucial. That same cooperation was also critical as long as the central government depended upon local taxes to finance the public school system.

Control over Textbooks

Much of the Meiji debate over local autonomy versus central control in education focused on textbooks, as it would still a century later. In 1881 the Education Ministry ordered schools to report on which textbooks they were using. Local educators were still permitted to choose so long as the book had not been specifically rejected by the ministry. This law changed in 1886 when both the new Primary School Ordinance and the new Middle School Ordinance stipulated that "Textbooks . . . shall be restricted to those authorized by the Minister of Education."[95]

The following year Minister of Education Mori Arinori instituted a new process for ascertaining whether a textbook was appropriate for use in classrooms. The Textbook Authorization Ordinance of 1887 required publishers who wished to sell textbooks to schools to have them scrutinized by a committee selected by the Education Ministry. The books that passed muster under Mori were filled less with traditional Confucian or samurai values than with more modern perspectives influenced by Western models, albeit not those stressing individualism or liberalism.[96] On the whole, the textbooks authorized during his tenure were more notable for their secular subject matter and low prices than for their moral message. Mori also attempted to sidestep the issue of morals textbooks by eliminating written materials for those courses entirely, although they were restored after his death in 1889.

In the decade between the Sino-Japanese War and the Russo-Japanese War, political pressure built for tighter central control over the teaching of morals courses in the primary schools. This sentiment was shared by many of the new political actors on the scene after 1890. These participants were neither associates of the oligarchy within the government nor self-conscious intellectuals criticizing Education Ministry policy from the outside; rather, they were elected members of the Diet.

The 1889 constitution, of which Itō had been the chief author, had created a bicameral parliament, or Diet, with an elected House of Representatives balanced against a House of Peers. The latter included members of the new peerage created in 1885 or their heirs. But among the most politically active of the members were the life peers, distinguished men whose support of the government earned them the honor of a seat in the House of Peers albeit not one inheritable by their offspring.[97] Members of the House of Representatives, by contrast, were elected by adult males who paid a certain level of direct taxes—usually land tax—in each electoral district. Although no bill passed by the representatives could become law without the approval of the peers, it was equally true that there could be no increases in government budgets without the approval of the representatives. Thus public schooling was now subject to a new kind of public scrutiny at the national level and the Diet members often reflected the local concerns of their constituents in matters relating to schools.

As a result, political parties were given a national forum from which to influence educational policy. The two most successful antigovernment parties in the 1890 election—the Liberals and the Progressives—had run on platforms that included planks on education. These were headed respectively by Itagaki Taisuke and Ōkuma Shigenobu, both of whom had long been critical of government educational policy. Itagaki's Liberals promised to "improve education and encourage the spread of learning."Ōkuma's Progressive Party was led by supporters closely associated with his private school, Waseda. At the same time, many elected to the parliament from these parties won their seats with the support of voters demanding lower taxes and greater autonomy for local communities. In this the Liberals and Progressives were joined by other parties. For example, the Daidō Party pledged "to entrust, as far as possible, the management of police affairs, public works, hygiene, education, and other matters to the organs of local self-government."[98]

It was in this context that the Education Ministry attempted to finesse the question of central versus local control. Its "Explanation of School Matters," issued in 1891, declared, "Ordinary administration of local school affairs should, as much as possible, be left to the local authorities. However, matters requiring special consideration . . . are fully under the guidance of the Ministry of Education." Lest there be any confusion about what matters might require special consideration, however, it also stipulated that the purview of the central ministry included "educational objectives, methods, teaching regulations, textbooks, teachers and pupils." The crucial matter of funding, however, was left to "every city, town and village."

Nor was the parliament necessarily averse to central control when it came to other matters. In 1896 a textbook bill was introduced in the House of Peers. Its sponsors argued that commercially produced morals textbooks were unduly expensive as well as being flawed in content. They proposed that a committee be created to draft them and a government bureau be established to publish and distribute them at public expense. The rationale for this change was couched in familiar nationalistic phrases:

> The essence of general education is the nurturing of those qualities that are necessary in a Japanese subject. If we ask where are the roots and foundations for this, they must depend chiefly upon morals education. If we are to say what it is that the spirit and vigor of this country are based upon, it is the attainments of its ordinary subjects. Therefore, [appropriate textbooks are necessary] in order that our country's strength continues to develop on a sound basis in the aftermath of our victory [in the Sino-Japanese War].[99]

This particular bill died in the parliament but by 1901 the Education Ministry was increasingly committed to a fundamental change in the manner in which textbooks were produced and adopted in the public schools. Although ministry certification had been required since 1886, publication had remained in the hands of private firms and choices among competing texts could be made at the local level. Kikuchi Dairoku, the erstwhile dean of sciences at Tokyo University who was serving as minister of education in 1901, explained that this system had a number of undesirable consequences. He spoke of the problems that the lack of standardization caused for pupils moving from one level to another as well as for those transferring from one school to another. He spoke also about the problems that remote school districts had in obtaining books through private publishers.

As it turned out, Kikuchi had glossed over a deeper problem. As early as January 1901 newspapers were reporting that the government was investigating graft involving textbooks. In the effort to market its products, the Kinkōdō publishing house had paid out as much as ¥10,000 in bribes, entertainment, and gifts to local education officials, government school inspectors, and political party functionaries.[100] As the investigation proceeded, the public learned this was not an isolated case but an incident of widespread corruption involving tens of thousands of yen paid out by as many as twenty publishing houses. By the end of 1902 government procurators brought charges against a total of 152 individuals, including principals of elementary, middle, and normal schools, other school officials, and bureaucrats as well as publishers. Eventually 112 were convicted.

In the meantime there were new stories that strengthened the hand of those who sought tighter state control over textbooks. In 1902 a test at the private Tetsugakkan School included the question "Is even regicide permissible for the sake of freedom?" Those scandalized by this blamed it on the use of morals textbooks translated from foreign languages, and the Education Ministry launched an investigation purportedly to determine whether it could continue to grant the waiver of middle school teachers' credentials examinations for the graduates of Tetsugakkan. That same year, critics of the existing system professed shock at a sexual reference in a textbook used at the Higher Women's School.

These developments opened the door to parliamentary action. The parliament first amended the laws to clamp down on bribery in book purchasing and then, in 1903, it gave the Education Ministry an exclusive mandate to commission and publish all elementary school textbooks. This would remain the system through World War II.

The textbooks in the morals courses were the most objectionable to liberal critics then and later. But several points need to be made here. First, it cannot merely be assumed, of course, that students educated with these state-published textbooks actually internalized all the ideals and norms that they preached. As one observer wrote in the early 1900s: "The young people of Japan listen to the principles of loyalty and filial piety as they would a sermon whined out by a Buddhist priest. At first they seemingly welcome it, but after it has been repeated time and time again they begin to yawn, and those with spirit stand up and argue back."[101]

Second, the actual number of hours devoted to morals courses in elementary schools was not very great, as Table 3.5 reveals.

Third, textbooks other than those used in the morals courses were not necessarily traditional in lessons they taught. Lower primary school children were taught little one way or another about history or geography, and the materials used in their Japanese language classes were not necessarily focused on traditional morals.[102]

Control of Private Schools

Government control over private schooling was a separate field for conflict. It seems quite clear that for a time in the 1870s and 1880s the government had

TABLE 3.5
Morals in Elementary Curriculum: Hours per Week Devoted to Subject, 1906

Grade	Hours	Percent of Total Time
Lower Elementary		
First	2	10
Second	2	8
Third	2	7
Fourth	2	7
Higher Elementary		
Fifth	2	7
Sixth	2	7

SOURCE: Calculated from Tsurumi, "Meiji Primary School Language and Ethics Textbooks," p. 248n.

attempted to curtail the growth of private schools—or at least those run by Japanese who had been demanding a more open political process. The Home Ministry had maintained police surveillance on such private schools, and the Education Ministry tightened its regulations on all private schools in the name of quality control. The 1879 Education Ordinance raised the standards for qualifying as middle schools. Whereas in 1879 there were 677 private academies fashioning themselves "middle schools," in 1880 the new standards had helped to reduce that number to only 50. Meanwhile, the number of public schools at this level increased from 107 to 137. When Keiō began to suffer severe budget problems in 1878 and 1879, Fukuzawa requested a government loan through Itō and Inoue Kaoru, political leaders who had been sympathetic to his financial needs in the past. They now turned a deaf ear.[103]

Between 1880 and 1884 a new series of revisions further reduced the number of private schools legally designated "middle" schools to only two. In February 1883, just four months after Ōkuma Shigenobu—who had left the government over the issue of greater popular participation in politics—opened a private school, all public officials including faculty at government schools were forbidden to lecture at any private school.[104] In December 1883 the regulations on military conscription were revised in such a way as to effectively eliminate exemptions for students at Fukuzawa's Keiō or Ōkuma's new school. It is claimed that at Keiō this change alone was responsible within a matter of weeks for over 100 dropping out of a student body of 588.[105] Similarly, Tokutomi Sohō's private academy in provincial Kumamoto, already being harassed by prefectural officials for using textbooks that taught Western concepts of "freedom, liberty, and democracy," suddenly lost most of its pupils.[106]

In January 1884, while private school administrators were still assessing the damage of the military conscription ordinance, there was yet another shock contained in the new regulations governing public middle schools.[107] One of the sources of employment for graduates from private academies had long been as faculty and staff in these secondary schools, whether public or private. Indeed, supplying this market for young teachers had been an important factor in the early success of Fukuzawa's Keiō, with as many as 450 graduates having been placed at such schools.[108] The 1884 regulations stipulated for the first time that at least a percentage of all staff of a school would have to have diplomas from either a certified teachers' training school or a university before it could be designated "middle."[109]

Nor did the government stop here. At the end of 1884 Keiō, Waseda, and other private academies had yet more reason for dismay. In December the Ministry of Justice received approval from the Council of State for its revised Judicial Appointment Rules, which instituted a new examination system for higher civil service personnel. From the standpoint of the private academies and especially private law schools, the key clauses were those granting exemptions from the examinations to Tokyo University law department graduates.[110] The latter had already been exempt from the bar exam since 1879 and now this special privilege was extended to recruitment into the system of judges and procurators. Nor was this discriminatory practice limited to the Justice Ministry. It was to be the precedent for a succession of regulations covering recruitment into other ministries.

Even some girls' schools were viewed by the authorities in this period as too politicized. In 1884 the small private academy run by Fukuda Hideko was ordered closed because of her activities on behalf of the Liberal Party. Fukuda was arrested the following year as part of a group of radicals attempting to smuggle guns to Korea.[111] It was perhaps not coincidental that in 1884 the government established a separate Peeresses' School independent of the now entirely male Peers' School.[112]

Under Mori Arinori in the late 1880s, governmental policy toward private academies took a much more positive turn. Whereas the policies of his immediate predecessors had curtailed the growth of private academies, Mori favored finding a place for them within a national system more broadly conceived. In 1886 he reversed some of the regulations that had hurt the fortunes of schools such as Keiō and Waseda as well as the more specialized private law schools. The judicial examinations were particularly important to Waseda and other private schools that offered training in law. Their graduates had to compete with those of Tokyo University. A compromise was arranged between the Ministries of Education and Justice, and a new Special Regulations for Supervision of Private Law Schools[113] granted certain privileges to law students graduating from Waseda, Senshō, Meiji, Tokyo Hōritsu, or Egirisu Hōritsu. If these schools submitted to an accreditation process under the supervision of Tokyo University law faculty, their students would be allowed to take a special examination administered at Tokyo University. Passing that test would grant them the same exemptions from the regular judicial examinations enjoyed by the Imperial University graduates. None of these designated law schools could afford to deny their students this special opportunity and initially all accepted these 1886 provisions for reporting to outside inspectors. The responsibility for inspection was subsequently transferred from Tokyo University to the Ministry of Education.

Private schools benefited in other ways from the new atmosphere under Mori Arinori. Keiō, besieged by budget problems in the late 1870s, found it possible to raise ¥127,000 in the 1880s and even received a donation from the imperial household.[114] This type of success allowed Fukuzawa to staff a more advanced curriculum in a new division that he insisted on calling a "university division" despite the government policy of limiting that title university to Tokyo Imperial University. Tokutomi Sohō's Ōe Academy in Kumamoto, which had been "on the brink of ruin and collapse," enjoyed a rebirth.[115]

Even Christian missionary schools enjoyed considerably more leeway in the 1880s. Dōshisha, Joseph Niijima's (Niijima Jo's) school in Kyoto, enjoyed a decade of prosperity with a fivefold increase in its student body, reaching an enrollment of over 770 males by 1889. The previous year Foreign Minister Ōkuma Shigenobu and Itō's close associate, Inoue Kaoru, had sponsored a fund-raising banquet for Niishima and raised the equivalent of US$31,000 for the school's endowment. Niishima's appeal for donations was based on the argument that "there does not exist in Japan a university which, teaching the new science, is also founded upon Christian morality. This is the foundation which our civilization needs." Meanwhile, in Niigata Prefecture, officials were actually subsidizing the budget of at least one school in which Christian missionaries tied to churches abroad served on the teaching staff.[116]

Conclusion

By 1905 Japanese government reformers had carried out a revolution in education. In comparative terms, Japan entered the twentieth century on an even par with England and Sweden and behind Prussia and France by only a few percentage points (see Figure 3.4). To measure it in another way, whereas in 1895 only 16 percent of Japan's productive-age male population (15- to 54-year-olds) had an elementary education, by 1905 the percentage had jumped to 42 percent. Thus over 40 percent of Japanese males between 15 and 54 years old now had some formal primary schooling in the new curriculum. Secondary and tertiary enrollments were less impressive, with only one out of eight males advancing beyond primary school; this percentage was even smaller for girls, 4 percent.[117] Nevertheless, Japanese women as well as men would find themselves almost literally in a different world by 1905. Just as Japan's success in the wars with China in 1894–1895 and with Russia in 1904–1905 would gain Japan a measure of acceptance by the Western imperialists, Japanese schoolchildren in the latter part of the Meiji period would accept much that had once been strange about Western ways.

More significant, the Japanese elite had committed itself to eclectic borrowing from abroad while preserving cultural traits deemed essential. Modernization need not simply be conflated with Westernization. Tokyo University philosophy professor Inoue Tetsurō summed up this approach when debating the issue of whether to import a Western alphabet to replace the existing system, which combined Chinese and Japanese script:

> Script accompanies the development of the human mind and has a close connection with the history of the development of a people's spirit. It is therefore different from other foreign imports such as railways and steamships. Suddenly to abolish the script which has grown along with the development of ideas since our ancestors' times and replace it with the entirely different *rōmaji* [Roman alphabet] would be to destroy the inner foundation stone of the nation and do violence to the people's feelings.[118]

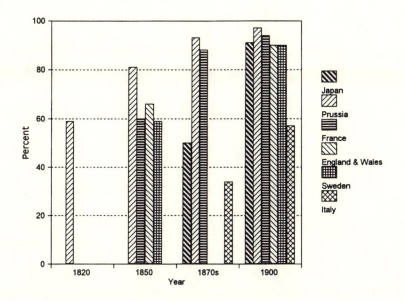

FIGURE 3.4
Elementary School Enrollments: Percent of Age Group Males, 1820–1900.
Sources: European data from Maynes, *Schooling in Western Europe,* p. 134; Japanese data from
Japan Ministry of Education, *Japan's Growth and Education,* pp. 156–157.

What this eclectic approach meant in practice, however, was that the struggle would now focus not on whether cultural traits were to be preserved but on
which ones were essential.

4

To Liberate Education from Bureaucratic Control: 1905–1931

I told [Procurator General Hiranuma Kiichirō] that recently university professors had become a gang of publicity-seekers and we could not sit idly by and ignore it while the abuses of publishing such absurd opinions were going on.

—Hara Takashi, Prime Minister[1]

Tokyo Imperial University should become the quarantine office for imported [ideologies]. If a thought is harmful, it should be treated as a harmful thought. For an ideology which is both harmful and harmless, the university should remove the harmful portion and import the profitable part.

—Takeuchi Kakuji, Lawyer[2]

The victory in the Russo-Japanese War of 1904–1905 signaled the fulfillment of the two main Meiji ambitions set forth in the slogan "Affluent nation and a strong defense." The Japanese army and navy were now recognized as the strongest military in East Asia, and Japan no longer needed to fear the threat of force in its diplomatic dealings with the Western powers. Indeed, Japan was now in a position to pursue its own imperialist designs in its colony in Taiwan, on the Korean peninsula, and in that portion of China north of the Great Wall known as Manchuria. Although it was still far too early to term Japan a rich country, it had successfully prevented the Western powers from establishing outside dominance over its economy—the fate of China as well as of so much of South and Southeast Asia—and the industrial programs begun in the 1870s and 1880s were beginning to change the country economically as well as culturally.

Success in dealing with the original Meiji agenda, however, generated yet other challenges. The period 1905–1931 was to be fraught with new tensions as the nation's leaders grappled with demands for greater equity and justice at home while protecting the country's economic and diplomatic gains on the Asian mainland. The First World War provided a powerful stimulant to the Japanese economy, drawing workers into the industrial workplace at an unprecedented pace. The speed of this hothouse growth and the series of sharp business downturns that followed created new gaps both between the work force and industrial managers as well as between the developing urban sector and the now depressed rural sector of the economy. Consequently, serious class strife between labor and management, on the one hand, and between tenant farmers and landlords, on the other, seemed imminent.

In 1918 riots over rice prices spread rapidly from region to region throughout the nation, leading to the resignation of the prime minister. As a consequence, the parliamentary parties were finally able to put their own leaders into almost all the key cabinet positions. Prime Minister Hara Takashi (Kei) devoted much of his attention, as did his successors over the next decade, to new strategies for coping with this perceived threat to social stability. Although these politicians owed their power base to the Western models of parliamentary government, they were much more comfortable with the elitist currents in Western political thought than with those moving in the direction of greater popular participation. They would pay lip service at times to such notions but their actions were more frequently aimed at suppressing the political left who championed these ideas. The latest in Western ideas came from this new political left. The small ideological fires set by Japanese socialists at the time of the Russo-Japanese War burst into flames at the end of the First World War, and Japanese political elites would expend enormous energy over the two decades of the 1910s and 1920s trying to put out this blaze.

The opposition to the political and business establishment in these years was quite diverse in nature, ranging from anarcho-syndicalism and Marxism through Christian and Fabian socialism on into contemporary British liberalism toward the center of the spectrum. When the holders of these various views did find common ground it was in their shared antagonism toward the concentration of political power in the hands of political and economic elites unwilling to address the social problems of an increasingly industrial nation. The mainstream of this movement thus demanded a reduction of the influence wielded by the nonelected House of Peers in favor of the power of the elected House of Representatives, the expansion of voting rights to include at least all male adults, and the selection of cabinet ministers more directly accountable to the majority in the parliament. These reformers also agreed on the need for stronger labor unions, tighter regulation of factory conditions, and more protection from the exigencies of a capitalist economy for workers and the deserving poor.

Japanese elites had reason to fear all these ideas, but in this period they were sometimes willing to compromise with the liberals and social democrats closer to the center while seeking to eradicate socialists and other radicals further to the left. The political system underwent changes between 1912 and 1925 that brought the parliamentary parties to the fore. Even if these were led most often by elitists who did not believe in popular democracy, they formed common cause with liberals in their campaigns to transfer control over the bureaucracy and military into the hands of the lower house of the Diet.

Education was a strategic theater in this political conflict for two reasons. First, some of the new liberalism involved ideas about the reform of the education system in terms of both values in the curriculum and access to opportunities beyond the primary level. Second, the campuses of higher schools and colleges became incubators for radical ideas and thus drew the ire of conservatives.

Ironically, this conflict resulted in part from the expansion of educational opportunities in the period 1905–1931. Schooling was both cause and effect in the spread of new ideologies. Increasing literacy rates made it possible to disseminate ideas about labor unions and other reforms. And the expansion at the secondary and tertiary levels produced a supply of graduates faster than the economy could absorb, creating more demand for reform.

Schools and Access to Opportunities

By 1905 enrollments in Japanese primary schools had exceeded 90 percent for both boys and girls, and in 1907 compulsory education was increased from four to six years, thus realizing the early Meiji vision. But now demand began to build for more. The success of universal primary schooling meant a larger population of elementary school graduates to compete for the far smaller number of places in public secondary schools. The Meiji vision—a massive elementary school base with only limited necessity for middle-level schooling and even smaller segments of society advancing to college—now slowly gave ground to the pressures for greater opportunity at the secondary and even tertiary levels. There were calls for extending compulsory education to eight years or even longer.

Nor was this heard only from the liberals or Marxists. Kita Ikki, the radical nationalist whose political ideals came to be shared by many young right-wing extremists in the military, called for an extension of compulsory education to "a period of ten years from ages six to sixteen" and said that "similar education shall be given to both male and female."[3] The platforms of even the conservative parties were promising to "promote education," "to reform and renew the system," or even "equalize opportunities for education," although they were not concerned with gender equality.[4]

The Expansion of Postprimary Schooling

The government eventually responded to this pressure by appointing an Extraordinary Commission on Education in 1917.[5] The result of the recommendations made by the commission was a number of significant changes in secondary and tertiary education, as can be seen by comparing Figure 4.1 with Figure 3.1 of the previous chapter. The Extraordinary Commission on Education had recommended extending compulsory schooling to eight years. This recommendation was not accepted in part because of the costs. Instead, the government expanded some facilities at the secondary level while keeping attendance voluntary. Between 1905 and 1920 the percent of males going on to secondary schools had already risen from 12 percent to 20 percent. For females, the earlier percent had been much smaller—only 4 percent—so the rise to 12 percent in 1920 was even more rapid even if the end result was less impressive. By 1930 the percent of males had stabilized at 21 percent whereas that of females continued to grow to 16 percent.[6] As unimpressive as these figures may be when contrasted with universal secondary education in the late twentieth century, at least the opportunities for males compared very well with other industrial nations in the 1920s.

Some of this growth at the secondary level came in institutions for vocational and technical training, as Figure 4.2 reveals. Another way of measuring the changes taking place for young adolescents is to look at the labor force participation rates for these decades. In 1920 approximately one out of four girls aged ten to fourteen were working. This meant that despite the raising of compulsory schooling to six years in 1907 many females in these early decades did not actually receive regular schooling. In 1940 only one out of nine were in the work force.[7]

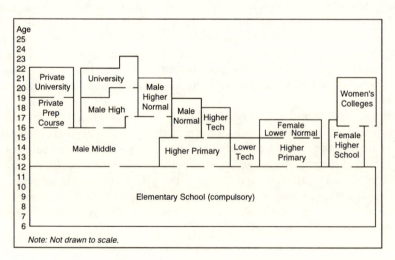

FIGURE 4.1
Main Tracks in Schooling, 1919.
Source: Adapted from chart in Monbushō, *Gakusei 80 nenshi*, p. 1031, as suggested in
Henry D. Smith II, *Japan's First Student Radicals*, chart 1, p. 3.

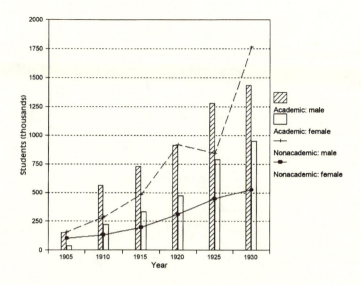

FIGURE 4.2
Secondary Schooling by Type: Number of Students, 1905–1930.
Source: Calculated from Japan Ministry of Education, Research Bureau,
Japan's Growth and Education, pp. 156–157.

The pace of growth in higher education, which had been relatively slow until 1917, exploded after 1918. (See Tables 4.1 and 4.2 and Figure 4.3.) The original five higher schools built for males under Mori Arinori in the 1880s were expanded to eight by 1910.[8] Together they enrolled over 6,300 students. Nine more state-supported higher schools were created by 1922; by 1930 there were twenty-five national schools and three supported at the municipal level. These twenty-eight public schools enrolled over 18,000 students, and four private schools that had emerged in the 1920s added another 2,000 males.

This system remained elitist in three senses. First, women's "higher schools" were still at the level of the males' middle school, accepting students directly from primary school. Second, even male higher schools never enrolled more than 1 percent of all Japanese males aged sixteen to nineteen years old. Third, all higher schools were not equal: The graduates of the First Higher School in Tokyo ultimately had much more success in entering the government bureaucracy.

By the late Meiji period, men seldom entered the ranks of the civil bureaucracy without first attending college. Although there was no legal requirement of a diploma, graduation from an imperial university or a legally designated private law school meant automatic exemption from some of the civil service examinations. In other careers as well, college attendance came to be the expected prerequisite by the early twentieth century.

TABLE 4.1
Higher Education for Males: Number of Schools, 1908–1933

	Higher School	College[a]	University
1905	8	50	2
1910	8	62	3
1915	8	66	4
1920	15	74	16
1925	29	85	34
1930	32	111	46

[a]Does not include technical *senmon gakko.*

SOURCE: Adapted from Monbushō, *Gakusei 90 nenshi,* tables 8, 9, 11.

TABLE 4.2
Higher Education for Males by Type of School, 1908–1933

	Higher School	College[a]	University
1905	4,904	23,822	5,821
1910	6,341	25,275	7,239
1915	6,259	29,643	9,693
1920	8,839	37,088	21,913
1925	16,858	40,711	46,666
1930	20,551	52,598	69,605

[a]Does not include technical *senmon gakko.*

SOURCE: Adapted from Monbushō, *Gakusei 90 nenshi,* tables 8, 9, 11.

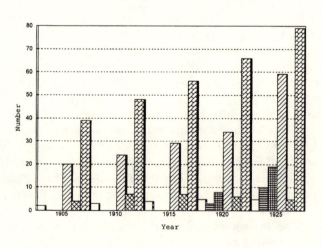

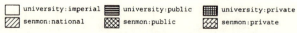

FIGURE 4.3
Institutions of Higher Education by Type, 1905–1925.
Source: Calculated from Amano, "Continuity and Change," p. 25.

Prior to 1918 the state monopolized the legal designation of "university," limiting it to Tokyo Imperial and its sister schools. Demands both for the opening of more state-supported universities and for elevating the more prestigious private schools to that legal status had grown in the 1900s. The privileged position of Tokyo Imperial as de facto personnel agency for the higher civil service came under particular attack from alumni of private schools now in prominent political or economic positions. One out of every four members of the House of Representatives in 1908 had attended one of the six major private schools in Tokyo. By 1917 the proportion had increased to almost a third.[9] Graduates of Tokyo and Kyoto Imperial universities combined made up only 6 percent of the members of the House of Representatives in 1908 and 15 percent in 1917. The alumni of these private schools and their allies initially targeted "imperial university privileges," the exemptions from certain qualifying examinations. In 1910 the parliament actually passed a bill extending exemptions to all graduates of certified private law schools. But the bill was opposed by the cabinet of Katsura Tarō and did not survive the House of Peers. Nevertheless, private colleges now had influential voices bringing pressure to bear through the parliament. Hara Takashi (Kei) and other leaders of the dominant party, the Seiyūkai, supported the attempt to reduce the role of Tokyo University as part of a larger effort to open up the civil bureaucracy to more party influence.[10] When the government stalled in implementing the reforms to end special privileges in the examinations for imperial university graduates, there were demonstrations by students outside the Diet building. The conservatives in government slowly gave ground in 1918 and again in 1923. By that year official university status had been granted to most of the private schools involved in the original campaigns.

Some of this expansion came in state facilities for higher education. The student bodies of the first two imperial universities were enlarged between 1913 and 1933, Tokyo by almost 160 percent and Kyoto by almost 320 percent (see Table 4.3). The government also created four more imperial universities

TABLE 4.3
Growth of Imperial Universities: Tokyo and Kyoto, 1913–1933

	Tokyo Students	Kyoto Students
1913	5,223	1,791
1918	4,904	2,033
1923	5,981	2,548
1928	7,820	5,170
1933	8,269	5,710

SOURCE: Naikaku Tokei Kyoku, *Nihon teikoku tokei nenkan*, vols. 45, 49, 50, and 54, Tokyo: Naikaku tokei kyoku, annual.

between 1905 and 1931: Tōhoku University (in Sendai) in 1907, Kyushu University (in Fukuoka) in 1910, Hokkaido University (in Sapporo) in 1918, and Osaka University in 1931. Two others were located in the colonies, one in Taipei, Taiwan, and one in Seoul, Korea, both of which were filled primarily with Japanese students. Not all of these new schools offered the full range of specialties available at Tokyo and Kyoto and they suffered other disadvantages in terms of prestige. Tokyo Imperial maintained much of its status as the "Mount Fuji" of universities.

Even Tokyo University students experienced changes, however. In the Meiji period the largest single employee of its graduates was the government. This was especially true of those who majored in *hōgaku,* or "law," where the faculty prided itself on training prospective administrators. Over one-third of all who had graduated in law prior to September 1908 were employed by the government; only one of eight was identified as a businessman or banker. By the early 1930s, the two categories had been reversed—19 percent were in the government and 29 percent were in business or banking. By 1928 almost two-thirds of all Japanese business executives had attended college.[11]

The legal designation "university" (*daigaku*) was generally withheld from private institutions until the 1918 reforms. In the next two years, eight private schools were formally recognized as qualifying. By 1930 there were twenty-four, including some of the more famous colleges and law schools founded in the early Meiji: Chūō, Dōshisha, Hōsei, Keiō, Meiji, and Waseda (see Table 4.4). Of these, Keiō and Waseda were the most exclusive, admitting only about one-fifth of the applicants in the 1920s. Most of the others admitted between half and three-quarters of those who applied.[12]

Places for Females

Although the number of girls in secondary schools had tripled between 1910 and 1920 to a total over 150,000, there were still no women's schools on a par with male universities and only a handful of females were enrolled at the tertiary level. Well over half of all Japanese women aged fifteen to fifty-nine were gainfully employed at the end of the 1920s and there were more jobs for

TABLE 4.4
Private Universities: Number of Schools and Students, 1918–1930

	Schools	Male Students	Female Students
1918	0	0	0
1920	8	9,891	0
1925	19	26,133	7
1930	24	40,725	52

SOURCE: Calculated from Monbushō, *Gakusei 90 nenshi*, table 11.

middle-class women in the 1920s then previously—for example, as nurses, office workers, department store clerks, and telephone operators. But these jobs were not seen as requiring university training. Among doctors, there were only 1,400 females in 1930 compared with 42,000 males.[13] However, by 1930 there were 100,000 female teachers, and normal schools continued to be the best opportunity for a woman to prepare for a white-collar career.

There is no statistical evidence regarding the social backgrounds of either the males or females who entered teachers' training programs in the late Meiji period. It is only possible to say that although it is true that teaching had attracted more samurai than commoners until the early 1900s, from then on the numbers of new teachers identifying their family background as samurai fell steadily. The data from at least one normal school indicated that by the early 1930s over 90 percent of students there were from the commoner class.[14]

Opportunities for women in teaching expanded after 1900. The creation of women's higher schools led to the addition of a second women's higher normal school in 1908. Job opportunities at coeducational primary schools expanded even faster. Much of this opportunity resulted from increases in attendance rates, and after 1907 the inauguration of six-year compulsory schooling replaced the older standard of four years, which meant more demand for primary school teachers. The ratio of females to males, moreover, also increased somewhat between 1907 and 1918—from 26 percent to 31 percent.

The increase in the ratio of women may have been caused in part by economic considerations: Salaries for women were lower than those for men, and a school district could thus stretch its budget by hiring women. The economic boom during the First World War also siphoned males into the private sector, and there were far fewer career alternatives for women. Whatever the reason, some members of the 1918 Extraordinary Commission on Education found this disturbing: "How long will it be before their number overtakes the number of male teachers? . . . When the responsibility for the education of the nation is put primarily in women's hands, we cannot cultivate vigor and virtuous simplicity in our citizens. . . . There should be a limit set on the number of female teachers."[15]

Apparently this voice went unheeded, since the percentage continued to rise—to 33 percent by 1927. As in the Meiji period, one reason may have been a combination of the low overall salaries, which drove males away from the profession, and the fact that women were cheaper to employ than men. Starting salaries for women were 10 percent less than those for men and the discrepancy tended to grow over time, especially in grades four and five of primary school.[16] Indeed, one 1920 survey indicated that very few school administrators thought women were suitable for teaching beyond the first four grades.

Criticism of women teachers also came from the political left. The feminist Itō Noe, who while in higher school had an affair with her male English instructor, expressed strong feelings on the subject of women teachers:

When I was in girls' school all our teachers taught us that to achieve happiness we
must learn to be satisfied with our lot. They taught us to eliminate all the impulses
that well up in our hearts. . . . There is nobody as hateful as the narrow-minded,
obstinate women educators of Japan. With the narrow outlook, opinionated views,
ignorance and superficiality, how could they expect to undertake true education?
. . . Your writings are amorphous and pointless. If they are indications of the kind
of person you are, you are not even worth spitting at.[17]

Because of, or in spite of, the character of schooling for females in this period, there was now a new generation of women more willing to become involved in the great political issues of the day than their Meiji predecessors had
been. Itō Noe was a well-known example, albeit an extreme one. Upon graduation she became the editor of the leading feminist magazine of the day, *Bluestocking* (*Setō*). In 1921 she also helped organize the Red Wave Society, a
socialist study group for women. The group was not large, having only several
dozen members, but it included Yamakawa Kikue, a Tsuda College graduate
who in the early 1920s was one of only three women in the first Japan Communist Party. Itō would die alongside her partner, the famed anarchist Ōsugi
Sakae, at the hands of the police in 1923. Yamakawa would survive to become
an important political figure after World War II.

The original editor of *Bluestocking* had been Hiratsuka Raichō, a graduate of
Japan Women's College and a trenchant critic of inequality in education:

Men and women are endowed by nature with equal faculties. Therefore, it is odd
to assume that one of the sexes requires [higher] education while the other does
not. . . .

I bemoan the fact that there is only one private college for women in Japan, and
there is no tolerance on man's part to permit entrance of women into many universities maintained for men.[18]

In 1919 Hiratsuka and another forceful woman, former elementary school
teacher Ichikawa Fusae, founded the New Women's Society. But Hiratsuka rejected the more radical views of the role of women proposed by the leftists Itō
and Yamakawa in favor of what the leftists stigmatized as a "bourgeois" acceptance of motherhood.

A less radical challenge to the educational orthodoxy was posed by the liberal New Education Movement of the 1910s and 1920s. Influenced by progressive theories imported from the United States and Germany, pedagogical
innovations aimed at stimulating self-motivation and individualized learning
were experimented with in elementary schools attached to women's normal
schools. These ideas were subsequently synthesized with indigenous values in
private schools such as Seijo Elementary School, founded by Sawayanagi Masa-
tarō, and the Freedom School (Jiyū Gakuen) for girls, run by Hani Motoko.[19]
Another influential figure in this progressive education movement was Shimonaka Yasaburō, a pioneer in the teachers' union movement and the founder
of the highly respected Heibonsha publishing house.

The Supply and Demand for Graduates

As the 1920s wore on, a new set of factors fueled discontent among students and teachers alike. The increase in the supply of university graduates could hardly have come at a worse time in terms of market demand. Although the government bureaucracy as a whole continued to expand in this decade, the pace of its expansion was much slower than in earlier periods, and the competition was correspondingly greater. One consequence was that graduates tended more often to seek jobs in the private sector. But in the 1920s the Japanese economy suffered a series of sharp business cycles that limited opportunities here as well. As a result, there were far more degree-holders than suitable jobs for them. Those school graduates who did secure employment often found themselves in positions far below their qualifications—in effect underemployed.

The situation became worse at the end of the decade. Japan entered an economic recession two years before the rest of the world when a huge bank failure cause a financial panic in 1927. Once the United States, Britain, and France began to cut back on imports and throw up tariff barriers following the Wall Street Crash of 1929, the Japanese economy went into a rapid tailspin. The impact on job opportunities was summed up in a June 1930 article in the Tokyo University student newspaper: "Having spent some seventeen years of preparation all the way from grade school through the university and about to enter the 'real world,' the graduate finds a situation of reckless over-supply and stands on the brink of joblessness, his status of 'Bachelor of Arts' having little value."[20]

The main ingredients that generated a new activism among students and teachers were a dismal economic environment, disillusionment with an older generation, a war in which the Central and Eastern European authoritarian monarchies had lost to the more democratic nations of Western Europe and North America, and revolutionary ideas winning out in the Soviet Union.

New Ideological Conflict

Student Activists

Participation of students in political causes did not begin in the 1920s. It can be traced back as early as the 1870s within the movement demanding an elected national assembly. Beginning in the 1880s the government had legally forbidden student participation in politics but was never very successful in actually preventing it. The issues, however, changed with time, and by the Russo-Japanese War the more radical causes that attracted student support were those championed by the Meiji socialists. There were two main concerns: the gap between rich and poor, which was exacerbated by capitalism, and the tendency for industrial nations to engage in imperialist wars.

Serious concern about the deleterious effects of industrial development in Japan dates from the turn of the twentieth century. Although a small labor union movement also arose about this time, it was too weak to sustain itself, and intellectuals were the first voices to successfully force attention to the problem of urban poverty. Initially the debate was primarily between two camps. A number of influential academics and high-level civil bureaucrats asserted the need for government intervention both to protect workers in the factories and to provide basic social welfare measures for workers and their families. In response, business leaders and their supporters in government argued that it was too soon to be worried about the negative effects of industrialization. Almost immediately, this debate was joined by more radical voices asserting that socialism was the wave of the future. What appeal they enjoyed probably stemmed less from their proposed solutions than from the tireless manner in which they probed the problems in the 1900s. As journalists, novelists, and public speakers, the small band of leftists relentlessly exposed the underside of Meiji economic progress.

Among the causes that drew significant numbers of protesters was the ecological disaster caused by Japan's first modern copper mine. The ruthless exploitation of the Ashio ore deposits polluted tens of thousands of acres of farming land and waterways with devastating effects on the lives of perhaps a half million people in Tochigi Prefecture, north of Tokyo. The plight of these farmers and fishermen eventually stirred large street demonstrations. Ōsugi Sakae, an anarchist whose own writings had considerable influence on student activists, described his first encounter with student activism in 1901 or 1902, when he was eighteen:

> [In my lodging house] there were five or six students from W [Waseda] University and one cold evening they went rushing pell-mell out of the house. I could hear the noise of what seemed a great crowd waiting outside. I opened the sliding window to look out. At least twenty students were there, all wearing the distinctive [Waseda] four-cornered cap with its tassel, milling about boisterously, holding aloft paper lanterns on poles and waving them like huge banners.
> "It's getting late! If we don't run all the way, we'll be late!"
> "But that's better! It's too cold to walk. Besides, we'll get a lot of attention if so many of us trot through the streets." . . .
> And they all flew off, shouting loudly to one another in high spirits.
> Even now the scene floats clearly in my memory: the flickering lights in the big paper lanterns illuminating the bold letters "Y [YANAKA] VILLAGE COPPER POLLUTION PROBLEM MASS MEETING." And I can still hear their voices chanting "Left, right; left, right" long after they were out of sight.[21]

At the center of this tiny socialist movement was the Commoners Society and its newspaper the *Commoners News*. During the Russo-Japanese War, most of the leading radical intellectuals of the day temporarily transcended their differences over religious faith and political theory to jointly oppose the war.

Ōsugi was one of many students who took part in the group's discussion meetings, sold subscriptions to the newspaper, and occasionally served as courier on clandestine errands. He lost his student status when he was arrested for taking part in a mass demonstration in support of the Tokyo streetcar strike of 1906. This small but vocal leftist movement suffered from external harassment by the police as well as from schisms within. In 1910 it was forced to suspend most of its activities when one of its most flamboyant leaders, the anarchist Kōtoku Shūsui, was arrested and subsequently executed for conspiring to assassinate the emperor.

The Russian Revolution and the victory of the Western democracies in the First World War were major stimulants to a revival of student activism, and it reached unparalleled heights on Japanese campuses in the early 1920s.[22] One of the first outbreaks came at Waseda University when a small group of students formed the Waseda Reform Society in summer 1917. They conducted rallies and marches to the drumbeat of a Russian tune with new Japanese lyrics, entitled "Waseda Revolutionary Song," and enough students joined the demonstrations to paralyze the campus for a month. The immediate issue was a clash among alumni, faculty, and school administrators over the college presidency, but it was a prelude to a greater politicization of the campus.[23]

Groups of students and recent graduates from Tokyo Imperial University had also been involved in political activities since the early Meiji period, but this intensified in the First World War as students were encouraged by social democrats among the faculty. Other students were involved off-campus as individuals in the moderate Yūaikai labor movement. In 1917 some of these organized a Worker-Student Society in Tokyo with the aid of a Waseda professor. A similar organization was formed in Kyoto with Dōshisha as well as Kyoto Imperial students under the influence of socialist intellectuals such as Professor Kawakami Hajime.

There were also right-wing patriotic student groups, especially at Tokyo Imperial and Kyoto Imperial universities. The best known was the Colleagues in Support of the Nation, formed by students of a Tokyo constitutional law professor, Uesugi Shinkichi. Uesugi was the sworn foe of all liberal interpretations of the Meiji constitution that implied that the Japanese monarch, like the British monarch, was legally bound to share power with his subjects. In this conservative view of the throne, Professor Uesugi had the support of powerful figures within the Japanese bureaucracy, notably Hiranuma Kiichirō, the leader of the dominant clique within the Ministry of Justice in the 1920s. On campus, Uesugi carried on a running debate with two of his fellow Tokyo Imperial professors, Minobe Tatsukichi and Yoshino Sakuzō.[24] This thrust the rightist Colleagues in Support of the Nation into direct confrontation with Yoshino's student supporters and brought both groups to the attention of the authorities.

The first enduring organization of student activists created without direct faculty leadership was the New Man Society of 1918, although its members included recent graduates who had been influenced by Professor Yoshino Sakuzō. In its statement of purpose the organization pledged itself to "work for and seek to advance the new trend toward the liberation of mankind, which is a universal cultural force."[25] Liberation for many activists came to mean not only reform at home but freedom for Japan's colonies, Korea and Taiwan. Their main focus was on domestic democratization, however. These students shared with many others in the early 1920s the certainty that a new era was dawning, and they asked rhetorically, "As we face the dawn, who, then, should take charge of reform of Japan today? How about the privileged classes who now occupy the positions of national leadership? How about the educated classes, the bureaucrats, the military, the party politicians, the capitalists, the university professors?" Scorn for their elders came through clearly in the answer: "Their lack of qualifications has been too eloquently proved by their behavior both now and in the past. Their record clearly shows too much wickedness, vulgarity, and lack of principle to win the confidence of the masses. We have already given up on the ruling class."

These radical student leaders directed some of their most vitriolic criticism at their own alma mater: "Tokyo Imperial University Faculty of Law . . . has to all appearance been a school for training lackeys of the civil bureaucrats bureaucracy and zaibatsu [big business]. . . . We aim to dissociate ourselves from university-oriented ideas." They also made explicit their rejection of Confucian and other traditional teachings that had formed the core of morals courses in compulsory schooling—"the old religionists and those who rely on ancestral virtue . . . [and] empty sermonizing and submissive morals." What was needed "in times like these" was for a new generation to wrest the levers of power away from the discredited older generation, including the academic elite: "The drive for reform must come from youth itself, youth whose conscience is pure, whose intellect is keen, whose spirit is afire. The blood of youth is untainted, the standpoint of youth is impartial, the ideals of youth are lofty. Has not the day come for youth to rise up as one?"[26]

In the meantime the organization made use of Tokyo University department classrooms to hold monthly meetings, which were attended mainly by other students, including some from women's secondary schools. Liberal and socialist academics were invited to speak to assemblies under the auspices of the New Man Society, sometimes drawing several hundred for an audience. In its eclectic mix of democratic ideals and social goals, the New Man Society accurately reflected the changes in the nation's ideological atmosphere at the end of the war. In the months that followed, however, the student movement, like the labor union movement and the left wing of the intellectual world, moved steadily toward a more systematic Marxist conception of what was needed.

Advocates of Marxist solutions were prominent among those student organizers who created a nationwide network of campus groups in the early 1920s. The first such organization of radical activists—the Student Federation, or

Gakuren—was created in autumn 1922 as an outgrowth of a campaign to raise money to aid famine victims in the Soviet Union. Waseda and Tokyo University students were in the forefront but the fifty-plus participants also included representatives from such private colleges as Hōsei, Keiō, Meiji, and Nihon as well as at least one women's medical college.

The movement soon spread to the higher schools, partly as the result of recruiting visits by radical university students. In January 1923 delegates from across the country met secretly at the First Higher School to form the Higher School League. The main purpose, they agreed, was to "engage in communist propaganda among higher school students."[27] The Japan Communist Party would eventually be dominated by men who began their political careers in this militant student movement of the early 1920s.

Politicized Professors

In large part the initial ideological stimulus and role models for political activism in the schools of the 1920s were provided by university professors. Among those destined to most win fame for his efforts to bring about social and political reforms was Tokyo Imperial University political science professor Yoshino Sakuzō, called "the apostle of democracy" for his attempt to synthesize Western liberalism with the Japanese system of monarchy. Keiō University professor Fukuda Tokuzō was an economist with the same goal. Waseda had several famous advocates for change, including the prolific essayist Ōyama Ikuo and the Christian socialist "father of Japanese baseball" Professor Abe Isoo. The economics department at Tokyo Imperial earned the nickname "Lenin Village" because young faculty such as Morito Tatsuo and Ōuchi Hyōe met with their graduate students late into the night to discuss the latest radical ideas from the West. At Kyoto Imperial the single most influential academic in this movement was Kawakami Hajime, who was moving steadily toward a Marxist view of what was required. These men either advised existing student clubs or drew around them clusters of college youth, which were the forerunners of independent student organizations.

Teachers' Unions

Political activism was not confined to students or faculty in higher education. In 1919 Shimonaka Yasaburō, a publisher formerly on the faculty at a prefectural normal school, founded what eventually became the Japan Teachers' Union Enlightenment Association. Until this time, the only nationwide professional organization for schoolteachers was the Imperial Education Association, chartered in 1883. Although the association came to be led in the 1920s by educators with progressive credentials, it remained politically conservative. Shimonaka's new group, which had 200 members at its first conference, was further to the left. It dedicated itself to "attain[ing] a just life based upon human rights . . . the basic rights of human beings and . . . their inalienable social rights," and its 1920 manifesto also proclaimed its support for the League of Nations and called for "an International Congress on Education to promote international understanding and world peace." However, Shimonaka and others in the leadership had great respect for the imperial throne and they stressed that their call for change was ultimately grounded in patriotism and loyalty: "We assert our sincerity as Japanese citizens and our desire to be loyal to the just and great principles of Japan. Therefore, we reject all irrational and unnatural laws, conventions and thoughts contrary to these principles."[28]

By its own count, membership in the Enlightenment Association quickly reached 1,500 by the mid-1920s. Although this association represented only a small fraction of the total public school teachers in the nation, it articulated several concerns that were being debated in the larger political arena: individual aspirations over the demands of the state; democratic rather than oligarchic decisionmaking; and greater equality of opportunity in education. More specifically, to increase democratic control, the group called for an end to both standardized curriculum and mandated textbooks and to place power in the hands of popularly elected national and local school boards.[29] Moreover, "in order to liberate education from bureaucratic control and to ensure the freedom of teachers, school administration should be organized by the teachers themselves." The teachers, in turn, should be allowed to join the union, for "without such a union of teachers, the government will usurp the control of education from the teachers."[30]

The Reassertion of Central Control

The Reaffirmation of "Japanese" Values

The first appearance in the 1900s of a socialist movement, as small as it was, greatly worried Japan's political elite and in 1904 the Home Ministry created a special unit of the national police to deal with subversive ideas. By 1911 this unit had grown into what came eventually to be called "thought police."[31] There were also measures to enhance the prestige of the Shinto religion. The Education Ministry, for its part, purged the history curriculum of confusion about the fourteenth century, when a deposed emperor had set up a Southern Court in exile to challenge the succession of the so-called Northern Court. Although the two courts were eventually reunited, scholars were divided over the question of which imperial line had been legitimate. One of the chief consultants to the Education Ministry on textbooks, a prominent historian at Tokyo University, made the government's position quite clear: "Historical disputes should be contained within the boundaries of historical discourse and should have no bearing whatsoever on history as it is generally taught in the nation's schools. I therefore think it wholly appropriate that no instruction be given in the lower schools regarding the problem of legitimate and illegitimate dynastic claims."[32]

The Education Ministry also ordered that morals courses be instituted in postelementary education, and in the following year, 1911, it revised the ethics textbooks used in the primary schools, increasing the stress on patriotism and the family at the expense of materials on individualism and internationalism. The 1918 textbook revisions continued the same trend.[33]

Also in 1918, the Extraordinary Commission on Education issued a resolution calling for a refocusing of Japanese education.

> Since the Restoration Japan has been so intent upon the importation of Western science and systems that she has failed fully to consider the merits and demerits before adopting them. . . . Although . . . her civilization has been enhanced and her national wealth and strength have witnessed a considerable growth, the indiscriminate adoption of Western science and systems has had the effect of disturbing the popular sentiments and seriously impairing the fine traditions of the country. . . .
> In removing these evils of the day, nothing is more important than to fix a common goal for which the people shall strive, and such a goal may be found in an endeavor to develop and protect Japan's peculiar civilization.[34]

More specifically the commission advised that "universities should pay more attention to moulding students' characters and to nurturing a spirit of respect for the State." In the 1918 University Ordinance, the Education Ministry amended the mission statement of higher education to include the phrase "Nurture the thought of the nation":

> It appears that the training of personalities and the nurturing of the patriotic thought of students in universities have not been satisfactory. . . .
> A desirable example to be followed even in our country is that of foreign universities which have magnificent chapels and well-equipped dormitories to provide students with enough assistance for this purpose. . . .
> Learning is nothing but an interjection to stimulate the specific development of the country by bringing culture to all levels of the people, because learning has infinite influence in the thinking of the nation. Accordingly, we must expect the really appropriate universities in the Empire to be able to keep the beauty of the individual characteristics of our country and to stimulate the thought of the State.[35]

Eventually, in the late 1920s, the Education Ministry launched a two-pronged initiative to supplement police campaigns to combat radicalism. To this end, a new section was created with a budget of over $200,000. Its purpose was to investigate and make proposals concerning the problem of student radicalism. It coordinated the efforts of ministry officials posted to each of the state-supported schools of higher education, an expansion of the existing system. On one side these officials introduced or broadened a wide range of programs:

> Employment counseling, mediation for part-time jobs, increased scholarships, loans at favorable interest rates, exemption from tuition payments for impoverished students, health and hygienic facilities, discounts on school-related supplies and equipment, and construction of new dormitories and student amusement facilities, . . . sports, . . . tours, picnics, and special entertainment.[36]

Along with faculty counselors in the higher schools, these government officials were also to identify students especially in need of "thought guidance," the label given to this campaign as a whole.

Key to this effort was the reaffirmation of indigenous values. In the words of the initial announcement by Minister of Education Mizuno Rentarō in 1928, "It is first necessary for those who educate and guide [the young] to ponder deeply, so that they may have convictions about the principles of the *kokutai* and about the nation's founding spirit which are firm and unswerving, and to serve as models themselves, that they may instruct by example within every area of daily life. It is also urged that they fathom the intentions of students, establish appropriate means of guidance, and eliminate the slightest opportunity for the interference of outside temptations. Thus we can nurture healthy, responsible citizens and assure the effectiveness of education."[37]

The values that Mizuno and his colleagues had in mind were made clear over the next decade in a series of manuals, lists of "good books," and panels of lecturers as well as in official reports.

Some women students also took part in the radical movements of the 1920s but in far fewer numbers than their male counterparts.[38] For conservatives, the more serious problem was the emergence off-campus of the "woman of the new age" or "modern girl." Whether in the feminist model of the cosmopolitan woman emancipated from the family or in the more popular model as "glittering, decadent, middle-class consumer who, through her clothing, smoking, and drinking, flaunts tradition in the urban playgrounds of the 1920s," the modern girl was a rebel against social convention and a threat to traditional morality.[39]

Thus conservatives were outraged. As in the Meiji period, their catchphrase was "good wives and wise mothers": "To make wise mothers and good wives, that is the meaning of a real education [for females], one which is able to develop completely the qualities of the 'old-fashioned woman' first, before attempting to train one in modern ways." Indeed, as the female proprietor of one private girls' school put it, "A modern woman has a tendency to be rational and individualistic. Both tendencies came from abroad, and it is lamentable that the long-established, good, and beautiful customs of Japan have been corrupted by such influences." The qualities of an "old-fashioned woman" included the customary virtues of humility, patience, and self-discipline, a willingness to sacrifice for the family. "Foreign-style education is important and indispensable at the present time," another private school mistress allowed, but "it would be very dangerous to over-emphasize such education and thereby lose the spirit of the people as well as that of the country."[40]

Suppression of Student Activism

In the period 1919–1931 the Japanese government responded vigorously to these challenges from student radicalism. The chief concern of the Education Ministry was on-campus activities. Surprisingly, its officials apparently did not realize until late in 1924 that there was a network of Marxist social science study groups running throughout the public higher school system. But once the extent of this network became apparent, the ministry asked the annual conference of higher school administrators to endorse a resolution calling for disbanding these student groups. Principals withdrew school approval for such study groups and pressured students to abandon their interest in radical ideas. The net effect may have been the opposite, as students maintained clandestine contacts through other channels—for example, debating contests.

The measures taken by the government to suppress student dissent on college campuses were more drastic. Although the Education Ministry did use its administrative channel in the attempt to solicit cooperation from college administrators, the police and Justice Ministry did much of the heavy work. Using the newly enacted Peace Preservation Law, Kyoto police swept down on the Student Federation in December 1925 and detained thirty-seven students from Kyoto Imperial and Dōshisha universities. Those arrested were released for lack of evidence but the police persisted over the next four months and eventually thirty-eight members from Kyoto and Tokyo colleges were tried and convicted of violating the Peace Preservation Law. Their punishment included jail sentences of eight to twelve months and expulsion from school.

Following this December 1925 police raid, the minister of education instructed administrators at the imperial universities to close down the Marxist social science study groups on their campuses. Only Kyushu Imperial University actually took immediate steps to do so in 1926. Two years later official recognition was granted to a new student group on the condition that it not affiliate with the national Student Federation. By this time the Student Federation had gone underground and its public role taken by a combination of the All-Japan Student League for the Defense of Liberty and local campus groups dedicated to "self-government":

> In higher schools, colleges, and universities throughout the country there exist no organs of student self-government. Wholly tyrannical schools are found in great number. Even where there are such organs, they exist in name only and do not

serve truly to represent the will of the students and to transmit it to the authorities. Student councils and assemblies, just like the Imperial Diet, are powerless. . . . Thus it is a system in which . . . the school, the very institution which claims to be independent of society, ironically manifests a system of oppression which is a replica of the Japanese state itself.[41]

In spring 1928, the government escalated its campaign to eradicate radicalism on campuses. On March 15 some 1,600 individuals were arrested on suspicion of planning, according to the official charges, "to overthrow the present organization of our country, and by a proletarian dictatorship to realize a communist society; [they have] organized a Japanese Communist Party, . . . infiltrated into the various kinds of labor and farmer groups to recruit new members for the [Communist] party and . . . broadcast handbills with inflammatory contents."[42]

Attacks on Faculty

Recognizing the influence of faculty on the student movement, the government made several concerted efforts during this period to rid the campuses of known instigators. This first attempt to rein in dissenting academics came at the end of 1919 when the Home Ministry censors suspended publication of the Tokyo University economics department journal on the grounds that it contained an article on anarchism. The publication of this article was deemed a violation of the press law because it allegedly threatened peace and order. The article by Associate Professor Morito Tatsuo, entitled "A Study of the Social Thought of Kropotkin," combined a scholarly analysis of anarchism with a personal endorsement of Pyotr Kropotkin's ideal society, in which each member enjoyed absolute freedom from economic as well as political oppression. Morito was critical of some aspects of Kropotkin's thought and expressed doubts about the likelihood of achieving such an ideal in practice. He also unequivocally eschewed violent means to these ends. Nevertheless, the university administration pressed him to issue a public apology. When Morito refused, both he and the journal's editor, Associate Professor Ouchi Hyōe, were indicted by the Justice Ministry.[43]

This action was unprecedented in two ways. First, although Home Ministry censorship of the press was commonplace in imperial Japan, government censors rarely concerned themselves with scholarly publications. Second, cases of faculty misconduct were ordinarily handled administratively by the Education Ministry, a procedure that in this case was bypassed in part because its officials lacked enthusiasm for the task. Instead, Procurator General Hiranuma Kiichirō, the leader of the dominant clique in the Justice Ministry, used unprecedented tactics against dissenting academics. Never before had an imperial university faculty member been indicted for publishing a scholarly article.

In this Hiranuma had the full support of the head of the majority party in the parliament, Prime Minister Hara Takashi, whose views are recorded in his diary: "I told [Hiranuma] that recently university professors had become a gang of publicity-seekers and we could not sit idly by and ignore it while the abuses of publishing such absurd opinions were going on."[44] A lawyer close to Hiranuma and his conservative circle expressed this point of view even more forcefully:

> Tokyo Imperial University should become the quarantine office for imported [ideologies]. If a thought is harmful, it should be treated as a harmful thought. For an ideology which is both harmful and harmless, the university should remove the harmful portion, and import the profitable part. . . . Mr. Morito has not only forgotten the duty of the quarantiner, but himself has become the importer of the harmful germ.[45]

A criminal indictment against a civil servant entailed automatic suspension pending resolution of the case. This unprecedented criminal indictment of an imperial university professor stirred the left and center of the Japanese intellectual spectrum into an impassioned defense of academic freedom. Hundreds attended a rally called by the economics department and a reported 1,000 people gathered in another open demonstration. When the prosecution formally requested jail terms for Morito and Ōuchi, a variety of student and intellectual groups sponsored a mass rally at the YMCA hall in the Kanda district. There speakers castigated Tokyo University administrators and the Education Ministry for abandoning the principles of academic freedom. One influential opinion magazine editorialized that bureaucrats were still incapable of understanding the simple truth that academic freedom was "necessary to the progress of the State . . . even if it sometimes opposed the interests of the State or rejects the State."[46]

A distinguished team of lawyers and academics as special consultants defended the two professors in court. Still other professors used the pages of national opinion magazines and gave interviews to popular newspapers to ridicule the government's case.

Two fundamental questions were raised in Morito's defense: Was the publication of a scholarly article on anarchism a criminal violation of those laws that gave the government the power to control the press? Did the actions of Morito and Ōuchi constitute a breach of their official responsibilities as university professors? Their lawyers did not attempt to defend anarchism or even to dispute the right of the state to control publications dangerous to the political order. Instead they based their case on the narrower grounds of the need to make certain distinctions. First, the determination of whether an article was indeed dangerous to peace and order must be based upon its actual influence upon society and not merely upon a reading of the text. Second, even if it were reasonable for censors in the Home Ministry to take steps to protect society from a dangerous influence, it did not necessarily mean that the Justice Ministry was correct in bringing criminal indictments against either the author or the editor:

> In cases where there is a danger in an article . . . it must be controlled. The only way to control such an article is to isolate it from the society where it is expected to disturb the peace and order. But legally the means to do this are limited to prohibiting the sale and distribution of the newspaper in which the article appears. . . . They definitely do not extend to imposing disciplinary punishment.[47]

Even closer to the crux was the question of the role of the university professor. Morito's defenders attempted to come to grips with the section of the 1918 University Ordinance that defined the functions of the university in terms that could be used against Morito and Ōuchi:

> According to the first article of the University Ordinance, the essential functions of the university are to be found in scholarly inquiry and scholarly instruction combined with attention to be paid to nurturing the thought of the nation. What does it mean to say "Nurture the thought of the nation"? This phrase appears for the first time in the new University Ordinance of 1918 . . . and one cannot find it used in [the regulations regarding] the university system before this. Actually the meaning of this phrase is unclear. . . . It may be thought that it is clear when considered [in some other context] separate from the University Ordinance, but as used in the University Ordinance regarding the responsibilities of university professors it definitely can not be said to be clear.[48]

On the one hand, the defense was asserting that the inclusion of this key phrase was done carelessly without any intent that it be used as a standard to judge behavior in specific cases. Whatever the words "nurture" or "the thought of the nation" might connote subjectively to the general public, their meaning was ambiguous in this legal context. On the other hand, Morito's lawyers sought to use the University Ordinance's call for scholarly inquiry as the basis for a logical defense of the freedom to publish the results of scholarly research.

Here then was a core argument that would be used over and over in the attempt to defend public university professors against the government during the 1920s and 1930s. The 1918 University Ordinance and the civil service regulations imposed upon professors the obligation to conduct research. For them to do so they must be able to examine controversial political subjects in a scientific manner. Anarchism was concerned with "the reasons for the existence of the State, a question which is a fundamental prerequisite for the study of the State." Therefore, by carrying out research on anarchism, Professor Morito was performing his duties as a scholar as provided for in the ordinance. That he and Ōuchi were legally higher civil servants assigned as professors to an imperial university rather than being employed at a private university did not alter their obligations as scholars.[49]

During the first trial of Morito and Ōuchi, these denials that the two econo-mists had committed any seditious act were well received in court. In early March 1920, the presiding judge ruled that the prosecution had failed to make its case for a violation of Article 42 of the Press Law. But he did not uphold the defense argument that in publishing an article on anarchism the two defendants were faithfully carrying out their legal responsibilities as university professors. Instead the judge found the defendants guilty of the lesser charge under Article 23, disturbing the public peace by spreading doubts about the legitimacy of the state. Morito as author was fined ¥70 and sentenced to two months of impris-onment; Ōuchi as editor was fined ¥20 and given a one-month sentence.

This, however, was not the end of the case. The Justice Ministry appealed the verdict and ultimately, in October 1920, the Supreme Court reversed the lower court decision, convicting the two Tokyo University faculty of acts in defiance of the imperial constitution. Morito's jail sentence was increased from two to three months. Ōuchi was given a year of probation in lieu of jail.[50]

The outcome of the Morito case held ambiguous portents for the future. On the one hand, the conservatives within government seemed to have found an effective new tool for bending the faculty of the imperial universities to their will. Whereas the Education Ministry had been unsuccessful in its attempts to pressure the faculty with the threat of *administrative discipline*, the Justice Min-istry had removed professors from their classrooms by means of formal *crimi-nal indictments*. Morito had been jailed and subsequently left the university in disgust; Ōuchi had been automatically suspended from the faculty during the term of his probationary sentence and thus effectively barred from the class-room for one year. The champions of academic freedom then and later have re-marked on the damage done to their cause by the decision of President Yamakawa and the senior economics professors to suspend Morito and Ōuchi even before the indictments were drawn.

But the government's success in prosecuting these cases had little if any neg-ative effect on the spread of radical ideas among students or future faculty. Quite the contrary. The press coverage of the trials had an impact far beyond that of any junior economist writing in an academic magazine: It made the term "anarchism" meaningful to a much broader public than previously. Stu-dents rushed out to buy any available copy of Kropotkin's *Mutual Aid* in their eagerness to discover what the conflict was all about.[51] Morito became a re-spected political commentator and a hero to Tokyo University students, who invited him regularly to speak at their gatherings. Ōuchi, once he served his year of probation while doing research in Europe, resumed the use of his pres-tigious position as an imperial university professor to criticize the political es-tablishment. Thus the 1920 confrontation resulted in something closer to a standoff than a victory for the government. Indeed, no cabinet would actually again use the weapon of criminal indictments against an imperial university faculty member for almost ten years.

This is not to say the enemies of academic freedom put down their cudgels. On the contrary, conservative leaders redoubled their efforts to find more effective means of controlling this radical dissent. In 1925 they secured from the parliament a new Peace Preservation Law with more severe penalties for challenging the legitimacy of the constitution. Surprisingly this turned out to have a new loophole for somewhat greater academic freedom, for it passed the Diet only with explicit assurances that academics would be allowed to conduct and publish research even on Marxism so long as they did not actually engage in political behavior deemed illegal.

Thus, whatever chilling effects they might have on individual professors, neither the precedents of the 1920 Morito case nor the intentions of the chief sponsors of the 1925 law produced effective controls over the faculty at imperial universities. Scholarly publication would be subjected to greater surveillance, but no indictments were to be brought against authors or editors of such scholarly works for their contents until after war broke out in China in the mid-1930s.[52] This does not mean there was no other official action against faculty dissenters in the late 1920s or early 1930s. Rather, because the use of the indictment weapon by the Justice Ministry was circumscribed by the need to produce admissible evidence of actual complicity in an illegal political act, the government's search for effective means of suppressing radical academics was forced into other avenues.

In April 1928 the cabinet gave Minister of Education Mizuno Rentarō approval for punitive measures against a list of faculty at the imperial universities in Tokyo, Kyoto, and Kyushu. The minister summoned the presidents of each of the imperial universities to tell them they must take steps to remove the leftist professors.[53]

The most famous of the names on the list was that of the celebrated author and patron of radical student groups, Kyoto economics professor Kawakami Hajime. Kawakami's home had already been searched in connection with the arrest of the Student Federation leaders in 1926 but no basis for legal action had been found at that time. Now the Education Ministry convinced the Kyoto University administration to demand Kawakami's resignation on three grounds: (1) Kawakami had taken an active part in the parliamentary election campaign of the leftist Farmer-Labor Party, (2) Kawakami had preached Marxism in his classroom lectures as well as in his scholarly writings, and (3) his influence as faculty adviser had incited students to acts of violence. In 1928 only the last action violated the letter of any Japanese law and whatever admissible evidence may have existed on this count had not been uncovered by the police during the March roundups. When a formal faculty meeting of the economics department was called to deliberate on the case, Kawakami's foes were unable to secure a majority vote for outright dismissal. Instead, they had to content themselves with a compromise motion stating that if Kawakami himself were to offer his resignation then the department should accept it. The Kyoto University president, armed with this resolution, confronted Kawakami. The president may have misrepresented the department action because Kawakami submitted his resignation apparently thinking the majority of his colleagues had explicitly demanded it.[54]

Also on the list were a number of faculty at other imperial universities who were part of a network of Tokyo University graduates. In addition to maintaining contact with the student movement on campus, some of these young social scientists formed close ties with off-campus radicals. Tokyo associate professor Ōmori Yoshitarō, for instance, became a leading member of the Labor-Farmer Faction, an important splinter group of communists and other radicals estranged from the Japan Communist Party because of their refusal to accept Comintern policy. Ōmori also took part in efforts to organize tenant farmers against their landlords. The government was particularly keen on ousting these men, but only at Kyushu Imperial University did this turn out to be a simple matter. There, the three associate professors targeted in the department of law and letters had little support among their colleagues. They were maneuvered into submitting their resignations despite their denials of having been involved in communist activities.[55]

At Tokyo University the Education Ministry's blacklist included, in addition to Ōmori, two other associate professors. But here things proved most difficult for the Education Ministry. Tokyo University president Onozuka Kiheiji, unlike his counterparts at Kyoto and Kyushu, had a reputation as a staunch advocate of university autonomy reaching back to his days as one of the "seven Ph.D.s" in 1905. He had subsequently taken a leading role in the 1913 clash with the Education Ministry over the administration of Kyoto University. Now he let it be known again that he would not yield easily to outside pressure—that Tokyo University would take care of its own internal housekeeping.

Nonetheless, Onozuka took a dim view of radical activism and did not intend to permit his school to continue to be torn asunder by political conflict. He thus quickly carried out the Education Ministry's order to disband the offensive student organization and questioned his young faculty members about the ministry's allegations that they were implicated in the illegal Communist Party. Onozuka particularly chastised Ōmori for articles published under a pseudonym in a radical journal and for excessive extramural political activity. But Onozuka took no action against these professors. Instead the president reminded them that the economics faculty had jurisdiction in its own personnel matters and should not be coerced in these cases.

The next step was taken by Ōmori. He resigned, apparently to spare his fellow activists on the faculty from further investigation.[56] As it turned out, Ōmori's resignation gave his fellow activists at Tokyo University only a two-year reprieve. In April 1929 there was yet another nationwide dragnet that arrested over 600 communist suspects. The proportion of students involved was even larger than in the previous year, now almost a third. Tokyo and Kyoto continued to produce the largest numbers, followed by the private schools of Waseda, Nihon, and Meiji.[57]

In early 1930 Tokyo associate professors Hirano Yoshitarō and Yamada Moritarō were again targeted for removal. This time the circumstances were such that a defense from within the university was much more difficult than it had been in 1928. In the intervening two years both Hirano and Yamada had been involved in efforts to rebuild the outlawed Japan Communist Party. Successful court tests of the 1925 Peace Preservation Law against communist political activity had given the government procurators all too solid grounds for moving against Hirano and Yamada. In 1930 officials of the Justice Ministry told the Tokyo University president that they would indict the two unless they resigned. Both did so, only to be indicted and convicted anyway.[58]

Neither these actions against faculty nor the police roundups of student leaders were successful in suppressing the turmoil on the campuses. Between 1928 and 1932 one campus after another experienced student strikes—over three dozen incidents in 1930 alone. Although Waseda was the hardest hit, the list included all types of institutions of higher learning and training. Students at women's schools such as Tokyo Women's College of Dentistry were among those attempting to shut down classes until their demands were met. These demands varied greatly from strike to strike but many had to do with greater independence for extracurricular clubs and others protested the cost and quality of education.[59]

Suppression of Teachers' Unions

The Japan Teachers' Union Enlightenment Association disbanded in 1928, in part because of Education Ministry pressure. But it spawned other efforts at organizing teachers, some of which had even more radical platforms. The leaders of the small Elementary School Teachers League, for example, had ties with the communist groups including the National Farmers Union. It advocated special schools for workers and explicitly condemned militaristic influence in education. Police arrested forty-five of its members in January 1930 for violations of the Peace Preservation Law of 1925. Thirteen of those were subsequently removed from their teaching posts.

Conclusion

The successes and failures of the early twentieth century Japanese educational system were clear for all to see by the end of the 1920s. On the positive side of the ledger, primary schooling had become universal for all classes and both genders. Whereas only one out of six Japanese had graduated from elementary school in 1895, by 1925 three out of four had done so.[60] (See Table 4.5.)

The system was still elitist by at least two important measures. First, only a small percentage of the populace had schooling at the secondary and higher levels. Of course, all societies were elitist by this measure in this period. If one uses contemporary international comparisons, Japan had about the same percent of the population enrolled in secondary schools in 1920 as did the United States—2.3 percent. This was more than twice as high as either France or Britain. Moreover, by 1930 both Japan and the United States had increased their percentages to three times that in England or France. (See Table 4.6.)

Second, females were far less likely than males to go past compulsory schooling. Whereas 20 percent of males were doing so in 1920, only 12 percent of females were. In 1930 the gap had closed only slightly—21 percent versus 16 percent. Even these figures exaggerate the degree of equality, since the curricula of secondary school for females was different from that of secondary schools for males.

The negative side of the ledger was further marked by heavy-handed attempts to suppress dissent. True, in the 1920s, the targets were a small minority of Marxist professors and radical students, but the violations of academic freedom were no less serious because of the relatively small numbers involved. The suppression campaign of the government was particularly ominous because of the increasing tendency to counter radicalism with indoctrination in neotraditional morals. Moreover, the trend toward tighter ideological control over higher education accelerated in the decade of the 1930s in the wake of military aggression on the Asian mainland and with the clouds of war enveloping the globe.

TABLE 4.5
Education Levels of the Productive-Age Population, 1895–1935

	Primary (%)	Secondary (%)	Higher (%)
1895	16	0.2	0.1
1905	42	0.9	0.2
1925	74	4.9	0.8
1935	82	9.2	1.6

SOURCE: Adapted from Japan Ministry of Education, Research Bureau, *Japan's Growth and Education*, p. 57.

TABLE 4.6
Secondary School Enrollments: Percent of Population, 1910–1930

	Japan	United States	England[a]	France
1910	1.6	1.2	0.4	
1920	2.5	2.3	0.9	
1925		1.1		
1930	3.7	3.9	1.1	1.2

[a]Includes Wales.

SOURCE: Japan Ministry of Education, Research Bureau, *Japan's Growth and Education*, table 1, p. 214.

5

Mobilizing the Spirit of the Nation: 1931–1945

Japan is made up of schools. Japan is a school, an Athens.
> —Nitobe Inazo, Christian Educator, 1931[1]

If we boil down to their roots the causes of the war which brought on Japan's recent defeat, we must call attention to our misbegotten education system.
> —Shidehara Kijūrō, Prewar Foreign Minister, 1946[2]

Although World War II did not begin for Europe until 1939 and for the United States until 1941, full-scale war for the Japanese began in China in summer 1937. The beginning of the "Fifteen-Year War" was dated in the official indictments at the war crimes trials in Tokyo and by some historians as 1931, when the Japanese seized Manchuria. Allegedly the Japanese military plan for an invasion of China and a wider war with the Western powers was already in place. Others would argue that this allegation relies upon a conspiracy theory that has not held up under historical scrutiny.[3] Under either interpretation it is clear that between 1931 and 1937 Japanese hard-liners used threats to expand their military and economic presence into the northern Chinese provinces. Disagreements over this foreign aggression as well as over domestic policies heated the political atmosphere within Japan until it exploded in 1936 with the mutiny of the First Division of the Imperial Guard.

This "February 26 Incident," led by extreme right-wing officers who favored the use of more force abroad and radical political reforms at home, was an attempt to overthrow the existing political system. The coup failed only when senior generals and admirals refused to join it and instead ordered the extremists overpowered. Nevertheless, within eighteen months, in July 1937, fighting between Chinese nationalists and Japanese troops broke out in the suburbs of

Peking. This was followed by a major military clash at Shanghai and the Konoe cabinet decision to invade central China in full force. By November 1938 Japanese army units had captured the Chinese nationalist capital at Nanking in an orgy of arson, looting, and rape intended to terrorize the Chinese into surrender. Instead it galvanized much of Chinese and world opinion behind the resistance, and the Japanese army marched deeper and deeper into a bloody quagmire from which they extracted themselves only with the defeat of Japan by the Allies in 1945.

Although the Japanese government chose not to label the invasion of China a "war," declaring instead that there was a "national emergency," wartime conditions existed at home for the next eight years. The Japanese military and its civilian supporters took advantage of the conflict abroad to move toward greater state control at home. Once war with the Western powers began in December 1941, there was little serious resistance to this effort, and government intervention into all corners of Japanese life increased relentlessly down to the end of World War II in August 1945.

Thus the history of Japan's road to war and defeat falls into three main stages: (1) the six years between the seizure of Manchuria and the invasion of China below the Great Wall in 1937; (2) the four years of conflict in China between 1937 and 1941; and (3) the larger war with the United States, Britain, and their allies between 1941 and 1945. Changes in education paralleled the growing intensity of each stage.

Military operations in Manchuria in 1931 gave the political right a new rationale for its campaign to eradicate Marxism and other Western ideologies that threatened to undermine national unity. The shift to the right in national politics and the popular mood that initially accompanied the coming of war against China in the 1930s precluded any further sustained, large-scale efforts at organizing protest or otherwise opposing the war effort. At the same time, there were new attempts made by the government to mobilize the resources and rally the people in a time of national crisis. As the Konoe cabinet stated in 1940, the goal was "renovation of education thoroughly in harmony with the fundamental principles of the national polity, and also the establishment of ethical principles of the nation stressing, above all, service to the state and eradicating all selfish and materialistic thoughts."[4]

Control of Dissent

Control of dissent in Japan during these decades continued to depend upon a combination of legal regulations and community pressure. That is to say, the more blunt methods of the fascist and communist police states of Europe were seldom resorted to in dealing with Japanese teachers or students. Instead, censorship laws covering the press, radio, and motion pictures were steadily tightened while intense public pressure was brought on academics and others to support the nation in its time of need.[5]

Much of the legal framework for restricting freedom of the press and other political liberties was already in place by the 1930s. The 1925 Peace Preservation Law aimed at suppressing communists or others seeking to change the "national polity" or overthrowing the system of private property had been amended in 1928 to provide more harsh penalties. In June 1936, following the attempted military coup, the Diet passed the Extraordinary Control Law for Seditious Literature, albeit over surprisingly strong opposition. The law broadened the categories of prohibited literature and prescribed jail terms of up to three years for "any one who publishes or distributes literature or pictures that defy the military order, confuse the financial world, or disturb the public peace." In April 1938, after the army invaded central China, the Diet passed the National General Mobilization Law, which included a ban on publications "containing items which hinder the national general mobilization."[6]

Later that year the Education Ministry made an unsuccessful attempt to reduce further the limited degree of autonomy enjoyed by the imperial universities.[7] It issued a statement intended specifically to reassure a group of right-wing critics within the House of Peers: "The universities are established, maintained and administered under the supervision of the Minister of Education according to the university ordinances, the university civil service system, and other regulations. University goals and the like cannot depart from those strictures, and so-called 'university self-governance' cannot be sanctioned."

Shortly thereafter Baron General Araki Sadao was appointed minister of education in the cabinet of Prime Minister Konoe Fumimaro. First as principal of the Army War College in the late 1920s and then as chief of educational administration within the army, General Araki had become a hero to militant nationalists for his advocacy of the "Imperial Way" (*kōdō*) ideology to counter the threat of communism at home and abroad. He had served as army minister from 1931 to 1934 but had then been placed on the reserve list in 1936 because he was thought to have approved at least tacitly the attempted coup of February 26. Nevertheless, in May 1938 Prime Minister Konoe gave Araki the education portfolio to appease the political right and show support for the "Movement for Mobilizing the Popular Spirit" behind the military offensives in China.[8]

Shortly after taking office Minister of Education Araki summoned all the imperial university presidents to a meeting in Tokyo and lectured them on the need to "mobilize the spirit of the nation" through "self-discipline and self-reflection." He specifically sought to reform practices at odds with a strict interpretation of the civil service regulations regarding imperial appointees. These included the customary faculty balloting for university presidents, limitations on terms for department chairs, and the faculty's effective control of the recruitment of new professors. Such practices, Araki contended, violated the letter and spirit of the constitution by disregarding the sovereign prerogatives of the emperor to appoint and dismiss all state officials.

The Tokyo University administration was determined to resist Araki's reforms, asserting that "self-government is the essence of the University. The University bears the privileged responsibility to the state of sustaining and promoting the vitality of that essence. Moreover, the state has entrusted higher education and research to the hands of the University." The minister of education was misguided if he thought a university could be subjected to a bureaucratic chain of command. Academics were not like bureaucrats; they rather resembled artists striving for creativity. If they were to lose their freedom there would be great damage. Faculty spokesmen also summoned up one of the most cherished values of the conservatives: the "spirit of familialism" that they claimed nurtured the university as an "independent society of colleagues."

> The relationship between professors within the University differs from that of high and low in the ranks of the bureaucracy. It is one of elder and junior, teacher and pupil—of colleagues—rather than one of dominance and submission. It differs precisely because of this degree of intimacy. . . . If someone who does not fit into this school tradition is forced in, or if someone is forced out by external power, the life of this family is impossible.[9]

Eventually the minister of education backed off and only small changes were made in the way that the university handled its internal personnel matters. But General Araki and his successors were to play key roles in achieving the ouster of individual professors from the classrooms through the use of other means.

Purging the Professors

The independence of imperial university professors had long been one of the more galling thorns in the side of the military and its nationalistic supporters throughout the 1930s. True, most of the faculty at Tokyo, Kyoto, and the other elite universities supported to a greater or lesser extent the use of force in China. But there were skeptics and even outspoken critics, especially in the initial stages when the fighting was confined primarily to Manchuria. Almost as serious in the eyes of the ultranationalists and super patriots were the Western orientation and even liberal bent of many professors in such departments as law and economics. In their view, the liberals aided and abetted the radicalization of the student bodies and the corruption of the nation's morals.

This dual concern for mobilizing public opinion behind the military effort on the mainland and for eradicating seditious or "non-Japanese" ideas at home led to a series of attacks on the autonomy of university self-government and to the steady erosion of academic freedom in the 1930s. Although we will deal here only with the ramifications for education, it should be kept in mind that these were part of a larger set of struggles for control of all the major institutions of political power and ideological influence in prewar Japan.

The efforts of the foes of academic freedom were complicated by the fact that although by law the Education Ministry had the administrative authority to dismiss individual professors from the imperial universities, in practice it could do so only with the cooperation of the faculty as a whole. One way around this impasse was to use the Home Ministry's powers of censorship and/or the Justice Ministry's authority to indict violators of criminal laws. This, of course, is what had been done in the Morito case of 1919. It was not even necessary to actually convict a professor for violating the press laws—an indictment was sufficient under the regulations covering all civil servants to force suspension from the classroom while the case wound its way through a notoriously slow set of court proceedings. More effective was the use of faculty peer pressure to force resignations, as we have seen in the Kawakami and Ōmori cases of 1928 and 1930. Still another scenario was played out in the so-called Takigawa affair at Kyoto University.

In the eyes of the right wing, Kyoto law professor Takigawa Yukitoki had apparently committed both of the two cardinal sins: (1) He was a liberal critic of the criminal court system and drew on Western criminology to criticize Japanese judges and (2) he had also criticized the Manchurian takeover.[10] He was not, however, a Marxist; nor was he unusually active in off-campus politics. Nevertheless, in the late fall of 1932 Professor Takigawa became a political target when the minister of justice informed Minister of Education Hatoyama Ichirō that complaints were being made about Takigawa's less-than-respectful attitude toward the judiciary. Education Ministry officials requested clarification of Takigawa's views from the Kyoto University president, who after consultation with the law department chair assured the Education Ministry that there was no serious problem with Takigawa's conduct.

The matter did not rest there, however. The following month, January 1933, a right-wing member of the Diet cited a book authored by Takigawa as an example of the type of material being taught by "red professors" at the imperial universities. More attacks soon followed in the radical right-wing press. In April there was finally formal action by the government: The Home Ministry issued a legal ban on further publication of two books by Takigawa. The Education Ministry summoned the Kyoto University president to the capital to insist that Takigawa be convinced to resign for the good of the university. The president and the Kyoto faculty leaders refused to cooperate. Instead they demonstrated a unified resistance quite unlike their cooperation in the purge of Kawakami Hajime five years earlier. The university president convened the university senate, which consisted of all departmental chairmen plus elected representatives. That body agreed to defy the Education Ministry and support the authority of the law department to deal with its own faculty affairs. The law faculty then voted to resign en masse if the Education Ministry did not back down.

When it became clear that the Kyoto University faculty were not swayed by these warnings, the minister of education brought charges against Takigawa in a formal civil service proceeding, a process never before used in the case of an imperial university professor. At the end of May, the Civil Service Personnel Review Board announced its recommendation: indefinite suspension for conduct unbecoming a civil servant.

The reaction of the law faculty chair was swift and decisive. He convened a general assembly of the more than 1,600 students to announce the cancellation of all law classes. He then forwarded to the university administration a letter announcing that the entire teaching staff of the department, from chairman to the most junior graduate assistant, were resigning in protest. The Kyoto University president submitted his own resignation to the Education Ministry.

In effect, the Kyoto law faculty had gone on strike with the support of their president. Closing of classrooms had been threatened before in the history of Japan's imperial universities—and in the famous 1905 case of the seven Ph.D.s, some professors at Tokyo Imperial University had actually suspended classes—but this was the first time a whole department had actually done so. This action pitched the campus into turmoil as right-wing, self-styled patriotic student groups clashed with liberal and leftist supporters of Takigawa. Large protest meetings of students and faculty were also called on the campuses of Tokyo and Tōhoku Imperial universities. Well-known liberal journalists joined hands with more radical intellectuals to write vehement rebukes of the government. These efforts were further coordinated with those of the National Association of Alumni of the Kyoto University Law Faculty, which held meetings in various cities to express concern. In short, support for the university in 1933 not only represented a broad spectrum of political ideologies but was also unusually well organized.

Faced with the firmness of resolve exhibited by universities and the widespread off-campus support for Takigawa, Minister of Education Hatoyama Ichirō began to maneuver in quest of a compromise. First, a number of retired professors emeriti were recruited as informal mediators in the dispute. The Education Ministry then privately assured the Kyoto University administrators that it would recognize their authority in future personnel matters, including the selection of a new president. Discussions were also begun about offering Takigawa a leave of absence abroad, whereby he could be reinstated once the political atmosphere had cooled.

Takigawa and his closest supporters in the law faculty refused these compromises. But a sufficient number of the Kyoto University faculty did come to the conclusion that further resistance was not in their or the university's best interests. In the election for a new president, they rejected a professor who had supported the strike in favor of another who, once in office, announced that he was accepting the previously submitted resignations of Takigawa and five other law professors. Seven other senior law professors withdrew their resignations, and eventually a total of eleven from what had been a thirty-one-man department resumed their duties. Thus the law faculty strike was broken in essence by vote of the university faculty as a whole.

One of the key agitators in these cases against liberal academics was an erstwhile Keiō University professor, Minoda Muneki, an "infamous denunciator" who although a writer rather than a government official served much the same function as Senator Joe McCarthy did in the United States of the 1950s.[11] Minoda published numerous articles and books listing Marxists and liberals who he demanded be fired from their positions. He lobbied the Justice and Home ministries to take legal action against them. In 1935 Minoda was involved in a concerted effort by a large number of right-wing nationalist groups to discredit liberal interpretations of the constitution. For Minoda and many others in this extremist camp,

> The Japanese nation, which preserves the myth of the national foundation and the national religion through its faith in the living god who is the present Emperor, will realize the destiny of humanity entrusted man by world history, which Confucianism, Buddhism, Christianity, and socialism have failed to achieve. When we faithfully serve our Emperor as a living god and defend our home country, we serve humanity.[12]

This was not the dominant view in the leading universities. The emperor was viewed by Japan's most prestigious scholars as a constitutional monarch not different in kind from those in Western Europe, an "organ" of the state rather than a "living god" who transcended the state. There had always been an energetic minority among the theorists at imperial universities who held that the Japanese throne was unique in the world, and this in general was the manner in which school textbooks treated the emperor.

Until 1935, public debate over these two contrasting views was muted. In that year, Minoda and his allies chose to use the issue against what they believed to be a clique of liberals who were preventing Japan from realizing its potential at home and abroad. The ultimate targets included high-ranking civil servants and advisers to the throne, but the chief public focus of this attack was retired Tokyo University professor Minobe Tatsukichi. Professor Minobe was the chief author of the "emperor-as-organ-of-the state" theory.[13]

The Military Reserve Association, which had branches in every community of any size, distributed Minoda's writings among its members with the following comment: "The emperor-organ theory is contrary to the essence of our unparalleled national polity and blasphemes the sacredness of the throne. It is absolutely incompatible with our traditional way of thinking. We must warn all Japanese to avoid involvement with this academic theory."

Members of one local branch actually burned copies of Minobe's books at the memorial shrine of the Meiji emperor, proclaiming, "A non-Japanese, blasphemous, Europe-worshipping ideology which ignores our three-thousand-year-old tradition and ideals is rife. This liberalism which threatens to turn us into Western barbarians is basic to Minobe's beliefs. His books must be burned to show how we [reservists] feel about his servile individualism."[14] Minobe was also subjected to editorial attacks on his patriotism in the press and physical assaults in his own home. He was eventually questioned by the police and several of his books were banned for allegedly misleading the public about the nature of the national polity.

Pressures were also brought upon other professors. Numerous law textbooks were officially banned from publication and some individual professors were even physically harassed by right-wing groups. One Tokyo University president, also a specialist in law, had his home placed under police guard after it was broken into by right-wing agitators. He also employed a judo expert as his private secretary.

As a result of the vehemence of this public campaign, Minobe ultimately resigned his seat in the House of Peers and all other public posts. No other professor was ousted in this campaign but the chilling effect these acts had on the academic atmosphere at the time was probably more significant than any official punitive measures against the faculty.

Prominent liberals were vocal in their reaction against Minobe's critics but were usually cautious about dissenting too blatantly from the traditional interpretations of the sacredness of the national polity:

> Faith is the peculiarity of beliefs concerning the national polity; legal studies possess the peculiarity of science. . . . If there is a violation in a legal theory, it is not a moral wrong; it is an error in reason. . . . It is not improper to oppose Dr. Minobe's theory, but the intention of eliminating that theory by violence and coercion is a sacrilege against learning. . . . To gag Dr. Minobe by threat of force . . . is a violation of the Imperial Rescript of the Meiji emperor, which enjoins us to respect the law and obey the constitution.[15]

The author of this defense, Professor Kawai Eijirō, was himself to be purged from the Tokyo University faculty in 1939.

The public attacks on Minobe stimulated a full-scale Education Ministry investigation into the textbooks and syllabi for courses on constitutional law at the nation's universities, but it did not lead to the dismissal of any professors at any imperial university in 1935 or 1936. Only after the beginning of the conflagration in China were the most vocal of the liberal and leftist faculty members at Tokyo Imperial University purged. This took place over a two-year period beginning in 1937.

The first Tokyo University professor to be pressured into leaving his post was Yanaihara Tadao, a Christian pacifist who was the department's leading expert on the results of previous Japanese imperialist ventures in Taiwan and Manchuria.[16] His reaction to the war was to condemn the military and call for peace. This stance put him into direct conflict with some of his colleagues who advocated a joint student-faculty march to demonstrate university support for the troops at the front. The polarization on campus was taken advantage of by enemies of academic freedom outside the university. Police investigated Yanaihara's writings and members of the House of Peers pressured the Education

Ministry to rid the school of such professors. The university president came to the conclusion that Yanaihara had to be sacrificed for the sake of the university.

Abandoned by the university administration and repudiated by a significant element of his own department, Yanaihara took it on himself to resign in December 1937.

> I have always been one who loved his country ardently and I think it is regrettable that the problem of my articles ever arose. Because I recognize my continuing at the University would cause it difficulties, I have submitted my own resignation to the president today.... Although the ideal University does have need of me, in the actual University my presence has come to be a disturbance.[17]

Within a month police carried out a fresh series of arrests aimed at destroying the Popular Front, an antifascist movement accused of following a communist strategy to undermine the military effort in China. Among those eventually arrested were Professor Ōuchi Hyōe, who had been prosecuted along with Morito in 1920. Two associate professors and several graduate students were also held by the police for questioning. Tokyo University found itself divided in the face of an external attack on its faculty. Once again the procurator's office and the Education Ministry sought to have Ōuchi and his fellow offenders suspended from the university even before formal indictments had been secured. Their defenders won a vote of support from their department, but this victory lost much of its significance once legal indictments were produced. The three indicted professors were all barred from the classroom under the automatic suspension provisions as their trial dragged through the courts for the next seven years. During this time they actually continued to receive their salaries from Tokyo University; officially they had only been suspended, not terminated, from their appointments. They were, however, legally prohibited during these years from either lecturing or publishing while their cases were before the courts.[18]

The chilling effect of these arrests in the Popular Front incident was felt throughout the Japanese academic community in spring 1938 as a new hail of allegations fell on "subversive" professors. The Tokyo University economics and law departments were characterized by one member of the House of Peers as "the headquarters and command post of the Popular Front." Professor Kawai Eijirō and others who publicly defended Ōuchi were castigated as being "only a hair's breadth away from communism."

Agitated students joined in harassing professors suspected of harboring Western liberal ideas or of lacking enthusiasm for Japan's mission in China. Right-wing students visited the classrooms of suspected liberals, and at other talks on campuses they frequently raised politically embarrassing questions. They visited professors in their offices to demand clarification of their interpretations of the national polity or an explanation of why a course syllabus was heavily weighted toward Western works on political science.[19]

Academics at private universities were not immune to such pressures. For example, Waseda University professor Tsuda Sōkichi was convicted in 1940 for *lèse majesté* in the contents of four books dealing with the imperial household in ancient Japanese history. He was initially sentenced to a jail term but it was dropped on appeal.[20]

Professor Kawai was finally removed from the classroom at Tokyo Imperial University in 1939.[21] Long a major critic of Marxism and ally of the anti-Marxists, Kawai had in recent years reassessed the threat to the liberalism he still ardently espoused. His criticism of "the evil of fascism [that] emerges from the military," and his outspoken defense of academic independence, made him a prime target of the right. By 1938 it had become an "open secret" that the Education Ministry desired to rid itself of Kawai. When the Home Ministry initiated action on old complaints about the liberal excesses in Kawai's writings by banning further sale of four of his books, the Education Ministry quickly ordered a board of inquiry to investigate Kawai's views in detail.

While this external investigation was in process, Kawai and his defenders were confronted with a new university president, engineering professor Hiraga Yuzuru. Hiraga had joined the Tokyo University faculty in 1931 after a career as a leading naval architect with the rank of vice admiral. He had just finished serving as chair of the engineering faculty, where he had made it known that he favored government plans to enlarge the facilities to aid the war effort. During the Ōuchi case earlier in 1938, Hiraga had also spoken out in favor of suspending faculty members even before they were indicted lest the university be perceived as indifferent to the problem of unpatriotic academics.

Hiraga proposed to deal with the Kawai case in an unprecedented fashion. He secured an agreement with faculty leaders to create a special ad hoc committee drawn from the economics and law representatives on the University Council. While completely rejecting charges that Kawai's books were procommunist or otherwise subversive, the committee report nevertheless did concede that Kawai's manner of expressing himself was, on occasion at least, less than proper for an imperial university professor. President Hiraga seized on this single major negative finding as a cause for advising Kawai to resign his professorship to spare the university any further difficulties. Although the president was willing to promise that efforts would be made to find the professor a nonteaching and less sensitive post within the university, Kawai refused any compromise. The economics professor pointed out that no indictment had been drawn by the Justice Ministry and that there had been no proper deliberations by his department. Soon after, the Procurator's Office in the Justice Ministry began preliminary questioning of Kawai to determine probable cause for an indictment for violation of the publications laws. Tokyo University president Hiraga then summoned Kawai once again, this time to inform the professor that Hiraga was invoking his authority as president to suspend Kawai.

Hiraga's actions in January 1939 aimed not only at ridding himself of the Kawai case but also at suppressing factionalism within the economics department. He suspended a conservative faculty leader, explaining to the Education Ministry that the liberal centrist Kawai and the conservative rightist Hijikata Seibi both shared responsibility for the internal turmoil that had for years disrupted the economics department. These suspensions touched off a furor within the department. No fewer than thirteen professors and staff tendered their resignations in protest at the failure of Hiraga to follow established consultative procedures.

The attack initiated from outside the university was now directed from within by President Hiraga. When faculty members in economics presented their joint resignations, Hiraga in effect declared the department in receivership by the surprise move of making himself department chair. As department chair as well as university president he accepted the resignations of five more faculty members and one graduate assistant. The others in the economics department allowed themselves to be persuaded to remain, but as this left Hiraga with only five full professors where there had been twelve a year earlier, the way was open for rebuilding the department.

After Pearl Harbor, there were few such cases. The mood on campus swung toward patriotic support of the besieged country. One Tokyo University law professor summed up the view of many of his colleagues as they stood to listen to Prime Minister Tōjō Hideki announce to the nation via radio the bombing of Pearl Harbor: "The feeling that we were now facing the inevitable made our mind clear. This was the moment at which all the Japanese people wholeheartedly felt their blood circulating in their veins." He also articulated a justification for the war that was shared by many:

> The true root of the present war is the hegemony Britain and the United States have claimed in Asia. They have asserted that maintenance of the status quo in this area is international justice. What appalling self-righteousness. They came to Asia from distant quarters of the earth in order to usurp the spoils. Their justice is nothing but keeping these spoils for themselves.[22]

Those leftist and liberal professors who remained on the faculties were understandingly cautious about teaching the ideas that had been so common in the 1920s and early 1930s, although even in the midst of the war some still had their students read Marxist works.[23]

Crushing the Student Movement

Controlling radical students in the school system was even more a government priority in the 1930s than it had been in the previous decade. Police surveillance, both overt and undercover, had intensified on college campuses in the wake of the earlier roundups of student radicals.[24] This surveillance was coordinated by the Home Ministry. The Education Ministry, for its part, convened a number of panels to advise solutions and upgraded its special section on student activities, renaming it the Thought Bureau in 1934. There were now almost 700 ministry officials posted at public and private schools of higher education to implement these policies. Student arrests began to fall off precipitously.

In fact, however, by 1934 the student left on campus was all but moribund, its organizational networks destroyed and far fewer students interested in striking to express discontent. Although the 1933 Takigawa incident at Kyoto Imperial University served once more to rally student support for academic freedom, enthusiasm for such protest could not be sustained. The last burst of left-wing student activity took place in the so-called Popular Front of 1938–1939, previously described.

By 1933 there were approximately 100 right-wing student groups. The great majority were not viewed unfavorably by government leaders but there were incidents in which extremists did pose a threat to peace and order. In one very dramatic incident in 1932, eight out of fourteen conspirators arrested for plotting political assassinations turned out to be students, most from either Tokyo or Kyoto Imperial universities.

But even after Pearl Harbor, the Japanese government never resorted to the more savage tactics of Hitler's Germany or Stalin's Russia, perhaps because they were unnecessary. The backbone of the radical student movement had been broken by the mid-1930s, and between 1938 and 1945 only 1,000 students were arrested under the provisions of the Peace Preservation Law, most of those prior to 1943. This was about a third as many as between 1925 and 1938. Most student organizations were closed down after 1941, replaced by patriotic activities led by school officials.

Disciplining the Teachers

Organized protest against the status quo by public school teachers grew smaller but more radical after the disbanding of the Japan Teachers' Union Enlightenment Association in 1928. Yet another attempt at nationwide organization was made under the leadership of the Educational Workers' Union formed in 1930. This group, technically illegal, openly advocated a united front with laborers and tenant farmers to give control of the schools to the people at home and resist military adventures abroad. Its commitment to using the strike as a weapon and its display of solidarity with communist labor unions led to the arrest of a number of members in several incidents during 1931, thus effectively ending its attempts to organize a radical teachers' union on a national scale. The shift to the right in national politics and the popular mood that accompanied the coming of war against China in the 1930s precluded any further sustained, large-scale efforts by teachers to organize protest. The police stepped up their surveillance of leftist activity among teachers. As a result, for example, 58 teachers were fired as part of the 131 arrested for fomenting radicalism in Nagano Prefecture in 1933.[25]

There were, however, continual attempts to keep some sort of movement alive, and some of these efforts were to plant seeds that eventually flowered after World War II. Perhaps the most important was the Institute for Proletariat Education formed in 1931 by members of the Educational Workers' Union. Since it avoided overt action, the institute was permitted to distribute its literature condemning "bourgeois and fascist educational principles" and "imperialistic education" while calling for the "adoption of educational principles and techniques based on a careful interpretation of Marx-Leninism" and "cooperation with international proletariat movements."[26]

In more concrete terms, these radicals were calling for tuition-free secondary schooling, especially vocational and technical, for working-class youth. In the classroom some teachers took advantage of the fact that there were no required materials for teaching composition and attempted to encourage essays on themes that were more liberal. This so-called life-in-education movement used creative writing as a means of awakening pupils to the ills of their society. Those teachers who went too far in this, however, were subject to punishment, including possible arrest for practicing "proletariat" education.[27]

Ultranationalist Values

Suppression of dissent through police actions and the purging of academics was only the negative side of the attempt to control radical ideas. The campaign to control seditious thought was accompanied by positive steps to define patriotic principles and national morality. Eventually, in 1937, a national spiritual mobilization campaign was announced by Prime Minister Konoe. Although sometimes pushed into the background by the zealots in the Home Ministry and the military, Education Ministry officials too redoubled efforts to persuade those within its jurisdiction to rally to the nation in its time of crisis. This educational response to ideological turmoil at home and to war abroad can be categorized by which group it was directed toward: The government attempted to persuade schoolteachers, university students, and professors that Japan was endangered by seditious ideologies. The aim for all, however, was to clarify the concept of *kokutai*—the national polity—and a return to the moral values supposedly embodied in the 1890 Imperial Rescript on Education.

Reeducating College Students

In March 1932, after the Japanese seizure of Manchuria, the Education Ministry released the report of its Student Thought Problem Investigation Commission.

It approved continued police measures and greater efforts to inculcate nationalist values as the best means of countering radicalism among college students. As a result, a National Spirit and Culture Research Institute was established by the Education Ministry.

The approach did not go unopposed. Two of the members of the commission itself—Tokyo University professors Kawai Eijirō and Rōyama Masamichi —published an extensive "minority report." In it they attacked the government for reliance on police power in an ineffectual attempt to impose a narrow version of nationalism. The commission had failed, in the eyes of Kawai and Rōyama, to comprehend the true nature of Marxism and the real reasons for its spread among the Japanese students. Marxism was composed of a commitment to four separate elements: historical materialism, the labor theory of value, violent revolution, and the dictatorship of the proletariat. It was only on the latter two grounds that Marxism could be viewed as "evil." Even here, however, the two authors contended that conservative arguments about Marxism contradicting the national polity were not only irrelevant but also false: "Marxism and the ideas of national polity are not totally antagonistic. The philosophy of dialectic materialism is, in part, perhaps antagonistic but violent revolution, socialism, dictatorship and the [Marxist] analysis of capitalism are not ideas directly antagonistic [to the values of the national polity]."[28] Indeed, the real evil political ideologies were those of fascism and right-wing radicalism. The dangers from the right and the left needed to be countered by stimulating faith in parliamentarianism, which meant strengthening the constitutional rights of freedom of speech so necessary to public debate.

While thus arguing for protection of the rights of Marxists, Kawai also criticized Marxists who themselves sometimes violated the academic freedom of others: "It is by no means only conservatives who oppose the principle of freedom of speech. There are Marxists who, because they are right now in the minority, advocate freedom of inquiry and publication but in their minds despise opposing views and tend easily toward suppression of them."[29] There should be certain limitations on the freedom of speech that Marxists must also abide by. Libel and blasphemy were not protected by the right to free speech. Furthermore, "because the university is the organ of scholarly inquiry, propagandizing, intimidation or struggle are not permitted."

Kawai was not advocating that either students or faculty take active roles in politics. As his colleague, Rōyama, put it in an article addressed to Kyoto University students in 1933: "It is absolutely impermissible in a nation such as Japan for university professors or students to be in movements colored by politics. Perhaps in China or South America, but it is impermissible in a civilized country."[30] Certainly the Education Ministry agreed with that much of Rōyama's argument.

By the mid-1930s, the enthusiasm of youth for politics tended to be absorbed in the wave of nationalism that swept the country in reaction to the Western condemnation of Japanese aggression in Manchuria. Indeed, many former leftists formally announced their conversion to patriotism in a process known as *tenkō*—apostasy or recantation. The authorities brought great psychological pressure on jailed students to recant their previous "non-Japanese" beliefs so that they could return to the national fold and spare their families further shame.[31]

Mobilizing the Public Schools

The response of the Education Ministry to the dangerous ideas infecting the nation's elementary and middle school teachers was to escalate its campaign to convince them that teaching was a heaven-sent calling, a sacred profession. Thus it was wrong to consider teachers as mere "workers" to be organized into labor unions. In normal schools the curriculum stressed that "the goal of education is for others. Therefore true education is attained when the teacher sacrifices himself for his students. Herein lies the reason why teaching is called a holy profession (*seishoku*)."[32] In 1934 a special conference was held for teachers throughout the nation with the goals of promoting patriotism and morality. In 1936 the Council on Innovation in Education and Learning issued a report that called for excluding from the classroom all ideas not in accord with the national polity.[33] The following year, in May 1937, the Education Ministry distributed the first of what eventually became 2 million copies of a booklet entitled *Fundamentals of Our National Polity*. Issued some months before the invasion of central China, this publication became the single most important statement of official educational ideology in the period 1937–1945. It was followed in 1941 by revisions of elementary school textbooks. By 1941 the radio was also a standard tool in the classroom: All broadcasts were of the government stations, so it was used to present the official version of war news.

The main purpose of these official pronouncements was to provide teachers and students with answers to the type of questions that appeared in the final examination for a 1941 ethics course:[34]

Why are loyalty and filial piety united in our country?
. . .
Discuss the necessity for overseas expansion.
Why is Japan's constitution superior to those of other nations?
What kind of spirit is required to overcome the present difficulties facing the nation?

How to reconcile the conflicting claims of political loyalty versus family loyalty commonly poses problems in state ideologies, and much space in the ethics textbooks was devoted to convincing students that the two were not in conflict. In essence the key was a realization that patriotism meant loyalty to the imperial house and that loyalty to the patriarchal emperor was itself an expression of filial piety:

It was some two thousand six hundred years ago when the Emperor Jinmu's first enthronement ceremony was held. Since that time our country, with the Imperial Family as the pivot of our activities, has enjoyed national growth like one big family. The successive Emperors have looked after their subjects like children; and we, the subjects, from the time of our ancestors, have venerated the Emperors as we would our own parents.[35]

The distinctiveness of the Japanese constitution lay in its origin as a gift from the emperor of the Meiji period "in accordance with the ancestral precepts and with the hope of bringing happiness to His subjects and prosperity to His country." Its superiority over those of other nations stemmed from the uniqueness of the Japanese imperial dynasty: "The manner in which we worship the Emperor as God and [the fact of] having the Imperial Household as the main stock of our family origin is something that is peculiar to the body politic of our country, there being no likeness of it throughout the world."[36]

Loyalty, patriotism, and respect for the "body politic"—the *kokutai*—were threatened by alien ideas of individualism and materialism. The 1937 *Fundamentals of Our National Polity* was quite clear on this:[37] "The various ideological and social evils of present-day Japan are . . . due to the fact that since the days of Meiji so many aspects of European and American culture, systems, and learning, have been imported, and that, too rapidly." At the heart of Occidental culture since the Renaissance were rationalism, positivism, and individualism. The doctrines of liberalism, socialism, anarchism, and communism "are all based in the final analysis on individualism." Western totalitarian ideologies such as fascism and Nazism, which in the view of the Education Ministry were also unsuitable for Japan, were reactions against the extremes of individualism. As a result, "both in the Occident and in our country the deadlock of individualism has led alike to a season of ideological and social confusion and crisis."

These evils flowed from the same wellspring, "a rationalism and a positivism, lacking in historical views." Because of this Western failure to grasp the importance of a nation's unique history, "importance is laid upon human beings and their groupings, who have become isolated from historical entireties, abstract and independent of each other." All of this overlooks the basic fact that "an individual is an existence belonging to a State and her history which forms the basis of his origins, and is fundamentally one body with it." These had to be countered with greater emphasis on the uniqueness of the Japanese spirit and the Japanese as a family extending back to their very beginnings.

Hence the Japanese should value what it is that they share as a people, especially the imperial dynasty unique in the world:

Our country is established with the emperor, who is a descendant of [the Sun Goddess] . . . to serve the Emperor and to receive the Emperor's august Will as one's own is the rationale of making our historical "life" live in the present; and on this is based the morality of the people.

The chief values in this morality should be loyalty, patriotism, and filial piety: Loyalty means to reverence the emperor as [our] pivot and to follow him implicitly. By implicit obedience is meant casting ourselves aside and serving the Emperor intently. . . . Offering our lives for the sake of the emperor does not mean so-called self-sacrifice, but casting aside of our little selves to live under his august grace and the enhancing of the genuine life of the people of the State.

In essence, loyalty to the emperor was the same thing as patriotism since the emperor and the state were one. In the same way, loyalty and filial piety were one, since "our country is a great family nation, and the Imperial Household is the head family of the subjects and the nucleus of national life." Of course, the family was conceived of as different from those in other cultures:

The basis of the nation's livelihood is, as in the Occident, neither the individual nor husband and wife. It is the home. . . .

The life of the family in our country is not confined to the present life of a household of parents and children, but beginning with the distant ancestors, is carried on eternally by the descendants . . . an unbroken chain that passes through from ancestor to offspring.

Individualism is the enemy of loyalty, patriotism, and the family because the possibility of harmony is destroyed "when people determinedly count themselves as masters and assert their egos. . . . The society of individualism is one of clashes between [masses of] people . . . and all history may be looked upon as one of class wars." The way to avoid such calamities is through self-effacement "that bids farewell to unwholesome self-interest."

The Education Ministry did not advocate the rejection of all Western ideas. Rather, like the imperial rescripts of the Meiji period, the *Fundamentals of Our National Polity* called for assimilation of the strong points in foreign culture, comparing the problem of dealing with modern Western culture to that of adopting Chinese writing in the ancient period:

In the inherent character of our people there is strongly manifested alongside this spirit of self-effacement and disinterestedness, a spirit of broadmindedness and assimilation. In the importation of culture from the Asian Continent . . . this spirit of ours has coordinated and assimilated. . . . To have brought forth a culture uniquely our own, in spite of the fact that a culture essentially different was imported, is due entirely to a mighty influence peculiar to our nation. This is a matter that must be taken into serious consideration in the adaptation of modern Occidental culture.

Japan is thus seen as uniquely qualified to produce a synthesis of "the strong points of Occidental learning and concepts [which] lie in their analytical and intellectual qualities," and those of the Orient, which "lie in their intuitive and aesthetic qualities." This synthesis is presented as the national goal: "Our present mission as a people is to build up a new Japanese culture by adopting and sublimating Western cultures with our national polity as the basis, and to contribute spontaneously to the advancement of world culture." Nevertheless, once war broke out with the United States and Britain, the English language was dropped from the secondary curriculum and a great many loanwords were replaced by Japanese equivalents—including a set of new terminology to use in baseball games.[38]

It followed from these convictions that patriotism was not a subject to be left to morals courses; geography and history were also subjects admirably suited to the purpose. Konoe Fumimaro, the most powerful prime minister of the 1930s, publicly endorsed this educational philosophy:

> The study of our nation's history is indispensable in strengthening an accurate understanding of our majestic national polity and splendid national customs; in making clear the origin of our nation, the nobility of our national polity, and the march of our national destiny; and thus filling our people with the faith and mission of citizens of our Empire. I believe that in making history a compulsory subject [in the civil service examinations], we can expect gradually to eliminate error in selecting men of ability to become higher civil servants.[39]

Many of Konoe's closest advisers belonged to the Shōwa Research Society. This organization created the privately funded Shōwa Academy, which offered lectures to "reeducate" university students among others. Ironically, the Shōwa Research Society itself came under fire as being procommunist. It was disbanded in 1940 and some government officials involved were arrested the following year.[40]

As the fighting in China intensified, the Education Ministry produced other materials for classroom teachers to use in explaining the national emergency to their charges. All textbooks at the elementary level had been compiled by the Education Ministry since 1904. In the morals courses, Western heroes such as Benjamin Franklin and Florence Nightingale were all but excluded and nationalistic values crowded out discussion of individual ethics even more so than in the 1933 editions.[41] The 1943 editions carried this process even further, although in the last stages of the war there was a great shortage of textbooks and other teaching materials.[42]

National myths were now taught even more literally than in earlier years. Indeed it reached the point where even primary school children are said to have sometimes expressed skepticism. Schools frequently arranged field trips to Shinto shrines. Much of the curriculum in middle schools was also affected, although until 1943 teachers at this level could practice some discretion by picking textbooks from an approved list.

A unique sense of filial piety and patriotic loyalty was thus at the core of the spirit needed to prevail in wartime.

> We, the Japanese people, are by nature peace-loving people. However, in the case of national crisis we, as the people, have made it our duty to serve the country courageously, unmindful of our personal sacrifices. . . .

In the case of national emergency all those under obligation to perform military duties . . . will be conscripted to go to the battle front. Thus to perform out duties and defend the country in this manner is one of the most important duties of the people and at the same time a great honor.[43]

Mandatory military drill was another means to drive this point home and inculcate proper attitudes for boys in upper elementary and middle schools. But they were also taught that duty was not limited to those at the front:

As war is fought nowadays is quite different from what it was in the past. It is total war between countries and for this reason, one cannot win a victory unless the entire people fight with one mind. Consequently the people back home have as important a job to do as the soldiers who fight at the front line. . . . We must mobilize all national resources to defend the nation.[44]

Structural Changes

Although education during the war years has been studied mostly for the upsurge of ultranationalism and suppression of academic freedom, there were other trends that should not go unnoticed. Some of these were continuations of directions already established in the previous two decades.

Higher Education

Expansion in higher education continued in the early 1930s (see Table 5.1). The proportion of the population enrolled in higher education reached 0.3 percent in the mid-1930s, twice that of either Britain or France. The number of both private and public schools at the tertiary level increased from a total of 245 higher schools, colleges, and universities combined in 1931 to 285 in 1941; in 1945 the number was 397.

TABLE 5.1
Higher Education for Males, 1930–1945: Number of Students Enrolled

	1930	1935	1940	1945
Higher school	20,551	17,898	17,719	21,687
College[a]	90,043	96,929	141,478	212,950
University	69,605	71,607	81,999	98,825
Higher normal	2,478	1,787	2,088	3,171
TOTAL	182,677	188,221	243,284	336,633

[a]Includes technical *senmon gakko.*

SOURCE: Adapted from Monbushō, *Gakusei 100 nenshi,* vol. 2, tables 10, 11, and 13.

The addition of Nagoya as the ninth imperial university in 1939 was the most important change in the public university system, although the school was comprised of only medicine, engineering, and science faculties. At the very end of the war, the government added three higher normal schools: two new ones for men and one for women.

The character of higher education also changed considerably in these years, especially after Pearl Harbor. Some of these changes were in somewhat surprising directions, given the conservative climate of the times. Although there can be disagreement over how to define higher education for women, by one count the number of female students increased substantially: from just 15,500 in 1935 to over 58,500 in 1945. Approximately 10,000 were in medical schools by the end of the war. These figures meant that whereas women had accounted for about 10 percent of students in higher education in 1937, they were now almost 14 percent—a jump of 40 percent albeit over a very small base.

Some of the other changes were less surprising. During the late 1930s and the Pacific War, far more students at the university level majored in science and technology than previously—science majors increasing by over 200 percent between 1935 and 1945, engineering up 477 percent. This change was in response to government and private initiatives in creating more facilities to meet the military and industrial demand for such specialties. It involved both growth in the number of technical colleges as well as expansion of these departments in the imperial universities or private universities. The government created a dozen new technical colleges, and another twenty-two were opened by the private sector.

Although higher education expanded in terms of numbers of schools and students, it suffered retrenchment in other dimensions. The most serious was the steady reduction of time that students spent in class after 1941. University school terms were shortened to accommodate the military conscription quotas, which began to affect large numbers of students in 1941. In 1942 the curriculum of higher schools was shortened from three years to two and middle schools from five to four.

Initially, university students had deferred conscription into the military until graduation, although in 1939 the government had ordered all college and university students to spend a week each year helping out on the nation's farms. By the opening of war with the United States, this service had been extended to a month and included work in industry. As the Pacific War wore on, there was greater need for manpower both at the front and at home. In late 1943 the government limited draft deferments to those in medicine, science, and other technical fields. Shortly thereafter the draft age was lowered from twenty to nineteen, so for the first time many students in higher schools and colleges were vulnerable. By this time, however, the mood among students is said to have been increasingly patriotic.[45] In 1944, seventeen- and eighteen-year-olds were registered in case they were needed to fend off an invasion attempt. Surrender came first.

Precollegiate Schooling

During the decade of the 1930s, there were continual calls for expanding schooling at the primary and secondary levels as well as in higher education. The Education Ministry again gave serious consideration to raising the compulsory education level from six to eight years of elementary school. The government backed off again, however, largely because of the cost. By the time it finally decided to make the change in 1941, wartime conditions prevented implementation.

Earlier, in 1935, the government heeded the military's call for expanded vocational training programs.[46] Vocational schools had existed at various levels since the Meiji period. For boys with six years of primary school who did not enter an academic or technical school at the secondary level, there were supplementary vocational courses, usually offered at night for working youth. In 1926 a separate set of Youth Training Programs had been created as part of the legal reforms that overhauled the military conscription system. Working males aged sixteen to twenty who were not full-time students elsewhere were given practical courses along with military drills in the evenings. In 1935 these and many private training programs were replaced with a system of Youth Schools, which offered two- to seven-year courses in industrial arts and agricultural science that could be taken on a full-time or part-time basis. In 1939 private companies employing at least 200 workers became legally obligated to provide training programs for them. Interestingly enough, these were placed under the supervision of the Ministry of Health and Welfare rather than the Education Ministry. Attendance at Youth Schools also became mandatory for those under the draft age of twenty who were not students elsewhere. By 1942 there were almost 24,000 such schools.

There is some question, however, as to whether these programs ever achieved their intended goal of producing more skilled manual workers since the curricula tended to favor commercial and clerical skills.[47] Moreover, many youth did not actually attend because they were needed on the job during the war years.[48] In addition to this instruction at the lower levels, in 1930 there were approximately 1,000 public technical schools at the secondary level offering courses in agriculture, business, fisheries, and assorted industrial arts. The government continued to expand this level—opening 800 more schools by 1945. By the end of the war, the government had consolidated the administration of all these vocational and technical programs into one centralized system.

As the war abroad went from bad to worse and living standards at home suffered accordingly, most schools could maintain only the facade of being educational institutions as their staff and students were drawn further into the war effort. By spring 1943 the need for labor on the home front led to the reduction of the length of the secondary school curriculum by a whole year. All male and female students above ten years old were ordered to perform mandatory labor service on farms and in war plants as well as in hospitals. They were often accompanied by their teachers as work leaders and sometimes Buddhist priests were present as chaplains to bolster morale. Many schools added workshops on their premises to aid in the war effort. The minimum number of hours of instruction required was eventually lowered to only six hours a week.[49]

In February 1945, when U.S. bombing began in earnest, the government had to face the reality that war devastation and shortages in all aspects of daily life made it virtually impossible to continue schooling. It therefore closed down the system, using the educational infrastructure at the primary school level to evacuate thousands of urban children to the countryside with their teachers. Those left behind held what classes they could in air raid shelters.[50]

Gender in Wartime

It is ironic that in the major nations involved in World War II, the drain on manpower offered women opportunities previously denied to them. This was the situation to some extent in education as well as in other spheres. More and more teachers in primary schools were women by the end of the war. In 1932 they had made up less than a third and the proportion remained that in 1935. But then it began to climb.

This need for new instructors did not, however, change the official ideology toward women in teaching immediately. A statement issued in 1938 by the Educational Inquiry Commission included the following expression of concern:

> Women teachers have increased to the extent found in the United States and Europe. This fact causes us great anxiety as to the future of our national system of education. Americans tend to base decisions on emotional considerations rather than upon fairness. This has resulted from the fact that 90 [sic] percent of all elementary school teachers [there] are women.[51]

TABLE 5.2
Schooling for Females, 1930–1945: Number of Students Enrolled

	1930	1935	1940	1945
Girls higher	341,574	383,861	518,584	875,814
Vocational higher	27,425	28,265	37,005	na
Jitsugyo gakko	51,670	92,522	156,439	247,314
Women's normal	13,938	10,429	15,159	21,593
Women's higher normal	897	871	977	1,362
TOTAL	435,504	515,948	728,164	1,146,083

na = not available

SOURCE: Adapted from Monbushō, *Gakusei 100 nenshi*, vol. 2, tables 5, 6, 11, 12, and 13.

One proposed solution was to restrict enrollments in women's normal schools to one-third of those at normal schools for males, about where it stood in 1932. But with the war in China draining off more males to battle or into war plants after 1937, there was too great a need for women for such a policy. The percent of women training to be teachers was allowed to reach 40 percent in 1940; by the end of the war females were in the majority, accounting for 54 percent (see Table 5.2 for numbers of female students during the war).

The 1943 educational ordinances upgraded ordinary normal schools by adding a sixth year to the curriculum, meaning that a graduate going on to teach primary school would have finished fourteen years of schooling. A more dramatic break with the past was to make these lower-level normal schools coeducational for the first time, merging the separate facilities that dated from the Meiji period.

In part these reforms in teacher training were aimed at strengthening centralized control by transferring these schools from prefectural jurisdiction to more direct central government supervision. However, the ability of the central Education Ministry to actually oversee the education outside of the main cities was steadily reduced as transportation and communication widened the gap between capital and countryside. The regulations for local education boards in the 1943 National School Ordinances may have included few substantial powers but in fact local governments must have been forced back on their resources more than ever in coping with the extraordinary strains in the last stages of the war.

Conclusion

In the decade and a half between the seizure of Manchuria and defeat in World War II, the Japanese school system was wrenched in several directions simultaneously. On the one hand, centralization increased as the state endeavored to whip the populace into greater and greater efforts to defeat the Chinese and stave off defeat at the hands of the Western powers. Both the vocational and normal school tracks were reorganized and prefectural jurisdiction was shrunk. The frenzied effort to indoctrinate students in more and more shrill versions of ultranationalism penetrated into almost every corner of schooling, although many liberal university faculty were able to survive by maintaining their silence and avoiding politically sensitive subjects in their teaching.

On the other hand, these years saw an erosion of the elitism that had characterized the school system since the Meiji period. Separation of the genders continued but to a lesser extent as normal schools became coeducational. Equality was a long way off, but women were more likely than ever before to be allowed schooling beyond the lower secondary levels. The war also thrust women into new occupations and new decisionmaking roles at home in the absence of husbands and fathers.

But perhaps the most significant consequence of the war was simply Japan's defeat. Whereas victory in the Russo-Japanese War forty years earlier had served to legitimize many of the educational reforms begun in the Meiji period, conquest by the United States and its Western allies served similarly to discredit the system in the eyes of many. The reformers in the American Occupation could thus count on many Japanese partners in their effort to overhaul it.

6

Stamping out the Bad, Stamping in the New: 1945–1950

Only a democratically educated Japanese people would be able to stimulate and defend political progress and build a frame of mind conducive to peaceful cooperation with other nations. . . . The goal of the educational programs would be the reeducation of the whole Japanese population.

—U.S. State Department[1]

The idea that a group of people who came to Japan with not even a child's knowledge about the Japanese education system could—in just 24 days in the country—get a grasp on how the system really works and propose a set of reforms is simply unbelievable. . . . My theory is that the whole [1946 U.S.] Education Mission was just a trick of the Occupation.

Kennoki Toshihiro, Former Minister of Education[2]

Japanese historians of education speak of the reforms of the immediate postwar as "the second revolution."[3] Like the first "revolution" of the Meiji era, these postwar reforms were initiated from the top down. This time, however, ultimate power lay in the hands of foreign conquerors rather than indigenous elites. For the six-and-a-half years between September 1945 and April 1952 the nation was under the rule of the Supreme Command Allied Powers, commonly known as SCAP. Although the USSR, Britain, and other victorious allies were nominally represented in the councils of SCAP, policymaking was in fact almost entirely in the hands of the Truman administration in Washington and the headquarters of General Douglas MacArthur in Tokyo.

Unfortunately, neither Washington nor the occupationaires were always fully aware of the realities of Japanese society past or present. Nor were they always in agreement among themselves about policy. But whatever the policy disagreements between Truman's advisers and MacArthur's staff, the results were shaped by their consensus about the diagnosis of what was wrong: The Pacific War had been caused by a Japanese nation that was not yet fully modern and therefore lacking the institutions and attitudes essential to a democratic and peaceful society. To ensure that Japan would never again be guilty of aggression against its neighbors, SCAP was given a broad mandate to carry out radical reforms in its political, economic, and social systems.

Among the earliest measures taken by the Occupation was the dismantling of the armed forces and a purge of almost a quarter of a million individuals in positions of wartime leadership. This action was followed by the stripping of power from the imperial throne and the abolition of state support for the Shinto religion. Simultaneously, the Americans who landed in Japan in autumn 1945 gave very high priority to transforming the educational system, convinced as they were that its schools had long been used to indoctrinate Japanese children "to accept authoritarian controls with unquestioning obedience" and to foster "the concept of loyalty and of Japan's militaristic and materialistic destiny."[4]

The task of reforming education was seen basically to involve attacks on three fronts simultaneously. First, the system was overly centralized. SCAP would have to dismantle the apparatus of centralized control by which the Education Ministry had usurped power from the local communities and initiative from teachers, who thus became "followers rather than leaders" with too little opportunity "to exercise professional freedom." Second, the curriculum was "ultranationalistic." It would be necessary to eliminate "existing curricula, textbooks, teaching materials, and instructional materials . . . designed to promote a militaristic or ultranationalistic ideology" and replace them with "new curricula, textbooks, teaching manuals, and instructional materials designed to produce an educated, peaceful, and responsible citizenry."[5] Third, the prewar system had been designed to provide "one type of education for the masses and another for the privileged few." It now had to be redesigned to be cured of the evils of such elitism.[6]

Educational Administration

The CI&E and the Education Ministry

To carry out reforms aimed at empowering the Japanese people to exercise democratic control over the schools, SCAP initially set up a highly centralized chain of command to facilitate leadership from the top down. Within the original six branches of the Occupation, responsibility for implementing reform of the school system was given to the Civil Information and Education Division (the CI&E). Its role has been described by one participant as "a mixture of policeman, auditor and ideological missionary."[7]

In practice, however, the Americans lacked the trained personnel and other organizational resources to administer the Japanese school system by themselves. Therefore, the CI&E, like other arms of SCAP, relied in the first instance upon existing Japanese governmental structures. Over the next six years the Ministry of Education would be both the chief liaison channel with SCAP and the main agency for implementing Occupation reform policy in the school system. Although this role of the Education Ministry may have been deemed a temporary expedient in the beginning, ultimately SCAP relegitimized the ministry by permitting its officials to continue, as they had before the war, to be the most important agents for administering the public school system.

The ministry did, it is true, undergo some major changes in the aftermath of the war. Just after the surrender, the transitional cabinet of Prince Higashikuni handed leadership in the ministry to Maeda Tamon, a former bureaucrat with a "liberal" reputation as well as personal experience with life in the United States. Maeda quickly closed down those ministry bureaus most concerned with controlling dissent and inculcating nationalist values and replaced a number of ministry officials with men more of his own persuasion. Among the most important of these was Tanaka Kōtarō, a former dean of the Tokyo University law department who, as a practicing Christian, was more acceptable to the Occupation than some others who had also remained at their post during the war.[8] Another of the key newcomers was Toyoda Takeshi, a specialist in medieval Japanese history from the Tokyo Women's Higher School who was brought in to help in the Bureau of Textbooks. These and other officials were in close touch with CI&E officers on such matters as curricular reform and the production of new textbooks.

The Purge of Ultranationalist Teachers

The impact of the defeat on Japanese schoolteachers was particularly great. In the words of one Tokyo University sociologist, it was "a shock produced by contradictory feelings of humiliation at the realization that the Japanese no longer controlled their own education and of their relief at the thought that the old education, which had required that they teach myths as truths, had been completely abrogated."[9] Many Japanese critics of the prewar system, however, stressed that the teachers themselves were as much a part of the problem as the Education Ministry:

> Next to army personnel, teachers of prewar Japan were the most nationalistic citizens in the country. This was especially true of those, who as primary school

teachers, . . . had complete responsibility for training their pupils to be the "loyal subjects" stipulated in the Imperial Rescript. Since they were required to teach ultranationalism, they themselves tried to acquire a firm belief in it.[10]

This was the view adopted initially by SCAP, which was determined to rid the system of ultranationalists. The CI&E issued the first directive in what would become a large-scale purge at the end of October 1945, an order to the Education Ministry regarding "Investigation, Screening and Certification of Teachers and Educational Officers": "All persons who are known to be militaristic, ultra-nationalistic, or antagonistic to the objectives and policies of the Occupation and who are at this time actively employed in the educational system of Japan, will be removed immediately and will be barred from occupying any position in the educational system."[11]

Among the first to be dismissed were administrators at Rikkyō Academy, a school founded by Christians. General MacArthur held them and others at similar schools especially culpable for violating religious as well as academic freedom. Presidents of some other private universities resigned and all institutions of higher education were ordered to reinstate faculty who had been driven out during the war. In November new administrators were named to head 140 public colleges and higher schools.[12]

Elementary and secondary teachers were included in the broader SCAP order of January 1, 1946, "Removal and Exclusion of Undesirable Personnel from Public Office." It is estimated that by then 105,000—one of out every six—wartime teachers and professors had already resigned or been dismissed. Faced with the Herculean task of dealing with the almost 1 million teachers and administrators still in service, the CI&E "essentially 'washed its hands' of the matter and informed the Ministry of Education that . . . [it] would permit them unconditional liberty in setting up the [purge procedures] provided that, as a minimum, they met the requirements of the general purge order."[13] By the end of 1947, the total staff who had left the school system since the end of the war reached almost 116,000, and by 1949 another 3,100 were purged.[14]

The next logical questions were who would replace them and by whom would these replacements be trained. But these matters could not be addressed until further decisions could be made about administrative authority in general. Would such decisions be made by a central bureaucracy or would power be handed down to the prefectural and local levels?

Reorganization at the Top

In January 1946 Minister of Education Maeda was replaced by another intellectual with a background deemed advantageous for working with the Occupation—Abe Yoshishige. Abe was a specialist in the history of Western philosophy who had taught at Seoul Imperial University as well as the First

Higher School. Minister Abe's welcoming speech to the 1946 U.S. Education Mission reflects the approach of conservatives to dealing with the Americans and provides a glimpse of why those outside of the government who favored more radical reform were so apprehensive. Minister Abe proclaimed the defeat in the war an opportunity for a brighter future: "We pray that the pressure brought upon us by [the U.S. victory] will help to make truth and justice permeate all our country, and serve as a chance for us to eliminate quickly and vigorously all the injustices and defects existing in our society." At the same time that he acknowledged "the weakness and evils underlying our national character and customs," however, he also expressed with rather remarkable bluntness the concerns he shared with many other conservatives within Japan: "There are some young idealists among the Americans coming to our country who tend to use Japan as a kind of laboratory in a rash attempt to experiment with some abstract ideals of their own, ideals which have not yet been realized even in their own country." These last remarks were considered sufficiently provocative that someone in the CI&E ordered them edited out of the report of the speech distributed to the Japanese educational community.[15]

Such remarks may also have hastened Abe's removal from office. When the Liberal Party leader Yoshida Shigeru formed his first cabinet in May 1946, Professor Tanaka Kōtarō was promoted to head the Education Ministry in Abe's place. Although the Occupation viewed Tanaka as a defender of academic freedom and political liberalism, his appointment was not at all reassuring to Japanese critics on the left, who feared the continued influence of prewar conservatism in the Education Ministry. They were not mollified until a socialist-led coalition of parties won the elections of May 1947 and brought one of their heroes in as minister of education—Morito Tatsuo, a professor who had been driven out of Tokyo University twenty-eight years earlier. By this time, however, some of the most important reforms of the Occupation were already in place.

The main legal framework for a new Japanese educational system was put into place in February and March 1947. As drafted by SCAP and endorsed by the Japanese Diet, the new constitution included several clauses of critical importance for education policy. Most directly relevant were Articles 23 and 26. The former stated flatly, "Academic freedom is guaranteed" whereas the latter granted equality of rights in schooling: "All people shall have the right to receive an equal education corresponding to their ability, as provided by law. All people shall be obligated to have all boys and girls under their protection receive ordinary education as provided by law. Such compulsory education shall be free." There was also significance in the constitutional provisions for gender equality in Article 14: "All of the people are equal under the law and there shall be no discrimination in political, economic or social relations because of race, creed, sex, social status or family origin."[16]

The U.S. Education Mission, which arrived in 1946, gave ample advice on how to apply these constitutional principles in the school system. The members stayed less than a month in Japan, but in the view of some within SCAP, "this mission was enormously important. . . . Although the mission had no official power in the Occupation, its recommendations were accepted almost as if law."[17] The main thrust of those recommendations was to decentralize administrative authority. Yet in the new Fundamental Law of Education, passed by the Diet in March 1947, the crucial question of power over the educational system was addressed only in rather vague terms: "Education shall not be subject to improper control, but it shall be directly responsible to the whole people. School administration shall, on the basis of this realization, aim at the adjustment and establishment of the various conditions required for the pursuit of the aim of education."[18]

In March 1947 the Diet also enacted a new School Education Law, and in 1949 it added an Education Ministry Establishment Law specifying the functions of the ministry. The ad hoc committee originally created to liaison with the U.S. Education Mission of 1946 was renamed the Educational Reform Council and was authorized to advise the government on a broad range of issues. The power to set the agenda for the council was given to a nine-member steering committee with three each selected from among CI&E personnel, Education Ministry officials, and the Educational Reform Council itself. This group was an active one, especially in the first six months when it held ninety-two general meetings. Between September 1946 and June 1952, the group met, on the average, as a committee of the whole twice a month and in subcommittees once or even twice a week.[19] In May 1949, however, Prime Minister Yoshida maneuvered to bypass this SCAP-sanctioned council by creating a cabinet-level committee as his "advisory board," the Bunkyō Shingikai, or Education Commission.[20] For higher education there was an All-Japan University Council appointed in 1947 to advise on all issues, and a University Chartering Committee was created in January 1948 to see that schools met the standards recommended by the University Accreditation Association.

The initial intent of these legislative acts was supposedly to circumscribe the powers of the central bureaucracy in dealing with educational matters. Rather than directing and managing the school system, the Education Ministry was to be restricted to "providing professional guidance," "preparing drafts of laws and orders concerning minimum standards," and "research."[21] But there would be years of fierce debates over how these functions differed from "improper control."

As initially envisaged by the reformers, the key to limited central power was control by lay persons at the local level. The 1946 U.S. Education Mission Report had strongly endorsed this means of decentralizing authority: "Powers at the National Level: Many present controls affecting curricula, methods, materials of instruction, and personnel should be transferred to prefectural and local school administrators." To further root the schools in the local communities, the Occupation first pushed for the formation of U.S.-style Parent-Teacher

Associations and then, in July 1948, created the Boards of Education Law, which gave elected local bodies the legal charge to oversee the schools. A U.S. participant at the local level called this law "the dividing line between authoritarianism and democracy in Japanese education . . . which throws the responsibility for Japanese education into the hands of the Japanese people and which breaks the legal back of Ministry of Education domination of Japanese education."[22]

The July 1948 law ordered the immediate creation of elected boards in each of the forty-six prefectures as well as in five of the largest metropolitan areas. The question of whether such boards should also be created at the level of lesser cities and towns was left to a special national commission charged with studying the matter. Its report, not completed until 1951, favored having the choice made by each locale. But the Liberal Party, which had originally opposed elected school boards altogether, soon sponsored legislation mandating such boards; by 1952 almost 10,000 had been created. These elected boards were to meet monthly with authority to "execute educational administration based on equitable popular will and actual local conditions, with the realization that education should be conducted without submitting to undue control and should be responsible to the people."[23] It was intended that these boards decide what schools should exist, determine the curricula and textbooks in those schools, recruit and terminate school officials to implement that policy, and draft budgets to fund all of these things. The local community boards were to make reports to the prefectural or metropolitan boards, which in turn would inform the Education Ministry about their policies and actions. But the central level was no longer to have administrative control over such policies and actions.

By giving power to representatives elected by direct vote of the people at the local level, the Occupation reformers intended to promote democracy through decentralization and lay participation. Surprisingly, some Occupation officials believed this could be done without politicizing the schools. The idealism as well as naïveté in these intentions can be glimpsed in the orders sent in August 1948 to regional military governments instructing them to "discourage political and partisan groups of any kind from maneuvering to get control of the boards. . . . Right now the political parties and the Teachers' Union, perhaps in good faith, perhaps not, are trying to get their representatives on the boards. This is not a political election. And it is not a happy hunting ground for self-seekers."[24] Despite such hopes, candidates backed by the Teachers' Union did very well in the initial elections.

On the one hand, the legal mandate of those elected was quite broad and it appeared that power now devolved down to at least the regional if not the local level. On the other hand, decentralization was in fact limited from the outset. SCAP had never intended the goal of decentralization to take precedent over the goal of purging Japan of those values that, in the official U.S. view, had caused the Pacific War. Thus SCAP retained at the central level the prerogative to set overall educational policy and to oversee the creation of a new curriculum

and new textbooks. In short, in the words of one Japanese historian who criticized the "colonialist character" of SCAP, "the new Occupation policy meant
the American rule of Japan under the guise of democracy."[25] Although central
control over the educational system might have been seen originally as a temporary accommodation to the requisites of carrying out revolutionary change,
nevertheless SCAP in effect sowed the seeds of the resurgence of the Education
Ministry in Tokyo.

SCAP did so in two ways. First, SCAP believed rightly or wrongly that it
could carry out its mission only by working through the existing central Japanese bureaucracy. Second, the failure of SCAP to set up adequate mechanisms
for local governments to finance their own programs independently of grants
from the tax revenues of the national government ensured at least an important oversight role for central government in education as in other spheres.

The dilemma of how to empower local communities while providing direction and financing from the top was almost the mirror image of what the Meiji
reformers had faced. In the 1880s and 1890s planners had been committed to
central control over education but were forced at times to compromise with
local communities because the national treasury lacked the funds to cover the
costs, thus giving local officials a certain independence. In the 1940s and 1950s,
the poverty of local governments strengthened the hand of the Education Ministry despite the reformers' commitment to grassroots control.

Other Political Players

Education Ministry officials, although in a position to have great influence on
SCAP reforms, were by no means the sole Japanese voices heard on educational
issues. There were other influential individuals and groups who played important parts in these years, often challenging the power of the Education
Ministry.

Government Advisory Boards

From the outset the CI&E utilized Japanese advisers separate from the Education Ministry, among the most prominent being Professors Kaigo Tokiomi,
Tokyo University specialist in education, and Kishimoto Hideo, a Tokyo University professor of religion. Kishimoto, who had done graduate work at Harvard, seems often to have facilitated backdoor communication between the
CI&E and the Education Ministry.[26] In early 1946, SCAP had also ordered the
ministry to create a special Committee of Japanese Educators to consult with
the U.S. Education Mission scheduled to arrive that March. Although this
group of Japanese would eventually endorse decentralization of administrative
control, a departure from prewar patterns, it warned against too radical a

change in other aspects. Its chair, Professor Nanbara Shigeru of the Tokyo University law department, shared Minister of Education Abe's caution about not destroying what was good in the people's "strong national consciousness" in the process of the "awakening of the individual human consciousness as an individual personality."[27] The membership of the committee was somewhat mixed in ideological views, but all could be characterized as right of center from the perspective of the new teachers' unions and their allies in the Japan Socialist Party, the other set of participants in the political struggle over education.

The Teachers' Union

Although the American Occupationaires were the most important reformers in the new politics of Japanese education, conservatives in the Education Ministry also found themselves facing an indigenous coalition of critics equally intent on reforming the system. Within the parliament there was a vigorous political opposition that objected vehemently to SCAP dependence upon bureaucrats and academics who had been part of the prewar educational establishment. There was particular criticism of the two dozen Japanese nominees put forth by the ministry to serve on the special Committee of Japanese Educators because it did not include leaders from the new teachers' unions.

As we have seen, the only large-scale organization of public school teachers in prewar Japan was under the aegis of the Education Ministry, that is, the Imperial Education Association. Efforts in the 1920s and early 1930s to create independent teachers' organizations that might challenge the authority of the government quickly dissipated as the winds of war grew stronger. But those prewar efforts had nevertheless left their mark, if only by creating political martyrs who stepped forward to champion reforms after the defeat in the war. Almost immediately after the beginning of the American Occupation, veterans of the prewar movement joined with new converts to attack the Education Ministry.

In Tokyo in December 1945, several rival groups claiming to represent teachers were formed. The leadership of the All-Japan Teachers' Union included one of the more famous of the wartime political martyrs, Hani Gorō. Hani, whose mother-in-law, Hani Motoko, had founded the private Freedom School in the 1920s, was imprisoned during the war for his advocacy of socialism. Released by SCAP, he became a founding member of the new Japan Communist Party. His comrade and prison mate, Kitamura Magomori, had been fired as a teacher in 1930 for his role in the prewar League of Elementary School Teachers and then jailed in 1941 for his efforts to organize machinists into a labor union. Not surprisingly, the mission statement of the All-Japan Teachers' Union restated many of the radical demands of the old Elementary School Teachers League of the 1920s, including an end to central control over curriculum and textbooks as well as the popular election of primary school principals.[28] More controversial among teachers were this union's connections with the postwar Communist Party and men like Hani Gorō, who publicly denounced the emperor as sharing in responsibility for the war.

To the political right of this group stood the Union of Japan Educators led by other prewar activists such as the Christian socialist Kagawa Toyohiko. Kagawa's anticommunist and pro–imperial throne position may have been shared by many, indeed perhaps the overwhelming majority of teachers, but his direct supporters were drawn mainly from faculty at secondary- and college-level institutions rather than from primary and middle school teachers.[29] To counter the influence of the communists, Kagawa and his colleagues proposed that teachers' unions ally only with the more moderate wing of the labor union movement and restrict their political endorsements to candidates in the right wing of the Socialist Party. This preoccupation with old prewar battles over politics undercut Kagawa's leadership, and other moderate elements in the new teachers' movement in Tokyo soon organized yet another group dedicated to more narrowly defined economic and professional issues.

Elsewhere regional groups had sprung up independently. These, in turn, were rapidly amalgamated into a national federation named the National League of Teachers' Unions, the forerunner of the Japan Teachers' Union. By autumn 1947 the CI&E estimated that this national federation had a membership of over 446,000, or 98 percent of the country's elementary school teachers. The leadership for this national movement spanned the whole political spectrum of left of center activists, including communists and left-wing socialists. Their demands included many of the more radical provisions of the prewar movement: freedom from the dictates of the central bureaucracy, popular control over schools, abolition of militaristic values in the curriculum. These were now, of course, very much in tune with U.S. policies.

For these activists, the mission of a teachers' union was not limited to educational matters; it was also an integral part of a larger political movement to bring about fundamental change in Japanese society. Thus from the outset, the Japan Teachers' Union not only cooperated with other labor unions that were expanding at an enormous rate but also its national leaders threw their support behind the two major opposition parties, the Japan Socialist Party and the Japan Communist Party. This is not to say that there was complete political consensus among the leaders, much less the members, of the Japan Teachers' Union. There was basic agreement on the rejection of the prewar system and great solidarity on the need to improve the economic lot of teachers as well as to empower them to take control of the classroom from the central bureaucracy. Nevertheless, union activists were deeply split over what tactics and which political party to support.

Initially, the Occupation had intended that the Education Ministry recognize and work with organizations representing teachers. But the Japanese in power were reluctant at best to negotiate with those they perceived to be their sworn political enemies. In late December 1946 there was actually a scuffle between police and a group of militants outside the office of the minister of education, former law professor Tanaka Kōtarō. This incident resulted in the arrest of several union leaders. The police quickly released all the participants, but the clash symbolized the growing tension between the ministry and the unions. The mutual hostility was exacerbated as the teachers' unions involved themselves with the nation's other labor unions in planning a general strike for February 1947. The Liberal Party cabinet counterattacked by proposing a bill that prohibited strikes by teachers as well as other government employees. Minister of Education Tanaka further proclaimed that legally the government was under no obligation to recognize as "real unions" those organizations that "aim at political or social movements."[30] The cabinet relented on the prohibition of strikes but Minister Tanaka continued to stonewall even the moderate union leaders on their demands for pay increases. All he would promise was to slow the reduction in numbers of teachers.

Shortly thereafter two developments paved the way to a compromise of sorts. In January Tanaka stepped down as minister of education. His place was taken by a retired Keiō economics professor who was more conciliatory toward the union. More important, later that month, when SCAP ordered all labor unions to call off a planned general strike, the teachers' leaders were quick to yield. The Education Ministry then entered into contractual agreements with the two largest organizations, the moderate National League of Teachers' Unions and the more militant All-Japan Teachers' Union. These negotiations recognized the unions' right to bargain collectively for their members, a historic recognition of the rights of teachers to organize.[31]

In addition to clauses regarding pay, fringe benefits, maternity leave, and working conditions, the March 1947 Collective Bargaining Agreement pledged "not to make any discrimination based on sex distinction against the members [of the union]," and the government subsequently addressed some of the salary disparities between male and female teachers. These precedent-breaking agreements further charged the two parties to "cooperate and be responsible for the enhancement of democratic education" as equals.[32] Moreover, the Education Ministry had previously issued a directive in January 1946 explaining that teachers and students had the right to take part in politics as long as such activities did not "interfere in any way with their normal duties." This right was now spelled out in greater detail in a separate memorandum.[33] Teachers were freed from many of the restrictions imposed upon them by the prewar civil service regulations. Later that year this new spirit of cooperation permitted a merger of the two major rival unions into a single Japan Teachers' Union. This organization thus emerged as one of postwar Japan's most important labor unions and therefore was among the more powerful participants in postwar politics.

This partnership between the new national union and the central government was not to last long. In July 1948 the American Occupation took action that effectively nullified the labor contracts and countermanded the Trade Union Law it had originally ordered the Diet to pass: It banned all public service employees, including teachers, from striking. This ban was eventually written into the December 1950 Local Public Service Law prohibiting the use of "strike, slow-down, and other act or dispute against their employer, who is the local people as represented by the agencies of the local public body."[34] This last clause also stripped the national leadership of the Japan Teachers' Union of the legal right to negotiate on behalf of its members—such negotiations with government officials were now sanctioned only at the local and prefectural levels, where the unions were also severely handicapped in their dealings with the local boards by these new statutes. The central educational bureaucracy immediately ceased to recognize federations of local or prefectural unions at the national level.

On the one hand, the 1950 law cost the teachers' union much of the legal ground it had gained in the first years of the Occupation. On the other hand, it probably served to strengthen the internal solidarity of the union, whose rank and file would show few signs of backing off in the struggles that were to mark education in the coming decades.

Zengakuren Students

Yet another set of players that emerged very early in postwar years was the All-Japan Federation of Students' Self-Government Associations, known best by its Japanese abbreviation, Zengakuren. Originating on the campus of Kyoto University in late 1945, it mushroomed into a national organization, linking some 145 colleges with an estimated membership of 300,000 students by late 1948.[35] Its leadership was firmly in the left-wing political camp and wielded a constant threat of student strikes for such causes as academic freedom and better physical facilities in higher education.

The Japan Socialist Party

The most important public arena for the political struggle over education under the Occupation was the Japanese parliament. The 1947 constitution transferred ultimate political authority from the ministers of the imperial throne to the elected representatives of the Japanese people. The old House of Peers, whose seats were filled almost entirely by either inheritance or imperial appointment, was replaced by a House of Councilors elected by prefectural and national constituencies. The powers of this chamber were also reduced vis-à-vis the House of Representatives, which was to have final say on the election of the prime minister and on several other key matters. For most of the years between 1946 and 1955, the House of Representatives was dominated by supporters of one or the other of the two right-of-center parties, the Liberals or the Democrats. Their main opposition came from the Japan Communist Party on the far left and other socialists toward the center who managed enough solidarity to remain in a single party, the Japan Socialist Party, at least during the Occupation. Among the major spokesmen for this opposition on educational issues were some intellectuals familiar from the prewar period, notably Morito Tatsuo, who would hold the education portfolio from May 1947 to March 1948 under Prime Minister Katayama Tetsu, until 1994 the only Japanese cabinet ever to be headed by a socialist.[36] These two leftist parties generally supported the legislation initiatives demanded by SCAP in the first years of the Occupation but often pushed for even more radical changes, particularly in the ideological content of the curriculum.

Ideological Reform

The socialists and their allies were deeply dissatisfied with the new laws reorganizing the administrative framework of the educational system. But they were even more concerned about revisions in the curriculum, demanding a clearer rejection of prewar ideology and expressing skepticism about the willingness of the conservatives to accept the new principles behind the educational reforms. There were indeed conservatives who openly questioned the main thrust of the U.S.-inspired changes. And once again, as sixty years earlier, the debates revolved around the issue of what to do with the 1890 Imperial Rescript on Education.

Initially the conservatives had hoped to retain the original rescript, arguing that it could provide the symbolic axis for constructing a new future. The first two ministers of education to serve after surrender, Maeda Tamon and Abe Yoshishige, both explicitly called upon the nation to "respectfully read the Imperial Rescript on Education" because "the Imperial Household is the nucleus of our national life. Let us, in these dark days following the end of the war, worship the Imperial Rescript on the New Year, and extol the Imperial will as it endeavors to construct a new State." The third postwar minister of education, Tanaka Kōtarō, concurred, arguing that since the Imperial Rescript was in accord with natural law, it "has existed for all historical time as the infallible, inviolable, and cardinal principle of Japanese ethics."[37] Some conservatives were willing to compromise: If the 1890 version was somehow no longer suitable then perhaps a new one could be issued.

The opposition left demanded nothing less than the formal repudiation of the document. Their reasoning was spelled out in the resolution ultimately endorsed by the Diet in June 1948:

> Whereas the Diet has legalized a Basic Law of Education . . . eliminating thoroughly the error of an education that would put our state at the center of the

universe and instead proclaiming solemnly the concepts of democratic education aimed at rearing a humanity that stands for truth and peace.

Whereas the Imperial Rescript on Education, as well as the Imperial Rescript to the Army and the Navy, the Imperial Rescript to the Students, and the like, have thereby lost their validity.

Whereas we fear that some ill-advised elements may entertain the notion that these documents still retain their validity and wish to make clear the fact that they are no longer valid and to cause the Government to collect all copies of such documents in the possession of universities and schools.[38]

Instead of a new imperial statement, the socialists endorsed the U.S.-inspired 1947 Fundamental Law of Education, a document written in a very different spirit. The first article of the law stated that the aim of education was "the full development of personality, striving for the rearing of the people, sound in mind and body, who shall love truth and justice, esteem individual value, respect labor and have a deep sense of responsibility, and be imbued with the independent spirit, as builders of the peaceful state and society." Philosophically, this constituted a stress on values that transcended such collectivities as the community or the state. Truth and justice replace loyalty and filial piety; individual and personality are privileged over group. There are also, of course, implications for social hierarchy in the call to "respect labor" and for antimilitarism in the call for a "peaceful state." The other ten articles of the law reiterated the new constitutional guarantees of academic freedom, demanded religious tolerance, and spelled out a commitment to coeducation.

As in the Meiji era, the issue of religion and state in the context of education had to be addressed. For example, in 1946 a member of the Liberal Party questioned the article in the draft constitution that banned religious teachings from the schools:

> The democratic nations of the world, particularly the United States, are built on a strongly religious foundation. . . . The Americans have still not lost that spirit. . . . What kind of a religious conviction is behind this Constitution, which is to serve as the basis of rebuilding our nation? . . . A statement [in the constitution] such as "religious belief is a personal matter" would encourage ordinary citizens to take religion lightly.[39]

Later, this representative, who identified himself as a morals teacher at a technical high school and an adherent of Buddhism, pressed the point: "Perhaps it is not acceptable to preach a particular faith in the classroom. But I would like you to clearly state that it would be acceptable to discuss religion as a way of building the character of students. . . . I have talked about my own convictions from the podium, although it might not be appropriate for me to urge students to believe them."

Minister of Education Tanaka, himself a Christian, responded sympathetically:

> The separation of religion and state . . . does not mean that it denies the importance of religion in human life. . . . As I understand it, . . . [this article] does not

mean that the state should remove teaching about religion, and religious enrichment, from education. . . . Within the sphere of school education, we would like to include stories that would inspire students such as those about the world's principal religions, biographies of great men of religions, etc. We would like to foster students' interests in religion and increase their appreciation.

Ultimately those opposed to these views managed to defeat any amendments aimed at specifically endorsing the teaching of "religious sentiments." The challenge now was how to implement this ideological reversal. The most tangible manifestation of the debate over these new ideas was to be seen in the process of revising the textbooks used in primary and secondary schools.

Textbook Revision

Even before the new constitution and the Fundamental Law of Education, the Civil Information and Education Section of SCAP had moved ahead with concrete reforms in the textbooks and the curriculum. The Americans prohibited all classroom materials that taught

1. The Greater East Asia Co-Prosperity Sphere doctrine or any other doctrine of expansion.
2. The idea that the Japanese are superior to other races and nationalities.
3. Concepts and attitudes which are contrary to the principles set forth in the Charter of the United Nations.
4. The idea that the Emperor of Japan is superior to the heads of other states and that the *tenno* system [of imperial sovereignty] is sacred and immutable.

The Education Ministry was specifically instructed to remove militaristic themes from textbooks and teaching materials. It banned

1. The glorification of war as a heroic and acceptable way of settling disputes.
2. The glory of dying for the Emperor with unswerving loyalty.
3. The idealization of war heroes by glorifying their military achievements.
4. The development of the idea that military service is the most patriotic manner of serving one's country.
5. The objects of military glorification: guns, warships, tanks, fortresses, soldiers, etc.[40]

Actually, SCAP to some extent had been beaten to the opening punch in the removal of the more obvious militaristic elements in the schools. At the end of August 1945, two weeks before the formal surrender, the cabinet headed by Prince Higashikuni had ordered the end to military training and the expurgation of militaristic sections from textbooks.[41] On September 20, the Education Ministry had issued a directive entitled "Concerning the Handling of Textbooks in Accordance with the Postwar Situation," which instructed schools that certain sections in the national readers should "be struck out either entirely or partly, or be handled with utmost care." These included materials "that

emphasize national defense and armament . . . [or] fostering fighting spirit . . .
[or] may be harmful to international goodwill . . . [or] have become obsolete as
being entirely removed from present postwar conditions and the everyday life
of the students."[42] The phrase "struck out" was intended literally; schoolchildren were given their first hands-on lesson in censorship when they were instructed to use ink to obliterate a list of designated passages.

This was not the last lesson. SCAP quickly created a Civil Censorship De-
tachment with over 5,000 "examiner-translators" who, until late 1949, practiced
much the same type of scrutiny of political ideas expressed in the press and
other media as had been practiced by the old Home Ministry in the prewar
era.[43] Once the Occupation forces were fully in place, the task of replacing objectionable material with new textbooks was undertaken with great zeal by the
CI&E. Its initial hope was to have new teaching materials available for all
grades in primary schools and middle schools by the beginning of the next
school year in April 1946. At the Education Ministry Bureau of Textbooks,
where Japanese army advisers had been replaced with SCAP personnel, fresh
materials were drafted with English translations that had been simultaneously
prepared for inspection by CI&E officers who did not read the Japanese language. Initially the process of producing these materials closely resembled that
of wartime Japan. Four of the surviving textbook publishers were designated
by the Education Ministry to print the books from manuscripts approved by
the military, albeit now the U.S. rather than the imperial Japanese army.

The enormity of the task of replacing the entire public school curriculum
began to set in by the end of December. There were over 200 courses affected,
most at the primary level but sixty-five at the middle school level and another
dozen in the normal schools. The rewriting of Japanese history proved particularly challenging, especially with regard to how to treat the Shinto mythology
surrounding the founding of the nation and the imperial throne. In December
1945, SCAP specifically banned "the dissemination of Shinto doctrines in any
form and by any means in any educational institution supported wholly or in
part by public funds." The emperor subsequently went on the radio to disclaim
any divinity in his nature. Eventually, Article 19 of the 1947 constitution read
in part, "The State and its organs shall refrain from religious education." A new
ten-person Committee of History Specialists was formed by the Education
Ministry in December 1945. It was composed of academics who were well established in the prewar system. They soon recommended a compromise in
which much of the material on the "age of the gods" would be relegated to the
teachers' manuals. But the key Textbook Bureau figure continued to be Tokyo
Women's Higher School professor Toyoda Takeshi, who proved stubbornly in-
flexible on such issues.[44]

To move ahead, CI&E resorted to temporarily suspending the most con-
taminated courses—that is, history, geography, and morals—in order to first

produce "stopgap" materials for less politicized subjects—for example, Japanese and foreign languages, mathematics, and natural sciences.

But the rewriting of Japanese history proved to be a far more time-consuming task than anticipated. Delays continued into May 1946, when the Americans finally lost patience. Professor Toyoda Takeshi was relieved of his duties in the Bureau of Textbooks, the ministry's Committee of History Specialists was disbanded, and the responsibility for overseeing the drafting of new texts was transferred to a committee from the Historiographical Institute, a prewar research facility located on the Tokyo University campus but separate from its regular faculty.

These moves were in keeping with advice of the U.S. Education Mission of 1946 Report of that spring. It called for the privatization of both preparation and publication, with supervision of the most politically sensitive subjects—history and geography—to be located outside the Education Ministry: "Councils of competent Japanese scholars should be established to develop authentical [sic] objective sources for the rewriting of Japanese history . . . [as] a basis for the preparation of textbooks." The mission acknowledged that "for economic reasons the selection of textbooks cannot be left wholly to the free choice of teachers. They should be selected by committees of teachers from a given area." But the chain of decisionmaking, as envisaged by the report, was bottom up: Teachers' groups would advise the "local school authorities" on textbooks and these local officials would in turn request authorization from prefectural officials.[45]

The 1947 Fundamental Law of Education was accompanied by more specific legislation to guide the implementation of its principles. This included the 1947 School Education Law. It provided that schools "shall use the textbooks approved or those the use of which is authorized by the competent authorities or textbooks published by competent authorities. Books other than the abovementioned textbooks and other teaching materials may be used, if they are good and suitable."[46]

In the interpretation preferred by the Education Ministry, this meant that textbooks had to be chosen from a list of titles certified by the ministry. It therefore issued a number of ordinances and regulations to implement this. The ministry did, however, make a gesture toward compromise with those critics who said it was trying to reinstate the prewar system. It appointed several dozen prefectural officials and others from outside to serve on a Standing Committee on Textbooks to provide advice to the ministry. This led in May 1948 to the creation of a Textbook Authorization Committee made up mainly of schoolteachers and professors with the mandate to select panels of experts to examine prospective textbooks and give final advice to the Education Ministry.[47] When in 1949 the Diet passed the Education Ministry Establishment Law of 1949 to specify jurisdiction and organization, it renamed this committee the Textbook Authorization and Research Council. Essentially, the government had returned to those procedures for selecting textbooks that were in effect in the Meiji period prior to the 1904 reforms.

It should be noted that by this stage in the Occupation it is sometimes said that the Americans in the CI&E were acting "essentially in the role of professional adviser," allowing the ministry more and more independence. Nevertheless, SCAP officials vetoed 247 textbook manuscripts submitted by ministry officials in 1948. It disapproved of 75 more submitted for the 1949–50 school year.[48]

The Red Purges

A more blatant use of central power for ideological aims was demonstrated in the so-called Red Purges that began in 1949. The growing hostility between the United States and the Soviet Union in the late 1940s inevitably had ramifications for Japan. Even before the outbreak of war in Korea, SCAP leaders expressed concern about communist influence in the classrooms and in the labor unions movement, which included the Japan Teachers' Union. In 1949 anger on the part of SCAP and Japanese conservatives at the influence of leftist ideology among Japanese educators and students boiled over.

CI&E adviser Walter Eells was perhaps the most outspoken of SCAP officials about the "Red Peril" in education. In a speech at Niigata University in July 1949 Eells made clear where SCAP stood:

> In the United States we have an important organization known as the Educational Policies Commission, composed of the leading educators of the country. . . . The Commission . . . only a few weeks ago issued a document which advocates and defends the discharge of proved Communists from the schools of America. This report has been approved by the United States Commissioner of Education and by President Truman.

Eells then asked rhetorically:

> Do the recommendations of this document violate the long and jealously guarded academic freedom of the universities? By no means. The basic reason for advising exclusion of Communist professors is that they are *not free.* Their thoughts, their beliefs, their teachings are controlled from the outside. Communists are told from headquarters *what to think and what to teach.* . . .
>
> It is clear that the university administration and the Ministry of Education . . . will not hesitate to take a positive and vigorous stand against Communist professors on its faculty.[49]

Even earlier, in September 1949, Education Ministry officials are said to have held a secret meeting with prefectural officials and superintendents of education in which they were allegedly ordered to find some pretext to fire known communist teachers. The Education Ministry is reported to have claimed it was only communicating orders from SCAP. Dismissal orders were then approved by local school boards either on the grounds that a particular teacher had been derelict of duty in refusing to follow regulations or, more simply, that the school district needed to reduce its staff. The total teachers purged in this way reached over 1,000.[50]

The outbreak of war in Korea in 1950 fueled these fires, provoking MacArthur to immediately ban over a hundred Japanese communist publications and to bar two dozen key party leaders from politics. In an official letter to Prime Minister Yoshida Shigeru, MacArthur explained the need for censorship:

> The international forces with which the Japan Communist Party is publicly affiliated have assumed an even more sinister threat to the preservation of peace and supremacy of the rule of law in democratic society. . . . In these circumstances, it becomes obvious that the free and unrestricted use of the media of public information for the dissemination of propaganda to such an ends by a minority so dedicated in Japan would be a travesty upon the concept of press freedom.[51]

The same logic had been used by the Yoshida Shigeru cabinet in outlawing the communist-led National Liaison Council of Japanese Trade Unions in August 1949. One month earlier, the government had carried out a massive retrenchment for economic reasons in the national railroads, firing 65,000 workers but placing alleged communists and other union organizers first on the list. This action stimulated over 500 private companies to carry out their own purges, firing an estimated 10,000 individuals.[52]

Expanding the System

In the eyes of SCAP, overcentralization of authority and ultranationalist values were only two-thirds of the set of ills that had afflicted the prewar Japanese school system. The report of the 1946 U.S. Education Mission had made clear the view that

> The Japanese system of education in its organization and curricular provisions would have been due for reform in accordance with modern theories of education even if they had not injected into it ultra-nationalism and militarism. The system was based on a nineteenth century pattern which was highly centralized, providing one type of education for the masses and another for the privileged few.[53]

Thus the existing system was also deemed elitist.

By elitist, the Occupation referred to two crucial features: (1) the small percentage of females who received an equal secondary education and (2) the tiny percentage of youth of either gender who had access to higher education. Article 3 of the 1947 Fundamental Law of Education quite emphatically made equality of opportunity a major goal:

The people shall all be given equal opportunities of receiving education according to their abilities, and they shall not be subject to educational discrimination on
account of race, creed, sex, social status, economic position, or family origin. The
state and local public bodies shall take measures to give financial assistance to
those who have, in spite of their ability, difficulty in receiving education for economic reasons.[54]

The CI&E was quite explicit about attacking the gender discrimination of
the existing system by altering policy toward postelementary schooling for females. Girls needed courses in home economics—"as every girl expects to be a
homemaker"—but females were also to be given the type of education that
would prepare them for "further specialized study and future jobs—law, medicine, science, etc."[55]

The 6-3-3 System

The 1946 U.S. Education Mission put forth some specific recommendations to
achieve greater equality of opportunity. These began with the lengthening of
compulsory schooling. Under the School Education Law of March 1947, all
Japanese became obligated by law to attend school through the ninth grade—
six years of primary and three years of middle school. By 1950 there were
14,000 such schools, with over 5,300,000 students.

This extension of compulsory schooling was not one of the more radical
changes. A steadily increasing percentage of Japanese primary school graduates
already had been going on to secondary schooling in the decades prior to the
war, and by 1940 28 percent of males and 22 percent of females were doing so.
Moreover, the Japanese government itself probably would have implemented
an eight-year minimum except for the war. The postwar system did, however,
replace the multiple tracks of the prewar system with comprehensive middle
schools into which all students, male and female, were to be tracked. Coeducational public high schools with three-year "comprehensive" curricula were an
even greater innovation, although these were not compulsory and there continued to be other tracks for those desiring to go on beyond middle school.

The objective of the comprehensive high school was "to ensure 'equality of
educational opportunity,' since it did not require a career choice early in the
student's schooling," in contrast to the prewar system that had "locked their
students into fixed career choices early in their lives in a 'multi-track' system."[56]
SCAP advocated "small" secondary school districts within cities large enough
to have more than one public high school. The ideal was to give each middle
school graduate an opportunity to attend a high school that offered a wide
array of curricula, including college prep. Moreover, if students' choices were
limited to the high school in their district, the logic went, no longer would
there be the steep hierarchy among schools. At the end of the Occupation
about half of the nation's public high schools were within such small districts

and the majority were offering a blend of academic and vocational subjects.[57] The total enrollment in 1950, however, was under 2 million, as many families were either unable or unwilling to send the children beyond compulsory education. Males still outnumbered females two to one.

The overall goal was to build what was referred to as a 6-3-3 system—six years in primary school, three in middle school, and three in high school. The course of study in the universities would be extended from three to four years, following the U.S. model (see Figure 6.1). There were major obstacles to achieving these goals. As a physical system, public schooling had been severely battered by the war. Thirteen percent of all school buildings had been destroyed. Many others, perhaps the majority, were in substandard condition because of the inability during the war years to carry out routine maintenance. Added to these shortcomings in plant facilities was the fact that the purge by the Occupation and postwar economic problems had combined to drive teachers by the tens of thousands out of the profession. Many of those remaining were almost as ill prepared for the ideological shifts in curricula as their Tokugawa counterparts had been in 1868.

To absorb the 50 percent more students created by the extension of compulsory education, schools were forced to institute double and even triple shifts. As late as 1954 almost a third of elementary school children were attending in shifts because of lack of adequate facilities. To provide them with teachers, the reformers compromised. The 1949 Teachers' Certification Law set new requirements that fundamentally altered the old normal school arrangements. Henceforth all new public school teachers would need a diploma from a four-year college. Temporarily a certificate from a two-year college would be accepted

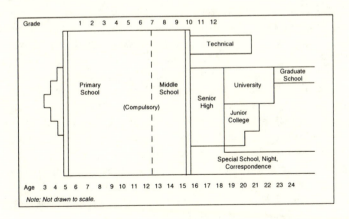

FIGURE 6.1
Main Tracks in Schooling, 1948.
Source: Adapted from Monbushō, *Gakusei 80 nenshi.*

and all teachers with ten years of service who had survived the Occupation purges were permitted to continue.[58]

Higher Education

Higher education was no less a concern for these reformers. Facilities at as many as one-third of the over 400 institutions of higher education had been destroyed or very heavily damaged by the bombing raids. Simply rebuilding prewar facilities, however, would not meet the needs of the nation. What was needed was "that the right of access of students to higher educational institutions should be broadened. . . . That the number of colleges and universities should be increased."[59] What the reformers had in mind was a complete reorganization along the lines familiar in the contemporary United States. Existing universities would become four-year institutions, recategorizing their third-year curriculum as graduate study and adding two years of lower-division work in general education for graduates of the new three-year high schools. Existing higher schools could either upgrade themselves into four-year institutions or move down to become three-year upper secondary or high schools for middle school graduates. Some of these with too narrowly designed curricula could merge with others to produce more comprehensive facilities.

The reformers recognized that orderly change without central mechanisms would be very difficult or even impossible and recommended "that a government agency should be responsible of approving the initial establishment of higher institutions, . . . but that once established such institutions should be free to pursue their objectives independent of government control."[60] An All-Japan University Council was appointed in May 1947. The chartering of universities was delegated to a University Chartering Committee created in January 1948. The committee was to apply standards recommended by the University Accreditation Association, a body formally independent of the government. The University Chartering Committee was made up of twenty-two members nominated by the University Accreditation Association, thirteen from the most recently accredited institutions, five from the government, and five lay persons. Only three of the forty-five were Education Ministry officials.

A total of 98 universities were chartered in 1948 and 1949: 12 private schools, 68 national, and 18 public schools at the prefectural or municipal level.[61] The total number reached 201 in 1950, enrolling over 205,000 males and 16,759 females in their regular programs.

One of the unsuccessful reform proposals was the SCAP plan to decentralize control over the old imperial universities by placing them under prefectural authority, as with the U.S. system of state schools. There was even a plan to introduce the U.S. system of university regents or trustees. When the Yoshida cabinet dutifully drafted a bill along these lines in late 1948, faculty and administrators joined Zengakuren students from scores of schools to close their classrooms and demonstrate in the streets. SCAP soon allowed the Yoshida cabinet to withdraw the bill.[62]

In 1949 CI&E offered yet another possibility for existing schools: to be reclassified as two- or three-year junior colleges or "short-term universities." This entirely new type of institution was meant as a solution for the problems faced by the hundreds of technical and vocational schools that did not fit easily into the three-year high school or four-year university pattern. They would supposedly expand their curricula to add courses in postsecondary general education as well as technical subjects. The following year 149 schools were put in this category, with 8,222 male students and 5,617 females.

Women's Schooling

More radical than any of these reforms were the measures aimed at closing the gender gap at the secondary and postsecondary levels. The Education Ministry had issued a New General Plan for Female Education Reform aimed at "reform[ing] female education with a view to giving equal opportunity of receiving education for men and women; raising female education to the level of men's education; and furthering mutual respect among men and women."[63] But the ministry also left considerable room for waffling, stating in February 1947, "But in determining whether this principle be adopted or not, opinions of the inhabitants of the cities, towns and villages within the limits of the attendance area should be respected." It was even less enthusiastic about coeducation in the high schools.[64]

Two of the national public universities were the former Tokyo Higher Normal School (renamed Ochanomizu Women's University) and Nara Women's Higher Normal School. These became women's universities, not being made coeducational although the former men's higher normal schools were. Five other private colleges for women only were chartered in 1948.

Conclusion

The American Occupationaires and their Japanese allies performed Herculean tasks in the first few years after the war. Still, most of the principles underlying their reforms were not totally new in Japan. Significant numbers of Japanese families had been choosing for decades to send their children beyond the six-year compulsory education minimum; raising that to nine years was not in itself revolutionary. There were even signs that females were making some progress in the school system prior to the Occupation. Even forms of decentralization complete with local school boards had been experimented with in the 1870s. Similarly, the postwar procedures for certification of textbooks rather than government publication had precedent in the Meiji period prior to

1904. It can even be argued that the liberalism ordered into the postwar text-books echoed some early Meiji values, although it is more plausible to point out that the extreme forms of ultranationalism and militarism being replaced dated only from the 1930s.

But it would be a serious mistake to cite such facts with the intent of depreciating the revolutionary character of what was attempted by these SCAP reforms. The real issue was the one raised increasingly after the end of the Occupation: Could the U.S. school system be transplanted into the Japanese environment? Certainly there were sceptics among Western as well as Japanese observers from the very outset. British criticism was particularly trenchant although not necessarily stated publicly. Officials in the British Foreign Office declined to "waste our energies on this sort of 'missionary' enterprise" and some even suggested that the prewar "ideological chauvinism" in Japan would not have been so extreme "if the Americans and ourselves had not so assiduously attempted to foist Christianity and Western culture on the Japanese." In this perspective, British foreign relations with Japan would be best served by waiting for the Japanese "reaction against too much Americanization" that would inevitably follow because the Americans "will be unable to refrain from ramming their pet ideas down the throats of the Japanese."[65]

There were also those among the Americans who took part in the reforms who did not believe that the reforms did not go far enough to win in what one called "the greatest educational experiment—and gamble—of our times."[66] Certainly some of the ground won by the liberals under the Occupation was to be lost in the political warfare of the next two decades.

7

Warfare Waged Between the Entrenched: 1950–1969

One may well ask whether policies which had emerged from the experience of professional education in American culture could invariably be the most effective ones to introduce into a tradition so different as that of Japan and whether, if introduced, they could take root without modification.

—Professor John W. Hall[1]

No Japanese institution in the postwar period has experienced more political conflict than public education. . . . [It has been] the kind of warfare waged between the entrenched German and Allied forces in World War I . . . [in which] many years of heated but indecisive battles have led to a stalemate but no general truce.

—Professor Thomas Rohlen[2]

Spring 1950 ushered in a new era for East Asia as a whole and for Japan in particular. The Cold War between the two postwar superpowers, the USSR and the United States, broke out into full-fledged combat in Korea and spurred negotiations leading to the San Francisco Peace Treaty in September 1951. This formally terminated the Allied Occupation of Japan in April 1952. Accompanying these developments were the first steps toward rearmament and an anticommunist military alliance with the United States. As result, during the 1950s Japan was repeatedly racked by mass demonstrations against the ruling Liberal Democratic Party and its close alliance with the United States—part of a long, concerted movement that eventually led in spring 1960 to the cancellation of a state visit by President Dwight D. Eisenhower and the resignation of Prime Minister Kishi Nobusuke. What most surprised many foreign observers at the time was the prominent role played in this campaign by young students from

Japan's elite universities and by middle-aged teachers from elementary schools who arrayed themselves alongside blue-collar workers in the often violent confrontations with Japanese police and U.S. marine guards.

The foreign policy disagreements were only part of the political turmoil. Educational policy was among a number of key domestic issues contested by the two camps. Not unlike school desegregation and busing in the United States, the educational reforms of the Occupation became the focus of broader power struggles and ideological controversies all the more fiercely fought because they involved families at the local level as well as leaders at the national level. The most significant of these battles at the precollegiate level were about such questions as who had the authority to determine curriculum? how were educational standards to be maintained? who was to select the textbooks? where was the proper place of morals in the curriculum? and more specifically, what should children be taught about the nature of Japanese society and its relations with the rest of the world, past and present? The lack of consensus on these questions led to hostile encounters on several fronts using a variety of weaponry in election campaigns, court contests, labor strikes, and mass media debates.

For the sake of clarity, these battles will be analyzed separately and not necessarily in chronological order. Yet it should be kept in mind throughout that they were integral parts of a single war being waged more or less simultaneously on several fronts. It should also be noted that through the 1950s and well into the 1960s Japan was still in the process of recovering economically from the devastation of the war. The Japanese "miracle" was not recognizable until the late 1960s. Finally, it is important to realize that these events took place prior to the U.S. defeat in the Vietnam War. All of these factors colored the political struggles in education as much as in other spheres.

The Warring Camps

The two warring camps that emerged from the Occupation period have most often been characterized as Conservatives and Progressives: That is, on the one side, the Liberal and Democratic parties, successors to the prewar Seiyūkai and Minseitō; and, on the other side, the Left, a loose alliance between Marxist and non-Marxist groups. The first part of this chapter is devoted to examining the most important of these belligerents in the conflict over education.

The Conservative Establishment

The Liberals and Democrats who merged in 1955 have usually been referred to as "Conservatives," although we shall see ways in which this label can be misleading if misunderstood as parallel to contemporary U.S. or British usage. Missing from the Japanese Liberal Democratic Party have been two key principles dear to Anglo-American conservatives of recent decades—antagonism to government intervention in the marketplace and commitment to local control over local affairs. Neither have characterized the views of Japanese conservatives in the postwar era. What the Japanese Conservative camp has shared with conservatives elsewhere in the world has been a commitment to anticommunism and a willingness to be allied with the United States in the Cold War.

Despite the original U.S. intent, the Education Ministry survived the Occupation largely intact. Like the rest of the central bureaucracy, this ministry then and now is staffed by professionals who enter the civil service after graduation from college and typically spend their whole careers within it. Although the top post of minister is a cabinet office, it is filled by an appointee chosen by the majority party in the House of Representatives. The average tenure of the nineteen appointments between 1960 and 1970 was just over eleven months. By contrast, the vice-minister and his fellow senior bureaucrats do not lose their posts merely because of cabinet changes.

Nor does the Education Ministry merely implement policy made elsewhere. Like other ministries, it is charged with crucial policy research, and in the 1950s and 1960s at least, conservative politicians depended heavily upon ministry bureaucrats for leadership in policy formulation. Even the advisory committees that were intended to augment the ministry typically drew a third to a half of their membership from among bureaucrats or ex-bureaucrats, albeit not necessarily all from the Education Ministry.[3] Such advisory committees were also means of linking the central bureaucracy with officials and administrators at the prefectural and local levels.

The supporters of the Liberal Democratic Party included intellectuals in the center as well as to the right. That is, in contrast to the Marxists and the "Progressive liberals" who supported the opposition parties, the Conservatives have often had the support of intellectuals whom I will label here "moderates" or "moderate conservatives" though others have labeled them "old liberalists" or "democratic conservatives." The point of any such labels is merely to distinguish them from their sometime allies among the ultranationalists even more to the right.[4]

We have already met some of these moderate conservatives because of the important political roles they played during the Occupation: for example, Tokyo University professors Tanaka Kōtarō and Nanbara Shigeru. Others were members of the Culture Study Group formed to advise Prime Minister Yoshida Shigeru on educational affairs. The core of this association was formed by academics: For example, Abe Yoshishige, minister of education in 1946, served as president of Gakushūin University; Koizumi Shinzō was former president of Keiō University as well as tutor to the crown prince; Takahashi Seiichirō, who served as Yoshida's minister of education in 1947, was emeritus professor of economics at Keiō; and Watsuji Tetsurō, Education Ministry adviser on history textbooks in the immediate postwar period, was a retired Tokyo University philosopher. They, like Yoshida himself, had opposed the Japanese military on occasion, but unlike the Progressive intellectuals, they were not identified with the prewar social democratic movement.

Other moderately conservative intellectuals served on the Central Council on Education, created in June 1952 to replace the Educational Reform Council organized under the Occupation. This policy advisory board attached to the Education Ministry was composed of academics and school administrators with a small number of seats reserved for journalists and businessmen. Morito Tatsuo and Rōyama Masamichi, whom we have met in their roles as academic victims of right-wing attacks in the prewar period, were among the more important council members in the 1960s.[5] All were anticommunists, although they did not necessarily agree on other political issues. For instance, Nanbara and Abe Yoshishige had advocated the abdication of Emperor Hirohito in favor of his son, thereby acknowledging war guilt but preserving the monarchy. Abe then became a member of the Peace Problems Symposium, which in the late 1950s helped lead the attack on the military alliance with the United States. On the other side, active in the attempt to rally popular opinion in favor of that alliance were well-known professors from such universities as Hitotsubashi, Keiō, Nihon, Tokyo, and Waseda.[6]

The "Progressive" Opposition

Opposition to the Liberal-Democrats came primarily from left-of-center liberals and socialists. In the parliament until the late 1980s, this camp has been represented by one large and several smaller parties: from left to center on the political spectrum, the small Japan Communist Party (JCP), the much larger Japan Socialist Party (JSP), and at any given time one or more splinter parties, most notably the Democratic Socialist Party. The Communist Party in the late 1960s counted as many as 15,000 schoolteachers as members as well as 10,000 to 15,000 students.[7] The relations between these three parties have vacillated greatly over the years, sometimes making common cause but at other times quite at odds. By the late 1960s, the two socialist parties were most often rejecting alliances with the communists in favor of arrangements with the new Clean Government Party. The ideological stance of this party, founded in the 1960s with the support of a large neo-Buddhist organization, has been less predictably left of center but typically opposed to the Liberal-Democrats.

The Progressive camp outside of the parliamentary parties has counted on the labor union movement—especially the Japan Teachers' Union—as well as various intellectual groups and a radical student organization. The main organization representing schoolteachers continued to be the Japan Teachers' Union—usually abbreviated Nikkyōso in Japanese or JTU in English. Over a half million strong at its peak with upwards of three-quarters of all elementary and junior high school instructors as members, this militant union has been a powerful player in postwar Japan politics. At times its influence has been felt far beyond educational issues, especially in the 1950s and 1960s. Although the JTU was a professional association concerned with promoting the goals of an interest group, it was also simultaneously part of a political movement dedicated to altering fundamental national policies by ousting the ruling party. As the second largest union in the General Council of Japanese Trade Unions, it provided critical support to the Japan Socialist Party. In return, JTU leaders have functioned as the major influence on the policies toward education of this Socialist Party. From time to time in this period, the union was independently strong enough to select and elect its own candidates to the national Diet albeit usually on the Socialist Party ticket. Hence the JTU ranked among the world's most powerful teachers' unions in this period.[8]

However, its place within the Progressive camp severely limited its direct influence on cabinet decisionmaking, Diet legislation, or Education Ministry administration. The political activism of Japan Teachers' Union members also on occasion cost the union much public sympathy, as in the 1949 elections, when some 150 Tokyo teachers were dispatched to the homes of their students to distribute Japan Communist Party campaign literature.[9]

In large part because of such activities, SCAP allowed and even urged the Liberal-Democrats in parliament to strip the union of the legal rights gained in the early years of the Occupation. Amendments in 1948 to existing legislation and the passage of a new Local Public Service Law in 1950 reversed earlier legislation that had permitted them to bargain collectively or even strike. Under the provisions of this 1950 law the JTU even lost its official status as a national labor union. The Education Ministry thereafter refused to recognize it as a legitimate bargaining agent and the teachers' movement became legally a mere collection of "personnel organizations" of public servants functioning only on the prefectural and local levels. Such "negotiations" as were sanctioned by the 1950 law therefore could take place only with prefectural school boards or town and village officials. Yet because of the central government's role in setting salary standards and providing funding for local school systems that were only nominally independent, it has seldom been possible to settle economic grievances satisfactorily at the prefectural or community levels. Moreover, it has been primarily the cabinet and the Education Ministry rather than local school boards or prefectural officials who have taken the offensive in heavily partisan campaigns to reform the curriculum, textbook selection procedures, student achievement testing, and teacher efficiency evaluations.

If the legal status of the union has been somewhat ambiguous over the years, the political stance of its leaders has been far less so. Union leadership oscillated between socialist-oriented "moderates" and communist-supported "extremists," but almost always both have agreed on the need to make common cause in the national arena to combat the steady trend toward consolidation of power in the hands of the central government. Although it could be argued that this centralizing trend merely parallels recent educational history in other industrial nations (including even the United States), in the eyes of the Progressives it has been seen as a reversal of American Occupation efforts at democratization, thus a setback to Japanese modernization and even a return to the "fascism" of the 1930s. The Conservative response was to denounce the union as under the control of communists. In the words of Araki Masuo, minister of education between 1960 and 1963, "These communist members are trying to work up a revolution by brainwashing the good teachers and children. . . . There is no choice but to get rid of the Union in order to pass on to the generations to come our culture and virtues developed through the efforts of our forefathers."[10]

In addition to the JCP, the left wing of the JSP, and the labor unions that supported them, through much of the postwar era there was a very active radical student movement organized by the Zengakuren, the All-Japan Federation of Students' Self-Government Associations (see Table 7.1).

There were a number of significant similarities in the student movements of the prewar and the postwar eras in terms of basic ideology, patterns of organization, and political techniques. Moreover, the prewar and postwar movements seem to have attracted roughly the same type of student in terms of such attributes as above-average socioeconomic background and high individual intelligence. Studies of the membership of this organization at its height in the 1960s indicate that many moved toward opposition to the status quo while still in secondary school.[11]

However, the Zengakuren was far more successful in playing an important role in the politics of the postwar environment than its prewar counterparts. Like the leaders of the teachers' union, the leadership of this student group conceived their role quite broadly. Although not neglecting such campus issues as tuition and physical facilities, the Zengakuren took a very active part in challenging the government on its policies toward schooling in general, joining in

TABLE 7.1
Zengakuren Membership Estimates, 1950–1960

	Proportion of Campuses with Affiliated Organizations (%)	Proportion of All Students (%)
1950	27	na
1952	11	6
1956	na	30
1958	22	44
1960	na	42

na = not available
SOURCE: Calculated from Shimbori, "The Sociology of a Student Movement," p. 308.

protests against textbook screening, teacher evaluations, and recentralization of administrative power. University students were also active on domestic controversies and especially effective in mass demonstrations against the foreign alliance with the United States against the communist Soviet Union and China.

Throughout the 1950s and 1960s, Japanese college students of both genders reportedly overwhelmingly favored the left-wing political parties in opposition to the government. A 1957 survey at the elite Tokyo University, for example, showed 50 percent of males and 59 percent of females supporting the Japan Socialist Party with only 11 percent and 5 percent respectively choosing the Liberal-Democrats.[12] The number of students in campus organizations once affiliated with the national Zengakuren is estimated as high as 300,000. Another measure of its influence is the numbers of students who took part in street demonstrations and other mass confrontations with the police in the 1959–1960 struggles against the renewal of the military alliance with the United States. The Zengakuren plan called for mobilizing as many as 10,000 for the dramatic storming of the Diet building in November 1959, and although it is not clear how many actually showed up, Zengakuren students were the core of the 1,000 or so who ultimately forced their way into the Diet compound. About 13,000 students also took part in an April 1960 demonstration, and on June 15, 1960, as many as 4,000 students made it into the compound of the Diet building in a bloody melee that killed one female student. This incident is credited with finally forcing the Kishi cabinet to cancel the state visit of President Eisenhower.

In the years following this political victory, the Zengakuren was plagued with internal factionalism and external harassment by the authorities. Nevertheless, in the late 1960s college students again emerged as important participants in political warfare when the Vietnam War fueled another flare-up over the issue of Japan's alliance with the United States.

These opposition parties, unions, and the student movement all benefited from the support of a large number of prominent intellectuals, including many academics at leading universities. Some segments of the antigovernment camp have been described by an unsympathetic observer as "progressive intellectuals [who] proclaimed feelings of guilt for their prewar and wartime silence or collaboration; under the motto 'Never Again!' they attacked all conservative policies and governments, regarding themselves as jealous guardians of the new democracy." Even this commentator conceded, however, that the men he was criticizing constituted "an all-star cast of Japan's academic world."[13]

It must also be noted that some of the most prominent of these progressive intellectuals were academics who had firsthand experience of political persecution in the late 1930s because they had not remained silent. In the postwar environment they reemerged in positions of influence in the universities and used their new prestige on behalf of the Progressive cause. For example, the Christian Yanaihara Tadao was reinstated at Tokyo University and became its president; the Marxist Ōuchi Hyōe also returned to Tokyo University and then served as president of Hōsei University; and Sakisaka Itsurō, who was fired from Kyushu University in 1928, was also reinstated and became an influential postwar activist.

Ōuchi was a leading figure in the Peace Problems Symposium formed in 1948. This influential group included academics who served as presidents of such prestigious institutions as Ochanomizu Women's College, Peers College, Ritsumeikan University, and Tokyo University. In the 1959–1960 struggles against the military alliance with the United States, many more professors became active. One new organization formed in 1959, the Treaty Problems Research Association, had 2,000 members. Some organizations even joined in the front lines, as did the Association of Faculty Members and Students at Christian Schools for the Protection of Democracy, drawn from five Protestant schools in Tokyo including Aoyama Gakuin, International Christian University, and Tokyo Women's Christian University. Some sixty-five of the group were injured in the June 18, 1960, demonstration at the Diet building.[14]

The Battle Rejoined

Moral Conflict

At the same time, there was taking place within the school system new clashes over what to teach. These struggles between the Conservative and Progressive camps became particularly heated as the American Occupation ended. Within a month of the signing of the San Francisco Peace Treaty, a top Japanese government advisory council issued a set of "Recommendations Concerning Reforming the Educational System." This report signaled the onset of an increasingly vigorous Conservative counterattack when it stated, "By basing our system on that of a foreign country where conditions differ, and pursuing only ideas, we have incorporated into our system many undesirable elements."[15]

The more moderate Conservative camp view was expressed by a number of intellectuals in the 1950s, including some prominent Christians. Kyushu University education professor Hiratsuka Masunori, author of such works as *The Educational Philosophy of the Old Testament* and an influential member of the Education Ministry's Central Council on Education, reproached those who would "entirely condemn prewar education": "I do not say that education in prewar Japan was without fault [but]. . . . It is extremely unwholesome to condemn earlier ways of doing things in favor of creating totally new ways. Such action only produces confusion for the development of society and the state; unless a link with the past is maintained, no healthy development is possible for human society."

Hiratsuka also quoted approvingly the views of Tanaka Kōtarō, a former minister of education who was then serving as chief of the Supreme Court: "Although the Imperial Rescript on Education emphasized loyalty, patriotism and social obligation, it also expounded ethical qualities many of which are of a universal nature." The solution for Hiratsuka and others of his persuasion was simply to separate education from politics—whether in the form of excessive government direction or teachers' partisanship: "Educators must have insight and express opinions on politics, but from a plane higher than that on which politicians and businessmen operate."[16]

Thus, in one sense, the Japanese faced a perennial problem in all modern societies: how to teach moral values in a secular world. But as previously in modern Japanese history, the battle was equally over the underlying cultural question that had plagued Japanese politics for a century: To what degree could foreign elements be incorporated into Japan without threatening its cultural identity and continuity in its history?

Embedded in this question was an even more specific issue: how to explain the disastrous war to a new generation. Conservatives in the immediate postwar years frequently expressed their fear that defeat in the war had left the nation in a state of anomie. The prewar expression of Japan's national ethos had been discredited and there was not, as it was supposed to exist with Christianity in the West, a shared religious doctrine that could sustain morality in these dark days. The result was not only a breakdown in family values accompanied by an increase in antisocial behavior but also the end of patriotic love of country. As the end of the Occupation neared, their voices grew louder. The Education Ministry under the cabinets of Prime Minister Yoshida was increasingly straightforward in its intention to use the school system to reverse these ominous trends.

These intentions were clearly reflected in the two concrete measures being debated publicly in 1950 and 1951. The Conservative camp strongly advocated some sort of official statement to express a common ethical creed or national ethos that might serve as a "moral prop." Linked to this was their campaign to put back into the curriculum courses that would focus directly on the standards of ethical behavior. The Progressives saw these efforts as a thinly disguised plot to resurrect the obsolete Imperial Rescript on Education and the defunct morals courses of the prewar era. Minister of Education Amano Teiyū denied that either of these goals was part of the government's agenda but he did express support for a set of ethical principles that could be used as the basis for guidelines to teachers who dealt with moral issues in the existing curriculum.

In November 1951 a Japanese newspaper published what it claimed was a draft of "An Outline of Ethical Practice for the Japanese People" and identified it as authored by Minister of Education Amano. The document immediately drew vehement attacks. The general tone of its language, it was pointed out, was fraught with associations with prewar moral teachings. Objection was also made to some of its explicit assertions about freedom as merely the opposite of self-indulgence and about the Confucian conception of the family, alleged dangers of social change, the transcendental moral character of the state, and Japan's peculiar emperor-centered national polity. The following excerpts illustrate some of the more controversial motifs.

DRAFT
An Outline of Ethical Practice for the Japanese People

Section I. The Individual

. . .

2. Freedom: . . . True freedom lies in not being the slave of insensitive animal self-indulgence or impulsive desires. . . .

Section II. The Family

1. Husband and wife: Marriage is a beautiful *jinrin kankei* [moral relationship]. . . .
2. Parents and children: . . . In order that they may give place to their children and allow them to create the succeeding age, parents have the responsibility for ensuring healthy growth for their budding lives. And since creation is impossible except on the basis of tradition, respect and love for parents is the happy duty of every child.

. . .

Section III. Society

. . .

2. Common sense: In order that society may progress, we must be prepared to abandon meaningless old customs and to live always anew. But this must not lead to the superficiality which is ever following the fashion of the moment.

. . .

Section IV. The State

1. The State: . . . The State is the parent body of the individual; without the State there can be no individuals.

. . .

2. Tradition and Creation: This State has its own traditions, and if we are to create a new age, it must be firmly rooted in these traditions. . . .

. . .

6. The Emperor: We possess an Emperor who is the symbol of the State, wherein lies the peculiar nature of our *kokutai* [national polity]. It is the special characteristic of our country that there has always been an Emperor throughout its long history. The position of the Emperor partakes of the nature of a moral focus as the symbol of the State.
7. The ethics of the State. Morality is the lifeblood of the State. The State, in essence, is founded more deeply on its moral than on its political or economic character. The Emperor possesses an objective moral character. . . .[17]

The major Japanese newspapers—especially *Yomiuri* and *Asahi*—were editorially in the Progressive camp in the early 1950s and they led the media bombardment on the Education Ministry. *Yomiuri* headlined one of its stories "The Amano Outline: A Declaration of War on Democratization" and dismissed the ethical views of Minister Amano as merely a rehash of prewar combinations of German philosophy and Chinese Confucian notions justifying the dominance of the state over the individual. The "objective moral" role assigned to the emperor in Amano's "Outline" was disparaged both in theory and in practice since the people's affection for the throne had been politically manipulated by the right in the prewar era.

The House of Councilors Education Committee immediately conducted hearings on the issue. The Education Ministry responded by backing away from this effort, if only temporarily. Within a year it was requesting that its Curriculum Committee study the issue in order to make formal recommendations.

The opposition of the Japan Teachers' Union to such efforts was spelled out in the mid-1950s. It emphatically rejected the notion of a separate morals course because "morals education . . . should be conducted constantly at school, in the home, and in society, with full cooperation of teachers, parents, and the general public. Morals education would thus be conducted during the whole course of education. A special ethics course will not be established." The opposition also defined what values should be fundamental: "Morals in the new age should be based on an awareness of human rights, love of independence, the education of an individual imbued with the spirit of peace, democracy and international friendship, and on respect for an individual who possesses practical knowledge and techniques and who has awakened to the principles of science."[18]

In 1958 the Education Ministry issued a *Guide to Ethical Education,* which once again led to a storm of criticism over its prewar tone. Minister of Education Araki poured more fuel on the fire in the early 1960s by saying such things as "There is no choice but to get rid of the [Japan Teachers'] Union in order to pass on to the generations to come our culture and virtues developed through the efforts of our forefathers."[19]

But there were also intellectuals who came to the support of reinstating a morals course in the curriculum. Something of the flavor of the more right-wing reactions can be sampled in a 1953 magazine article entitled "Win Back the Students from the Reds!" Kitaoka Juishi, a college professor and adviser to a right-wing student organization, called for a renewed emphasis on morals coupled with the suppression of the communists regardless of their freedoms guaranteed in the constitution:

> The Japanese people, perhaps because they are deficient in culture, perhaps because their life is so hard, are apt to misuse the freedom that they have been

granted. When they are given the freedom to gamble, both adults and youth run amuck at bicycle-races and *pachinko* [pinball] parlours; when the control of morals is relaxed, the harlots shamelessly parade the streets; when censorship is abolished, the book-shops bury their counters with erotic magazines. It is doubtful whether such a people should in fact be granted too much freedom.[20]

Somewhat more restrained were the opinions of Ōshima Yasumasa, a professor of ethics at the Tokyo University of Education: "[The criticism of the Education Ministry] is not a responsible view because it incorrectly equates prewar moral education with postwar ethical education. Such an equation results from a lack of understanding of what ethical education consists of as defined by the Ministry of Education; it shows that certain historical developments are not understood."

For Ōshima, "Japan's prewar ethical concepts died with the nation's defeat in the war" and it was "not possible for a certain political party or even a minority of the nation's leaders to recreate the conditions that existed before the war." He denied that the Education Ministry's *Guide to Ethical Education* was in any way a return to the past. Indeed, the real concern was that because "moral education before the war . . . [made people] unable to judge things independently and to act accordingly," in the postwar period too many people "began to think of the Soviet Union and Communist China as utopias."[21] This political danger, not "the various forms of decadence such as juvenile delinquency and sexual laxity," were the long-run problems that required ethical teaching in the schools.

Honda Akira, a scholar of Western literature, was less quick to condemn the past or to treat juvenile delinquency so lightly:

> While moral education as taught before the war was feudalistic and placed too much emphasis on the relationship between superior and inferior, feudal ethics in themselves are not completely and totally wrong. One feudal ethic derived from Buddhist teachings is that it is wrong to kill. . . . Good relations among children, harmony between man and wife, kindness to friends, and consideration for the weak are moral concepts which would not be all out of place in the world today.

Like Kitaoka, Honda was particularly incensed about the left's misunderstanding of the concept of freedom: "Children demand such willful freedom, and it is considered in today's social climate to be undemocratic and even reactionary for parents and teachers to interfere in children's freedom. Good breeding and good moral education under these circumstances are not possible; children will just grow up to be rascals." What did that mean in behavioral terms? "The young today think they have the 'freedom' to strike teachers, to occupy two seats instead of one on streetcars and make the old people stand, to ignore traffic regulation and to race along on motorcycles and impose on the freedom of the pedestrian. Indeed, Japan is today a paradise of freedom!"[22]

Doubtless many ordinary citizens and parents found such arguments persuasive. Thus the opposition attempted to rebut arguments at this level. For example,

Professor Osada Arata, a former president of Hiroshima University and in 1958 the president of the Japan Pedagogical Society, wrote that

> according to [proponents of the morals courses], children have bad manners, speak impolitely, are egoistic and selfish, do not listen to their parents or teachers, are immodest and lack self-criticism and introspection. But the reason that the critics are making such an outcry is that they are measuring today's children with yesterday's yardstick. . . . The members of the older generation . . . are too quick to equate the idea of ethics with the outmoded forms of loyalty and filial piety pursued in the prewar period.

Although Osada, as a specialist in Pestalozzi, was an advocate of the importance of the home environment in shaping children, he was not opposed to ethics also being taught in the schools: "Students should be taught in school to develop the ability to decide independently about ethical problems that arise in their lives." The emphasis, however, should be on "independently," and he opposed "special courses which aim at cramming the students with ethical concepts and principles. . . . As morals were taught before the war, children were not permitted to think for themselves; they were taught to do just what the teacher told them."[23]

"Improper Control"

In addition to the controversy over the reinstitution of morals courses in primary and middle schools, the 1951 Education Ministry report also contained three other inflammatory recommendations. It called for tighter control over textbooks by the central government and the abolition of elections to fill local school boards. The 1951 Advisory Committee for the Reform of Government Ordinances also recommended multiple tracks at the middle school level to better prepare vocationally those students not going to high school. This view was endorsed the following year by the powerful Japan Federation of Employers' Associations in a statement entitled "Demand for Re-examining the New Educational System."[24] Taken as a whole, the report thus raised the twin specters of recentralization of control and the reintroduction of ultranationalism while simultaneously, in the view of the opposition, threatening to reinstate elitism in the secondary school system by creating inferior tracks.

The political momentum needed to deal with "undesirable" aspects of the SCAP reforms accelerated with the successful merger of the two Conservative parties in 1955. Kiyose Ichirō, minister of education in the third Hatoyama cabinet, explained the new Liberal Democratic Party's agenda for education in the following terms:

> The fundamental reforms of the education system carried out after the end of the war were epochal in the history of Japanese education and played a considerable role in educational development, but on the other hand, since the reforms were carried out hastily under the special conditions of the occupation, there are quite a few points at which they do not accord with reality.[25]

Thus the Conservatives once again opened fire on the issue of the distribution of power between the central, prefectural, and local governments: Was the Education Ministry primarily an advisory and coordinating agency or were its directives legally binding? If the latter, then what was the role of the local school boards?

In this controversy over who had legal authority over what in the school system, the primary focus was often on how to interpret the 1947 Fundamental Law of Education, especially Article 10: "School Administration: Education shall not be subject to improper control, but it shall be directly responsible to the whole people. School administration shall, on the basis of this realization, aim at the adjustment and establishment of the various conditions required for the pursuit of the aim of education."[26] The interpretation of this article favored by the Japan Teachers' Union, the Japan Socialist Party, and their supporters was summed up by Tokyo University education professor Munakata Seiya, who served on an advisory committee for the JTU:

> The new system . . . involved three principal reforms: the democratization of education, the decentralization of government control over education, and the freeing of the administration of education from the influence of politics. . . . The principal function of the administration of education is to arrange for external matters, such as physical facilities required by education and to draw up budgets . . . not [to] interfere internally by influencing the "aim of education" itself.[27]

Anything more would constitute "improper control."

This idea was unacceptable in the eyes of the Liberal Democratic Party and those of the professional staff within the Education Ministry. Their view was that the law empowered the central government to set policy for the school system as a whole and particularly in such matters as curriculum and standards. As asserted by one high-ranking Education Ministry official, Adachi Kenji,

> A part of providing the "various conditions required for the pursuit of the aim of education" involves a kind of education administration which sets standards for the content of curricula. . . . Therefore, [they are] wrong in saying that "the various conditions required" do not entail the government being involved in such *internal* matters as curricular content.[28]

But to those who resisted the state's power, the phrase "directly responsible to the whole people" meant that parents and teachers, not bureaucrats, should control the schools: "Decisions . . . must be made by those who have educational rights; those who possess educational rights are parents and children. . . . Educational rights which teachers possess are derived from the educational rights of children. The teacher represents culture and truth and the child has the right to inherit culture and to learn the truth."[29]

Adachi responded with the argument that because taxpayers were the source of the revenues that made public education possible, "the right to educate the student belongs to the whole of the people who have the right to express their views and make decisions on education." The members of the Diet, "who are representatives of the people of the country" enacted legislation reflecting those views and the prime minister and the minister of education, who administered those decisions, "bear their responsibility toward the whole of the people of the country."

Adachi further dismissed any claims that government involvement in such matters infringed upon the guarantees of academic freedom specified in the 1947 constitution:

> Academic freedom is something which should be enjoyed by people in institutions of higher learning. Free research and study is the public mission of university professors but not of primary and secondary school teachers. Their public mission is to impart fundamental knowledge to students. Primary and secondary school teachers may and probably should conduct free research and study but only as private individuals.[30]

Adachi did not address as clearly the counterargument that "to have the state decide on matters relating to our value system, or to be more concrete, on what the contents of a course on ethics should be, is in conflict with our Constitution which guarantees freedom of thought and conscience."[31]

Thus the two camps squared off. For the Conservatives on the right the 1947 law gave authority over education to the state, and the representative parliament then delegated the authority to administer the national school system to the Education Ministry. The phrase "improper control" meant that education should be politically neutral, free from partisan interference by political parties or labor unions or any other pressure group. For the liberals and the left, "improper control" meant domination by the state, which would violate the people's educational authority by denying the right of children to learn as well as the academic freedom of teachers and the freedom of expression of authors of teaching materials. By this logic the Education Ministry was therefore itself partisan and the Japan Teachers' Union called for "abolition of the position of minister of education, appointed by the prime minister representing a political party, and establishment of a Central Education Council whose members will be elected democratically. The Ministry of Education will be revised to become the Secretariat of the Central Education Council."[32]

Spokesmen for the postwar Conservative camp often argued that centralized government is "natural" for a culturally and racially homogeneous people who occupy a small geographical area. Some have gone so far as to assert, somewhat disingenuously since the reference is to an era of several hundred years, that centralized government is the historical tradition "except for a relatively short period of decentralized feudalism which, in the mind of many Japanese, represents a time of chaos." The failure to understand the differences in the historical traditions of the United States and Japan was what had led SCAP to ignore the need for what Kiyose Ichirō, minister of education in 1956, called clear "lines of command in the educational structure."[33]

Certainly the administrative chain of command that had emerged from the American Occupation was complex and at times quite tangled. The Ministry of Education was charged with oversight over the national school system as a whole but the 1946 U.S. Mission report had said that "the control of the instructional program should be more dispersed than at present; vertical lines of authority and responsibility should be definitely broken at certain levels of the system."[34] The 1949 Education Ministry Establishment Law had eliminated many of the prewar powers and functions, supposedly refocusing its activities toward advisory and coordinating roles rather than direct control.[35] By the terms of the 1948 Board of Education Law, the task of administrating the local primary and middle schools was supposed to be left to five-person local school boards of which four members were elected by the municipality or village and one appointed to represent the local assembly. By 1952 this pattern would be established in almost 10,000 communities across the nation.

At the regional level there were fifty-one prefectural and metropolitan boards of seven members each, six elected and one appointed by the prefectural assembly. These regional boards were directly responsible for the high schools as well as the certification of teachers and administrators throughout the prefecture and, in the case of the five largest cities, the metropolitan area. Local regional boards hired superintendents, principals, and teachers and authorized textbooks for their own primary and middle schools. Regional boards did this for high schools and certain special schools. Both drew up budgets, although funds came out of the general revenues and had to be authorized by the appropriate assembly.

As the struggle over who was to control the Japanese school system heated up, school boards were soon in the middle of the battlefield. When Minister of Education Kiyose Ichirō called for clearer "lines of command in the educational structure," what he really meant in the view of many was that the candidates of the Japan Teachers' Union were winning too many seats on the school boards—up to a third by the 1950s. Although they were required to resign their teaching positions if elected, it was nevertheless seen as a problem even by the Second U.S. Education Mission of 1950, which had expressed concern about the influence of the Japan Teachers' Union on administration and suggested that the school boards set policy but leave implementation to the professional administrators.[36] For the Japanese Conservatives a more drastic solution was needed, and they sought first to reduce the independence of these school boards by abolishing elections.

The Hatoyama cabinet dangled the carrot of increased central funding to badly strapped local governments, suggesting that it might increase the central government's share of the budget for teachers' salaries from 50 percent to 100 percent. In return, it insisted on assurances that the schools were being competently managed. In the Conservative view, elections could never produce competent school boards if for no other reason than because schoolteachers were eligible.[37] For heads of local government, there was also the carrot of increased patronage since it would be they who would select the members of the reformed boards. Perhaps in part because of these carrots, the proposal to reform school boards gained a majority among two influential groups of elected officials—the Association of Prefectural Governors and the Association of Municipal Heads. The two groups did not fully endorse a return to the centralized administration of the prewar period, but they did condone the reduced independence for the school boards in two ways. First they urged that elections be dropped in favor of appointment by the governors (at the prefectural level) and mayors (at the municipal level). Second, they argued for consolidating the heretofore separate budgetary functions into the general budgetary procedures of the prefectures or municipalities. These two changes were part of a bill—Law Concerning the Organization and Management of Local Educational Administration—submitted to the parliament in 1956 by the Hatoyama cabinet. This bill also included provision for ministerial nullification of school board actions in certain circumstances. Simultaneously the Hatoyama cabinet introduced a bill to require primary and middle school textbooks to be certified by the Education Ministry before being purchased with public funds. Both bills were highly controversial and touched off months of political conflict. Let us take them one at a time, beginning with the school board controversy.

Inside the parliament, the Hatoyama cabinet proposals were vehemently opposed by the Socialists and Communists. Holding only 36 percent of the seats in the lower house, the opposition resorted to a variety of blocking tactics. So violent did these parliamentary debates become that police actually entered the Diet building to restore order. Outside the parliament there was equally vigorous opposition. The Japan Teachers' Union, which had successfully used the election process to place many of its own candidates on local school boards, opposed revision. In this they were joined by the National Associations of Prefectural and Municipal Boards of Education and hundreds of academics on the university campuses. Tokyo University president Yanaihara, himself once driven from his professorship by political pressure in the 1930s, headed a list of two dozen major university presidents from the Tokyo and Osaka metropolitan regions who objected to the proposed strengthening of nonelected officials. The Zengakuren organization rallied an estimated 10,000 students in street demonstrations and perhaps a quarter of a million students in campus strikes that affected 150 schools.[38]

Since the new Liberal Democratic Party remained united on the question, however, it was able to use its majority to push the bill through the parliament in June 1956. Prefectural and Local Educational Committee members were thenceforth appointed rather than elected. As the opposition feared, this move has reduced the influence of the Progressive camp at this level, or at least where the governors and mayors were not in their camp. At the prefectural level, Conservative governors have often appointed former bureaucrats from the Education Ministry.[39] In cities such as Kobe, however, mayors have appointed distinguished lay persons who left most matters to the municipal Office of Education. This agency has been run mainly by professional educators recruited from the ranks of teachers, although they are not usually teachers who have been very active in union affairs. These administrators are in charge of such personnel matters as recruitment of new teachers and transfers as well as most negotiations with the union. They also oversee the work of school principals, who themselves have invariably been former teachers.[40]

One innovation from the Occupation years that continued into the post-Occupation era with undiminished vitality was the Parent-Teacher Associations. These ostensibly voluntary groups not only served to provide lay persons with input into school affairs but also served as an important training ground for community leaders.[41]

By the end of the Occupation, the Education Ministry could attempt to exert direct influence over what was taught within the classrooms of primary and secondary schools in two ways: by issuing curriculum guidelines and by screening textbooks. Until 1958, ministry curricular guidelines, entitled "Course of Study," were quite abstract and generally of less importance than the teachers' guides provided by the textbook publishers or the sample examinations for high school and college admissions.[42] Nevertheless, these first post-Occupation guidelines were met with fierce objections. In 1953 a group of education professors at Tokyo University sounded the tone that would be heard repeatedly over the next decades when they asserted that "the Government's suggestion that the Social Studies course should be reconstructed appears to us to conceal extremely dangerous intentions. . . . It is not a Social-Studies course that they want, but a State-Studies course. . . . These are nothing more nor less than the educational ideals of Fascism."[43]

Not until 1958 did the Education Ministry make these guidelines part of the mandatory criteria for the textbook selection and only then did the government have a truly effective means of enforcing its will on curriculum. Thus the first attempts to roll back key SCAP reforms focused initially on school textbooks, especially those in use in the social studies classes, which the Conservatives alleged were often little better than propaganda media for the Progressive camp. The procedure that had been instituted by the Education Ministry in 1950 to replace the Occupation system had centered on an appointed advisory Textbook Certification Investigations Council, which received reports on proposed textbooks from panels of part-time "investigators."[44] This textbook council was originally composed of sixteen members and was nominally only advisory to the minister. More than 600 investigators, part-time teachers or others with expertise, were assigned to subject panels in groups of five to read each proposed textbook. Once cleared by this certification process, the textbook was placed on a list from which selections were made at the local level, most often by groups of teachers. In 1955 the new Liberal Democratic Party fired its first salvo in the form of a pamphlet entitled "The Problem of Deplorable Textbooks." It denounced the Japan Teachers' Union for disseminating communist ideology disguised as democratic values.

This was followed by a Textbook Bill aimed at giving the Education Ministry much more control over textbooks.

The 1956 Textbook Bill failed in the Diet, but the ministry went ahead to make a number of substantial changes that it claimed did not require new legislative action. The 1956 replacement of the elected school boards gave the Education Ministry a further excuse to tighten its textbook certification procedures. The Textbook Council was expanded to eighty, in part at least to place more right-minded bureaucrats on it. Forty ministry employees were now appointed as full-time internal "examiners" who filled two places on each of the five reader panels. The remaining three readers were external to the ministry and served part-time; two of these three were still to be drawn from the ranks of teachers in service. The panels were collectively to report on whether the work met the "Absolute Conditions," which included a ban on any religious or political bias. But the Education Ministry also tightened up its criteria when it instructed the panels to evaluate accuracy, balance, originality, suitability of content, and other aspects of the drafts. Then the panels were to suggest or demand revisions before finally advising the minister on whether to reject or to certify. After 1957 schoolteachers no longer had as much input into the selection, as the new appointed education committees exercised more control over this process.

The selection process at the local level was altered again in 1963, this time by parliamentary action. The occasion now was the undertaking on the part of the central government to provide free textbooks throughout the compulsory grades. The nation was carved up by population into 458 Regional Unified Selection Districts, often cutting through prefectural and local school board boundaries. Sometimes there was only one selection district to a prefecture, as in the case in Aomori, but sometimes there were dozens, as in the case of Tokyo. The relevant local Education Committees together appointed a Unified Selection District Council, which in turn relied upon anonymous experts to decide on a single textbook for each course for all the schools in the Unified Selection District (see Figure 7.1).

Thus, although all schools in a Unified Selection District adopted the same texts, different districts could and did use different ones. For example, Ienaga Saburō's senior high textbook, *A New History of Japan*, published by the Sanseido Company, was a best-seller in Tokyo, Osaka, Fukushima, Nagano, and Hokkaido, where the Education Committees were either weak or more liberal. But the book was seldom selected in more conservatively oriented prefectures such as Toyama, Wakayama, or Kagawa.

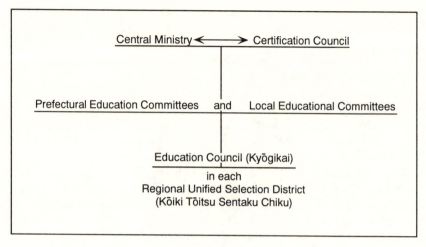

FIGURE 7.1
Certification of Textbooks

Intellectuals and others once again made common cause with the Japan Teachers' Union in opposition to this system of textbook selection. The newspaper *Asahi* editorialized as early as 1952 about the Education Ministry's bias against "all facts . . . that might injure the prestige of 'The Great Japanese Empire'" and warned, "Is this the first sign that all our efforts since 1946 to bring about a fundamental change in the teaching of history in schools is going to be all in vain, and that history is to go back to it prewar form?"[45] Beginning in 1965 the JTU established its own system by which it has regularly published reviews of textbooks in an attempt to influence the profession. It also supported a series of court battles in an attempt to challenge the government on constitutional grounds.

Perhaps the most famous history textbook in modern Japanese history has been Ienaga Saburō's *A New History of Japan*, although its fame has been due less to the number of people who actually read the work than to the number who heard about it because of almost thirty years of courtroom litigation. In June 1965, after many months of negotiations over several hundred separate passages in the scheduled revision of this 400-page text, Professor Ienaga brought the first of three suits against the Education Ministry.

While this first civil suit was still in Tokyo District Court, Ienaga filed an administrative suit in June 1967 to force the restoration of six passages in the book that he had originally agreed to alter under threat of loss of certification. Some of these objections dealt with Ienaga's treatment of Japanese mythology as mere political propaganda constructed by an ancient elite seeking to legitimize imperial rule. The Education Ministry held that Ienaga failed to give appropriate weight to ancient texts as historical sources as well as violated the principles laid down in the ministry curriculum guide for history, which stated that a goal of history courses should be "to cultivate an attitude of intimate respect for and deepen their understanding of the arts, religion, thought and learning in our nation's cultural heritage." Ienaga's lack of respect for the imperial house in later periods was also criticized.[46] In a related complaint, the ministry even demanded that he remove the captions "People as the Mainstay of History" from the four illustrations of "the working masses" used to open each historical period.

A second more general complaint was that "the overall tone [was] too negative" and Ienaga should remove some of the more graphic illustrations, such as those of people suffering in war.[47]

Third, there were specific problems about war guilt. Some were quite narrowly focused. For example, Ienaga had described the 1941 Russo-Japanese Neutrality Pact as a Japanese strategy to open the way to move south and invade Southeast Asia. The Education Ministry insisted on adding a sentence to indicate that the USSR had initiated the negotiations. More general objections were raised to Ienaga's language in explaining how the war began because "from a worldwide perspective, it is too harsh to affix blame on only Japan." The officials were even more adamant about references to atrocities: "If atrocities by Japanese troops are described, similar actions by Soviet forces should also be included or the text will be biased. And what about the Americans?"[48]

Ienaga argued that these changes were part of a government effort to protect the imperial throne, refocus history on rulers rather than common people, and shift blame for aggression.[49] More fundamentally, Ienaga's suit contended that the textbook certification system as a whole violated the children's constitutionally guaranteed educational rights, an author's freedom of thought and expression, as well as his and the schoolteacher's right of academic freedom. He further argued that this system was in violation of Article 10 of the 1947 Fundamental Law of Education, which, in his interpretation, had taken decision-making authority on textbooks away from the central ministry and given it to the teachers. Ienaga therefore demanded an end to the existing selection procedures as well as damages for lost royalties and mental distress.

In the early stages of these legal battles, the suit received great attention in the mass media as dozens of prominent experts were called by each side to testify on the accuracy and balance of Ienaga's treatment of history. The government spokespersons responded that the parliament had in the 1947 School Education Law charged the Education Ministry with the authority to approve all textbooks before selection by the local school authorities. In this view there was nothing unconstitutional or illegal about its procedures for carrying out its mandate.

As is typical in modern Japan, the wheels of the judiciary ground slowly. The Tokyo District Court did not hand down its ruling on the first suit until 1974.

Meanwhile, in 1970 the court had already reached a decision in the second Ienaga suit. In the so-called Sugimoto decision, the Tokyo District Court found the textbook screening system constitutional in theory but flawed in practice. Judge Sugimoto Ryōkichi held that educational rights did belong to the people, not the state, and that "the intervention of State authority must be vigorously averted." But he also found that it is society's obligation to arrange for the education that is each child's innate right. Therefore the parliament, representing the people, may legislate administrative arrangements to screen textbooks. Such screening is not necessarily censorship unless the government were to reject a work on ideological or philosophical grounds. Since the Education Ministry had indeed challenged Ienaga's theories and opinions, in this case the government had been guilty of censorship.

On the crucial point of textbook adoption and the academic freedom of public school teachers, the Sugimoto decision was more ambiguous. It held that the teacher is "on the one hand . . . the person bearing the official responsibility to fully nurture the right to learn; [but] at the same time the teacher bears a responsibility to accept the parent's and the People as a whole's ideas about education." Having said that, Judge Sugimoto went on to find that some matters must be left to the teacher, for whom "educational 'neutrality' is a personal responsibility . . . and its autonomy must be guaranteed."[50] The government immediately appealed to the Tokyo Higher Court, and five more years would pass while it pondered the Sugimoto decision.

Textbook screening was but one of several fronts upon which the war between the Liberal-Democrat government and the Japan Teachers' Union was fought in the 1950s and 1960s. Proposals to evaluate teachers' performance and test student achievement were other fields for pitched battle.

The purge of left-wing activists that had begun under the Occupation continued into 1950, provoking a hail of protest from liberals and leftists, a storm that was punctuated by student demonstrations on university campuses. Two such incidents in October 1950 were particularly notable, in part because they took place at elite universities and in part because both involved use of the police. Early in the month the well-known academic Nanbara Shigeru, acting as president of Tokyo University, called in the police to restrain some 2,000 students from disrupting the operations of the school. Nanbara was a proponent of central government intervention in prefectural and municipal universities as well, arguing that Japan's institutions of higher learning were all national in the sense that their students came from throughout the country.[51] Two weeks later an estimated 600 students at the private Waseda University stormed a meeting of the school's regents and were evicted only through force.

The main organizational network for such student action was the radical Zengakuren. Minister of Education Amano and the chief of the Metropolitan Police Board quickly announced that the government considered this association subversive and ordered it to be disbanded. Despite, or perhaps in part because of, these official threats, the Zengakuren continued throughout the 1950s and 1960s to mobilize thousands of young people in political demonstrations opposing conservative party policies. Although their tactics were primarily disruptive rather than truly violent in these decades, they received considerable media attention when, for example, a large contingency surrounded the emperor's vehicle in November 1951 and forced him to listen to them sing the "Communist International" as a means of protesting the military alliance with the United States.[52]

The government's response to student activism was not only to attempt to suppress it with police force but also to increase pressure on teachers whom it blamed for inculcating such subversive ideas in primary and middle schools. Its main weapon was a teachers' evaluations procedure by which local school administrators were encouraged to reward or punish their teachers on the basis of annual efficiency ratings.[53] It was first attempted in 1956 as part of a budget retrenchment in a remote school district facing fiscal difficulties.

Prefectural authorities temporarily backed off from the evaluation procedure in the face of hunger strikes by local union leaders but reinstituted it the following year. This time the newly elected Kishi cabinet announced that it was going to enforce nationally the eight-year-old Local Public Service Law of 1950: "The appointing authorities shall periodically evaluate the work performance of personnel and shall take such appropriate action as the result of evaluation may call for."[54]

Each principal was charged with filing an annual personnel report on each teacher. The form called for a five-point scale ranging from excellent to inferior in a number of categories, including the principal's assessment of how sincere, reliable, and cooperative a teacher had been. Not surprisingly, the Japan Teachers' Union rejected such judgments as overly subjective and largely irrelevant to effective classroom teaching. It claimed that the real purpose was to provide a rationale for punishing activists and undermining the union.

Tsuji Kiyoaki, a prestigious Tokyo University professor of political science, rebutted the arguments of the Education Ministry on three main points. First, the ministry's arguments about the 1950 Local Public Service Law mandating such ratings entirely ignored the fact that for eight years it was not so interpreted and no rating of teaching was deemed necessary. Equally disingenuous were ministry claims that rating would be left entirely in the hands of local officials; after all, the ministry intended to write the standards for the ratings. Third, and most important, was the failure of the ministry to make the crucial distinction between "objective efficiency," which was properly relevant to teaching performance, and "normative efficiency," which improperly focused on teachers' "personal sincerity, his [sic] regard for education, and the guidance he gives to students."[55]

The Japan Socialist Party was split on the issue but Prime Minister Kishi's Liberal-Democrats held firm in backing the Education Ministry. In September

1958, JTU leaders launched a counterattack by urging a nationwide one-day work stoppage. In this it had the backing of the more militant of the other national labor unions, who urged their rank-and-file workers to show solidarity by keeping their children home from school on September 15. The Zengakuren also mobilized its student members and an estimated 21,000 joined in strikes at sixty different campuses.

These were the first in a series of protest actions that in the next three years led to almost 57,000 cases of administrative punishments and/or reprimands and over 4,000 criminal actions by government authorities against teachers.[56] Technically, all disciplinary action was taken by school boards at the prefectural or local levels, and the Education Ministry consistently refused to engage in negotiations with the Japan Teachers' Union leadership. But there was no mistaking that the real war was between the Education Ministry, backed by the majority of the parliament, and the national Japan Teachers' Union, backed by the majority of the teaching profession. The press and public opinion surveys most often damned both sides for their intransigence.[57] But in some cases parents sided vigorously with the government: The Parent-Teacher Association in a Kochi Prefecture village shut the regular teachers out of the school and conducted their own classes. When officials from the national union attempted to intervene on behalf of the teachers, they and some teachers were physically beaten.[58]

Some relatively moderate commentators noted, "There is a very real threat that the Teachers' Efficiency Rating System may be used as the means of implementing the educational policies of the Liberal Democratic Party which tries to suppress the Japan Teachers' Union."[59] But other moderate Conservatives joined in with attacks on the dangers that the teachers' union posed to education. For example, the author of the following account, Professor Honda Akira, was a respected expert on English literature and was formerly on the faculty at Kyushu Imperial University and Tokyo Women's Higher Normal School. In his view, "The word 'freedom' is often improperly used" by the left: "They believe that under democracy the individual is his own master and has the right to act with complete freedom and liberty without regard for the rights of others."

Professor Honda then cited an example of such wrongheadedness:

> The following episode is illustrative of "democracy" as it is understood in postwar Japan . . . [in] a certain prefecture where the struggle against the Teachers' Efficiency Rating System was particularly sharp. There I asked the leaders of the local chapter of the Japan Teachers' Union what was meant by "democratic education." They answered, "For us educators democratic education is getting rid of the controls over education held by the Ministry of Education and school principals."

He concluded that "'democratic education' for those teachers was also a one-way street, and the fact that they think that way is despotic; theoretically even fascists could provide a 'democratic education.' . . . It is because there are teachers with such misconceptions that education is in a confused state today and the children are not learning anything in school."[60]

Eventually the issue of teacher rating ended in stalemate rather than compromise. The Education Ministry continued to direct the school boards to order their principals to use the designated form for annual reports. The local chapters of the union, however, were largely successful in rendering the exercise meaningless. In a large number of schools the teachers usually have rated themselves and principals have preferred to avoid confrontations on this issue unless viewed as absolutely necessary.[61]

The issues involved in the use of teacher evaluations had parallels in the evaluation of students. During the 1950s the Education Ministry had sporadically used achievement tests in a limited number of subjects and in selected schools for the purpose of evaluating how well national goals were being met. This practice expanded with the implementation of the 1958 Course of Study, and in 1961 the Education Ministry proposed a systematic use of such tests for all second- and third-year middle school students. Its announced aim was to identify geographical regions where special efforts might be necessary to bring their schools up to national standards.

The Japan Teachers' Union and its supporters, not surprisingly, perceived the motivation differently. In their view, the ministry would use the tests to "strengthen the Ministry of Education's control over the intellectual growth of Japanese children and to test the loyalty and commitment of teachers to the aims and values which the State sought to impose under the guise of its administrative expertise."[62] The tests constituted "improper control" in violation of the 1947 Fundamental Law of Education.

The opposition further objected on the grounds that achievement testing could be used to stigmatize poor learners or make invidious comparisons between teachers or schools, blaming them for results when the causes lay elsewhere. Business corporations might then avoid investing in areas with bad scores. Teachers also warned that such examinations would lead to "teaching for tests" and detract from the goal of educating students.[63] The Education Ministry was also criticized for failing to involve classroom educators in the process of creating testing instruments.

Nevertheless, beginning in October 1962 the Education Ministry enjoined the school boards to direct their administrators to carry out testing. The union fought back with both political and legal weapons. In some areas, the union was initially strong enough to effectively block testing altogether. One tactic was for the teachers to simply refuse to handle the test materials. Some teachers then prevented outside testers from entering their classrooms, and in many other areas local school officials modified the ministry's instructions. It was later said that school authorities actually encouraged slow learners to be absent the day of the exams to inflate the results.[64] Most prefectural school boards, for example, agreed with the union that individual students should remain anonymous.

The Education Ministry forced the issue by calling upon the local educational authorities to retaliate with court actions against teachers for failing to perform their duties. This move gave the opposition the chance to test the constitutionality of such central control in court. Between 1962 and 1976 there were seventeen separate judgments. In ten cases achievement testing was found illegal, but in seven cases it was found legal. For example, a Kyushu district court ruled in 1964 that such testing did indeed violate the prohibition against "improper control" in Article 10 of the 1947 Fundamental Law of Education. But a district court in northeast Japan less than two years later found for the government: "In the final analysis it must be said that the People, through their representatives in the Diet, entrust the State with the power to execute their general educational will. In this context it is only natural that the central government have the responsibility for determining appropriate national standards and making sure that they are upheld." This verdict was then overturned in 1969 on appeal to the Sendai Higher Court, which cleared the protesting teachers of any crime. Although the government had legal authority to manage the school system, "educational administration . . . should observe reasonable restraints with regard to those aspects of education that impinge upon the internality of human character or the professionalism of teachers." Particularly noteworthy was the interpretation of the prohibition against "improper control" in the 1947 Fundamental Law of Education as aimed specifically at the "prewar State's bureaucratic domination of education . . . as a result [the framers] produced an unambiguous affirmation of the principle that the independence and autonomy of education must be guaranteed."[65] Teachers who refused to obey the directives regarding testing were within their rights.

Again, the outcome of this clash between unionized teachers and central bureaucrats was a stalemate. As early as 1964 the Education Ministry had to settle for sampling schools rather than attempting the whole nation annually, thus forgoing the use of the results to punish or reward schools.

Radicalism on Campus

An area where the Conservatives were even more frustrated in their attempts to assert central control was the governance of the universities.[66] In 1951 the Yoshida cabinet had drafted legislation to establish a national universities committee to serve as a board of trustees for all public universities. It would have included nonacademics on the board. A second bill would have returned to the Education Ministry the legal veto it had over the appointment of public university presidents in the prewar period. This bill was proposed under the guise that it was merely making permanent a temporary arrangement authorized by the Occupation when the new charters were issued to reorganized schools. Postwar faculty, especially those at the successors to the old imperial universities, were highly sensitive to attacks on the procedures by which the faculty chose their own administrators and strong reactions against encroachments on university autonomy forced the Conservatives to back off temporarily.

Student activism kept the issue of central government control alive throughout the 1950s. Usually the confrontations with the police in this period came in demonstrations off-campus, but in one notorious 1952 case a police undercover agent was discovered spying on the Tokyo University campus. This and other government "antisubversive" campaigns led to bloody clashes on May Day of that year. The following year the Education Ministry formally requested that the Central Council on Education consider a plan to strengthen government authority over university administrators regardless of how they were selected. Once again, at the heart of the plan was the appointment of outside lay persons along with faculty to boards that would oversee faculty governance. The ministry shortly thereafter took the first steps in that direction by administratively ordering the establishment of such councils, albeit without outsiders. When these two new policies sparked great protest, the government then dropped the former but kept the latter, thus winning a partial victory in its drive to erode faculty autonomy.

In 1960 Japan's most serious postwar political crisis exploded. At issue were the foreign and domestic policies of Prime Minister Kishi Nobusuke, a prewar bureaucrat whom many in the opposition labeled a fascist and a war criminal. Demonstrators numbering tens of thousands forced the cancellation of an official visit by U.S. president Dwight Eisenhower and the resignation of Kishi.[67] Students, backed by their faculty mentors, played an enormously important role in these protests and Kishi's supporters were more determined than ever to bring the universities under tighter government rein. The Ikeda Hayato cabinet, which succeeded Kishi's, again considered introducing the bill authorizing the Education Ministry to veto appointments of public university presidents. Ikeda would later make his intentions quite clear in a 1962 speech: "When we consider the present condition of Japan, should we not be strongly disturbed by the fact that education is being used as a stepping stone to revolution . . . ? We must devise satisfactory measures to cope with this." Other Liberal-Democrats, citing "the problem regarding the political activities of university personnel," threatened even tougher measures to establish "limits to self-government."[68]

Perhaps the most drastic threat was one party leader's suggestion that the government abolish humanities and social science departments so that the national universities would be dominated by the more conservative faculty and students in the natural sciences and technical fields. The focus was on national universities, although the conservatives were concerned about all public institutions and there were even discussions of how to curtail political activity at private universities.

Most of the government proposals stopped short of giving the Education Ministry power to hire and fire faculty. But they would have concentrated more decisionmaking power at the top within the university by curtailing the rights of faculty, especially those in the lower ranks perceived to be filled with radicals, in choosing their departmental leaders and participating in the governance of the institution.

There was no shortage of protest to this latest attack on academic freedom, although the leftists had some difficulty reconciling their democratic ideology, which included support for elected school boards, with their opposition to lay persons having input at the university level. One opponent explained his opposition by saying, "Setting up within the university advisory bodies that include outsiders will not necessarily reflect popular opinion in university administration. It may do nothing more than provide a way for capitalists and those in positions of authority to express opinions and exert pressures."[69] This, of course, was precisely what the Conservative camp had in mind.

The Ikeda cabinet finally decided to shelve the bill in the face of opposition not only from the Progressive camp and the media but also from among the moderately conservative academics who were typically more receptive to measures aimed at controlling radicalism. The Association of National University Presidents rejected the notion that university presidents needed greater powers over their faculty; it supported maintaining the self-governing traditions of each separate institution. It did make one significant gesture toward compromise: "In cases where it is necessary to hear such opinions [from nonacademics] within the university, and to the extent that it does not interfere with the independence of the university, there should be no impediment to the establishment of organs in which suitable outsiders participate."[70]

Public opinion swung more toward the Conservative view of university autonomy at the end of the 1960s. This trend resulted in part from the long series of student strikes, sit-ins, and demonstrations that succeeded in shutting down most major universities at one time or another. This resurgence of radical student action began primarily over the issues of poor-quality facilities and high tuition. There were also renewed demands for student input into school governance, particularly at private colleges, which had increased their share of college-age enrollments to 71 percent by 1965. Surveys by the Japan Association of Private Colleges and Universities revealed that the number of campus disputes increased more than fivefold between 1965 and 1968, up from 20 to 115.

This trend climaxed in 1967–1970 with the movement against the Vietnam War and the renewal of the military alliance with the United States. Beginning with an attempt to block Prime Minister Satō Eisaku from visiting Saigon in October 1967, there took place a year and a half of rallies and demonstrations that some claimed drew a total of 18 million participants.[71] The most violent confrontations with the police involved splinter groups from Zengakuren. In October 1968, thousands of helmeted radical students, some armed with staves and Molotov cocktails, attacked train stations, police boxes, and even the Self-Defense Agency headquarters in Tokyo. The main Education Ministry building was one focal point. In April 1969, some 8,800 radical students, denied a police permit to take part in the huge antigovernment rally in Tokyo, temporarily took over parts of the city's central shopping area, the Ginza.

At the movement's peak in 1969, there were a total of over 900 incidents on campuses—public and private—and 3,500 student arrests, although remarkably few deaths. Tokyo University was the hardest hit, as students shut it down for most of an entire year until a massive mobilization of police force, including water cannon if not firearms, rooted them out of the main buildings.

This type of radicalism led to the formation of a separate antiwar national student organization in September 1969, an alliance of Joint Struggle Councils, or Zenkyōto. Thirty thousand students from forty-six universities met in Hibiya Park just outside the Imperial Palace in an attempt to redirect energies into the antiwar campaign away from violent confrontations. Yet the most violent protests of these years took place the very next month.

The Conservatives used this spectacle of street violence and campus turmoil to resurrect the issue of central control. The professionals within the Education Ministry were actually less bellicose than in previous years but in June 1968 the politically appointed minister, Nadao Hirokichi, stated that "no one can assert that [the student problem] is a problem that can be solved by the universities themselves. . . . Great limits must inevitably be recognized on the autonomy of the universities and . . . emphasis on university autonomy must be kept in tune with contemporary realities in order to insure the understanding and support of society in general."[72] Eventually, in August 1969, the Liberal Democratic Party majority enacted legislation that empowered the Education Ministry to "determine emergency measures which shall be taken to assist the independent efforts by universities to restore order"[73] after six months of such disorder. This University Administration Emergency Measures Law, better known as the University Control Law, was widely interpreted to mean the government would take over the administration of any university in such circumstances.

The government sweetened the medicine by offering private universities government subsidies and guarantees for loans. Inflation and resistance to tuition increases had placed even some of the more famous private schools in serious risk of defaulting on the bank loans that had funded their postwar rebuilding and expansion.[74] To funnel funds to such needy institutions, the Diet authorized a Foundation for the Promotion of Private Schools in 1970.

The Expansion of Educational Opportunities

Higher Education

The problems of both public and private universities in the 1950s and 1960s were due in part to rapid expansion to meet the new demand for postsecondary education. (See Figure 7.2.) The system mandated under the Occupation in

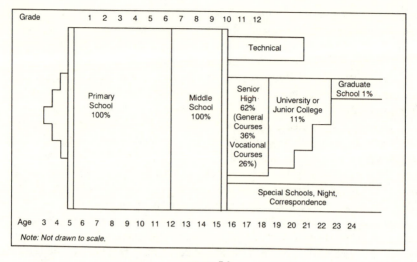

Note: Not drawn to scale.

FIGURE 7.2
Main Tracks in Schooling, 1961.
Source: For percents of age group, Cummings,
"Japan's Science and Engineering Pipeline," pp. 190–191.

1948 had taken shape in the early 1950s with over 200 four-year universities granted charters. This number compared to less than 50 at the end of World War II. By 1970 there were almost over seven times as many university students than in 1950—1,670,000 versus 240,000 (see Table 7.2). The percentage of Japanese in the twenty to twenty-four age group who were attending school was now on a par with or higher than the capitalist nations of industrialized Europe. Only the United States and the USSR remained significantly ahead. By this measure, progress toward the goal of opening greater educational opportunities looked quite impressive. However, the system remained elitist by two other measures—the hierarchy of prestige among postsecondary institutions and the persistent differences in schooling of females.

TABLE 7.2
Postsecondary Schooling: Students by Type of School

	Total Students	Students in College	Students in Junior College
1950	240,021	224,923	15,098
1955	601,240	523,355	77,885
1960	709,878	626,421	83,457
1965	1,085,209	937,556	147,653
1970	1,669,740	1,406,521	263,219

SOURCE: Monbushō, *Gakusei 100 nenshi*, tables 20 and 21, pp. 455–456.

The "new" universities of postwar Japan were often in fact the products of reorganizations and/or mergers of prewar institutions.[75] The old imperial universities became "national" (*kokuritsu*) institutions by virtue of their direct relationship to the central government. In some cases they absorbed the former higher schools as lower divisions for general education courses. Other existing public universities as well as old normal schools and some higher schools were recategorized as prefectural or municipal institutions because they were under the jurisdiction of, and received their primary funding from, those regional and local governments. As such they retained much of their previous reputations. That is, the more prestigious schools in the prewar period—particularly Tokyo and Kyoto among the old imperial universities and Keiō and Waseda among the private colleges—still had significantly more prestige than their competitors.

One reason for their continued prestige has been the public awareness of their dominance in supplying recruits for the administrative elite—those in the higher-echelon civil bureaucracy, which plays a much more central role in Japanese politics than that in the United States.[76] Each year since the war, between 20,000 and 45,000 applicants have taken the Type-A Higher Civil Service Examination to qualify as candidates for entry into the government ministries and more powerful agencies where the most successful will rise to bureau chief or vice-minister. Only 1,200 to 1,500 pass the examination—an average rate of about 3 percent to 6 percent. National university graduates have a success rate of about double this. The only other schools from which students come close to doing as well have been top-echelon private colleges—Waseda and Keiō—and certain municipal universities—Osaka City (not the same as Osaka University) and Tokyo Municipal. Tokyo University and Kyoto University together accounted for a third in 1967.

Tokyo University graduates made up a large proportion of Diet politicians as well. In 1963 they made up 27 percent of the total members of the two houses combined. More surprising, perhaps, they also constituted as much as a fifth of the left-wing party leaders.[77]

As with the government recruitment, so too it has been with private companies. A college graduate's chances of being recruited by one or another of those larger corporations that offer both security and a relatively high standard of living are considerably enhanced by a diploma from one of these same universities. Indeed, many recruiters have limited their search to a small list of what they perceive to be the top schools. Since the most successful companies have their headquarters in Tokyo or Osaka, regional schools could not balance this by having an edge with large companies based in their area, as is true in more decentralized economies such as that of the United States. A 1965 study of 9,743 business executives listed 33 percent as having attended Tokyo University with Kyoto University second with 13 percent. The former Tokyo School of Commerce, now renamed Hitotsubashi University, plus the leading private colleges, Keiō and Waseda, accounted for another 24 percent—meaning that five universities produced 70 percent of the total (see Table 7.3). Most of these executives, it can be assumed, had gone to school under the prewar system, but the practice of national companies selecting from a limited number of universities was continued in the postwar period.[78]

This practice, of course, becomes a self-fulfilling prophecy as the most ambitious and well-prepared students are attracted to those schools because they believe it will increase their chances of being successful. Their success in entering the higher civil service or top corporations thus reinforces the reputation of the school quite apart from other measures of quality. As with the prewar elite universities, admissions continued to be determined primarily on the basis of test scores in achievement examinations designed and administered by the schools themselves.

This elitism is one in which the winners are chosen primarily on the basis of academic merit since theoretically nothing else—wealth, social status, attendance at elite high schools, extracurricular activities, letters of recommendation—is of any importance other than the admissions tests. The results are elitist in the sense that the expansion of higher education did not create an equality of outcomes. There is also a huge discrepancy in how this expansion affected the genders.

Women in College

If one looks only at the aggregate figures for all institutions of higher education, the increase in the number of women in the 1950s is not unimpressive. Between 1950 and 1960 their number more than tripled whereas male enrollments increased by 54 percent. This increase meant that in 1960 there were almost 140,000 female students where there had been only 40,000 ten years

TABLE 7.3
Postwar Business Executives: College Attended, 1944–1965

	1944 (%)	1954 (%)	1959 (%)	1965 (%)
Tokyo University	27	41	21	33
Kyoto University	6	5	7	13
Hitotsubashi University	9	10	6	6
Keiō University	9	6	7	8
Waseda University	3	3	4	10
Foreign universities	3	na	na	na
No college	18	na	na	na

na = not available

SOURCES: Data for 1944 and 1965 from Aonuma, *Nihon no keieisō*, table 8; data for 1954 and 1959 from Yanaga, *Big Business in Japanese Politics*, tables 1 and 2.

earlier. By 1970 the number had tripled again to 459,000. The increase in the proportion of men to women, though improving, was less impressive: It was one in ten in 1950, one in five in 1960, and not much better in 1970.

Moreover, these figures hide an important truth: Most women were not attending the same type of colleges that men were. The overwhelming majority of female students in higher education in the 1950s were in junior colleges, which were new two- or three-year schools granting terminal degrees that could not be transferred directly toward a four-year university degree. Women made up less than half of junior college student bodies until 1953, when they reached 52 percent. Over the next seventeen years their percentage soared until in 1969 they made up over 80 percent of those enrolled in these two- and three-year schools (see Figures 7.3 and 7.4).

Four-year universities in the 1950s were still male dominated (see Table 7.4), and in 1960 fewer than one in six students was female. The ratio improved only slightly by the end of the 1960s to just over one in five (see Table 7.5). Gender-related differences must also be measured in other significant dimensions. Most women in postsecondary schooling—whether four-year or junior colleges—were in majors that did not lead to great economic success or high social prestige.

Success in entering the best corporations as well as the higher civil service in the postwar period, as in the prewar period, was correlated with degrees in

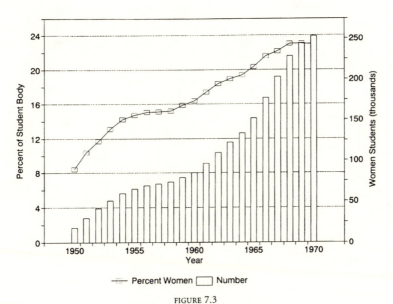

FIGURE 7.3
Women in Universities: Number and Percent, 1950–1970.
Source: Calculated from Monbushō, *Gakusei 90 nenshi,* pp. 652–653.

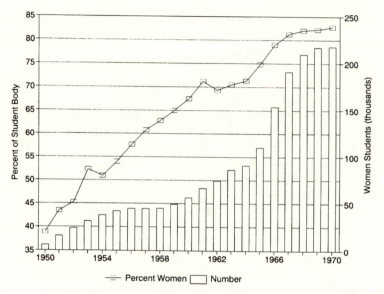

FIGURE 7.4
Women in Junior Colleges: Number and Percent, 1950–1970.
Source: Calculated from Monbushō, *Gakusei 90 nenshi,* pp. 652–653.

TABLE 7.4
Postsecondary School Students: Percent of Age Group, 1955–1970

	Total Enrolled in Postsecondary (%)	*Male (%)*	*Female (%)*
1955	10	15	5
1960	10	15	6
1965	17	22	12
1970	24	29	18

SOURCE: Adapted from Burkham, ed., *The Occupation of Japan,* p. 277.

TABLE 7.5
Postsecondary Schooling: Women as Percent of Students

	Total	*University*	*Junior College*
1950	9	8	37
1955	17	15	53
1960	19	16	66
1965	24	20	74
1970	27	23	82

SOURCE: Calculated from Monbushō, *Gakusei 100 nenshi,* tables 20 and 21.

certain majors granted by the faculties in the main divisions of universities. The division of *hōgaku*, or law, of most universities was still a separate upper-division college that taught a wide variety of courses aimed at training future administrators, whether in the public or private sphere. It was largely self-contained, its students focusing almost all of their coursework within the division once having completed required general education courses in their first and second years. Switching major divisions was much like switching universities in that it was not permitted without retaking entrance examinations and losing much of the course credits accumulated in other divisions. This was also true of economics and commerce as well as the sciences and engineering.

These were the fields that supplied most of the recruits into managerial positions in corporations and government. Yet there were few female students in these fields. They, by contrast, clustered in the *bungaku*—literature or more broadly the humanities—or in home economics and education. Since students did not place their names and other identifying information on entrance examinations and since letters of recommendation or high school transcripts were not used, theoretically it was not school quotas that determined this outcome but prior factors such as family or peer pressures.

In any case, women in overwhelming proportions took degrees in fields that did not prepare them to compete in the better-rewarded careers. The exception was education itself, one of the few professions relatively open to women. Primary schools employed more women teachers than men. But middle schools had about a two-to-one ratio in favor of males, and it was extremely rare for a woman to become a school principal at either level.

Although not unnoticed, these imbalances were not raised as a major question of educational equality in the 1950s or 1960s, as they would be later. The 1952 Japan Teachers' Union "Code of Ethics for Teachers" made vague references to social and economic limitations placed upon the individual but there was no specific mention in this section or elsewhere of opportunities for women. Nor did its 1957 recommendations for reforms address the issue.[79] Of course, the union was almost entirely composed of those teaching in primary and middle schools, where the genders were less segregated.

Issues of Multitracking

The institutionalization of coeducation at the higher secondary level came with deliberate speed in the first two decades after World War II. Since these schools were administered at the prefectural and metropolitan level, however, there was some regional variation. The cities of Osaka and Tokyo, for example, approached it in different ways. Osaka paired up former boys' schools with former girls' schools and exchanged half of the students and staffs from each. Tokyo initially settled for moving a third. Moreover, it was not until the mid-1960s that there were roughly equal numbers, and in rural areas it was not surprising to see a senior high school with less than 10 percent females. Other prefectures opted to continue gender segregation by keeping some schools just for girls.[80]

Questions about educational if not gender equality in secondary schooling were raised immediately after the end of the Occupation. The U.S. vision of a comprehensive high school enrolling all students in a district did not materialize in the postwar period, in part because of resistance from the outset by those who believed that youth should be tracked into vocational training at an earlier age. Although the advocates of a multitrack approach talked about "education appropriate for the ability and aptitudes of students," in a more fundamental sense it was a disagreement about what it was that schooling should contribute to society.[81]

In 1958 the Central Council on Education had strongly recommended that the 6-3-3 system be augmented by two new tracks: (1) a 6-6 track, which would replace the middle schools and senior high academic track with six years of vocational training, and (2) a 6-3-5 track, which would shunt middle school graduates immediately into advanced technical training. The 1962 Education Ministry publication *Japan's Growth and Education: Educational Development in Relation to Socioeconomic Growth* justified public schooling primarily in terms of "educational capital" and attempted to measure its contribution to industrialization. Two other reports, one in 1963 by the Economic Council Manpower Policies Committee and another in 1966, "On the Expansion and Development of Upper Secondary Education," issued by the Central Council on Education, continued the controversy by stressing "diversity by ability" and advocating different tracks for secondary students with different aptitudes.[82]

Critics attacked the notion of "education as an investment" as too narrow a utilitarian view. The 6-6 track proposal—to create vocational schools for primary school graduates—did not survive the attacks by the opposition. Some of these critics also took aim at the Scholastic Achievement Test that the government wanted to institute, arguing that it was intended "to play a strategic role in laying the foundations for the diversification of upper secondary education demanded by our current industrial structure. In short, economic values have been used to deny the validity of all pedagogic objectives which are vital for preserving the autonomy of education."[83]

Meanwhile local governments were making their own choices regarding "tracking." After three decades the original SCAP attempt to create "small" districts each with a single comprehensive high school was a dead letter. By the early 1970s, approximately one-third of all high schools offered precollegiate curriculum without vocational courses, and another third had a curriculum based on vocational courses.[84] In other words, only about one out of three senior secondary schools could be labeled "comprehensive" in so far as they combined academic and vocational course offerings.

Eventually, however, students in over 70 percent of the nation's 542 school districts were no longer channeled into specific high schools on the basis of the

district in which they resided.[85] In Kobe, for example, the city had divided itself by 1953 into three subdistricts, each with eight high schools. Until 1967
Tokyo was divided into thirteen subdistricts with a total of eighty-nine academic high schools, but this was altered to a more complex pattern of "groups,"
each with either two or three academic high schools, and students were assigned in such a way as to equalize the achievement level of the student bodies
with the goal of ending quality distinctions between schools.[86] Elsewhere in the
nation, in extreme cases, a subdistrict might have as many as ten or even more
academic high schools, as was the case in sixty-nine instances—13 percent of
the nation's districts.

Thus, in most cities, graduates of middle schools who wished to continue
their education needed to be directed into one or another track. Usually this
was done on the basis of entrance examinations, although there were variations
in how this system worked. For example, in Osaka in the 1970s each student
could apply to one and only one high school in the city. In Hyogo Prefecture,
where the city of Kobe is located, students were "guided" to apply to particular
high schools on the basis of teachers' evaluations of their grades and scores on
achievement tests. In Tokyo, however, students residing in a particular district
were assigned by computer to the high schools in the district "groups" on the
basis of examinations with the goal of having each school within the group
have a similar mixture of high achievers and lower achievers.[87]

Parents not happy with the results of this process could send their children
to private high schools. Twenty-nine percent of senior secondary students were
in private institutions in 1960; this increased slightly to 33 percent in 1965 and
then leveled off at 30 percent in 1970. Although there are some private religious schools in Japan, they enroll only a minority of private students. The
overwhelming majority of private prep schools are secular and exist not to
transmit a particular worldview but to enhance a student's chance of gaining
entrance to a more prestigious university. They are not necessarily better at this
function than the best of the public high schools; nor are they necessarily easier to enter, since those with the highest reputations also use entrance examinations to assure themselves the type of high achiever whose subsequent
success will help to maintain the reputation of the student's alma mater.

Just as with the highest-ranked public schools, there is a strong likelihood of
self-fulfilling prophecy at work in the private sector: Most of the students in
private schools are successful because, as measured by test-taking skills, they
are the better students in the first place. However, the private high school is
also somewhat more free to gear itself directly to preparing for the university
entrance examinations than would be its public counterpart. If students attend
a high school attached to a private college, they also commonly receive preference in admissions at that school.

Whatever the causal factors, by 1970 private school graduates had dramatically increased their share of entering classes at prestigious universities.
Whereas almost 90 percent of the Tokyo University entering class had been

from public high schools in 1955, the percent had shrunk to under 60 percent by 1970.

The prestige of the old higher schools did not necessarily suffer after the war. It was well known, for example, that many of the posts in the upper civil service were filled with bureaucrats who had graduated from the old higher schools on their way to the university. One sample of those in office in the 1949–1959 period revealed that over half had attended one of the original eight higher schools, with one out of four having been to the First Higher School in Tokyo.[88]

Objective examinations have long been the single factor weighed in admissions decisions at major universities. The combination of large high school districts with diversification in types of curricula also led to a heavy reliance upon entrance examinations to determine which students would have the opportunity to attend which high school. This in turn led to what critics have called "cutting the student population in slices" within a hierarchically stratified system of secondary schools. That is to say, "the exam system tends to provide each high school with a student body homogeneous in its academic ability."[89]

In this period the Japan Teachers' Union took no consistent position on entrance examinations other than to say that high school should be compulsory for all youth. The 1952 Japan Teachers' Union *Code of Ethics for Teachers,* which was drafted by a committee dominated by academic intellectuals, proclaimed that "equal opportunity in education and respect for the dignity of the individual, as guaranteed by the Constitution, are today still dead letters."[90] Interestingly enough, the only particular cases mentioned under the heading "Teachers Shall Fight for Equal Opportunity" were "the multitudes of working young people or mentally and physically handicapped." But this type of meritocracy, or "exam-ocracy," is the opposite of the democratic ideal of the Occupation reforms in the view of some in the Progressive camp:

> The result is that differences in quality among secondary schools have widened sharply. As secondary schools are polarized into those designed to prepare students for entrance to elite universities and those organized to educate those classified as non-achievers, the democratic ideal of a unified secondary school education has disappeared, and secondary education itself sinks deeper and deeper into a dangerous and destructive morass.[91]

Conclusion

Clearly the campaigns during the first two decades after the end of the American Occupation had mixed results. The fiercest fighting came in 1957–1959 when the Education Ministry sallied forth simultaneously on four fronts: school board reform, textbook screening, teacher evaluations, and student achievement testing. Although the government gained considerable ground on the first two fronts, it was far less successful on the latter two. Certainly the battles over what values should be taught to children were inconclusive.

Nor was the issue of multitracking resolved. Compulsory education was successfully extended through the ninth grade, something planned only under the wartime regime, but the two opposing camps could not agree on whether there should be more than one type of public middle school. Senior high school, once an elitist institution, became more and more expected of youth in all classes and sights were being raised steadily to include college itself.

Perhaps none of these developments were as revolutionary as the routinization of coeducation in all public middle schools and the majority of public high schools. The percentage of adolescent females going on beyond compulsory school showed marked increase in the decades following the Occupation. Thirty-seven percent of female middle school students continued their schooling in 1950. In 1960 over half did, and by 1970 the number reached 83 percent, which was comparable with the percent of males. About a quarter of these, however, were attending private girls' high schools. In some of the less industrialized and urban areas even some public high schools, particularly those that had existed in the prewar period, were segregated, although this had become relatively rare in the major cities.[92] Coeducation was also the single most radical change at the level of higher education, although here it was felt that very little in the courses on economics, law, and other subjects was needed to prepare for the best-rewarded careers after graduation. The gender ratio in the natural and applied sciences changed little despite the opening of departments in the humanities to women.

Least changed, it seemed, was the political polarization between the Conservatives and the Progressives. Their extreme differences on the three issues of administrative control, moral values, and multitracking seemed to block further improvement in the system. Yet in the 1970s the Conservatives girded their loins again, this time employing a fresh set of weapons supplied by a series of reports issued by the Central Council on Education. But by this time the opposing forces had undergone some modifications.

8

The Challenge of a New Era:
1970–1989

*Today, we are confronted with an entirely different set of problems, the
challenge of a new era which mankind has never seen the likes of before.*
—Report of the Central Council on Education[1]

Look at the University of Tokyo, the funsō *[disturbances], the riot! They are
the result of the post-war reforms.*
—Hosokawa Ryōgen, Council Member[2]

Japan entered the 1970s a more affluent nation and stable society than either
the Meiji oligarchs or the SCAP reformers could have imagined. Nevertheless,
a truce on the question of what to teach its children still eluded the warring
camps of Conservatives and Progressives. Ironically, this struggle dragged on
amid a phenomenon unprecedented in the postwar era—widespread expres-
sions of admiration from abroad. During the late 1970s and early 1980s many
foreign observers, Americans in particular, wrote paeans of praise about the
success of the Japanese school system. Not only had Japanese youth consistently performed extraordinarily well by international measures in mathematics and science but in comparison with the United States, at least, the average
Japanese teenager seemed to these observers to be miraculously both better be-
haved and better educated. Study after study indicated that Japanese children
were starting school earlier, attending class more regularly, doing more home-
work, taking drugs less frequently, becoming pregnant more rarely, and graduating from high school more often than their U.S. counterparts.[3] Furthermore,
some claimed, "We are looking at an unusually open society educationally, and
at a society that displays strong pragmatism with little of the traditional elitism
that has characterized educational development at secondary and higher levels
in much of Europe, at least until recently."[4] It is not surprising that U.S. and

British publishers suddenly awakened to the commercial possibilities of books on Japanese schools with subtitles like "Lessons for the West" or the "Japanese Challenge."[5]

Perhaps partly in reaction to the "bright" views of some foreign and domestic commentators, critics both within and without restressed the "dark" side.[6] The political and social costs to the society as well as the psychological costs to the nation's youth were, in this view, simply far too high. As in the past, the most important disagreements were over moral values and the danger in the central government playing the key role in determining the curriculum.

The cannonades in the 1970s and 1980s were more scattered. This may have resulted partially from the decline in the strength of three of the participants of the earlier period: the radical student organizations, the Japan Teachers' Union, and the Japan Socialist Party. But there were also changes within the Liberal Democratic Party as neoconservatives like Nakasone Yasuhiro rose to positions of leadership.

Changes Within the Camps

Apathetic Students

The radical student movement never recaptured the heights it had climbed in the struggles against the military pact with the United States.[7] Beginning in 1970 a variety of factors, including internal factionalism as well as external suppression, brought about an extended cease-fire on the campuses of Japan's universities. The national Zenkyōtō student organization, the main successor to the Zengakuren, eventually dissolved in 1971, and off-campus student activism declined dramatically as the end of the Vietnam War neared. On-campus disturbances also dwindled to a post-1945 low and more often than not involved clashes among rival student groups rather than between students and authorities.

Political events—the return of Okinawa to Japanese rule, overtures by the United States toward the People's Republic of China, and U.S.-USSR arms agreements in the 1970s and 1980s—also helped defuse the explosive potential of the Cold War within Japanese domestic politics even before the breakup of the USSR in the late 1980s ended it officially.

These factors helped produce a much more apolitical mood on Japanese campuses by the 1980s. A 1978 survey of incoming undergraduates taken by the Tokyo University student newspaper found that only the Liberal Democratic Party had any substantial support. This shift away from the Progressive camp was confirmed in more scholarly surveys in 1980 and again in 1983.[8]

A Weakened Teachers' Union

Although from the vantage point of the 1990s it would become clear that the fortune of the Japan Teachers' Union had been ebbing at least as early as the 1970s, the union still maintained sufficient strength to hold off the Education Ministry on a number of important fronts. The stalemate regarding teacher efficiency ratings still held, as did the one over national achievement testing. Moreover, the union blocked full implementation for years of the plan to create a quasi-administrative echelon of *shunin*—"teaching coordinators" or "master teachers"—from within the ranks in the primary, middle, and secondary schools. This plan had been proposed in 1974 during the tenure of the scholar Nagai Michio, who was a surprise appointment as minister of education by Prime Minister Miki Takeo. From the union's point of view, Professor Nagai had sold out to the Conservatives and was using "salami tactics" to divide the teachers by creating new middle management positions within the ranks of the teaching staff. The head of the National Association of Reformist Mayors—a constituent part of the Progressive camp—denounced the scheme in familiar if no less scathing terms: "The implementation of the *shunin* system is a political problem, for it plays a leading role in making the country into a fascist state."[9]

But the old tactics of frequent strikes and other obstructive actions in the 1960s had cost the union considerable public sympathy.[10] Moreover, the Japan Teachers' Union was perceived to be declining in membership despite its denials. It entered the 1980s claiming a membership over 727,000—71 percent of primary and secondary teachers combined and 90 percent at the primary level. Education Ministry statistics, which count all educational personnel including principals and other administrators who have not legally been permitted to join the union since 1966, gave much lower figures. By the ministry's measures, membership had dropped to as low as 50 percent by 1985 (see Figure 8.1).

In the mid-1980s the union leadership began to suffer the most serious schisms since the late 1940s. Two factions actually held separate national conventions and police protection was called in at one. These events occurred just as the labor union movement as a whole was undergoing a massive realignment that threatened to weaken the Progressive camp in the Diet.

Anemic Opposition Parties

As some wag noted many years ago, Japanese politics during the 1960s became a matter of a party and a half. Despite an election process probably only slightly more corrupt than most in the industrial world, one party—the Liberal Democratic Party—won at least a substantial plurality in every national balloting for the House of Representatives between its formation in 1955 and the 1993 election.

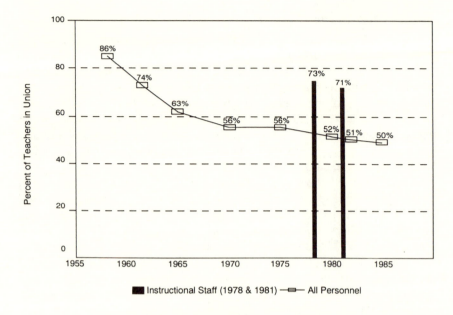

FIGURE 8.1
Japan Teachers' Union Membership, 1958–1985.
Source: Calculated from Ota, "Political Unionism in Japan," pp. 254–256.

Its main challenger in the early postwar era, the Japan Socialist Party, has been unable even to maintain solidarity among the left much less come close to winning enough seats to form a government. In the 1980s there were actually two other left-wing parties claiming the heritage of the original socialist movement, and the Japan Communist Party's share of the votes at the national level dwindled into insignificance. Second place among the opposition was captured by the Clean Government Party, originally the political arm of a neo-Buddhist religious organization. Although less nationalistic than the Liberal Democratic Party, it is nevertheless more conservative than its sometime socialist allies in its view of moral education and related issues. A further blow to the socialists came at the end of the 1980s when the labor union movement underwent the most thorough realignment since World War II. The result has been the loss of funds, organizational networks, and automatic votes that the Japan Socialist Party and its allies had once counted on.

This decline of support for the militant left sectors of the student and teacher constituencies was caused in part by the economic successes of the 1960s. Socialist support dwindled as the so-called economic miracle of postwar Japan became fact both objectively and subjectively for the middle classes. Neither the brief spell of near economic panic at the "Oil Shocks" at the beginning of the 1970s nor the longer downturn following the too-rapid rise in the stock and real estate markets in the late 1980s translated into support for the Progressive camp in the parliament.

This does not mean that ideology was dead or that the Conservatives were to have their way entirely on educational issues. Rather, what had been in the 1950s a war of maneuver had by the 1970s settled into a war of attrition with the left only slowly if inexorably giving ground. At times, however, the main impediment to serious change within the system was caused by frictions within the Conservative camp itself.

Mutations Within the Establishment

The Liberal-Democrats in the Diet suffered a number of severe blows in the early 1970s—embarrassments that strained party unity and weakened the party's hand in such matters as educational policy. In 1972 Prime Minister Satō's claim to true partnership with the United States, already under criticism over the Vietnam War, led to greater skepticism when President Richard Nixon suddenly reversed U.S. policy toward Communist China without giving Satō sufficient time to reverse his own stance. After the fierce intraparty strife that followed Satō's resignation, Tanaka Kakuei emerged as his successor but was soon deeply mired in a series of political funding scandals. He was ultimately charged and convicted of taking bribes from the Lockheed Corporation—the most serious postwar political scandal up to that time. In the midst of these political setbacks, the party also suffered politically because of its handling of the economic aftershocks stemming from the 1973 oil embargoes by the Organization of Petroleum Exporting Countries. The high rate of bankruptcy among small and medium businesses and the loss of many jobs was accompanied by sudden price inflation in a number of consumer necessities, including toilet paper. This rise in prices prompted consumer advocates to accuse the government of allowing price gouging by its business allies.

As a consequence of these developments, the Liberal-Democrats lost twenty-seven seats in the House of Representatives in the general election of December 1976. Since the size of the House of Representatives, the more important of the two parliamentary chambers, had actually been expanded by twenty new members, this loss of seats meant an overall loss from a comfortable majority of 58 percent to a bare majority of only 50 percent. Not since the party had been formed in 1955 had it won such a small majority of the vote or of seats in the House. Although the party bounced back in the 1980 election, it has never regained the combination of strong prime ministers and solid parliamentary majorities that it enjoyed in the 1960s. In 1993 the Liberal Democratic Party was to lose its first election ever as Japanese politics moved into a new era.

Over these years there were also very important changes within the Liberal Democratic Party. Particularly important in this context was the emergence of informal cliques of Diet members with specialized policy concerns and expertise who were capable of challenging both the party leadership and the civil bureaucracy for influence. These cliques existed in the sphere of education as well as in agricultural, transportation, and other policy areas. Members of this educational policy clique, the "education tribe," have sometimes functioned as allies to the Education Ministry in blocking hostile legislative initiatives. In the late 1960s and 1970s some acted as the party's field commanders in pushing for changes to subdue the turmoil within the universities. But in the 1980s these Liberal Democratic Party members more often had their own agenda and were instrumental in forcing changes upon the Education Ministry bureaucrats while thwarting the will of party elders or prime ministers such as Nakasone Yasuhiro.[11] These Liberal Democratic Party members were no longer content to follow the lead of the bureaucrats within the Education Ministry. In the words of one such official:

> In the 1950s and '60s, MOE [Ministry of Education] officials played the leadership role. . . . In the later 1960s, these Diet members got together and set up study sessions to learn about education policy. . . . I was called on to lecture to these meetings—as an MOE elder to the younger Diet members. Today [in the 1980s] those same Diet members are able to come up with their own ideas and formulate their own policies. They tell the MOE what to do.[12]

Morals Revisited

As had been the case since the Occupation, the target for much of the fire from all sides in the 1970s and 1980s was the content of the textbooks used in primary and secondary schools. In the 1970s the lawsuits brought by Ienaga Saburō were once again in the spotlight as they worked their way through the lower courts toward the Supreme Court.

Patriotism and Textbooks

In July 1974 yet another ruling was handed down on Professor Ienaga's 1965 civil damage suit against the Education Ministry. Tokyo district judge Takatsu Tamaki did not see the law in the same light as Judge Sugimoto had in 1970. Whereas Sugimoto had located educational rights with "the People," Judge Takatsu held that "the Constitution empowers the State to provide the People with the education they require." On the question of what the 1947 Fundamental Law of Education intended by the clause "Education should be conducted without improper controls as a direct responsibility to the nation as a whole," the Takatsu decision held that the threat of control came from groups other than the state: "Improper controls should be interpreted to mean partisan pressures of political parties, labor unions, or other segments [of society] which are not the nation as a whole, and as also including, insofar as they are improper, controls under administrative power over education."

Textbook screening was not, in Takatsu's judgment, "improper control." The state may "carry out textbook screening in order to maintain the quality of educational opportunity and to continually raise the level of educational standards in accord with the appropriate developmental stage of the student."[13] Thus the state's "jurisdiction does not end simply with the establishment of and maintenance of external conditions for education; it can also extend into the content of education."[14]

With regard to the rights of the teachers and authors, Judge Takatsu explicitly ruled that in textbook screening, "the freedoms of expression which are otherwise guaranteed to citizens must necessarily be withdrawn." The principles of academic freedom applied to research and teaching in higher education, but not to the selection of textbooks at the primary or secondary levels:

> Because children do not sufficiently possess the ability to criticize what they are taught, it is necessary to exercise great discretion and educational consideration appropriate to the stage of their intellectual development. By no means should we allow the [precollegiate] classroom to become a forum for teachers' exposition of their own theories or for their insistence upon the correctness of the results of their own inquiry. This imperative is one of the most important reasons why we must impose limitations or restrictions on the educational freedom of teachers and textbook authors.[15]

Having spurned Ienaga's constitutional challenge, the court did agree that the Education Ministry had made errors in applying its own standards to Ienaga's book, thereby illegally ordering him to make certain revisions. The court ordered the government to pay Ienaga the equivalent of approximately U.S.$300 for mental distress. At the same time its verdict left Ienaga having to pay almost all the much more substantial court costs out of his own pocket.

Despite Ienaga's defeat on the constitutional issues in this case, the government decided to appeal to the Supreme Court, challenging the right of an author to sue the ministry over revisions in the first place. In this appeal the government took the position that only a publisher had that right since technically only a publisher requested certification.

Six months after the loss in the Takatsu decision, Ienaga won a new round. The Tokyo Higher Court rejected the Education Ministry's appeal of the Sugimoto ruling on Ienaga's original suit, albeit only on narrowly defined grounds. Unfortunately for Ienaga's cause, the government was determined to exercise its own right of appeal and thus the struggle continued through the 1970s, the 1980s, and into the 1990s at the level of the Supreme Court. In 1976 the Supreme Court, in yet another ruling, came down squarely on the fence: "There are two diametrically opposed viewpoints with regard of to whom . . . the authority and competence to determine the contents of children's education properly belongs. . . . However, because each of these positions is too extreme in its basic orientation, this court is unable to find either one of them suitable for complete adoption."[16]

The 1980s brought renewed public attention to the question of what was in the nation's textbooks. In summer 1980 a minister of education again asserted that patriotism was being ignored in schools, provoking the media to yet another extended discussion of the true meaning of love of country. By the end of the year, the Liberal Democratic Party had created a new internal committee on textbooks, which eventually echoed the title of the 1955 party report by publishing *The Problem of Deplorable Textbooks*. Again the allegation was heard that textbooks were espousing communist ideas. Again Conservative intellectuals called for textbook revision. And again Professor Ienaga Saburō filed a lawsuit, his third, in the hope of raising public consciousness if not actually winning a legal victory.

There were, however, three developments that distinguished the resumption of these skirmishes from previous engagements. First, textbook treatments of Japanese aggression became linked directly with foreign diplomacy. Second, a new prime minister came to office more determined than his recent predecessors to do battle over education. And third, public support for Ienaga weakened with the decline of the Japan Teachers' Union and the Zengakuren student organization.

The position of the government on textbooks had changed little from the 1960s. Mainstream Liberal-Democrat members of parliament continued to complain that schoolchildren were being misled by textbooks and teachers who preached unilateral disarmament and attacked the capitalist system. Education Ministry officials continued to pressure publishers to produced "balanced" works more suitable to the age of the pupils, by which it meant that the Conservative view of capitalism, national defense, and past history should receive as much if not more attention than that of the Progressives.

Conservative intellectuals denied the claims that textbook revision necessarily meant parroting the Liberal Democratic Party line but argued that civics courses overemphasized individual rights at the expense of teaching people's obligations to society. They also blamed the schools for confusing their pupils about national defense issues by substituting pacifism for patriotism. Outside the halls of the government or academia, there was also continued criticism from organized business interests.[17]

In June 1982 the Education Ministry, as it had every three years throughout the preceding decade, released an up-to-date list of certified textbooks. The influential newspaper *Asahi* immediately attacked the government for "reverting to a prewar tone," reporting that the Education Ministry had suddenly changed by insisting that textbook authors cease using the word *shinryaku*—invade or commit aggression—in favor of the word *shinshutsu*—advance, march in—in describing Japanese penetration in north China in the years prior to the beginning of widespread fighting in 1937.[18] Within days, other newspapers and magazines were reporting the story.

In fact this account was not accurate, and eventually *Asahi* and some other newspapers ran retractions of sorts. In the first place, the Education Ministry had actually been consistent throughout the 1970s in its recommendations about the use of the word "aggression." Second, there was no evidence of any changes in the 1981 textbooks beyond the substitution of one expression meaning "invade"—*shinko*—for another that may have slightly different connotations—*shin'nyū*.[19]

Such linguistic subtleties were not of interest, however, to Japan's critics in the People's Republic of China or the Republic of Korea, who once again were indignant that the Japanese government was hiding the truth about wartime atrocities from its schoolchildren. Within a few days the mass media in both countries had taken up the story in its original form and Beijing had issued a formal complaint to the Japanese Foreign Ministry. As the Foreign Ministry attempted to smooth the issue over, a member of the Suzuki Zenkō cabinet fired back, warning against foreign interference in internal affairs and accusing Korean history textbooks of having their own flaws: "For example, Korea describes the annexation [of 1910] as an act of aggression. But in view of the Korean domestic situation at that time, I don't know which is the accurate description."[20]

In August the government of the Republic of Korea formally protested the use of euphemistic descriptions of Japan's imperialist expansion into Korea between 1875 and 1910 as well as colonial policies on religion and language. Koreans were particularly sensitive about the textbooks having left out the phrase "forcibly drafted" in mentioning Koreans serving in the Japanese Imperial Army. The Korean media now focused renewed attention on the history of Japanese sins and a public campaign was mounted against Japanese travelers visiting Korea.[21]

In response, a variety of conciliatory gestures were made by Japanese government spokespersons in the weeks following, although the Education Ministry continued to resist Foreign Ministry pressure to back down. When the Suzuki cabinet did finally issue several official statements in late August, it expressed sorrow over the past: "The Government and people of Japan are deeply aware that, in the past, Japanese actions have inflicted great suffering and injury on the peoples of Korea, China and other countries of Asia, and we have embarked upon the path of a nation of peace in the penitence and determination that such events must never be repeated."[22]

But Prime Minister Suzuki also said, "Evaluation of our country's actions in the past needs to await the judgement of future historians. But it is a fact that there are severe judgements, criticisms, and understandings about them on the part of the world including China. The government must recognize them."[23] The Education Ministry instructed the schools to note the controversy and be sensitive to the feelings of foreign nations but to use the textbook until their next scheduled revision. It did make one concession by promising to shorten the usual cycle for revisions from three to two years. The chief cabinet secretary, Miyazawa Kiichi (later to become prime minister), reassured the public that the Liberal Democratic Party was in favor of textbooks that would foster "the friendship and good will of neighboring Asian countries."[24]

This conciliatory stance stirred a backlash from right-wing Japanese nationalists. One group calling itself the "National Congress to Safeguard Japan" sponsored the writing of a senior high textbook that would express their particular views of the Pacific War. In 1986 the Education Ministry authorization panel insisted on correcting certain errors and toning down the rhetoric in the draft—a total of 241 mandatory revisions and twice that many other recommendations. The group responded by holding a reception for the press in which they attacked the new prime minister, Nakasone Yasuhiro, for caving in to foreign pressures. This in turn stimulated officials of the People's Republic of China and the Republic of Korea to lodge yet another protest with the Japanese Foreign Ministry about militarism in textbooks. The Education Ministry then decided on the extraordinary procedure of holding an additional review round. Eventually, however, a heavily revised version of this textbook did receive certification.

Thus the main questions remained: Was the textbook certification system merely a facade for a government-sponsored domestic propaganda campaign? Could the state ever practice such certification without engaging in political censorship? Was there any way to teach history without partisan bias?

Professor Suzuki Hiroo, a historian of education at Tsukuba University, argued both yes and no:

> Any method of screening that compels textbook authors and publishers to revise individual words or phrases is alien to [a free society]. . . . Since diversity and relativity of values are the hallmark of a democratic society, it is inherently contradictory for the Education Ministry to run a screening system with the same mentality that prevailed when state preparation of textbooks was the rule.

He recommended that the function of screening textbooks be given to a new independent research institute separate from the Education Ministry.

In a somewhat more novel vein, Professor Suzuki asserted that there were other fundamental problems that could not be avoided so long as it was public policy to provide free textbooks:

> First, the system hides school textbooks from the public view; it is a closed system that does not allow public criticism of the process by which textbooks are screened, adopted, supplied, and put into use. . . . Second, to the publishers, textbooks are commodities [whose] sale is guaranteed [so long as they pass screening]. . . . It is these two characteristics that prevent publishers from producing better textbooks.

Suzuki's solution was to involve parents in the direct purchase of the textbooks, granting a tax allowance to compensate for the costs. "In this way parents will be made to go through the process of purchasing (and hopefully examining) their children's textbooks, thus preventing Education Ministry bureaucrats and teachers belonging to a Nikkyōso [labor union] from making the books their exclusive province."[25]

Hata Ikuhiko, a specialist in World War II history, was equally optimistic that there was "a middle way between rigid screening and no quality control at all" if the authorization process was removed from the Education Ministry and if the writing was no longer "left to ideologues."[26]

This 1982 textbook controversy centered on the Pacific War and no doubt encouraged Ienaga Saburō's third lawsuit against the Education Ministry. This time Ienaga zeroed in on the ministry's demand that he delete references to a bacteriological warfare unit that had operated secretly during World War II in Manchuria. Since after the war the U.S. Army had suppressed all information on the existence of this unit and its atrocities to make use of some of the experimental data it had collected, very little had been known about it until scholars such as Ienaga began to bring it to public attention. The Education Ministry had reacted to the inclusion of such information in a textbook with the following comment: "No credible scholarly research—articles or books—have yet been published on this issue; it is premature to discuss it in a textbook."[27]

Ienaga then went to court once more in 1984, charging that the Education Ministry had violated his freedom of speech by insisting he alter the references to Japanese atrocities during the war. In 1989 the Tokyo Court of Appeals found only one count in Ienaga's favor and awarded him the equivalent of about U.S.$700 in damages. The government appealed to the Supreme Court.

In the meantime, in this confusing pattern of judicial leapfrog, the government's appeal of Ienaga's second suit, originally filed in 1967, had reached the Japanese Supreme Court in 1982. That court overturned the ruling of the Tokyo Higher Court on a technicality and sent the case back to it for reconsideration. In March 1986 the Tokyo Higher Court reversed itself and gave the victory to the government. Ienaga's legal team immediately began preparing their own appeal in yet another attempt to force the Supreme Court to rule on the broader constitutional issues.

Thus a forty-year-old legal campaign against the system of central government authorization of textbooks was kept alive into the 1990s.[28]

The "New Conservative Logic"

The political right also played its part in refusing to allow these conflicts to subside. In 1982 the prime ministership passed into the hands of Nakasone Yasuhiro. Although Nakasone's own faction was the smallest among the Liberal Democratic Party in the Diet, he turned out to be one of the more forceful of postwar prime ministers. It was his assertive approach to foreign policy and military defense that most marked his tenure but he also made educational reform central to his "new conservative logic."

Early in Nakasone's political career he had served as vice-chairman on the Liberal Democratic Party committee that issued the pamphlet "The Problem of Deplorable Textbooks," which accused the Japan Teachers' Union of propagating communist ideology. He had subsequently called for reform of the system as a whole because "only piecemeal improvements have been carried out within the framework of educational philosophy and institutions transplanted from abroad by the Occupation authorities about thirty years ago." In his view, there were intrinsic "confusions" in "transplanting" foreign policies into Japan: "[The Occupation reformers] were filled with abstract idealism and universalism, splendid products of the history of mankind. However, education should not ignore the particular uniqueness, history, climate and social constitution of each nation." As prime minister he was more specific: "My interpretation of the [1947] Fundamental Law of Education, . . . is that patriotism and filial piety must be taught as the goal of education."[29]

The prime minister acted out this rhetoric when he paid a highly publicized visit to the Yasukuni Shrine on August 15, 1985, the fortieth anniversary of the surrender to the Allies. Although analogous to the U.S. Arlington Cemetery in so far as both are dedicated to war dead, Yasukuni Shrine is closely associated with prewar state Shinto as well as with militarism.[30] Since the end of the Occupation there had been groups advocating that the government provide financial support for it, and beginning in 1969 the Conservatives in the Diet had tried repeatedly to pass a bill to declare the shrine a national monument rather than a religious facility, a change that would permit the government to fund it without violating the constitutional separation of church and state. In 1975 Prime Minister Miki Takeo had paid a visit billed as a personal visit in his capacity as a private citizen and every prime minister thereafter had done the same. But Prime Minister Nakasone made his visit in an official capacity to coincide with the anniversary of the end of World War II. This provocative act stirred even greater criticism from the opposition because of Nakasone's well-known nationalist views.[31]

Nakasone completed his tenure as prime minister in 1987 but the Education Ministry, which had fought with Nakasone on a number of other matters, proved quite willing to keep faith with him in the larger battle over patriotism. In 1985, responding to reports that only a small minority of Japanese primary or middle schools were displaying the Japanese flag or singing at graduation the prewar anthem "Kimigayo"—a song focused on the imperial dynasty—the ministry decreed that these patriotic symbols should be part of school ceremonies.[32] This policy statement renewed the argument over whether—as critics maintained—these were symbols of militarism and emperor-worship or—as the ministry and its supporters asserted—they had evolved into symbols of a peaceful culture. At least some principals, perhaps reacting to the pressure from teachers and parents, have simply ignored the ministry.

Patriotism was not the only textbook issue. The Japan Teachers' Union accused the Education Ministry of also "carefully rejecting disadvantageous facts for the government such as . . . the environmental pollution, or the poor administration in social welfare."[33] This view was countered from the right by some within the Liberal Democratic Party and others in the powerful Federation of Economic Organizations, who pointed to what they characterized as a socialist bias against business in the treatment of economics in the social studies.[34] Concern about schooling on the part of corporate Japan was to carry into other areas of the curriculum as well.

Remarkable Successes?

Easily lost sight of in the smoke of this ideological combat and judicial firefights over textbooks has been the enormous changes and what some at least would term remarkable successes during the four decades from 1950 to 1990.

Declining Japanese birthrates slowed the growth of enrollments in the compulsory grades and by 1986 had produced an absolute drop in the number of primary school pupils, a harbinger of future drops in the secondary school numbers. Nevertheless, the national system of schooling as a whole actually grew in the 1970s and 1980s. This growth resulted from two trends: (1) At the lower end more parents voluntarily sent their children to kindergarten and (2) at the upper end a larger percent of those completing compulsory education were going on into senior high school and beyond.

About two-thirds of all preschoolers were attending some type of formal program by the 1990s. Much of the growth at this level was in the private sector. Whereas in the 1980s less than 1 percent of primary school students attended private schools (versus nearly 25 percent in the United States) and only 3 percent of middle school students attended private schools, about three-quarters of all preschools were private.[35] Although preschool child care issues have emerged as extremely important in the United States, more important to the politics of schooling in Japan was the growth in the upper levels. By the mid-1970s Japan had surpassed every other capitalist nation except the United States in the percentage of male and female youth attending a secondary or postsecondary school. And by the early 1990s, 96 percent of those graduating from middle school went on to attend the noncompulsory upper secondary schools. To measure it another way, whereas over half of the fresh workers in the manufacturing sector in 1965 had only a middle school education and 8 percent had gone beyond high school, 100 percent had middle school diplomas by 1985 (see Figure 8.2), with a third having gone beyond high school. In the service industries such as banking and insurance, the number of new recruits with some higher education had almost quadrupled in those two decades.[36]

One result was that by the early 1980s "a considerably larger proportion of Japanese (90 percent) than Americans (73 percent) or Europeans (in most countries below 50 percent) finish the twelfth grade, and a greater proportion of males complete university B.A. degrees in Japan than in any other country."[37] Japan ranked second only to the United States among capitalist countries in the percent of college-age individuals in higher education.[38]

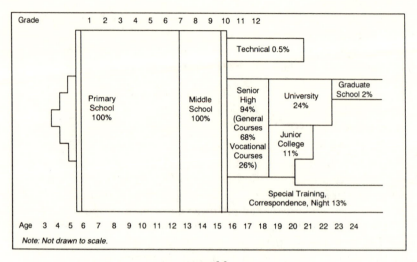

FIGURE 8.2
Main Tracks in Schooling, Mid-1980s.
Source: For percents of age group, Dore and Sako, *How the Japanese Learn to Work*, p. 21;
and Schoppa, *Education Reform*, p. 35.

The reputation abroad of the quality of Japan's schools improved greatly in the 1970s. In part this was in recognition of the role the schools were playing in providing managers and workers in Japan's "economic miracle." As a distinguished British sociologist put it:

> School [in Japan] serves ... to teach the classic Protestant ethical doctrine that life is primarily about fulfilling one's assigned duties and meeting deadlines and only secondarily about happiness or enjoyment. It teaches, too, the pleasures of achievement, and the dangers of resting on laurels and not recognizing the challenge of even greater possible achievements. ... School also teaches the pleasures of socialization, the shared pleasure of group accomplishment. It prepares people not only to accept as natural, but also to get comfort from, the patterns of co-operative effort, constant consultation, group responsibility and group sharing in achievement which seem to contribute to the efficiency of Japanese enterprises and to sustain their character as "learning organisms."[39]

Also at this time the foreign press increasingly noted that elementary and junior high students were scoring at or near the top in international competitions in the natural sciences and mathematics. The comparative proficiency of Japanese schoolchildren in music and the graphic arts also came to the attention of Americans.[40] Indeed, a U.S. observer of Japanese high schools stated, "It would not be an exaggeration to say that in many respects the average high school graduate in Japan is equal or superior to the average American college graduate in science, math, geography, history, music, art, and foreign language skills."[41] Another American stressed the basic egalitarian aspects of such achievement: "Japan's distribution of cognitive skills is probably more equal than that of any other contemporary society."[42]

Of course, not all Japanese schools were perceived as equal in quality. Faced with more applicants than places, prestigious national as well as other universities both public and private continued to rely chiefly upon entrance examinations almost to the complete disregard of high school transcripts, recommendations from former teachers, and extracurricular activities. Because the applicant is identified only by a number on these examinations, even gender and age are supposedly masked.

The role of family influence and/or the extent of examination cheating in gaining admittance are less clear. Certainly some lesser private colleges in need of funds have allowed "backdoor admissions" in exchange for hefty donations (a practice not unknown among those U.S. Ivy League schools that give preference to alumni children). It is also asserted that powerful political figures are able to gain admissions for their own children and those of their constituents.[43] From time to time, cases have been uncovered where faculty or staff have taken bribes, particularly for admissions to medical schools. Infrequently, this practice has even reached into the very best of universities. For instance, it was discovered in 1991 that admissions to a private university of excellent reputation had for some time been corrupted by a staff member arranging for proxies to take the examinations.[44] Perhaps the only generalization that should be made is that the more exclusive a Japanese university the less likely it tolerates such practices but the more likely that individuals are tempted to try them.

Because of the admission examinations system, some scholars were arguing by the late 1970s that "class distinctions stemming from a person's birth or parentage are minimal in contemporary Japan," and because of low tuition rates and the national scholarship system "few superior students are forced to give up a University Education simply because their parents cannot afford it."[45] Authors of a 1981 study of a sample of 7,000 male students and their fathers emphasized in their conclusion "how many students from poor homes managed nevertheless to enter the gates of the national universities."[46] Although these claims are subject to some skepticism, they seem to have widespread credibility among the Japanese public.

Even more striking were the changes in the upward mobility of female students within the school system. In the mid-1970s, 93.5 percent of all girls finishing compulsory middle school were going on to either senior high school or higher technical schools versus 92.6 percent for all youth. In other words, by this measure females had actually surpassed males.

The percent of women going on to postsecondary schools expanded from 18 percent in 1970 to over 32 percent a decade later. Male attendance also grew, from 29 percent to 43 percent. For males, if not for females, educational achievement has continued to be by far the single most important factor in opening up opportunities for success in later life. It is even claimed that there is a much tighter correlation between schools attended and income or social status than in most industrial societies.[47]

Disastrous Failures?

Although there has been little argument that the school system made enormous progress from the days prior to World War II, many on the right as well as the left have found that the benefits of the system do not outweigh the costs. In the words of one early skeptic among U.S. observers:

> What is given short shrift are the costs of this system in terms of stifling individual creativity, failing to accommodate and deal with deviant groups (be they minority groups, individual deviants such as left-handers, or "drop-outs"—who have become a public issue since the early 1970s), and not fostering attitudes appropriate to dealing effectively with sharply different cultures.[48]

By relying on achievement in the schools to determine occupational roles and therefore income, social status, and even political power, society had produced a system of "exam hells" that stifled individuality and creativity while penalizing underprivileged families and inflicting psychological damage on all youth.

In Japan, as much if not more than in other industrialized nations, both society and its school system remain highly stratified. More than most industrial societies, ladders within the school system determine on which tier of society the individual will ultimately land. But not all ladders begin or end in the same place. The trick for the ambitious is to get started as soon as possible up that set of ladders that reaches to the highest tier with the fewest delays or detours.

It is probably fair to say that compulsory education varies less in Japan than in other industrial societies, not only because the quality of public primary and middle schools varies less from community to community but also because private schooling plays a relatively small role at these compulsory levels. But this situation is not so for grades 10 through 12: These grades have not become legally compulsory in Japan, although by the mid-1980s they were nearly universal with some 94 percent going beyond middle school.

But upper secondary schools differ much more widely in reputation than those at the compulsory levels. Since vocational high schools are in some sense meant to be terminal—that is, they do not provide ladders beyond the skilled labor or service worker tiers in the occupational structure—we will focus here on the "ordinary" or "comprehensive" senior high school, which does purport to prepare students for the possibility of college.

As we have seen, there are three categories of senior high schools in Japan: public, "national," and private. The great majority of public schools are under local jurisdiction and there is considerable variation in quality even among those that are considered "academic" as opposed to vocational. This variation is a result of local decisions to create a hierarchy of schools within the district that has already been described (see Chapter 7). Facilities and other conditions in lower-ranked high schools are usually inferior to higher-ranked schools in the cities, but the facilities are not usually what is ranked. It is largely the reputation for moving students into the "best" universities that determines the difficulty of gaining entrance to a particular high school.

The second type of tax-supported schools are termed "national" because they are attached to national universities and, unlike other public schools, are funded from the central government, which has been generous under the guise of sponsoring educational research. These national schools often have attached kindergarten, primary, and middle schools, in which case the high school student body commonly consists of large numbers who got on the "escalator" at these lower levels. Regardless of when they admit students, these schools normally have residential district restrictions so that they are not supposed to draw students from throughout the country.

At the senior high school level, private schools begin to play a significant role, enrolling more than one-fourth of all upper secondary students (versus roughly 6 percent in Britain and 13 percent in the United States). These private schools are not necessarily higher-quality institutions; they vary greatly in facilities as well as in price of tuition. As with public high schools, these are ranked in the public mind by their degree of success in placing their graduates in the most desirable universities. Some private high schools have established a nationwide reputation for this and draw students from all over the country. Others are last choices for would-be college preparatory majors before they settle on a public vocational school. Which middle school graduate gets on which ladder to climb to which of the next tiers depends almost entirely upon scoring well on entrance examinations.[49]

Although course grades and, especially in more recent years, teacher recommendations from the middle school may be considered, applicants to the best schools must score high on the competitive examinations. To get past this obstacle, parents may place their children in private primary schools or even kindergartens affiliated with private high schools to get on the right ladder. But even private schools must protect their rankings by admitting as many high achievers as possible, so entrance exams are critical here as well. Thus the parents of middle school students who do not do well on entrance exams are faced with choices among lower-ranked high schools whether they be public or private.

Failing to gain admission to a highly ranked school is, of course, a deep disappointment to ambitious students, and materials designed to help them adapt to senior high school sometimes address it explicitly, as did this pamphlet: "At least a few of you think that you are in a second-rate school . . . and would like to transfer into a school with a better reputation so that you'll increase your chances of passing the entrance examination of a good university. That attitude is a big mistake." The mistake was said to be twofold. First the pamphlet argued, "High school is the most important period for character-building and for the cultivation of a student's broad sensibility to life. If all one learns is what he needs to pass the [university] entrance examinations, he really isn't educated." But at the same time, the authors held out the hope that some students even from "so-called second-rate high schools" would get into good colleges.[50] One suspects that such pamphlets were not often distributed at the most prestigious high schools.

Success in the entrance examination to the right college is even more critical for ambitious students because colleges vary in quality even more widely than do secondary schools, and transfer of credit between them is seldom allowed. Once again, quality is equated with results in placing graduates into jobs. Whereas lesser schools may produce local or regional leaders,[51] only national universities—especially Tokyo and Kyoto—and the very top private schools—Keiō University and Waseda University—can assure relatively easy access to managerial posts in leading corporations or the higher civil service.

The annual average success rate for candidates taking the civil service examinations has been between 2.5 percent and 6.5 percent, but graduates of national universities have rates far higher than that. Those from other public as well as private schools regularly fall below the average (see Figure 8.3).

Among the national universities, graduates of the Universities of Hokkaido and Tōhoku trail far behind Tokyo and Kyoto, which together regularly supply 40 percent to 55 percent of successful candidates despite that their enrollments—

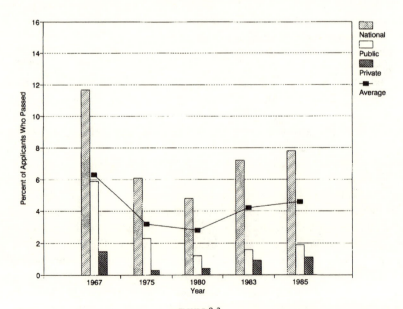

FIGURE 8.3
Success in Civil Service Examinations: Percentage of Applicants Who Passed, 1967–1985.
Source: Data from Koh, *Japan's Administrative Elite,* p. 88.

14,440 for Tokyo and 11,500 for Kyoto—are considerably smaller than such private schools as Waseda (40,500), Chūō (30,700), or Keiō (22,800).[52] (See Figure 8.4.)

Waseda and Keiō do much better in placing their graduates in key positions in the business world but here too the universities of Tokyo and Kyoto combined dominate the highest echelons. A 1992 survey of 2,105 presidents of major companies listed in the First Section of the Tokyo Stock Exchange revealed that alumni of Waseda and Keiō combined for about a quarter of the total. But once again, they were behind Tokyo and Kyoto, whose graduates together accounted for almost half.[53]

The advantages of attending a government-supported school can also be measured in terms of income earned in the private sector. There is a strong correlation in Japan between size of firm and size of remuneration, and there is a strong correlation between size of firm and pecking order of colleges. In other words, graduation from a national university is correlated with working for a larger firm and receiving larger paychecks and more generous fringe benefits. Larger firms also offer greater security in the form of the expectation of "career-long employment." Graduates of the prestigious national and private schools are four to five times more likely to be employed in the elite companies, either because of or despite what actually was learned as undergraduates.[54]

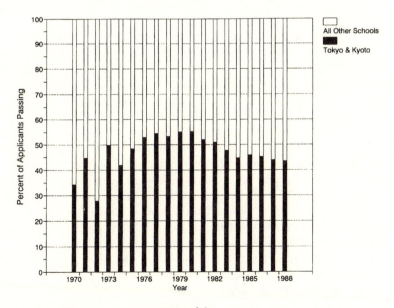

FIGURE 8.4
Schooling of Administrative Elite: Percent of Graduates Passing Civil Service Exams, by College.
Source: Calculated from Koh, *Japan's Administrative Elite*, p. 86.

As might be expected, the demand for places in such schools is very high. Annually some 12,000 apply for one of the 3,000 seats in the entering class at Tokyo University. Over half of those successful will have taken the exam once before and a third will have taken it twice before. One out of ten will pass only on their fourth annual attempt.[55] Moreover, it should be remembered that for everyone who does apply there are doubtless many others who decided instead to try a less selective school. By no means are all postsecondary schools so exclusive. In the 1980s over 88 percent of college applicants applied to and three out of four attended private colleges, many of which have long accepted applicants who scored well below the median.[56]

There are also other types of postsecondary schools. The number of junior colleges—or "short-term colleges," as they are called—grew from 479 in 1970 to 517 by 1980. These enrolled over 370,000. During the 1970s higher technical schools—postsecondary schools with various engineering courses—enrolled another 47,000 or so. Both types of schools offer only terminal programs in the sense that credit earned is not usually transferable to a regular four-year college.

The emphasis on gaining entrance to the more exclusive high schools in order to gain entrance to the more exclusive universities has stimulated the explosive growth of what are referred to most often simply as *juku*.[57] The term *juku* has a long tradition as a designation for private academies of various types. In contemporary parlance, however, it can most often be translated as "after-school academies"—for-profit tutoring enterprises that offer classes in the late afternoons, early evenings, and/or weekends. Although *juku* is sometimes misleadingly translated simply as "cram school," there is actually a wide variety of these schools, including those that specialize in sports, traditional arts, and other skills that may not be in the regular school curriculum (*keiko goto juku*). There are also *juku* that concentrate on preparing youth for examinations (*yobikō, shingaku juku*, or *shiken juku*) or catching up in school (*gakushū juku, hoshū juku*). As Kondō Sumio of the Children's Research Institute in Tokyo has noted: "It is far from uncommon for a child to be getting extra tutoring on Monday, Wednesday and Friday, and lessons on painting on Tuesday, piano on Thursday and swimming on Saturday."[58] (See Table 8.1.)

"Academic" *juku* may both tutor slow learners and prepare students for entrance examinations, although the term *yobikō*, or "prep school," is used most frequently for those that offer instruction specifically aimed at the college entrance exams, enrolling recent graduates from senior high school who have failed one or more college entrance exams in the past—what the Japanese call *rōnin* in reference to samurai without lords.[59]

The popularity of *juku* increased rapidly over the years. A 1943 Education Ministry survey identified only about 2,300 such institutions; a 1977 survey counted some 50,000, with 60 percent having been established after 1966 and another third in the early 1970s. Depending upon what is included, estimates of the total number of *juku* in the 1990s range as high as twice that many.[60] By

TABLE 8.1
Elementary Students Enrolled in After-School Lessons, 1968 and 1972

	Second Grade		Fifth Grade	
	1968 (%)	1972 (%)	1968 (%)	1972 (%)
Any lessons	69	74	70	83
Subjects[a]				
Academic	11	5	20	26
English	0	5	0	10
Abacus	4	2	23	30
Music	32	26	15	14
Calligraphy	29	39	25	36
Painting	9	8	4	5
Sports	2	9	3	13

[a]May take lessons in more than one subject.

SOURCE: Adapted from Kondo, "Off We Go to Our Lessons," graph 1, p. 16.

the mid-1980s these were enrolling 4.5 million primary and middle school students, one of every four in the nation. The largest of these are incorporated chains with tens of thousands of customers, including some organized in networks of franchises and some even with foreign branches for children of families working abroad. At the other end of the scale, especially in rural areas, there are many that are quite small with as few as a dozen students.

Males are somewhat more likely than females to be sent to a *juku* and the percentage of both groups increases with grade level in school. These data reflect the importance of entrance examinations as well as the bias toward giving a priority to the educational success of the male. Other variables include urban versus rural and income levels of the families. (See Figure 8.5.)

The concern about the impact of the cost of preparing for the entrance examinations on equal opportunity was raised long before the trend became as pronounced as it had by the mid-1970s.[61] Table 8.2 illustrates those trends. These data show a steady tendency toward underrepresentation by students from families in the lower income strata. This is somewhat more true of private universities, which make up the largest proportion of students despite costing much more than the public schools. At national universities (the best of the public schools), the percent of students from lower income strata in 1965 was remarkably equitable. By 1976, however, the students from families in the lower income strata had lost considerable ground to those from families with higher incomes.

It should be noted, however, that such breakdowns may tell us less in the case of countries like Japan or Sweden than in the United States or Britain because the disparity in incomes—the distance between the bottom and the top

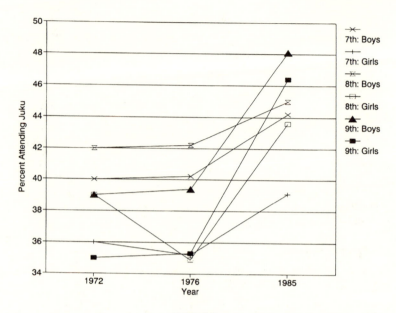

FIGURE 8.5
Middle School Students in *Juku* by Grade and Gender, 1972–1985.
Source: Data from Tsukada, *"Yobiko" Life*, passim.

incomes—is less pronounced in Japan. In the early 1970s, the before-tax quintile ratio, which compares the income of the richest 20 percent with that of the poorest 20 percent, was about twice as great for the United States (12), France (11), or Canada (10) than for Japan (6).[62] After-tax ratios in Japan were about the same as in Sweden or the United Kingdom but still much lower than that of the United States. Moreover the 1970s saw a very slight trend toward greater equality, although there were still wide differences. Perhaps the clearest evidence of disparate outcomes of the school system was statistics on male and female students going beyond compulsory levels. Females still lagged behind males in the percent moving from high schools to colleges—33.6 percent of women whereas the total for both genders was 38.6 (44 percent in the United States, 19 percent in West Germany, 20 percent in England, and 25 percent in France).[63]

Moreover, these figures hide an important truth: Most women were not attending the same kind of postsecondary schools that men were. The overwhelming majority of female students in higher education in the early postwar period were in junior colleges, those two- or three-year postwar institutions that granted only terminal degrees for credit not usually transferable directly toward a four-year university degree. Those who wished to go on to a four-year college had to take the entrance examination along with recent graduates from high school. The programs offered were either narrowly vocationally oriented or intended for young ladies preparing to be housewives.

TABLE 8.2
Social Equality and Universities: Students by Type of School and Income Strata

	1965 (%)	1970 (%)	1976 (%)
All four-year universities			
Lowest 20%	8	9	7
Next to lowest 20%	10	8	9
Middle 20%	13	14	12
Next to highest 20%	22	22	25
Highest 20%	46	47	47
National universities			
Lowest 20%	16	17	13
Next to lowest 20%	15	14	12
Middle 20%	19	18	15
Next to highest 20%	23	21	25
Highest 20%	28	29	35
Private universities			
Lowest 20%	5	6	7
Next to lowest 20%	7	6	9
Middle 20%	11	13	12
Next to highest 20%	21	22	25
Highest 20%	56	53	47

SOURCE: Adapted from Cummings, "Expansion, Examination Fever, and Equality," table 5.3, p. 102.

Moreover, although originally conceived of as coeducational schools in the postwar years, they ceased to be so by 1960. Whereas women made up less than half of junior college student bodies until 1953, their percentage soared until in 1960 they made up more than three-quarters. In 1970 women constituted 83 percent and in 1980 almost 90 percent. Put another way, over 40 percent of women enrolled in higher education in 1970 were actually in second-class institutions (see Figure 8.6). In that year less than 7 percent of females graduating from high school were enrolling in four-year colleges and they constituted only 18 percent of the student bodies of four-year institutions. Although the numbers of females attending postsecondary schools increased greatly over the next three decades, these proportions did change significantly: In 1991 over 40 percent of postsecondary female students were enrolled in junior colleges.

Another significant measure of de facto gender segregation in higher education can be seen in the statistics on student majors. Whereas males in four-year universities are concentrated in the social sciences and technical fields that lead to jobs that have higher prestige and income, women are concentrated in education, humanities, and home economics, degrees that are not closely associated with high-paying, high-status careers.

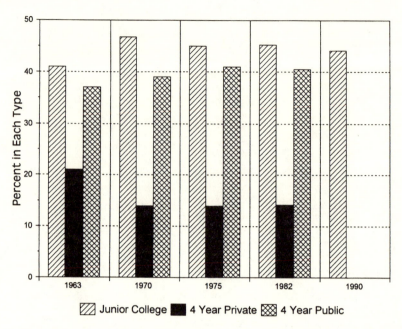

FIGURE 8.6
Women in College by Type of School Attending, 1963–1990.
Source: Calculated from Monbushō, *Gakusei 90 nenshi*, pp. 652–653.

Here again one can assume some aspect of self-fulfilling prophecy at work. Middle-class females, whose families and peers as well as prospective employees expected them to work only briefly before marriage and childbirth, were channeled into majors suitable for that future. Those who then by choice or necessity stayed in the paid work force had far more limited options than their male counterparts who had majored in other fields.

However, it would be shortsighted to stress only the connections between college and work opportunities. Political scientist Susan Pharr has stressed the broader impact of higher education on changing how women view their roles over this period:

> "Higher education" is really a shorthand term for number of variables that go along with increased educational exposure. Going to college gives the individual the opportunity to enter into new relationships with peers and with teachers whose ideas may be markedly different from those of the family, and the option, available in the university setting more than in almost any other major institutional setting in most societies, to try out new ideas and types of behavior in a subculture where experimentation is accepted and even valued.[64]

Although the disparate outcomes for women are the most obvious way in which the system fails to provide equal passage up the educational ladders, they are by no means the only or even the worst evidence of discrimination in the Japanese system. There are some sizable ethnic and racial minorities amid the supposed homogeneity of Japanese society, especially the Okinawans, Ainu, Burakumin, and Koreans. All of these have been disadvantaged to one degree or another. In the words of the Japan Teachers' Union, "We had or still have a shameful history of discrimination against the Korean, the Chinese, the Okinawan, the Ainu race, and the inhabitants of 'unliberated hamlets' called Buraku."[65]

Over 1 million Japanese citizens reside in the Okinawan island chain. They are sometimes considered ethnically distinct from the mainland although others would dispute this. What is indisputable is that despite centuries of close cultural relations since their political incorporation in the seventeenth century, these areas remained economically disadvantaged in comparison with the main islands. Education is one of the key spheres in which Okinawa Prefecture is commonly said to lag behind the rest of Japan.

The Ainu include a number of groups of clearly racially distinct indigenous peoples who were forced off the main island onto the northern islands of Hokkaido, the Kuriles, and Sakhalin over the course of a thousand years. The harsh living conditions on these islands plus their inferior political status contributed to the reduction of their numbers to fewer than 17,000 at the end of the nineteenth century, when the parliament passed the first "Law for the Protection of the Former Natives of Hokkaido" after several decades of government-sponsored expropriation of Ainu lands by Japanese from the main islands. A 1986 survey of Hokkaido identified some 25,000 living there. Almost all had some ancestors who had intermarried with Japanese. Between 1901 and 1937 there were separate curricula for Ainu schools. Since then they have supposedly been integrated into the regular school system. Although a great deal of assimilation has taken place over the centuries, those who remain identified as Ainu are still thought of by many, perhaps most, other Japanese as separate and do not have equal opportunities in schools or jobs. The Ainu Association of Hokkaido, with a membership of some 16,000, is also committed to maintaining a separate cultural identity while working for equality of opportunity.[66]

Prejudice is also widespread against the large numbers of Burakumin, a people who though racially Japanese have nonetheless suffered many centuries of social and economic discrimination as outcasts from mainstream society. The origins of this minority are the subject of considerable disagreement. But it is clear that by the Tokugawa period most Burakumin had been ghettoized primarily in areas around cities in central Japan such as Osaka and Kyoto. There they worked in occupations that were disdained by others: for example, grave digging, butchering, leather tanning, and garbage collecting. Legally emancipated by Meiji reformers in 1871, they have nevertheless commonly continued to be the victims of severe prejudice. Because many prefer not to be identified, precise numbers are difficult to obtain. Estimates in the 1970s ranged between

1,200,000 and 3 million. In 1965, in part because of the efforts of two rival organizations—Buraku Liberation League and the National Liaison Council for Buraku Liberation League Normalization—the government created a commission to make recommendations on how to integrate these Japanese into mainstream society. This has included incorporating information on the problem into the school curricula.

Much more ethnically but not racially distinct are those Koreans who reside permanently in Japan. Beginning with the Japanese annexation of Korea in 1910 and accelerating during the Pacific War, Koreans either voluntarily migrated or were conscripted to work in Japan, bringing the total wartime number to perhaps 2 million. Although they legally held the status of imperial subjects, they were commonly discriminated against in ways not unlike those suffered by Irish Catholics in England. The partition of Korea after its liberation in 1945 complicated enormously the repatriation issue, but by 1981 the number was down to 668,000. Although the overwhelming majority have been born in Japan, the modern legal code has never recognized mere fact of birth in Japan as sufficient to establish citizenship and naturalization has always been difficult. The 1952 Nationality Law recategorized many of these former colonial subjects as aliens. In a sense this law has been tantamount to a twin set of disadvantages: social prejudice and legal barriers. This is also true for other "foreign" residents in Japan, including over 50,000 Chinese residents in Japan. In the case of the Koreans, however, sharp political divisions between supporters of North Korea and supporters of South Korea have complicated their efforts to bring about change.[67]

On the legal front, there was some progress in the 1970s. In 1974 a Korean resident won a Supreme Court case against a large private corporation on the grounds of job discrimination despite having been hired in the first place only after hiding his Korean nationality on his application by using a Japanese name. In 1977 a Waseda University graduate seeking to practice law won a Supreme Court case against the Ministry of Justice, which had denied him the opportunity to pass the bar because he was technically an alien.[68]

Beginning in the 1960s but intensifying in the 1970s and 1980s, these minorities became much more politically visible in their struggles against discrimination. In the early 1970s there was a flurry of incidents of vandalism and bombings that were done in the name of Ainu liberation if not necessarily by Ainu themselves. One of the bombings destroyed part of an ethnographic exhibit at the University of Hokkaido. These incidents were followed by a violent backlash against Ainu and their supporters. A decade later the Ainu Association of Hokkaido spoke for many when it demonstrated to protest remarks by Prime Minister Nakasone and others who spoke of Japan as a "monoethnic" society.

The more sustained protest against discrimination in the schools has arisen over the treatment of Burakumin. On a number of occasions, activists from the

Buraku Liberation League have confronted teachers over issues of counseling, remedial instruction, and related questions. Two incidents in particular have received extensive media coverage. In April 1969 a group of Osaka school-teachers were held captive by members of the Hyogo Prefecture chapter of the league in a "public denunciation session," ostensibly for their failure to use league-endorsed teaching material but also because they were Communist Party supporters who favored the approach of the rival National Liaison Council. The league members involved were initially convicted of unlawful detention but their appeal was not heard until 1975. Meanwhile, in November 1974, activists from the same Hyogo Prefecture chapter clashed violently with teachers at the prestigious Yōka High School, a conflict that resulted in forty-eight persons being hospitalized. The key issue this time was the teachers' resistance to the organization of Burakumin student study groups. This case also resulted in years of trials.[69] The long-term issue for educational officials, however, has been the recurring incidents of student physical and/or verbal harassment of Burakumin classmates. By the end of the 1970s the Education Ministry was allocating increased subsidies to schools with large numbers of Burakumin, especially in the Kansai region of central Japan. One U.S. observer, William Cummings, reported that many schools there had increased their efforts to alter student attitudes. But in 1990 five faculty members at the private Hiroshima Shudo University were dismissed in a controversy that involved their efforts to educate students about discrimination.[70]

Another prime target for critics of Japan's schools has been the entrance examination system. The "exam wars" or "examination hell" and the link to the "*juku* boom" or the "runaway *juku* era" have been roundly condemned for doing serious damage to Japan's youth. Fresh denunciations of the educational system come with each new study that shows an increase in some undesirable behavior, or the greater need for eyeglasses and a decrease in physical stamina as measured by national surveys, or even a decline in numbers of medals at the Olympics.[71] Since the early 1950s it has been commonplace to attribute Japan's high suicide rates to the strain of the entrance exams.

The evidence of cause and effect here, of course, is usually tenuous at best and sometimes the data simply do not fit. For instance, suicide rates among those age groups that were under the most pressures to perform in schools actually declined after the 1950s (see Figure 8.7).

Moreover, even during the decades when suicide among Japanese youth was at its highest, the difference between male and female rates was surprisingly small—surprising because it is supposedly the males who are under the intense pressure to succeed. In the 1980s suicide among U.S. youth surpassed that in Japan despite that entrance examination pressures were supposedly far less in the United States (see Figure 8.8).

Although suicide can no longer be seen as a chief symptom of a dysfunctional school system, there is no shortage of other candidates put forth. As the

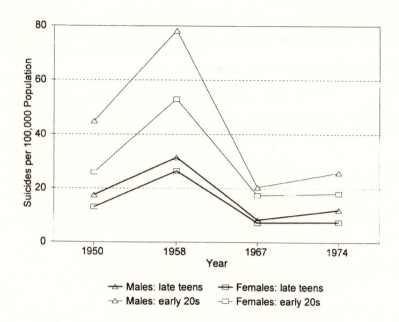

FIGURE 8.7
Suicide Rate Among Japanese Youth by Age Group and Gender, 1950–1974.
Source: Data from U.S. Department of Education, *Japanese Education Today,* table 9, p. 79.

businessman who headed the Hiroshima Prefectural Education Commission in 1983 phrased it: "Behavioral problems and decreasing scholastic achievement are concrete manifestations of the collapse of education. . . . Schools have been unable to develop an educational setup that can keep up with the changes in the world at large, and also because the educational function of the family has broken down." By speaking of behavioral problems, he was referring to "school violence and juvenile delinquency," which he asserted were "rampant today, and the age level of the children involved is becoming lower. In the schools affected, the teachers have their hands full dealing with these problems; in consequence, the other students are distracted and the overall level of scholastic achievement has dropped."[72] (See Figure 8.9.)

This concern was shared by the chief spokesgroup on education issues for the national business elite, the Japanese Federation of Employers, when it issued a report on school violence in 1983. But these businessmen focused more specifically on the effects that the school environment was having on potential workers:

> It being one of the objects of school education to teach students about the relationship between society and the individual, the disrespect of rules inherent in school violence . . . cannot be tolerated.

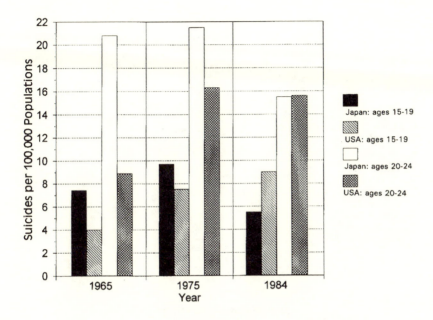

FIGURE 8.8

Suicide Rate Among Japanese and Americans by Age Group, 1965–1984.
Source: Data from U.S. Department of Education, *Japanese Education Today,* table 9, p. 79.

We must try to maintain the Japanese worker's diligence and group-consciousness which have been so crucial in helping to push up the nation's economy. Thus it is vitally important that the schools guide students in such a way that they have a proper outlook on society and work.[73]

Another commentator in the mid-1980s, a former official from the Ministry of International Trade and Industry, labeled the violence in schools a "consumer revolt" and argued for "supply-side competition" among the "suppliers of education, namely teachers and administrators" to drive out "inferior products."[74]

Police statistics did indeed show a rise in juvenile delinquency in the 1970s. Particularly alarming was the proportion of juvenile crimes committed by those still attending school: It was up from 48 percent to 72 percent between 1960 and 1975. This increase was correlated with the decreasing age of juvenile delinquents—fewer high school–aged and more middle and even primary school students. However, many of these arrests were for such offenses as smoking cigarettes and the incidence of violent offenses by juveniles—such as murder, rape, and other bodily harm—actually fell between 1960 and 1980. Moreover, the numbers of Japanese minors being arrested for any kind of offense were significantly smaller than in the United States or much of Europe.[75] Not all the physical violence in schools is committed by students. Increasingly in the 1980s the media carried stories of teachers who habitually used physical

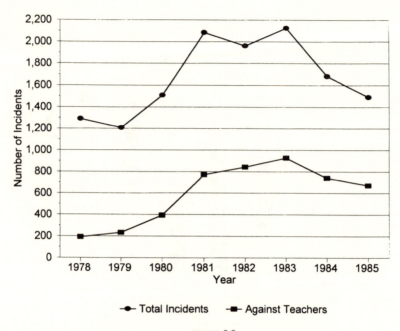

—●— Total Incidents   —■— Against Teachers

FIGURE 8.9
Incidence of Violence in Japanese Schools, 1978–1985.
Source: Data from Schoppa, *Education Reform*, p. 52.

beatings to maintain discipline.[76] There was in the 1980s also new evidence of an increased dropout rate among senior high school students and truancy at primary and middle school levels, although only a fraction of the rates in the United States.

Quite apart from worry about these statistically measurable symptoms, there is also concern about less tangible effects on adolescents' psyche and social adjustment. Healthy development is said to be jeopardized by the paucity of extracurricular activities such as athletics or lack of time for an active social life. Certainly the last years of junior high and especially the last two years of high school are very stressful passages for both parents and youth with ambitions for white-collar jobs. It is a time of far fewer extracurricular or social activities such as dating, parties, and recreation than for U.S. teenagers.[77]

One of the factors that supposedly has led to so much stress among youth is the prevalence of mothers willing to spend enormous time and energy tutoring their children as well as interacting with school and *juku* in the attempt to assure academic success. The popular term for these mothers, going back to the 1950s and 1960s, has been *kyōiku mama*—"Education Mother" or "good-education crazy mums"; others labeled them "excessive education mothers" or even "monster mothers." In the 1970s and 1980s this type of mothering seemed to become expected behavior, or at least a necessary evil, as "home education" was viewed as essential to student achievement. Just how many families are actually caught up in this competitive scramble to the extent portrayed in the stereotypical descriptions is not clear. Some estimates are as low as 10 percent. That is to say, there is reason to believe that the ambitions of most families do not extend to such extreme limits.[78]

By the late 1960s there were also numerous commentators who attributed the malaise in Japan's universities to the strain endured by students passing through "exam hell." These critics did not attempt to link this kind of post-exam stress syndrome to suicide but rather to other problems, including an inability to think creatively. As the *New York Times* summed it up in the heading for a 1973 article, critics were charging that "Japan Has Highly Trained Elite, but It Lacks Creativity."[79]

Increasingly in the 1980s Japanese television roundtable discussions and magazines carried somber exchanges on this question of *dokusō*—originality/creativity. Criticisms of the schools by Prime Minister Nakasone Yasuhiro helped to focus attention on alleged shortcomings from the lack of creativity: Were the Japanese schools, with their heavy emphasis on memorization and test-taking, nurturing the mindsets that would permit Japan to be successful in the postmodern world? It was said that education for a new Japan would have to produce these qualities in greater abundance because Japan could no longer depend upon importing technology from abroad. The irony of industrial success was that Japan was no longer playing catch-up and would have to take its turn blazing the trails of the future.

Related to this issue was the question of Japan's relative isolation from the world. In the 1980s the term *kokusaika*—to make international or to "internationalize"—became a buzzword in discourse on the school system as well as in other spheres.[80] The goal, pushed under Prime Minister Nakasone, was to create "international persons" and thereby an "international society." "Internationalization" included the goal of increasing both foreign professors and foreign students at Japanese universities. In 1980 there were only 1,127 full-time foreign faculty members at Japanese universities. Almost three-quarters of these were at private colleges.

Another area of concern in this regard has been the small numbers of foreign students in Japanese universities. Whatever the causes, whether the language barriers, high living expenses, failure to recruit, or lack of administrative flexibility, Japanese institutions have not enrolled students from abroad in numbers comparable to other industrialized countries. Although during the Meiji period there were numerous Chinese studying in Japan, and during the Pacific War the Japanese government to some extent encouraged students from the Greater East Asian Co-prosperity Sphere, in the postwar era the numbers have been small. In 1980 Japan ranked twenty-second in the world in numbers of foreign students, far below Italy, Lebanon, and Egypt, not to mention North American and Western European countries. Almost all of these—over 80 percent in 1983—have been from South, Southeast, and East Asia. They have been about equally distributed between private and public schools.

Renewed Calls for Reform

There had been little common ground between the Conservatives and the Progressives during the three decades from the end of the American Occupation and the end of the 1970s. One exception was a shared belief that the school system should grow in size. In the 1980s, however, the two opposing camps both shifted their attention toward the internal health of the now maturing system. Again both concurred that there were signs of serious afflictions. But there was painfully little agreement on how to diagnose these ailments much less prescribe a cure.

Between 1969 and 1971 the Central Council on Education issued a series of reports covering everything from the expansion of kindergarten schooling to the administration of graduate school research. Central government funding did increase, including more aid to private schools, but much of the rest of the reform agenda of the early 1970s remained on the drawing board. Then in the mid-1980s Prime Minister Nakasone initiated a fresh reform process. In the election campaign of 1983 he pushed a "Seven-Point Proposal":

1. Reform of the 6-3-3-4 school system.
2. An improvement in the system of high school entrance examinations—including reform of the *Kyōtsūichiji* [common] entrance examinations.
3. Improvement in the university entrance examination system.
4. Incorporation of work-experience activities and overnight camps into the education system.
5. An increased emphasis on morals and physical education.
6. Continued promotion of the internationalization of education.
7. An improvement in the quality of teachers.[81]

The following year Nakasone took the problem out of the hands of the standing committees in the Education Ministry and the Diet by appointing a new Ad Hoc Council on Education to report directly to his cabinet. In the next three years the commission issued four major reports listing as reasons for drastic change most of the symptoms discussed above. Much of this, although by no means all, was familiar from previous government reform proposals. And, as it turned out, Nakasone was no more successful than his predecessors in forging a consensus.

Control of Higher Education

The Liberal Democratic Party and the Education Ministry, spurred on by business leaders, did not relent in their efforts to exert more centralized control over the school system. But neither did these efforts bear much in the way of tangible fruit. The 1969 University Administration Emergency Measures Law had authorized the government to step in when university administrators were deemed to have lost control of their campus, but whatever the law's chilling effect on university policies, it was not used in the 1970s or 1980s. In the early 1970s, the government pushed for more consequential legislation.

The Central Council on Education issued the *Draft Outline of the Preliminary Report on the Basic Design of the Reform of Higher Education* in December 1969.[82] It cited a great number of areas for improvement, including the quality of teaching, the problem of underfunded facilities, and disparate missions of different types of schools. The council also underlined the need for further expansion of higher education to meet the demand among the people.

To meet these needs and "to avoid the evil effects arising from present disparities in the financial resources of national, local and private institutions," the council assumed that the national government was going to foot a large part of the bill for this government funding. This carrot of financial aid was welcomed by private schools, most of which were in deep debt as a result of their rapid expansion in the preceding decade. Subsidies in the form of research grants had been available to private colleges since the 1960s, but now some of Japan's major banks joined in lobbying the Diet to provide more generous public funding to prevent the collapse of the private sector as a whole.[83]

Beginning in the early 1970s the Diet responded. Postsecondary schools received grants and subsidized loans from the national treasury up to half of the operating costs per enrolled student. The government retained the ability to manipulate the formula in the attempt to maintain certain enrollment targets and student-faculty ratios in private colleges as well as to encourage the search for other funding sources. This latter feature has actually benefited the private schools with the highest prestige because they usually maintained the lowest student-faculty ratios and were the most successful in raising funds from alumni. A by-product of this was a considerable improvement in the salaries of teachers in the private sector. Other funding increases were included, albeit for private as well as public schools. However, the government restricted the future expansion of private schools.

The Central Council on Education did not intend that these increased expenditures to public and private universities come without strings attached. On the contrary, its draft report stressed that "the coordinating functions of the central government are increasingly required." The section in the report entitled "The Necessity to Guarantee the Autonomy of Universities and the Need to Overcome Their Isolation" focused on desired changes within university administration. "It is necessary to prevent the universities from becoming too isolated from society, by an excessive insistence on their independence, and from fulfilling their social obligations. If they become smugly self-contained, their activities in research and teaching will decline." More specifically, the council charged that "the universities are reluctant to listen to outsiders. Their sense of responsibility to the country is ambivalent, they are reluctant to cooperate with industry. They feel that bureaucratic administrative practices interfere with the creative activities expected of university persons."

A final council report, entitled *Basic Guidelines for Reform of Education,* was presented to the Education Ministry in June 1971. Under the heading "Institutional Reform Concerning Administration and Management of National and Local Public Universities," the council insisted:

> Whatever the measures finally decided on for rationalising the administration of higher education, the principle of non-institutional representatives participating in university administration is essential. In view of the "public nature" of higher educational institutions, the administration of each should include a certain number of officers chosen by each of three concerned parties: the institution itself, the government and the non-academic world.[84]

If Conservatives were particularly enthusiastic about these administrative recommendations, Progressives as well as university leaders were, not surprisingly, generally suspicious. This is not to say that university faculty and staff simply ignored these recommendations; public criticism was too great for that. Indeed, there took place in 1970 what has been described as an unprecedented "'boom' in university reform proposals"—some eighty schools undertaking self-examination and over 300 reports being produced.[85] By 1972 a large number of schools could boast of having made some changes in governance. Even Tokyo University had augmented its president's permanent staff during 1969 to enhance intramural coordination and respond more effectively to changed circumstances.

But for the most part these changes were small, and no major public university was willing in practice to yield internal policymaking to a board dominated by outsiders, whether from the government or the nonacademic world. Theoretically more attractive was the major alternative discussed, a model from the British system of each university being chartered as a corporation independent of the government except for funding. This would, however, still have required on the part of the Progressives considerable trust that the government would treat funding in a nonpartisan manner. Trust on either side, of course, has long been in short supply.[86]

In a stormy Diet session in 1973 the Liberal Democratic Party did manage to pass legislation aimed at implementing some of the recommendations of the Central Council on Education. It abolished the Tokyo University of Education—the successor to the prewar Tokyo Men's Higher Normal School—and replaced it with a radically new type of university to be located in the rural "science city" of Tsukuba. It was intended as a model for the reorganization of all national universities.

Some of the innovations involved the internal organization of teaching and research, but the most important breakthroughs were in governance. In the original bill, Tsukuba was to have a faculty senate, as in the typical public university, but the president would be much more powerful than usual. Moreover, he or she was to be advised by a committee that would include outsiders. Foes also made much of the fact that, unlike other major Japanese universities whether public or private, Tsukuba was placed well away from any major city—a location that would inhibit student involvement in off-campus politics.[87]

In the final analysis, these changes were not quite as radical in practice as in theory. Nor have other public universities been reorganized on the Tsukuba model. Thus in the 1980s, the Conservatives tried a new tack. The Ad Hoc Council on Education created in 1984 under Prime Minister Nakasone reintroduced the notion of a new Central University Council to oversee higher education. It also called for more diversity in postsecondary schooling and for changes in the admission examinations.

The Education Ministry has been largely unsuccessful in implementing any of these suggestions. It did persuade university administrators to make some small alterations in the entrance examination system in the late 1970s by adopting measures aimed at standardizing the examination system. All government schools agreed to hold entrance tests on the same day, eliminating the possibility of students taking exams at more than one such school in any given year. However, private schools were reluctant to sign on; thus students could continue to apply to a mixture of public and private colleges in any given year. The government also attempted to institutionalize a single National Common Examination administered by a separate national institute. Tokyo University and other elite universities had to accept this in principle but they then required applicants to also take a second test, using the first only as a screening device to winnow out a portion of the candidates. Interestingly enough, the candidates themselves were not to be told the results of the first exam.[88]

Control of the Compulsory System

Nor have the Conservatives been happy with the limited success that the national government has had in recentralizing control over the other levels of the system. The almost 3,500 appointed Educational Commissions that replaced the elected School Boards have managed to maintain some semblance of decentralized administration at the prefectural and local level. This has been especially true where the opposition parties have been able to elect governors and mayors and/or a substantial proportion of the assemblies, since it is these politicians who control the appointment process. There is technically a rule that no commission has a majority from either the Liberal Democratic Party or its opposition, although this can be finessed by appointing friendly "independents."[89]

Leaders in one district even challenged the appointment process itself. The huge Tokyo metropolitan area is organized like a prefecture with subdivisions having their own Educational Commissions. In 1978 one of these subdivisions, Nakano Ward, insisted on local elections for commission seats. The Education

Ministry opposed this as a violation of the statute, so in 1980 a nonbinding public poll was substituted with the head of the ward committing himself to making appointments on the basis of their results even though the elections had no legal status—a not untypical Japanese solution.[90]

As always, however, the economically dependent status of prefectural and local governments has meant that the central government can bring great leverage to bear. The Education Ministry budgets and allots central funds as subsidies in order to equalize the differences in the tax bases of affluent communities and those below average. A third of the funding of public primary and middle schools has come from central revenues, with prefectures and municipalities sharing about equally in the remaining burden. The prefectures have paid most of the costs of the senior high schools (80 percent) and universities (65 percent), but the national government has paid a 87 percent share for technical schools and a 36 percent share for junior colleges. This does not guarantee equal funding across the nation, but whereas the levels of per capita student expenditures in U.S. communities vary as much as 100 percent, in Japan the variation in ordinary public schools at the compulsory levels is only about 25 percent. This, of course, is a direct effect of the fact that the share of public elementary and secondary school funding in the United States from local revenues (between 40 and 50 percent) has been larger than in Japan in the 1970s and 1980s and because the share of the federal government funding (between 6 percent and 10 percent) has been smaller. Central government funding of higher education is also much smaller (13 percent to 14 percent in the 1980s) than in Japan.[91]

This does not mean that there are no significant regional variations in other aspects. For example, although the Education Ministry standards call for primary schools to have no fewer than twelve and no more than eighteen classes with between forty and forty-five students each, in the 1980s only 21 percent of schools actually were within the guidelines on the number of classes and the average number of students was thirty-four.[92] Nevertheless, most observers report that regardless of the politics of a community, the Education Ministry curriculum guidelines on "Courses of Study," which include specific objectives for each semester of each course at each grade, are generally followed in primary and middle schools.[93] To vary too greatly might jeopardize the students' opportunities to do well in the competition for places in the universities at the national level. Although students judged to be seriously handicapped either mentally or physically are segregated into special schools, there is usually no division between gifted and slow learners within a class and students are assigned to homerooms with an eye to combining mixed abilities. Hence, regardless of region, the general goal of each public school is to have every child approach the national targets. As a result, "Japanese young people of any given age and grade level experience a greater communality of cognitive exposure than do their American counterparts." Moreover, administrators generally follow practices aimed at minimizing social distinctions between youth while in school:

The stress on uniform pronunciation of the Japanese language, field trips paid out of the school budget rather than family contributions, the insistence that all children either walk or use public transportation between home and school, and the use of uniforms by secondary students, tend to obscure the class origins of individual Japanese students.[94]

As elsewhere in the industrialized world, those in the business world in Japan have long pressured for schooling that would meet their demands as employers. Their influence has been felt especially within the Liberal Democratic Party because of its close financial and policy ties with the business world. During the 1970s and 1980s it became commonplace to talk about the need for a "third wave of reform." This phrase was said by some to mean completing the postwar efforts of the American Occupation in the 1945–1950 period and the initiatives of the Central Council on Education in the late 1960s; others intended it to mean a grander reform that would rival the Meiji and Occupation reforms as a "third educational revolution."[95] For Japan to adapt to its unprecedented status as an economic power, if not superpower, schools would need to make major changes.

Spokespeople for major corporations, especially those in the electronics and auto business, capitalized on their success in world markets by calling domestically for a review of the existing system. Intellectuals and politicians of various stripes joined in the chorus. The 1972 report of the Central Council on Education, *Basic Guidelines for Reform of Education*, had already set the tone:

> Modern school education in Japan is equal in quality to that of other advanced countries. . . . However, . . . it is wrong to think that the contemporary school system which was hurriedly established under the supervision of the American Occupation Administration during the unusual situation following World War II will be satisfactory for all time. Today, we are confronted with an entirely different set of problems, the challenge of a new era which mankind has never seen the likes of before.[96]

The 1972 report of the Central Council on Education was in some ways more balanced in its rhetoric than earlier reports: It blamed both camps for the deadlock on reform.[97] Indeed in 1972 for the first time a representative from labor unions joined the academics, journalists, and businessmen on this advisory board. Some Progressive nuances were reflected in the report, especially when it spoke of "equal opportunity for education to all peoples" and "the justifiable demands for education of different social groups" or discussed the aim of education as "to enable individuals to realize their desirable objectives" and "to develop students' individual abilities and interests."

But the 1972 report was much more conservative when it echoed earlier Education Ministry statements about the individual being embedded within society and its traditions: "The individual does not exist in isolation from State or Society. He is only able to develop his individuality and demonstrate his creative ability within the context of the cultural tradition of the society in which he lives."[98]

Hence it is not surprising that this call for change was seen by the political left as part of "monopoly capitalism's structural reorganization plans" in which business was "advocating their naked excessive demands for labour and profit."[99] Critics reacted similarly to some of the conservative themes sounded by the members of the 1984 Ad Hoc Council on Education. For example, "[The statement in the 1947 Fundamental Law of Education] that the purpose of education should be the creation of 'complete persons' is vague as to what kind of person should be completed. Clearly, the idea that a person should be raised in the culture and traditions of the country where he was born is connected to this idea of 'complete persons.'"[100]

In addition to such rhetoric, the Conservative camp also tried more direct means to gain support for reform. In the early 1970s the Tanaka cabinet recommended to the Diet that teachers' salaries be increased by 50 percent—an amount that was eventually reduced to 10 percent when it passed in the parliament in 1974. In the 1980s similar recommendations came from Prime Minister Nakasone's Ad Hoc Council on Education. But these offerings were coupled with expanding government aid to private schools, and the Japan Teachers' Union, most of whose members were in public schools, was understandably opposed to diverting more funds into the private sector. It responded by accusing the government of intentionally undermining the public school system:

> This is clear from the emphasis on diverse new private educational institutions visible in [the Ad Hoc Council's] call for "an increase in the establishment of private elementary and middle schools." These policies simply promise an acceleration in the privatization of education and a speeding up of the process in which schools are increasingly being treated as just another piece of merchandise.[101]

Such opposition has not prevented the government from continuing to aid private schools. At the high school level, aid has been offered through a combination of local and national government subsidies and the formula for funding can vary somewhat from prefecture to prefecture.

"Diversification" in Multitracking

Differences of more substance were found in the recommendation that students be tracked earlier in their school careers so that they could develop more skills useful in the job market. The leadership of the Japan Teachers' Union was scathing in its 1975 denunciation of this capitalist version of "ability-first with its plausible propaganda . . . the very root of all disasters in education today":

> The ability-first policy played a certain role for democratization of society and education in a certain period of time, as long as it emphasized equality of [people].

But . . . it has gradually shifted to overemphasizing ability which industries just need, and at last it introduced a new discrimination. . . . In a capitalist society "equal opportunity according to ability" means nothing but mechanics for alienating the inferiors.

In practice this meant, the statement went on to explain, that

schools become a system of selecting children to be classified with ability. Just as an orange sorter selects oranges into each grade of A, B, or C with its respective price and destination, our school[s] classify children for each destination appointed by the demands of industries. . . .

Under this policy the elite at the top of the social hierarchy must sacrifice humanity instead of ability, because to be the elite is nothing but to be heartless, intolerant, and to kick their fellows down.

The policies advocated by business would also continue discrimination against the poor and segregation of "most of the mentally and physically handicapped children [who] are excluded from compulsory education and deprived of their right to education" despite the 1947 Fundamental Law of Education, which guaranteed "education according to ability." That is to say, "Equal opportunity should provide everyone with access to education without any discrimination such as of social status or family origin. In a capitalist society the 'equal' opportunity is almost closed to poor children, and they say it is proper for the rich to have rich education but for the poor to have a poorer one according to their capacity."

As opposed to "ability-first," "education according to ability" should mean "education satisfying every need of development." The document concluded by declaring, "Thus against the government's educational policy based on distinction of ability, we must declare a principle of justice in education for the full and wholesome development of every child."[102]

Among the top priorities within the recommendations issued by the Central Council on Education at the beginning of the 1970s was the proposal to change the 6-3-3 school system. This was not a new issue. Spokesmen for the Conservative camp had favored altering the single-track primary and lower secondary school systems since the end of the Occupation. But the June 1971 council report differed in that it actually proposed "pilot projects" to determine which alternatives might best serve the national interest. The possibilities that were suggested included ending elementary school at either the fourth or fifth grade and creating four-year lower and senior secondary schools. Little came of these proposals, in large part because there was no agreement within either the Education Ministry or the Conservative camp on how to implement multitracking.[103]

Despite the lack of consensus among the Conservatives and the opposition of the Progressives, de facto differentiation and specialization at the postcompulsory level was already quite marked by the time these particular proposals appeared. By the mid-1970s the comprehensive high schools envisioned by the reformers during the American Occupation were a fast-fading ideal. Approximately one-third of all high schools offered precollegiate curricula without vocational courses, whereas another third had curricula based on vocational courses stressing such subjects as business, agriculture, machine shop, and/or home economics.[104] In other words, only about one out of three upper secondary schools could be labeled "comprehensive" in so far as they combined academic and vocational course offerings. This trend would continue and by 1983 almost half of all schools at the high school level overwhelmingly stressed precollegiate studies and only a little more than one out of four were comprehensive high schools.

Looked at from the point of view of the courses being taken by high school students, however, the proportions appear a bit differently. In 1985 about one-fourth were in vocational programs and over two-thirds in general or academic programs. Nor should it be assumed that vocational programs in high schools ignore general education entirely. At least a third of the curriculum must, by Education Ministry regulations, be devoted to such academic subjects as social studies, mathematics, science, and art plus physical education. If English language courses are counted, then in the 1980s even students in vocational high schools were spending half their class time in general education courses.[105] However, the examinations system has been attacked by some critics because high schools may concentrate so greatly on exams for college that they do not give full consideration to those not planning to go to college.

Prime Minister Nakasone's Ad Hoc Council on Education also recommended fundamental changes in the articulation of the various levels in the system. This included reviving the question of a 6-6 system that might exist alongside the 6-3-3 to benefit the academically gifted. Some of the council's members were particularly enthusiastic about ending the practice of promoting on the basis of age rather than ability, arguing that the brightest should be permitted to move up faster. This was part of what was called the "liberalization" of the system, a concept upon which there was rare agreement within the Japan Teachers' Union and at least some factions within the Education Ministry: They both opposed it.[106]

Powerful lobbies such as the Japan Federation of Employers Associations had long pushed for even greater differentiation and specialization at the postsecondary level.[107] Public opinion polls also revealed that Japanese in the street overwhelmingly agreed with the statement that their countrymen placed too much emphasis on educational background.[108] Some intellectuals expressed concern about the problem of "overeducated society" and what it might mean politically as well as economically.[109] One U.S.-trained professor of sociology wrote,

> The supply of university graduates has come to exceed the economic demand for
> them. . . . This excess of higher education is also effecting fundamental changes in

the social structure of employment and in internal corporate organization. As a result of these changes, the employment difficulties encountered in the current recession seem to have brought on problems fundamentally different from those in past recessions, when the university-educated population was not as large.

"Overeducation" led not only to this new type of unemployment among white-collar workers but also to *underemployment* of university graduates within corporations where "those occupational posts which have been considered suitable for well-educated people are now overflowing." This in turn was a cause for "discontent and a deterioration in the will to work among those highly educated people who consequently had to do more routine work." Ultimately such failure of fit between education and occupation "may even become a source of social unrest" and "a revolt of the intellectuals."[110]

The solution in the eyes of the business lobby and some others was to create more vocational training programs for those who did not need a college education while retooling the universities to produce more science and technology majors. The Japan Teachers' Union has constantly opposed these separate ladders: "We believe it is fundamentally wrong to segregate higher education on the basis of ability-first-ism and divide schools into so many distinct types." Instead it called for equalizing funding among all schools, private as well as public, while giving priority to "the purpose of humanistic education that is contained within general education."[111]

The debate went on, in part fueled by a new furor over the nature and quality of general education at Tokyo University. All its undergraduates in the postwar era have taken two years of general education courses in the College of Arts and Sciences on the Komaba campus before moving into one of the ten upper divisions or "faculties." A disagreement over the hiring of a new professor on the Komaba campus triggered a larger quarrel among the faculty over general education versus specialized training. The dispute resulted in three senior men resigning and publicly denouncing their former college as "on the verge of ideological and intellectual bankruptcy."[112]

Others seized the opportunity to attack the university for ignoring real world problems, including the need to "internationalize." Tangible results of the internationalization campaigns of the 1980s are hard to measure but there have been some significant increases in foreigners on some campuses. In 1993 there were over 52,000 foreign students in Japan, up from about 8,000 in 1982. In 1982 the Diet lifted the ban on aliens being given tenure in public universities, although their appointment still technically requires Education Ministry approval and they cannot be selected to head departments.[113] Moreover, although the Tokyo Metropolitan Board of Education employed eleven legal aliens in 1975 and some served as regular teachers, most prefectures did not certify any such permanent residents for teaching posts in this period.

Conclusion

In the 1980s there was movement in the lines that separated the warring camps. The Ad Hoc Council on Education gained some ground by creating a new ideological packaging for the Conservative reform agenda. Multitracking was now referred to less as differentiation and more as "liberalization." There were also some more substantive changes in that Prime Minister Nakasone and his supporters were arguing less in terms of centralized control to ensure standardization in the curriculum—the position long held by the Education Ministry—and more in terms of a decentralized system of diverse public schools coupled with a larger private sector to promote "individuality, individual dignity, freedom, autonomy, and self-responsibility."[114]

But the decade nevertheless ended without the Nakasone reform agenda being implemented. A sudden economic downturn and a new series of political scandals so weakened the Liberal Democratic Party that Nakasone's immediate successors were too preoccupied to pursue educational reform while attempting to cope with more pressing issues. Moreover, during much of 1988 the nation as a whole was preoccupied with the long illness and impending death of the emperor.

9

Our National Identity as Japanese: Post-Shōwa Japan

The death of Emperor Hirohito was an occasion for remembrance, not of a day or a decade, but of more than a half century of unprecedented turbulence and change. . . . For the Japanese, it created a moment that linked the past with the future.

—Professor Carol Gluck[1]

School reform movements in Japan and the United States are developing in opposite directions.

—Professor Nobuo K. Shimahara[2]

The End of an Epoch?

The death in January 1989 of Emperor Hirohito ended a reign that spanned several distinct historical periods—not unlike the reign of Queen Victoria, which also covered sixty-four years. And although in neither case did the end of one imperial reign and the beginning of a new one signal a necessary change in politics, the death of the Shōwa emperor coincided with a number of events of momentous importance for the nation. In foreign affairs, it was coincidental with the collapse of the USSR and the end of the Cold War, which for over four decades had determined so much of the Japanese view of the world and their place in it. Economically, its end coincided with a serious crisis in Japan's financial institutions that rocked the nation's confidence in its economic success at a time when trade friction with the United States was reaching new highs. Politically, it occurred just at the beginning of a series of new revelations about corruption that eventually led to the defeat of both the Liberal Democratic Party and the Japan Socialist Party in the election of 1993.

But equally significant for many Japanese was the psychological impact of the death of the Shōwa emperor himself; for them it meant the end of what has been called "the long postwar": "Long after Germany and nearly every place else had closed out their domestic *après-guerre*, . . . the postwar retained its prominence in Japan's contemporary consciousness. Despite frequent pronouncements, the earliest in 1956, that the postwar was over, the Japanese postwar went on and on and on—rhetorically."[3] The notion of "postwar" was a cultural concept as much as a political one—a period in which, in the eyes of its most influential intellectuals at least, Japan had striven to become fully "modern." Ironically, Japan reached this modernity just as the "postmodern" began. The question here is what the post-Shōwa, the post-postwar, or the postmodern era would mean for the politics of Japanese education.

The first years of the Heisei emperor have given little clear indication of what lies in store for the nation, but it is obvious that political changes with important implications for the educational system are at work. During the late 1980s there took place a massive realignment of the labor union movement with the amalgamation of the major unions into a new national federation known as Rengō. This amalgamation cannot but affect the role of the Japan Teachers' Union. But there was still skepticism in the mid-1990s that it would achieve its stated goal of unifying the left into a single political party. And in the 1993 election, the postwar Progressive opposition suffered serious losses. The Liberal-Democrats, for their part, were mired in a series of political scandals that threatened to paralyze the government response as the economy stumbled into a deep recession. The party also suffered from an internal crisis of leadership as the relatively charismatic Nakasone was succeeded by a rapid series of politicians who were too busy coping with trade friction, economic recession, and political scandals to focus much attention on school issues.

Nevertheless, the bureaucrats in the Education Ministry and their Conservative supporters in the Diet have given no sign of retreating from the field in the 1990s. At the end of the 1980s the Education Ministry had resumed their campaign to have schools display the Japanese flag and sing the prewar anthem "Kimigayo." In an intriguing bit of reasoning, the minister of education asserted that internationalization required the use of these national symbols: "In this period of internationalization, we will be jeered by other countries unless we resolutely develop our national identity as Japanese."[4] This 1985 call for showing the flag at schools on opening day and at graduation did not meet with much public protest, but despite the ministry's efforts over the next four years, there were still large numbers of primary and secondary schools that were not featuring the prewar anthem at school ceremonies. High school administrators were particularly negligent: Only a little more than half were in compliance. Even in primary schools, a fourth did not sing "Kimigayo" on the opening day and over 40 percent failed to do so at graduation.

Less evident has been any commitment to internationalization that might mean actually hiring more foreigners on a regular basis. The question of hiring foreign nationals as teachers in secondary schools has long been entangled with a related question about the treatment of Koreans and others who are permanent residents but not legally citizens. Certification of secondary teachers is handled at the prefectural levels and prior to the 1990s very few prefectures outside of Tokyo certified Korean residents for teaching posts. In January 1991 a diplomatic agreement between Japan and South Korea was supposedly to encourage other school districts to permit Korean residents to take the certification tests. But the Education Ministry then enjoined local officials to employ legal aliens only as instructors since to appoint them to administrative posts or even hire them as regular teachers would violate the law limiting public decisionmaking posts to Japanese nationals: "Regular teachers must be Japanese nationals, because they directly take part in school management presided over by principals, and thereby are considered participants in public decision making."[5]

There has been somewhat more movement on the recommendations of the Educational Programs Council aimed at a more "relaxed education."[6] One potential means to this goal was the elimination of Saturday classes. School combined with *juku* accounted for five hours each Saturday for the average child in 1990.[7] In September 1992 the Education Ministry implemented the first phase of its plan to shorten the school week, paralleling a broader government campaign for a five-day workweek in private companies. Forty-seven thousand public elementary and middle schools with a total of 18 million students did drop Saturday classes but only every other week. Six hundred forty-two other test schools are trying a two-year experiment with no Saturdays at all.

This move was accompanied by pleas that this not be seen as merely an opportunity to increase time at the *juku*. Early surveys indicated that this plea was being heard. An Education Ministry survey of 8,000 pupils following the first day off found less than 2 percent attending *juku*. However, an independent survey of 290 schools reported that administrators were compensating for the lost time by cutting back on class excursions, athletic meets, art classes, and other extracurricular activities. Nor were parents overjoyed by the change. A third of the parents in a sample of 2,116 pupils replied that they could not use this time for family activities because they were working. A total of 42 percent answered "undecided" when asked whether they approved of the plan.[8]

Another sign that the Liberal Democratic Party had begun to heed some of the critics was the appointment of a special panel to investigate dropout rates in senior high schools. Part of the problem was identified as mismatching students to schools. From the mid-1960s on the common practice has been for middle school teachers to use commercially prepared achievement tests combined with information from high school staffs to advise students on which high schools to apply for admission. The Education Ministry has sought to ban this practice, citing as reasons the increasing dropout rates and the growing availability of space as the teenage population declines. When the special panel issued its report in December 1992, the minister of education endorsed its call for more attention to the individual overall potential rather than depending mechanically upon test scores to advise middle school students on which high schools to apply.

Having noted all the condemnation of the secondary school experience, however, it comes as something of a surprise to find that student survey data do not necessarily support the criticism. One opinion survey in 1990 had considerably more senior high school students reporting more general satisfaction with life (87 percent) than their predecessors in 1970 (69 percent).[9]

One group for which the satisfaction curve does seem headed in the opposite direction is advocates of gender equality. Although the percentage of female high school graduates who go on to postsecondary education continues to be comparable to that of their male classmates, far more females than males still enroll in junior colleges rather than four-year universities. Forty percent of all women "college students" in 1991 were in junior colleges. And these institutions continue to be primarily schools for women. Ninety percent of their students in 1989 were women. Moreover, the majority of women in four-year programs have continued to eschew majors in public administration or technical fields in favor of less marketable degrees in, for example, the humanities. The field of education remains something of an exception, and women have achieved parity as primary school teachers. But they remain underrepresented in secondary schools and constitute only a tiny minority of the faculty in higher education. Moreover, relatively few women have achieved administrative posts at any level in the school system. One exception to this generalization came in 1992 when Prime Minister Miyazawa Kiichi selected the first woman ever to serve as minister of education—Moriyama Mayumi—almost simultaneously with President Clinton selecting the first woman to head the U.S. Department of Education.

Given the continued existence of disparate ladders of upward mobility in schooling and the de facto gender segregation among college majors, it seems hard to argue with the observation that "the co-existence of the principles of egalitarianism and inequality characterized the Japanese educational system."[10] How fast this can change in the absence of an enormous shift in public opinion, even if a central government were to formulate radical new policies, is a matter of speculation. Moreover, it is by no means clear to what extent it is even possible to provide equality and quality in the same system. This, after all, is not a policy dilemma unique to Japan.

Persisting Dilemmas

There are other dilemmas that have persisted over the course of the modern era. The contemporary Japanese political world has changed in so many ways that comparisons with the prewar or even immediate postwar periods are not only difficult but also potentially misleading. That said, however, it is also evident that within a decade of the end of the Occupation the Education Ministry had regained a significant portion of power it had held in the prewar period. Its mandate to create curriculum guidelines and determine standards, when coupled with its procedures for certifying textbooks, gives it indirect influence over much that goes on in every elementary and secondary school. Moreover, since postsecondary institutions depend upon funds voted by the parliament, often budgeted only after the ministry's recommendation, true autonomy is tenuous even for the most prestigious universities, whether public or private.

Thus, the late twentieth century has seen in Japan a continuation of the attempts to find a midpoint between the horns of the dilemma of control. Politically, how much centralization is possible and desirable in a national school system? Can any society flourish if there is no uniformity in its educational standards? But can there be any such standardization without control by an undemocratic bureaucracy?

There is a case that can be made for central leadership:

> One can make the argument, and many Japanese do, that their centralized system ensures that every child—from Okinawa to Hokkaido—enjoys "equality of opportunity" because of substantially equal physical facilities throughout the archipelago, a uniform curriculum administered by a single Ministry of Education, equal access to the same textbooks, teachers of relatively equal competency, and a uniform set of national standards.[11]

Yet this rosy picture is not shared by all and there remains the concern expressed so concisely in the 1971 report to the Organization for Economic Cooperation and Development:

> When uniformity is achieved through central government control it always entails the danger that the government in power (particularly in countries where a single party has a longstanding monopoly of power) may use its control to enforce a conformity designed primarily to perpetuate its rule ... [and] its opposition may tend to see education in terms of its potential for political indoctrination.[12]

To effectively challenge the power of the Education Ministry, the Japan Teachers' Union has always sought recognition at the central level, seemingly contradicting its own demands for local control over schools. But then it should be remembered that neither the Japan Teachers' Union nor its allies among the left-wing political parties have stressed local political control as an intrinsic good in the manner, for example, that those right of center in U.S. politics have. The problem, one senses, is not that big government is inherently antidemocratic but that any government dominated by the Conservatives is ipso facto at odds with the true will of the people. In that sense, neither the Conservatives nor the Progressives are traditional in that neither would return to the early nineteenth century style of local control. The unresolved question was and is who dominates the mechanisms of central control.

Meanwhile, the main battlegrounds continue to be the cultural content of
the curriculum and the socioeconomic outcomes of schooling. Culturally, how
can schooling in a modern society not include moral training? How much ethical diversity can a society tolerate? Can social cohesion be promoted without
a form of cultural nationalism that stresses the separateness and uniqueness of
the Japanese? Increasingly in the 1980s ideas of such uniqueness gained popularity in the press and other media. The debate had a new label—"*Nihonjinron,*"
or "discourse on the Japanese identity"—but in essence it was a revitalized version of the prewar ideological struggles and the successors to the Nativist tradition of the nineteenth century. One of the more mild versions simply starts
with the premise that "national characteristics (*minzoku tokushitsu* [literally,
the special characteristics of a nation's people]) are the product of racial, cli-
matic and historical conditions. . . . It is not a question of 'good' or 'bad,' but a
matter of 'character.'"[13] Other versions give greater stress to genetic roots, and
many at least insinuate cultural superiority. Almost all stress the persistence of
loyalty to family and other collectivities as central to Japanese identity.

The schools cannot avoid being battlefields in this continued strife since neither side has believed that morals could or should be left to the home or
church. Both sets of belligerents are committed to the premise that the school
must teach one set of ethical values and, by the same token, only one version of
historical truth. In socioeconomic terms, the main question is, What is the
proper balance between meritocratic and egalitarian goals in a school system?
When does equality of opportunity give way to the greater recognition of excellence? To what extent should the state correct economic inequalities stemming from family background by subsidizing educational costs for all? The
Liberal Democratic Party has persisted in the meritocratic traditions of the late
nineteenth century, although tempering these with programs that provide student aid and subsidies to private schools to reduce somewhat the inequalities
in family means as well as lessen the differences between colleges. It has not,
however, seen fit to expand public higher education in a way that might flat-
ten the hierarchy at the postsecondary level. Indeed, it has advocated a system
with more clear-cut differences in the various postelementary tracks for students destined for particular slots in the job world.[14]

The opposition on the left, for its part, has demanded cheaper schooling and
more concerted efforts to minimize the distinctions between institutions of
secondary and postsecondary education while opposing multitracking and the
accompanying intense pressures to do well in the entrance examinations. The
main obstacle to any cease-fire in the "examination wars," of course, is not at
the lower levels but at the higher reaches of the system. So long as the government bureaucracy and business corporations legitimize the system by using it
to select new recruits, it seems unlikely that much will change. But judging
from trends elsewhere among industrialized societies—especially Germany and
the United States—there may actually be more, not less, pressure to expand

publicly funded vocational training. This would seemingly produce a greater difference between the various tracks.

It seems unlikely that the political deadlock on fundamental reform will be broken until there is a sustained period of major election victories swinging the pendulum decisively one way or the other among the various parties. The Liberal Democratic Party, which had ruled for almost four decades, clearly lost its political mandate in the momentous election of July 1993, but so did the newly renamed Japan Social Democrat Party, which had spearheaded the parliamentary opposition throughout the post-Occupation period. Until the process of political alignment has produced a new stability, electoral politics are unlikely to produce any clear directions for education.

Instead, there may be more duels between the warring camps in the courts. Both sides have managed to draw blood at the lower levels of the judiciary system but appeals to the Supreme Court have usually ended either in victories for the Education Ministry or, in a few instances, very narrowly defined rulings that have given neither side much satisfaction. The Japanese Supreme Court, which for three decades avoided pressure to cut the Gordian knot in these political entanglements, did come closer in March 1993. It upheld the constitutionality of the textbook screening system and rejected Professor Ienaga Saburō's claims that the Education Ministry had violated his right to academic freedom by refusing to certify his high school history text. Writing for the court, Justice Kabe Tsuneo endorsed the principle of standardized textbooks for use in the national school system while pointing out that Ienaga had not been deprived of his right to publish his work. But Ienaga, now almost eighty years old, vowed to continue the legal actions, and in October 1993 the Tokyo High Court did grant him damages against the Education Ministry for its censorship of his accounts of wartime atrocities. At the same time, however, it upheld the constitutionality of the textbook screening system. As one commentator summarized the logic of this: "A history textbook should not be turned into a 'criminal history of Imperial Japan.' There must be a balance. The effect on the students should also be taken into consideration."[15]

Ienaga may already have his spiritual successor. In spring 1993 Takashima Nobuya, a social studies teacher at the Tokyo high school attached to Tsukuba University, announced that he planned to sue the Education Ministry for forcing changes in a high school textbook he coauthored. The passages in contention involved quotations regarding Japan's mission in East Asia from the works of the famous nineteenth-century educator Fukuzawa Yukichi.

Since these court cases have focused on textbooks, the question has arisen of how to measure the influence that textbooks, be they slanted left or right, have had on Japanese students. Or to put this more bluntly, as in the title of one magazine article, "So What If the Textbooks Are Biased?"[16] If, as many Conservatives assert, the teachers have been primarily left-wing sympathizers, then what goes on in the classrooms may not ever have actually reflected the Education

Ministry preferences whatever the textbooks say. But then what about the all-important high school and college entrance examinations? Do they reward only one version of the truth? Some have argued that it does not matter. According to the National Institute for Educational Research, "Very few questions of an ideological nature appear on high school entrance exams because the basic policy in formulating these tests is to choose questions in areas that are covered by all textbooks used in the given prefecture and that are based on the objectives and content of the Education Ministry's curriculum guidelines."[17]

It is not clear exactly why the last clause is not itself reason for concern about ministry influence. Moreover, what happens in prefectures where there is ideological bias? Nevertheless, the point that textbooks are only part of the equation is well taken. Surely, teachers' handling of the material is also crucial. But if we judge from the recent turbulence within the Japan Teachers' Union, it is also true that the ideological orientation of Japanese public school teachers may be in flux and the gap between teachers and the Education Ministry may be diminishing.

In short, as the last of the prewar generation move out of positions of leadership, polarization in education may diminish. This may open the way to more innovative attempts to cope with the dilemmas of schooling in a post-Shōwa Japan. But one is reminded of an assessment of early attempts at reform: "Success in the past has depended on a 'Big Bang,' a profound international and domestic crisis that instigates a reform movement and skillful leadership 'from above' for that movement."[18]

Notes

Notes to the Introduction

1. For more on the centrality of history in contemporary Japanese discourse, see Gluck, "The Past in the Present."

2. John W. Hall, "Education and Modern National Development," p. 408.

3. See Japan, Ministry of Education Research Bureau, *1962 White Paper on Education.* For a less self-serving treatment, see Evans, "The Contribution of Education to Japan's Economic Growth."

4. For a clear and concise statement of this, see "Introduction to the Comparative History of Educational Change," in Maynes, *Schooling for the People,* as well as Maynes's *Schooling in Western Europe.* I have included the modern tertiary level in my focus.

5. Tsurumi, *Japanese Colonial Education in Taiwan.*

Notes to Chapter 1

1. From "Preface to Collected Commentaries on Chu Hsi's Regulations for the School of the White Deer Cave," as translated in Tsunoda, de Bary, and Keene, comps., *Sources of Japanese Tradition,* p. 364.

2. From "The Kansei Edict," as translated in Tsunoda, de Bary, and Keene, comps., *Sources of Japanese Tradition,* pp. 502–503.

3. For a comparison of Tokugawa with early modern states in Europe that does emphasize the degree of centralization, see White, "State Growth and Popular Protest in Tokugawa Japan."

4. A major exception to this generalization, the practice of temporary promotions and "acting ranks," is discussed by Thomas C. Smith in "'Merit' as Ideology in the Tokugawa Period."

5. For elaboration on this point, see Dore, *Education in Tokugawa,* p. 291.

6. These estimates are based on Taueber, *The Population of Japan;* see the summary in Passin, *Society and Education,* p. 57.

7. See Moriya, "Urban Networks and Information Networks."

8. Passin, *Society and Education,* p. 57. Thomas C. Smith's "Ogura Nagatsune and the Technologists" treats materials published for cultivators. Irokawa Daikichi has argued forcibly for the high level of sophistication in the countryside; see the English translation of Irokawa, *The Culture of the Meiji Period.*

9. For more about Tokugawa women, see Bernstein, ed., *Recreating Japanese Women*.

10. See Harootunian, *Toward Restoration;* Webb, *The Japanese Imperial Institution in the Tokugawa Period;* and Craig, *Chōshū in the Meiji Restoration*, pp. 138–143.

11. The best English source on Tokugawa science is Bartholomew, *The Formation of Science*.

12. See the account in Sansom, *Western World and Japan*, pp. 259–265.

13. Much of the following is based upon Rubinger, *Private Academies*. He translates *shijuku* in the more usual way as "private academies" but Najita uses the term "personal school" to distinguish them from what I have called "community schools"; Najita, *In Search of Virtue*, p. 63.

14. For exceptions see Robertson, "The Shingaku Woman."

15. Much of the following is based upon Dore, *Education in Tokugawa*. Dore as well as many others refer to daimyo domains as "fiefs" and hence these schools as "fief schools."

16. Passin's estimates are in *Society and Education*, table on p. 44.

17. Dore, *Education in Tokugawa*, p. 97. Unless otherwise indicated, ages have been recomputed in the Western fashion rather than appearing in the traditional Japanese fashion, which adds one year the first of each calendar year regardless of the individual's birthdate.

18. See data presented in Dore, *Education in Tokugawa*, pp. 116–120.

19. Dore, *Diploma Disease*, p. 37.

20. Bartholomew, *The Formation of Science*, pp. 13, 27.

21. Passin estimated an average attendance of about 30,000 in the 1860s: *Society and Education*, table on p. 44.

22. That is, 92 out of the 244 domains that responded to an 1883 Meiji government survey. Dore, *Education in Tokugawa*, pp. 219–220.

23. The best description in English of these schools can be found in Dore, *Education in Tokugawa*, pp. 252–290.

24. Passin, *Society and Education*, table on p. 44; Dore, *Education in Tokugawa*, p. 256; Kobayashi Tetsuya, *Society, Schools and Progress in Japan*, p. 17.

25. Dore, *Education in Tokugawa*, pp. 320, 257–260.

26. Kobayashi Tetsuya, *Society, Schools and Progress*, pp. 17–18.

27. Passin, *Society and Education*, p. 28.

28. On the difficulty in making a precise estimate, see Dore, *Education in Tokugawa*, appendix 1; and Passin, *Society and Education*, appendix 3.

29. For an example, see Rubinger, *Private Academies*, p. 165.

30. Beauchamp and Rubinger, eds., *Education in Japan*, p. 24.

31. Walthall, "The Life Cycle of Farm Women in Tokugawa Japan."

32. Dore, *Education in Tokugawa*, pp. 97–98.

33. As described by Dore, the dormitories of the Yonezawa fief school housed some twenty *shosei*, who were subsidized and performed duties analogous to those of graduate assistants of modern U.S. universities except that their students were at the primary and secondary levels; Dore, *Education in Tokugawa*, pp. 74–78.

34. For more on *yugaku*, see Rubinger, "Education," p. 198.

35. See Dore, *Education in Tokugawa*.

36. Najita, *Visions of Virtue in Tokugawa Japan*, pp. 72–76. See also the description of the Gansuidō in Hirano City, ibid., pp. 62–63.

37. Robertson, "The Shingaku Women."

38. Kobayashi Tetsuya, *Society, Schools and Progress*, p. 22.

39. Evans, "The Satsuma Faction," p. 17.

40. Bartholomew, *The Formation of Science*, p. 31.

41. See Evans, "The Satsuma Faction," pp. 12, 15.

42. Passin, *Society and Education*, p. 54.

43. See Kobayashi Tetsuya, *Society, Schools and Progress*, p. 21.

44. Rubinger, among others, would stress more the roots in the Tokugawa: see "Education," p. 228. As is clear from the description of the Tokugawa structure here, I accept much of Rubinger's point but nonetheless lay heavier stress on the radical departure involved in the emergence of the new state as well as the new purposes to which it put schooling.

Notes to Chapter 2

1. For other translations see Spaulding, "The Intent of the Charter Oath."

2. From an internal government memorandum; a translation of the whole document can be found in Lu, ed., *Sources of Japanese History*, 2:49–50.

3. General accounts of this period in English can be found in Ivan Hall, *Mori;* Passin, *Society and Education;* and Rubinger, "Education."

4. McLaren, *Japanese Government Documents*, 1:27.

5. Monbushō, *Gakusei 90 nenshi*, p. 8; a translation of the March 4, 1870, Daigaku Regulations can be found in McLaren, *Japanese Government Documents*, 1:20n.

6. Monbushō, *Meiji ikō*, 1:95–96.

7. Quoted in Ōkubo, "Meiji shonen no gakushinmatsuri ni tsuite," p. 60.

8. Tōdai, *50 nenshi*, pp. 51–52, 75–90.

9. As quoted in Harootunian, "The Samurai Class During the Early Meiji Years," p. 71.

10. The organization of the central government remained in a state of flux in these early years—indeed to as late as 1885—and this creates special problems in translating the names of major bureaus and agencies. Some would use "department" for the first phase and "ministry" only later, but I have chosen to use "ministry" throughout to reduce the potential for confusion. It should also be noted that the Monbushō, in addition to its responsibility for schools, originally had jurisdiction over a wide variety of cultural and scientific activities, including, for example, testing the purity of drugs and water and, eventually, regulating the sport of sumo. In 1983 it changed the official English translation to Ministry of Education, Science and Culture.

11. See Hardacre, "Creating State Shintō"; Hardacre, *Shintō and the State;* Collcutt, "Buddhism: The Threat of Eradication"; and Ketelaar, *Of Heretics and Martyrs in Meiji Japan.*

12. Hardacre, "Creating State Shintō," p. 46.

13. Quoted in Havens, *Nishi Amane*, p. 87; Fukuzawa, *Autobiography*, p. 215.

14. Tsurumi, "Meiji Primary School Language and Ethics Textbooks." Tsurumi also makes the point that language texts used to teach reading and writing were full of moral lessons with traditional slants.

15. The Japanese historian Amano Ikuo, among others, stresses that "the idea that a genuine education should have a *moral* purpose transcending self-advancement was

something Japan derived from its Confucian past, not from its American or French advisers" (Amano, *Education and Examination*, p. ix).

16. Quoted in Passin, *Society and Education*, p. 14.

17. Quoted in Eppstein, "Musical Instruction in Meiji Education," p. 4.

18. Maynes, *School for the People*, p. 5. Thomas Havens would add "a deep undercurrent of insecurity . . . concerning Japan's precipitate rejection of her feudal tradition" (Havens, *Nishi Amane*, p. 87).

19. Monbushō, *Gakusei 100 nenshi*, 2:11–22. There are partial English translations of this seminal document—sometimes called the "Fundamental Code of Education"—in a variety of sources, e.g., Passin, *Society and Education*, pp. 210–211; Centre for East Asian Cultural Studies, ed., *The Meiji Japan Through Contemporary Sources*, 3:5–7; and Nitobe et al., *Western Influences*, pp. 34–35.

20. Monbushō, *Gakusei 100 nenshi*, 2:11. The preamble is translated in full in Passin, *Society and Education*, pp. 210–211. See also Centre for East Asian Cultural Studies, *The Meiji Japan Through Contemporary Sources*, 3:5–7.

21. Nagai, "Westernization and Japanization," pp. 47–52; Passin, *Society and Education*, pp. 69–70; Ivan Hall, *Mori*, pp. 331ff. Patricia Tsurumi reminds us that it is easy to overestimate the influence of any one of these foreign advisers, "Toward a Case Study of the Overseas Educator," p. 492.

22. Eppstein describes Izawa's experiences at one of them and the process by which his recommendations became policy; "Musical Instruction in Meiji Education."

23. Griffis, *The Mikado's Empire*, pp. 370–371.

24. That is, *Chūgaku kyōsoku*, reprinted in part in Monbushō, *Meiji ikō*, 1:487; see also Rubinger, "Education," p. 218.

25. Monbushō, *Meiji ikō*, 1:486; Amano, *Education and Examination*, p. 76.

26. Monbushō, *Gakusei 100 nenshi*, 2:14.

27. Amano, *Education and Examination*, pp. 84–91.

28. Monbushō, *Gakusei 80 nenshi*, pp. 64–67; and Tōdai, *50 nenshi*, 1:163–181. Ōkubo Toshimichi and Kido Takayoshi were among the strongest supporters. For information in English on overseas studies, see Conte, "Overseas Study in the Meiji Period"; Jones, "The Meiji Government and Foreign Employees," pp. 352–357, table 7 on p. 177, table 18 on p. 384.

29. Quoted in Conte, "Overseas Study in the Meiji Period," p. 53.

30. Ibid., chapter 2.

31. See Marshall, *Academic Freedom*, pp. 32–39.

32. Sakurai, *Omoide no kazukazu*, pp. 345–346.

33. For the law and literature faculty, see Marshall, *Academic Freedom*; for scientists and physicians, see Bartholomew, *The Formation of Science*.

34. Monbushō, *Gakusei 100 nenshi*, 1:11.

35. There was criticism of this practice but attempts to prohibit it were not successful in the Meiji period; see Bartholomew, *The Formation of Science*, p. 105.

36. Combining tables 8.2 and 8.4 in Rubinger, "Education," pp. 219 and 224; note Rubinger's warning about the reliability of these official statistics, p. 218n.

37. For example, the schools run by Kageyama Umeko and her daughter Fukuda Hideko in the 1870s and 1880s; see Hane, ed., *Reflections*, pp. 30–31, 34–36.

38. Keiō, ed., *Keiō 100 nenshi*, pp. 321–337.

39. See Griesy, "The Dōshisha."

40. See Notehelfer, *American Samurai*.

41. Monbushō, *Gakusei 100 nenshi*, volume 2, p. 11. This principle was reiterated in the textbooks used in the schools; see the quote in Nagai, "Westernization and Japanization," p. 56.

42. Quoted from *Nichi Nichi* editorials in late March 1875 in Huffman, "Fukuchi Gen'ichiro," p. 302.

43. Havens, *Nishi Amane*, p. 88.

44. Harootunian, "The Economic Rehabilitation of the Samurai Class," p. 435; see also Harootunian's dissertation, "The Samurai Class During the Early Years of the Meiji Period"; and Harootunian, "The Progress of Japan and the Samurai Class."

45. Spaulding, *Imperial Japan's Higher Civil Service Examinations*, pp. 20–32; Amano, *Education and Examination*, pp. 42–49.

46. See Evans, "The Satsuma Faction," pp. 34–35, 52–53.

47. Quoted from an 1878 issue of *Nagai kyōiku shimpō*, in Amano, *Education and Examination*, p. 67.

48. Quoted in Conte, "Overseas Study in the Meiji Period," pp. 49–50.

49. The two older girls did not remain abroad long but Yamakawa Sutemitsu stayed ten years, graduated from Vassar, returned home with a nursing license, and married one of the most powerful figures in the Japanese military, Field Marshal Ōyama Iwao. The next-youngest, nine-year-old Nakagi Shige, returned in 1881 and also married a high-ranking officer, Admiral Uriu Sotokichi (Mulhern, "Hani Motoko," p. 209). Clearly, there was little stigma attached by these members of the early Meiji elite to women with advanced educations. See also Kuno, *Unexpected Destinations*.

50. From Mori's article in the November 1874 issue of *Meiroku Zasshi*, which is translated in its entirety in Braisted, *Meiroku zasshi*. I have followed Ivan Hall in the translation of the second sentence, from Ivan Hall, *Mori*, p. 231.

51. Quoted in Passin, *Society and Education*, pp. 222–223; see also Ivan Hall, *Mori*, pp. 183–187. However, U.S. "experts" of the day such as Harvard's Edward Clarke, the author of *Sex in Education*, and Herbert Spencer warned about women becoming "reproductively disabled" by too much education; see Rose, *Tsuda Umeko*, p. 55.

52. March 1875 issue, Braisted, *Meiroku zasshi*, p. 376.

53. Ibid., p. 386.

54. Fukuzawa, *Fukuzawa Yukichi zenshū*, 5:291; also see Fukuzawa, *Fukuzawa Yukichi on Japanese Women*.

55. March 1875 issue, Braisted, *Meiroku zasshi*, pp. 401–402. For much interesting information on the Gakushūin and its student body, see Lebra, *Above the Clouds*, pp. 264–283.

56. Monbushō, *Gakusei 80 nenshi*, table 12 on p. 1067, table 14 on p. 1072.

57. Quoted in Karasawa, *Kyōshi no rekishi*, p. 107. A photo follows p. 122.

58. Nolte and Hastings also stress this point in "The Meiji State's Policy Toward Women," p. 169.

59. Karasawa, *Kyōshi no rekishi*, p. 110. Unfortunately, there is as yet no English-language history of women's normal schools in Japan.

60. See table 8.1 in Rubinger, "Education," p. 213; and Passin, *Society and Education*, pp. 73–74.

61. See table 8.1 in Rubinger, "Education," p. 213; for the question of attendance versus enrollment, see ibid., note 39, p. 212.

62. Amano, *Education and Examination*, p. 69.

63. Nagai, "Westernization and Modernization," p. 58; Brown, "Kido Takayoshi (1833–1877): Meiji Japan's Cautious Revolutionary," p. 156.

64. Nagai reports that 10,996 schools—almost half—did waive tuition in 1876 (Nagai, "Westernization and Japanization," p. 57). On this point also see Hastings, "Plotting Escape from the Slums," p. 1.

65. For a summary of the sometimes ambiguous attitude of this class toward schooling, see Waswo, *Japanese Landlords*, pp. 33–34, 85.

66. A translation of the whole document is reprinted in Centre for East Asian Cultural Studies, ed., *Meiji Japan Through Contemporary Sources*, 2:184–211.

67. Nagai, "Westernization and Japanization," pp. 54–55.

68. Rubinger, "Education," pp. 211–212.

69. E. P. Tsurumi makes this point very forcefully in her article "Meiji Primary School Language and Ethics Textbooks"; see also Amano, *Education and Examination*, p. 69.

70. For example, the riot of Shinshū Buddhist adherents, which is cited in Nagai, "Westernization and Modernization," p. 54.

71. As adapted in Eppstein, "Musical Instruction in Meiji Education," pp. 22–23; see also Malm, "The Modern Music of Meiji Japan."

Notes to Chapter 3

1. As quoted in Eppstein, "Musical Instruction in Meiji Education," pp. 34–35.

2. Quoted in Ivan Hall, *Mori*, p. 397.

3. Ibid., p. 344.

4. Among the best accounts in English for this period are Ivan Hall, *Mori;* and Passin, *Society and Education*.

5. These voices included those of Inoue Kaoru and Yamagata Aritomo; see materials quoted in Kokuritsu Kyōiku Kenkyūjo, ed., *Nihon kindai kyōiku 100 nenshi*, 3:1175–1179.

6. Monbushō, *Gakusei 80 nenshi*, pp. 715–716. A slightly different but complete translation can be found in Passin, *Society and Education*, pp. 226–228.

7. This was the forerunner of the Imperial Academy, created in 1906, and the Japan Academy of Learning in the post–World War II era.

8. Quoted in Ivan Hall, *Mori*, p. 338.

9. Nagai, "Westernization and Japanization," p. 68.

10. As translated in Fukuzawa, *An Outline of a Theory of Civilization*, p. 70.

11. There were two other lecturers—a specialist in Nativist Studies and, until 1875, the scholar of Western Studies—as well as those who appeared less frequently, Katō Hiroyuki (Shively, "Motoda," pp. 310–311).

12. From a lecture to the emperor in or about 1878; quoted in ibid., p. 327.

13. Monbushō *Gakusei 100 nenshi*, 2:7. There is a complete translation in Passin, *Society and Education*, pp. 226–228.

14. Nagai, "Westernization and Japanization," p. 63.

15. Passin, *Society and Education*, p. 227.

16. For an excellent discussion of this distinction between "essentials" and "useful" in the Chinese context, see Levenson, "'History' and 'Value.'"

17. Itō, "Opinion on Education," reprinted in Miyahara, *Shiryō Nihon gendai kyōiku shi*, 4:27–28. A slightly different but more complete translation can be found in Passin, *Society and Education*, pp. 229–233.

18. *Shōkai jōrei*, reprinted in *Shiryō Nihon gendai kyōiku shi*, 4:69. A slightly different but complete translation can be found in McLaren, *Japanese Government Documents*, 2:496–497.

19. See Shively's essay "Nishimura Shigeki," especially p. 200, where Shively argues that "it would only be misleading to speak of him as a Confucianist except in the loosest Meiji usage."

20. Quoted in ibid., p. 233.

21. The *Shōgaku shōshin kun;* Ivan Hall, *Mori*, p. 351. E. P. Tsurumi notes that the text illustrated Confucian virtues with materials drawn from the West ("Meiji Primary School Language and Ethics Textbooks").

22. Quoted in Shively, "Motoda," p. 328.

23. Duke, *Militant Teachers*, p. 15.

24. From a January 1889 speech as translated in Ivan Hall, *Mori*, p. 398. The original "Gakusei no mokuteki" is reprinted in Seiichi et al., eds., *Shiryō Nihon gendai kyōikushi*, 4:126.

25. As translated in Ivan Hall, *Mori*, p. 398. This extraordinarily interesting biography remains the best English treatment of Mori's ideology. There is fascinating detail on what Hall calls Mori's "pedagogical folly" on pp. 424–437.

26. Quoted in Shively, "The Japanization of Middle Meiji," pp. 101–102.

27. Ivan Hall, *Mori*, pp. 10–12.

28. In addition to Shively, "Motoda," see Nolte, "National Morality and Universal Ethics."

29. Official English translation as reprinted in Supreme Commander for the Allied Powers, *Political Orientation of Japan*, 2:584. This translation is the one most often quoted but see also the translation in Stead, *Japan by the Japanese*, pp. 5–6; for interpretations, see Horio, *Educational Thought*, pp. 130–138; and Gluck, *Japan's Modern Myths*, p. 154, where she notes the positive reaction of contemporary foreigners to the official English translation.

30. See Pittau, "Inoue Kowashi," pp. 103–107; Ivan Hall, *Mori*, p. 349.

31. Quoted in Pyle, *The New Generation in Meiji Japan*, p. 127.

32. The regulations are reprinted in Seiichi et al., eds., *Shiryō Nihon gendai kyōikushi*, 4:115–116. For more on the use of school ceremonies to instill patriotism, see Yamamoto and Konno, *Kindai kyōiku no tennōsei ideorogi*.

33. There are many accounts of this incident and the uproar it caused; see Lande, *Meiji Protestantism*, pp. 52–53. Uchimura's letter to an American friend explaining the incident is reprinted in Tsunoda, de Bary, and Keene, comps., *Sources of Japanese Tradition*, pp. 852–853. It is often said that school authorities who mishandled the ceremonies associated with the Imperial Rescript or imperial portrait were driven to suicide to atone. I have yet to see any statistics on this phenomenon but there is an amusing anecdote in Ōsugi, *The Autobiography*, pp. 75–76.

34. Gluck, *Japan's Modern Myths*, pp. 125–126.

35. See the translation of Ōnishi's essay on the rescript in Nolte, "National Morality and Universal Ethics," p. 290, and her introduction.

36. As translated in Passin, *Society and Education*, p. 234.

37. Quoted in Pyle, "The New Generation in Meiji Japan," p. 146n.

38. See Itō Mikiharu, *Kazoku kokkan no jinruigaku*, p. 9. I owe the citation to Fujitani, "Japan's Modern National Ceremonies," p. 298.

39. See Warren W. Smith, Jr., *Confucianism in Modern Japan*.

40. Quoted in Keene, "The Sino-Japanese War," p. 154.

41. Quoted in Pierson, *Tokutomi Sohō*, pp. 239, 241.

42. On the emergence of this intellectual movement, see Shively, "The Japanization of Middle Meiji"; and Pyle, *The New Generation in Meiji Japan*. The quotations are from Pyle.

43. Still one should be cautious about assuming too much for the efficacy of these educational efforts. Ella Wiswell's 1935 field notes on a rural community report that most of the women in their fifties and even forties were not functionally literate despite having been of school age in the 1890s and 1900s. Older villagers themselves attributed some of the differences between their worldview and that of younger (post-Meiji) generations to the latter having actually gone to elementary school. Smith and Wiswell, *The Women of Suye Mura*, pp. 11, 129.

44. Amano asserts that "mainly the children from economically and socially privileged families went to these higher elementary schools" but does not attempt to define the category more precisely (Amano, *Education and Examination*, pp. 145–146).

45. Ibid., p. 146.

46. Ibid., p. 148.

47. Quoted in Roden, *Schooldays*, p. 40; this is the single best English source on these schools.

48. For details, see Amano, *Education and Examination*, pp. 151ff.

49. Donald Roden has commented that the Japanese higher school still drew "from a wider spectrum of the rural and urban middle classes than was presumably the case in elite boarding schools in the West" (Roden, *Schooldays*, p. 52).

50. Ibid., pp. 68–69n.

51. Seiichi et al., eds., *Shiryō Nihon gendai kyōikushi*, 4:124.

52. Karasawa, "A History of Japanese Teachers," p. 18; Duke sums up this evidence in *Militant Teachers*, table 1, p. 8.

53. Karasawa, *Kyōshi no rekishi*, pp. 86–87.

54. Shimizu, *Tōkyō Daigaku hōgakubu*, table 3, p. 48; also see Abe, "Education of the Legal Profession." Fuller detail on this process can be found in the various official histories of Tokyo University, Tōdai, *50 nenshi*, and Tōdai, *Tokyō Teikoku Daigaku gakujutsu taikan* (henceforth cited as Tōdai, *Gakujutsu taikan*). For the situation regarding legal studies, there is a convenient summary in English in Spaulding, *Imperial Japan's Higher Civil Service Examinations*, pp. 70–71.

55. Roden, *Schooldays*, appendix 3, table 4.

56. Amano, *Education and Examination*, p. 84.

57. Monbushō, *Gakusei 80 nenshi*, p. 745.

58. Bartholomew, *The Formation of Science*, pp. 64, 103.

59. Monbushō, *Gakusei 80 nenshi*, p. 1150. See also Amano, "Continuity and Change in the Structure of Higher Education," pp. 15, 21; Passin, *Society and Education*, pp. 105n, 306; and Spaulding, *Imperial Japan's Higher Civil Service Examinations*, p. 132.

60. Ahn, "The Japanese Cabinet Ministers," table 19 (p. 110), table 21 (p. 138).

61. Takane, "Factors Influencing the Mobility of the Japanese Political Elite," table 7.1, p. 251.

62. Aonuma, *Nihon no keieisō*, table 8, pp. 116–117.

63. Beauchamp, "Reform Traditions in the United States and Japan," p. 11.

64. See appendix in Marshall, *Academic Freedom*.

65. From Ahn, "The Japanese Cabinet Ministers," table 19, p. 110.

66. For more on vocational training in the Meiji period, see Toyoda, ed., *Vocational Education in the Industrialization of Japan*.

67. As reprinted in Seiichi et al., eds., *Shiryō Nihon gendai kyōikushi*, 4:27–28.

68. Quoted in Pittau, "Inoue Kowashi," p. 109.

69. Satō, "The Development of Vocational Continuation Schools."

70. As in Passin, *Society and Education*, pp. 233–236.

71. Monbushō, *Gakusei 80 nenshi*, p. 930.

72. Quoted in Fujimura-Faneslow and Imamura, "The Education of Women in Japan." p. 231.

73. Fukuzawa, *Fukuzawa on Japanese Women*, p. 13.

74. Quoted in Shively, "Nishimura," pp. 229–230. Until 1885 daughters of the nobility had attended school on the same campus as male offspring. Lebra, *Above the Clouds*, pp. 265–266.

75. See Hastings, "Women Educators."

76. As translated from the 1891 "Gakuji Setsumei-sho" in Passin, *Society and Education*, p 235.

77. Monbushō, *Gakusei 90 nenshi*, table 5, pp. 606–607.

78. Monbushō, *Gakusei 80 nenshi*, p. 820.

79. Hane, *Reflections*, p. 15.

80. Hastings, "Women Educators."

81. See the experiences of the socialist Kutsumi Fusako recounted in Hane, *Reflections*, pp. 140–141.

82. Robins-Mowry, *The Hidden Sun*, pp. 49–51; the quotes are from Nakajima, "Naruse Jinzo," pp. 72–76.

83. This and the following quote are from Yamazaki, "Tsuda Ume," pp. 125, 140. Also see Rose, *Tsuda Umeko and Women's Education in Japan*.

84. Larson, "Yosano Akiko," pp. 27–30.

85. Hastings, "Women Educators."

86. Hani, "Stories of My Life," pp. 247–249. After a failed marriage and a pioneering career as a female journalist, she eventually returned to the role of educator, cofounding with her second husband the renowned Jiyō Gakuen (Freedom Academy). For more on the level of sophistication among rural youth, see Kinmonth, *The Self-made Man in Meiji Japanese Thought*; and Ōsugi, *Autobiography*, chapters 2 and 3.

87. As quoted in Uno, "Death of 'Good Wife, Wise Mother'?" pp. 298–299.

88. Quoted from an 1884 press interview in Ivan Hall, *Mori*, p. 300; Hall analyzes at length Mori's scheme for reconciling the principles of elected representation with bureaucratic expertise.

89. Ivan Hall, *Mori*, pp. 450–451.

90. See the biography by Hackett, *Yamagata Aritomo*, pp. 90–124. On local government a very concise summary is available in Baxter, "Local Government," and longer treatments can be found in Steiner, *Local Government in Japan*; Staubitz, "The Establishment of the

System of Local Government (1888–1890) in Meiji Japan"; and Waters, *Japan's Local Pragmatists.*

91. As quoted in Waters, "The Second Meiji Transition," p. 307.

92. Baxter, "Local Government," p. 64.

93. See the Liberal Party manifesto reprinted in Mason, *Japan's First General Election,* along with those of other parties in his appendices.

94. Monbushō, *Gakusei 100 nenshi,* 2:90–97. The only English-language treatment of these early school boards seems to be Kerlinger, "Educational Affairs Boards."

95. There were no such provisions in the 1886 ordinances for normal schools, higher schools, or the university; Monbushō, *Gakusei 80 nenshi,* pp. 770, 817, 848, 866–868.

96. Tsurumi, "Meiji Primary School," p. 255.

97. There was also a small number elected by the largest taxpayers in each prefecture.

98. See Mason, *Japan's First General Election,* on the election for the first Meiji Diet.

99. Quoted from Diet proceedings for February 1896 in Karasawa, *Kyōkasho no rekishi,* p. 193.

100. Quoted in Karasawa, *Kyōkasho no rekishi,* p. 202; see also Nakamura Kikuji, *Kyōkasho no shakaishi,* pp. 112–113.

101. Karasawa, "Changes in Japanese Education," p. 56.

102. Tsurumi makes this point in "Meiji Primary School," p. 259.

103. Keiō, ed., *Keiō 100 nenshi,* 1:737, 753–754.

104. Waseda Daigaku, ed., *Waseda 80 nenshi,* p. 68; Waseda, *Hanseiki no Waseda,* p. 92.

105. Keiō, ed., *Keiō 100 nenshi,* 1:805–816; see also Waseda Daigaku, ed., *Waseda 80 nenshi,* pp. 73–75.

106. Pierson, *Tokutomi,* p. 104.

107. Monbushō, *Gakusei 100 nenshi,* p 126.

108. This figure is as of 1890; no statistics are offered for the initial 1868–1883 period. Keiō, ed., *Keiō 100 nenshi,* 1:807.

109. Ibid., 1:806.

110. Spaulding, *Imperial Japan's Higher Civil Service Examinations,* pp. 58–63. Technically, the exemption applied to all who passed the bar exam.

111. Hane, ed., *Reflections,* pp. 36–37.

112. Despite its name, the school was open to girls from some families who were not in the peerage; see Lebra, *Above the Clouds.*

113. Spaulding gives a succinct account of these new arrangements in *Imperial Japan's Higher Civil Service Examinations,* pp. 70–72. See also Sugihara, "In the Schools of Law," p. 143; and Amano, *Education and Examination,* p. 127.

114. Tamaki, "The American Professors' Regime: Political Economy at Keiō University," p. 78.

115. Pierson, *Tokutomi,* p. 104.

116. Griesy, "The Dōshisha," pp. 130–132; Howes, "Japanese Christians and American Missionaries," p. 354.

117. Japan, Ministry of Education Research Bureau, *Japan's Growth and Education,* table 5, p. 38.

118. Quoted in Twine, "Toward Simplicity," p. 132.

Notes to Chapter 4

1. Hara, *Nikki*, 8:457.

2. As quoted in Mitchell, *Thought Control*, p. 41.

3. From Kita's "Kokka kaizō genri taikō" as translated in Lu, *Sources of Japanese History*, 2:136. For more on Kita's influence, see Wilson, *Radical Nationalist in Japan*.

4. For examples see the translations from the party platforms in Quigley, *Japanese Government and Politics*, pp. 411–418; see also Havens, "Japan's Enigmatic Election of 1928."

5. There are no extensive treatments of this important commission in English; in Japanese there is Kaigo, ed., *Rinji Kyōiku Kaigi no kenkyū*.

6. Japan, Ministry of Education Research Bureau, *Japan's Growth and Education*, table 5, p. 38.

7. See Hunter, "Women's Labour Force Participation in Interwar Japan," p. 108; also E. P. Tsurumi, *Factory Girls*, pp. 68–69.

8. One each in Tokyo (1886), Sendai (1887), Kyoto (1887), Kanazawa (1887), Kumamoto (1887), Okayama (1901), Kagoshima (1901), and Nagoya.

9. That is, Waseda, Keiō, Meiji, Chūō, Nihon, or Hōsei; calculated from Ramsdell, *The Japanese Diet*, table 3-1, p. 60.

10. For details, see Spaulding, *Imperial Japan's Higher Civil Service Examinations*, pp. 136–162.

11. See tables in Suh, "The Struggle for Academic Freedom," p. 297; and in Marshall, *Academic Freedom*, table A-6, p. 195.

12. Henry D. Smith II, *Japan's First Student Radicals*, pp. 14–15n.

13. See Nagy, "Middle-Class Working Women During the Interwar Years"; and Hunter, "Women's Labour Force Participation in Interwar Japan."

14. Karasawa, "A History of Japanese Teachers," table on p. 18.

15. From table 3 in Elizabeth Mouer, "Women in Teaching," p. 162; 42 percent of the faculty at girls' schools were also women. The quote is on p. 164.

16. See table 4 in Elizabeth Mouer, "Women in Teaching," p. 166.

17. Quoted in Hane, ed., *Reflections*, p. 22.

18. From the first issue of *Seitō* (Bluestocking) as translated in Lu, ed., *Sources of Japanese History*, 2:118–119. There is as yet relatively little on prewar Japanese feminism available in English, but on the diversity of the movement see Maloney, "Feminist Ideology in Prewar Japan."

19. For Sawayanagi, see Mizuuchi's contribution to Duke, ed., *Ten Great Educators*, pp. 149–165; on Hani, see the essay in Mulhern, ed., *Heroic with Grace*.

20. As quoted in Henry D. Smith II, *Japan's First Student Radicals*, p. 214.

21. Ōsugi, *The Autobiography of Ōsugi Sakae*, p. 95.

22. Much of the following is drawn from Henry D. Smith II, *Japan's First Student Radicals*.

23. See Powell, "Through the Writer's Prism."

24. The views of Yoshino and Minobe are more commonly analyzed and quoted in English works; one of the few treatments of Uesugi's views in English can be found in a short article by one of his contemporaries, Oda, "Mikadoism."

25. Quoted in Henry D. Smith II, *Japan's First Student Radicals*, p. 54.

26. Quoted from Shinjinkai publications in ibid., pp. 56–60.

27. Quoted in ibid., p. 106.

28. Duke, *Militant Teachers*, p. 15; Nakano, "Shimonaka Yasaburo," p. 176.

29. Thurston, *Teachers and Politics*, pp. 34–35.

30. Nakano, "Shimonaka Yasaburo," pp. 178–179.

31. See Mitchell, *Thought Control*, pp. 22–27; and Tipton, *The Japanese Police State*.

32. Mikami Sanji as quoted in Horio, *Educational Thought*, p. 101.

33. See the graph in Karasawa, "Changes in Japanese Education," p. 58.

34. Quoted in Olson, "Hara Kei," p. 278.

35. Some English translations of this report and the ordinance can be found in Suh, "The Struggle for Academic Freedom," pp. 101–114.

36. As translated in Henry D. Smith II, *Japan's First Student Radicals*, p. 202.

37. Ibid., pp. 200–201.

38. Ibid., pp. 183, 217.

39. See Silverberg, "The Modern Girl as Militant."

40. Quoted in Elizabeth Mouer, "Women in Teaching," p. 167.

41. Quoted in Smith, *Japan's First Student Radicals*, pp. 197–198.

42. Quoted in Mitchell, *Thought Control*, p. 84.

43. The Morito case is treated at greater length in Marshall, *Academic Freedom*. For studies of censorship in modern Japan, see Mitchell, *Censorship in Imperial Japan*; and Kasza, *The State and Mass Media in Japan*.

44. Hara, *Nikki*, 8:457, entry for January 12, 1920.

45. As quoted in Mitchell, *Thought Control*, p. 41.

46. "Daigaku oyobi seifu no kokkakan ni tsuite," p. 1.

47. Sasaki, "Daigaku kyōju no kenkyō no genkai," p. 22.

48. Ibid., pp. 27–28.

49. Ibid., pp. 37, 40.

50. The court proceedings are analyzed at length in Miyaji, "Morito jiken."

51. Arisawa, *Gakumon to shisō to ningen*, pp. 21–22.

52. For English-language studies of the 1925 law and the political circumstances of its passage, see Mitchell's analysis in *Thought Control*, where it is noted that academics did not mount an attack on the law (pp. 65–73).

53. Monbushō, *Meiji ikō*, 7:10–11. For a partial translation of the minister's instruction to administrators at state schools, see Suh, "The Struggle for Academic Freedom," pp. 159–162. See also Nanbara et al., *Onozuka Kiheiji*, p. 159; and Henry D. Smith II, *Japan's First Student Radicals*, pp. 200–205.

54. For more on Kawakami, see Bernstein, *Japanese Marxist*.

55. Henry D. Smith II, *Japan's First Student Radicals*; and Bernstein, *Japanese Marxist*, p. 142.

56. See the reminiscences of former Kyoto professor Suegawa Hiroshi in Tanaka Kōtarō et al., *Daigaku no jiji*, pp. 55–59; also Ienaga, *Daigaku*, p. 53; as well as Kawakami's autobiography, *Jijoden*, pp. 157–159, 243.

57. Tanaka et al., *Daigaku no jiji*, p. 65. For details in English on the Communist Youth League, see Henry D. Smith II, *Japan's First Student Radicals*, pp. 209–212; and Beckmann and Okubo, *The Japanese Communist Party*, pp. 188, 193–195.

58. Nanbara et al., *Onozuka Kiheiji*, pp. 159–167; Hirai gave a somewhat different account in *Individualism and Socialism*, pp. 122–123.

59. Henry D. Smith II, *Japan's First Student Radicals*, pp. 213–219.

60. Percentages taken from Japan, Ministry of Education Research Bureau, *Japan's Growth and Education*, figure 16, p. 57. Note that these figures are for productive population—fifteen to fifty-four years old—rather than the population as a whole.

Notes to Chapter 5

1. Nitobe, *Japan*, p. 231.

2. Quoted in Horio, *Educational Thought*, p. 107.

3. See, for example, Minear, *Victor's Justice.*

4. Translated in U.S. Department of State, *Foreign Relations of the United States: Japan, 1931–1941*, 2:108–111.

5. See Mitchell, *Censorship in Imperial Japan*; and Kasza, *The State and Mass Media in Japan*.

6. Mitchell, *Censorship*, pp. 277–279, 292.

7. For more detail on this attempt and the sources for the quotes, see Marshall, *Academic Freedom*, pp. 167–175.

8. See Berger's expert examination of the Konoe cabinet and the "mobilization" movement in *Parties Out of Power*, pp. 187–188.

9. See Marshall, *Academic Freedom*, pp. 170–172.

10. The Takigawa case is covered in greater detail in Marshall, *Academic Freedom*. Takigawa's autobiographical writings differ on why he thought he was singled out but his "Affidavit" is reproduced in Pritchard and Zaide, eds., *The Tokyo War Crimes Trial*, 1:990–993, 1004.

11. Miller, *Minobe Tatsukichi*, pp. 203–206, 33n. The characters for Minoda's personal name are sometimes read as "Kyoki" or even as "Muneyoshi."

12. As quoted in Tsurumi Shunsuke, *An Intellectual History of Wartime Japan*, p. 28.

13. See Miller's exhaustive treatment in *Minobe Tatsukichi*.

14. Smethurst, "The Military Reserve Association and the Minobe Crisis of 1935," pp. 8–9.

15. Kawai, "Minobe mondai no hihan," pp. 12–16.

16. Fujita gives a portrait of Yanaihara in his "Yanaihara Tadao"; for details of his resignation, see Marshall, *Academic Freedom*, pp. 159–162.

17. Yanaihara, *Watakushi*, pp. 101–102.

18. The first trial of the "Professors' Group" resulted in an acquittal for all but two, who were convicted for having contributed to the Marxist magazine. Because Japanese law permitted appeals by the prosecution as well as the defense, Professor Ōuchi and the other participants who were originally found innocent were retried two years later, again to be acquitted.

19. Yabe, *Nikki*, 1:74–81, 83–84, 92, 97, 142, 150.

20. *Kodansha Encyclopedia of Japan*, 8:112.

21. For details of the attacks on Kawai see Hirai, *Individualism and Socialism*; and Marshall, *Academic Freedom*, pp. 171–179.

22. Quoted in Nagao, "Did the Kokutai Change?" p. 145.

23. Shillony, "Universities and Students," p. 782.

24. This section, as well as earlier sections on the student movement, draws heavily from Henry D. Smith II, *Japan's First Student Radicals*, pp. 201–202, 218–230.

25. Karasawa, *Kyōshi no rekishi,* p. 179.

26. The Shinkyō's platform is translated in Duke, *Militant Teachers,* p. 17.

27. Duke, *Militant Teachers,* pp. 20–21; Ienaga, *The Pacific War,* pp. 101–106.

28. Kawai and Rōyama, *Gakusei shisō mondai;* see also Henry D. Smith II, *Japan's First Student Radicals,* pp. 204–205; and Suh, "The Struggle for Academic Freedom," pp. 283–302.

29. Kawai, "Daigaku no jiū to wa nani ka," pp. 119–120.

30. Rōyama, "Kyōdai gakusei ni atauru no gaki," p. 52.

31. In addition to Henry D. Smith II, *Japan's First Student Radicals,* see Steinhoff, "Tenkō: Ideology and Societal Integration."

32. Quoted in Duke, *Militant Teachers,* p. 21.

33. There is a summary in Anderson, *Japan,* p. 116.

34. Ienaga, *The Pacific War,* pp. 107–109.

35. Robert King Hall, *Shūshin,* p. 119.

36. Ibid., pp. 102–103, 76.

37. A complete translation is available in Hall and Gauntlett, *Kokutai no hongi.* Long excerpts can be found in Tsunoda, de Bary, and Keene, comps., *Sources of Japanese Tradition,* pp. 787–795; all quotes here are from the latter source.

38. Havens, *Valley of Darkness,* pp. 27–31.

39. As quoted in Spaulding, *Imperial Japan's Higher Civil Service Examinations,* p. 177.

40. Spaulding, "Japan's 'New Bureaucrats,' 1932–1945," pp. 63, 666; "Shōwa" in the title refers to the era that began in 1926.

41. Karasawa, "Changes in Japanese Education," pp. 58–59; see also Wray, "A Study in Contrasts"; and Caiger, "The Aims and Content of School Courses in Japanese History."

42. Havens, *Valley of Darkness,* p. 142.

43. Robert King Hall, *Shūshin,* p. 94.

44. Ibid., pp. 94–95.

45. Shillony, "Universities and Students," pp. 782–784.

46. Anderson, *Japan,* p. 40; Levine and Kawada, *Human Resources,* pp. 101–103; Kaigo, *Japanese Education,* p. 888; Kobayashi Tetsuya, *Society, Schools and Progress in Japan,* p. 39.

47. This is the assessment of Levine and Kawada, *Human Resources,* p. 103.

48. Havens makes this point in *Valley of Darkness,* p. 28.

49. Anderson, *Japan,* p. 45.

50. See the photograph in Havens, *Valley of Darkness,* p. 140.

51. Quoted in Elizabeth Mouer, "Women in Teaching," p. 168.

Notes to Chapter 6

1. Burkman, ed., *Occupation of Japan,* p. 33. The phrase "stamping out the bad, stamping in the new" in the chapter title is attributed to a U.S. brigadier general in Robert King Hall, "The Battle of the Mind," p. 63.

2. Quoted in Schoppa, *Educational Reform in Japan,* p. 37.

3. Some of the best general treatments on the SCAP educational reforms are included in Burkman, ed., *Occupation Of Japan;* see also Nishi, *Unconditional Democracy.* For an excellent treatment of U.S. planning for educational reforms, see Mayo,

"Psychological Disarmament." For accounts of the Occupation as political history, see Dower, *Empire and Aftermath;* and Schaller, *The American Occupation of Japan.*

4. Quoted from the July 30, 1945, Bowles draft on educational reform in Thakur, "Textbook Reform in Allied Occupied Japan," pp. 114–115.

5. Duke, "The Textbook Controversy," p. 251; see also Trainor's memoir, *Education Reform in Occupied Japan.*

6. U.S. Department of State, *Report of the United States Education Mission to Japan,* p. 1.

7. Robert King Hall, "Education in the Development of Postwar Japan," p. 126.

8. See Department of State document reprinted in Beauchamp and Vardaman, eds., *Japanese Education Since 1945,* pp. 65–66. For one Japanese view of the conservative character of Maeda and Tanaka, see Nishi, *Unconditional Democracy,* pp. 143–159.

9. Hidaka, "The Role and Aims of Social Studies Education," p. 77.

10. Ogawa, "Reflections on Postwar Education," p. 24.

11. Supreme Commander for the Allied Powers, *Education in a New Japan,* 2:29. For a historian's perspective on prewar Japanese nationalism, see Wilson, "Ultranationalism."

12. Nishi, *Unconditional Democracy,* pp. 170–171; see pp. 173–176 on MacArthur's special concern with promoting Christianity.

13. Robert King Hall, "Education in the Development of Postwar Japan," pp. 121–123.

14. Nishi, *Unconditional Democracy,* pp. 143–159.

15. Thakur, "Textbook Reform," p. 214.

16. The 1947 constitution is reprinted in various sources; for a recent analysis see Inoue, *MacArthur's Japanese Constitution.*

17. Robert King Hall, "Education in the Development of Postwar Japan," pp. 129–130; Hall terms the second mission, which visited in 1950, "merely a follow-up of this first mission." For a critical account of the mission, see Nishi, *Unconditional Democracy,* pp. 186–233.

18. An English translation can be found in Beauchamp and Vardaman, eds., *Japanese Education Since 1945,* pp. 109–111.

19. Kobayashi Tetsuya, *Society, Schools and Progress in Japan,* p. 41.

20. For SCAP's negative reaction see Nishi, *Unconditional Democracy,* pp. 157–158.

21. An English translation of the 1949 law can be found in Supreme Commander for the Allied Powers, Civil Information and Education Section, *Postwar Developments in Japanese Education,* 2:2–3.

22. Kerlinger, "The Development of Democratic Control," p. 85; see also Nishi, *Unconditional Democracy,* pp. 210–219, which stresses the disagreements within SCAP itself on this issue. Important clauses are reprinted in Beauchamp and Vardaman, eds., *Japanese Education Since 1945,* pp. 117–118.

23. Kobayashi Tetsuya, *Society, Schools and Progress,* p. 78; for more on the political structure within which these boards operated, see also Quigley and Turner, *The New Japan,* pp. 392–394.

24. Reprinted in Kerlinger, "The Development of Democratic Control," pp. 232–233.

25. Ogawa, "Reflections on Postwar Education," pp. 25–26.

26. See, for example, Thakur, "Textbook Reform," p. 249.

27. Quoted from a February 11, 1946, speech in Thakur, "Textbook Reform," p. 219; for more on Nanbara, see Barshay, *State and the Intellectual in Imperial Japan.*

28. Thurston, *Teachers and Politics*, pp. 53n, 55.

29. The reluctance of high school teachers to belong to the same associations as those at the elementary level has been a constant obstacle to union organizers; in 1950 a separate union was formed, eventually to be known as the Nihon Kōtōgakkō Kyōshokuin Kumiai (Nikkōkyō), the Senior High School Teachers' Union.

30. Thurston, *Teachers and Politics*, pp. 63–65.

31. For a translation, see appendix A in Thurston, *Teachers and Politics;* or Duke, *Militant Teachers*, pp. 214–217.

32. Thurston provides a translation of one of these contracts in appendix A, *Teachers and Politics*, pp. 273–278.

33. Duke, *Militant Teachers*, pp. 211, 217.

34. As quoted from Article 37 in Thurston, *Teachers and Politics*, p. 199; see also pp. 180–181.

35. Usami, "Zengakuren"; see also Halliday, *A Political History of Japanese Capitalism*, p. 410n, for bibliography.

36. Morito would later attack some of the reforms he helped realize; see his *Daisan no kyōiku kaikaku*.

37. As quoted in Horio, *Educational Thought*, pp. 132–133. Tanaka's role is also described in Nishi, *Unconditional Democracy*, pp. 150–157, 167.

38. The resolution is reprinted in *Political Reorientation of Japan*, 2:585; see also Yamazumi, "Educational Democracy Versus State Control"; and Nishi, *Unconditional Democracy*.

39. This and the following quotes are from Inoue, *MacArthur's Japanese Constitution*, pp. 149–153.

40. Supreme Commander for the Allied Powers, *Education in a New Japan*, p. 1.

41. Thakur, "Textbook Reform," p. 146; Caiger, "Ienaga Saburō and the First Postwar Japanese History Textbooks."

42. Thakur, "Textbook Reform," p. 149.

43. Rubin, "From Wholesomeness to Decadence"; Beer, *Freedom of Expression*, pp. 78–82; see also Nishi, *Unconditional Democracy*.

44. See Thakur, "Textbook Reform," pp. 247–252.

45. Quoted in Duke, "Textbook Controversy," p. 252.

46. Ibid., p. 346.

47. See ibid., pp. 345–347.

48. Robert King Hall, "Education in the Development of Postwar Japan," p. 129; Duke, "Textbook Controversy," pp. 346–347; also see Thakur, "Textbook Reform."

49. Reprinted in Beauchamp and Vardaman, eds., *Japanese Education Since 1945*, pp. 118–122. Italics added.

50. Duke, *Militant Teachers*, pp. 89–91.

51. Swearingen and Langer, *Red Flag in Japan*, p. 243.

52. Johnson, *Conspiracy at Matsukawa*, pp. 23, 60, 83, 119.

53. U.S. Department of State, *Report of the United States Education Mission to Japan*, p. 10.

54. There is a translation in Duke, *Militant Teachers*, pp. 218–219.

55. Quoted from a CI&E memo in Pharr, "Soldiers as Feminists," p. 29. The Women's Section of the CI&E included a number of graduates of Tsuda College, the private women's college.

56. Robert King Hall, "Education in the Development of Postwar Japan," p. 136.

57. Amano, "Educational Crisis in Japan," p. 28.

58. Kobayashi Tetsuya, *Society, Schools and Progress,* p. 43; Ogawa, "Reflections on Postwar Education," p. 29.

59. Supreme Commander for the Allied Powers, *Education in a New Japan,* p. 1. In addition to published sources, the following makes use of two doctoral dissertations: Miwa, "Analysis of the Effect of Major American Ideas upon the Organization of Japanese Higher Education from 1946 to 1967"; and Murata, "A Study of the Impact."

60. Supreme Commander for the Allied Powers, *Education in a New Japan,* p. 1.

61. Murata, "A Study of the Impact," pp. 92–95.

62. For the origins of these SCAP proposals, see Nishi, *Unconditional Democracy,* pp. 224–226.

63. Supreme Commander for the Allied Powers, *Education in a New Japan,* 1:256.

64. Quoted in Murata, "A Study of the Impact," p. 89.

65. John W. Hall, "Education and Modern National Development," p. 415; the quote from the Foreign Office is on pp. 460–461.

66. Robert King Hall, "The Battle of the Mind," p. 70.

Notes to Chapter 7

1. John W. Hall, "Education and Modern National Development," p. 415.

2. Rohlen, *Japan's High Schools,* pp. 210–211; see also Rohlen, "Conflict in Institutional Environment."

3. Pempel, *Patterns,* pp. 71–73; see also Kitamura and Cummings, "The 'Big Bang' Theory," pp. 309–310.

4. See Dore, "The Ethics of New Japan," p. 149; and Packard, *Protest in Tokyo,* p. 145; and Gluck, "The Idea of Showa," p. 6. Nishi discusses the confusion in the use of the term "liberal" during the American Occupation in *Unconditional Democracy,* pp. 169–170. For more on the ultranationalist right in the early postwar period, see Morris, *Nationalism.*

5. Kobayashi Tetsuya, *Society, Schools and Progress in Japan,* p. 77; Schoppa, *Education Reform in Japan,* pp. 220–222.

6. Dore, "The Ethics"; Nakamura, *The Japanese Monarchy,* pp. 118–119.

7. Langer, *Communism in Japan,* pp. 58–59.

8. Thurston, *Teachers and Politics,* pp. 118–122, 248–257.

9. Swearingen and Langer, *Red Flag in Japan,* p. 170.

10. Quoted in Duke, "The Textbook Controversy," p. 248.

11. Henry D. Smith II, *Japan's First Student Radicals,* p. 231; and Krauss, *Japanese Radicals Revisited.* See also Shimbori, "The Sociology of a Student Movement"; Wheeler, "Japan's Postmodern Student Movement"; and Halliday, *A Political History of Japanese Capitalism,* pp. 251–259.

12. Survey cited in Morris, *Nationalism,* p. 308.

13. Packard, *Protest in Tokyo,* pp. 26–31. Packard's is one of the best descriptions of these events and the estimates of student participation. For more on the mindset of progressive intellectuals see Gluck, "The Past in the Present"; and Koschmann, "Intellectuals and Politics."

14. Packard, *Protest in Tokyo,* pp. 287–299.

15. As translated in Yamazumi, "Educational Democracy Versus State Control," p. 96.

16. Hiratsuka, reprint of "World Education and Japan," pp. 13–15. Hiratsuka would head later the National Institute for Educational Research supported by the Education Ministry.

17. For a full translation of the text and an insightful analysis see Dore, "The Ethics."

18. Quoted in Duke, *Militant Teachers*, p. 137.

19. Quoted in Duke, "The Textbook Controversy," p. 248.

20. Quoted in Morris, *Nationalism*, p. 287.

21. Ōshima Yasumasa, "Japan's Defeat and Ethical Education," pp. 70–72.

22. Honda, "The Barren Social Climate of Postwar Japan," pp. 65–67.

23. Osada, "Problems Involved in Providing Ethical Foundation," pp. 67–69.

24. Kobayashi Tetsuya, *Society, Schools and Progress*, p. 91.

25. As quoted by Yamazumi, "Educational Democracy Versus State Control," p. 103.

26. An English translation can be found in *Journal of Social and Political Ideas in Japan* 1, no. 3 (December 1963): 122–124; it is also reprinted in Thurston, *Teachers and Politics*, pp. 285–287.

27. Ienaga, "The Glorification of War," p 127. See also Mochizuki, "Munakata Seiya," especially pp. 226–227.

28. Adachi, "An Interpretation of Article X," p. 59.

29. Munakata, "The Fundamental Law of Education," p. 57.

30. Adachi, "An Interpretation of Article X," p. 61. For a brief glimpse of the emotional aspects of the shrine, see Kiyama, "Meeting at Yasukuni Shrine."

31. Munakata, "The Fundamental Law of Education," p. 56.

32. Duke, *Militant Teachers*, p. 137.

33. Kobayashi Tetsuya, *Society, Schools and Progress*, pp. 83–85; very marked decentralization had characterized Japanese political history from at least the twelfth to the nineteenth centuries.

34. U.S. Department of State, *Report of the United States Education Mission*, p. 25.

35. See Anderson, *Japan*, pp. 83–85, for more on the "new" ministry.

36. See Anderson, *Japan*, p. 81.

37. For a comparative perspective, see Friedman, "Education as a Political Issue in Japan," pp. 250–257.

38. Shimbori, "The Sociology of a Student Movement," table on p. 307.

39. Dore, "Textbook Censorship," p. 548.

40. See Rohlen's description of school administration in Kobe, *Japan's High Schools*, pp. 215–221. He cites an interesting case of a former activist who broke from the union to become an administrator (p. 220).

41. Dore, *City Life*, pp. 233–235, 414–415; Singleton, *Nichu*, p. 14; Higuchi, "The PTA."

42. This point is made by Duke, *Militant Teachers*, p. 144; for more on these Education Ministry guides, see the summary of the 1951 "Social Studies Outline For Primary School" in Dore, *City Life*, pp. 407–410.

43. Dore, *City Life*, p. 412.

44. I follow the translations in Beer, *Freedom of Expression*, pp. 260–261. His account of the process is among the more detailed in English, but see also Duke, "The Textbook Controversy." Dore translates the name of the *bangikai* as "Textbook Examination Research Committee" ("Textbook Censorship," p. 549).

45. Dore, *City Life*, p. 412.

46. An account of the inner workings of the ministry can be found in Satō Kōmei, *Kyōkasho kentei no genba kara*. I thank Itaba Yoshihisa for this reference.

47. Beer, *Freedom of Expression*, pp. 265–266; Ienaga, "The Historical Significance of the Japanese Textbook Lawsuit."

48. Ienaga, "The Glorification of War," p. 125.

49. For more details, see Dore, "Textbook Censorship."

50. As translated by Platzer in Horio, *Educational Thought*, pp. 191–192.

51. Nishi, *Unconditional Democracy*, p. 225.

52. Swearingen and Langer, *Red Flag in Japan*, p. 248n.

53. Duke, *Militant Teachers*, pp. 138–143; Thurston, *Teachers and Politics*, pp. 191–194, 205–209.

54. Quoted in Thurston, *Teachers and Politics*, p. 191.

55. Tsuji, "Toward Understanding the Teachers' Efficiency Rating System," p. 52.

56. Duke, *Militant Teachers*, table 8, p. 154.

57. Thurston, *Teachers and Politics*, pp. 205–206.

58. See Sugimoto, "Quantitative Characteristics of Popular Disturbances in Post-Occupation Japan," p. 299n.

59. See the excerpt from Tsuji Kiyoaki's 1960 book, *Seiji o kangaeru shihyō*, translated as "Toward Understanding the Teachers' Efficiency Rating," in *Journal of Social and Political Ideas in Japan* 1, no. 3 (December 1963): 51–54.

60. Honda, "The Barren Social Climate of Postwar Japan," pp. 65–66.

61. Thurston, *Teachers and Politics*, p. 208.

62. Horio, *Educational Thought*, pp. 214–215.

63. Thurston, *Teachers and Politics*, p. 210.

64. Horio, *Educational Thought*, p. 216.

65. As quoted in ibid., pp. 183–184.

66. In this section I have relied heavily upon Pempel, *Patterns*, pp. 97–135.

67. On the 1960 crisis, see Packard, *Protest in Tokyo*.

68. Quoted in Pempel, *Patterns*, pp. 103–104.

69. Munakata, "The Task of Universities and the State," p. 93.

70. Quoted in Pempel, *Patterns*, p. 110.

71. Havens, *Fire Across the Sea*, pp. 133–136.

72. Quoted in Pempel, *Patterns*, p. 121.

73. As quoted in Cummings, "The Conservatives Reform Higher Education," p. 424. Note that Cummings believes university administrators privately supported such legislation.

74. See James and Benjamin, *Public Education and Private Education in Japan*, especially chapter 11.

75. See Miwa, "Analysis of the Effect of Major American Ideas upon the Organization of Japanese Higher Education"; and Pempel, *Patterns*, especially pp. 44–46.

76. For more on this administrative elite, see Koh, *Japan's Administrative Elite*.

77. See Yanaga, *Big Business in Japanese Politics*, table 3, p. 25; Colbert, *The Left Wing in Japanese Politics*, pp. 303–304.

78. See Azumi, *Higher Education and Business Recruitment in Japan*.

79. See Duke, *Militant Teachers*, p. 137.

80. Dore, *City Life*, pp. 235–238; Singleton, *Nichu*, pp. 19–20.

81. Schoppa, *Education Reform*, p. 101.

82. Kobayashi Tetsuya, *Society, Schools and Progress*, pp. 101–105.

83. Horio, *Educational Thought*, p. 220.

84. Victor N. Kobayashi, "Japanese and U.S. Curricula Compared."

85. Amano, "Educational Crisis in Japan," p. 28.

86. See James and Benjamin, *Public Policy and Private Education*, pp. 174–178.

87. For more detail, see Rohlen, "Is Japanese Education Becoming Less Egalitarian?"

88. Kubota, *Higher Civil Servants in Postwar Japan*, table 17, p. 62.

89. Amano, "Educational Crisis in Japan," pp. 129–130; see also Frost, "'Examination Hell.'"

90. Translated in *Journal of Social and Political Ideas in Japan* 1, no. 3 (December 1963): 129–131; reprinted in Thurston, *Teachers and Politics*, appendix III; see also pp. 84–85n.

91. Horio, *Educational Thought*, p. 299.

92. Fujimura-Fanselow and Imamura, "The Education of Women in Japan."

Notes to Chapter 8

1. *Basic Guidelines for the Reform of Education, 1972;* an English translation is available in Beauchamp, ed., *Learning to Be Japanese*, pp. 372–396. Prime Minister Ōhira later called it a "new age transcending the age of modernization" (Gluck, "The Past in the Present," p. 72).

2. Quoted in Schoppa, *Education Reform in Modern Japan*, p. 179.

3. Notable recent attempts to summarize the evidence can be found in Lynn, *Educational Achievement in Japan;* and Leestma and Walberg, eds., *Japanese Educational Productivity.*

4. Bowman, *Educational Choice and Labor Markets in Japan*, p. 104. Simmons puts this claim even more concisely: "Japan, perhaps more nearly than any other nation, approaches the ideal of equal educational opportunity for all, with students' futures decided by their academic merit" (Simmons, *Growing Up and Going to School in Japan*, p. 80).

5. Schooland, in making this same point, cites one case of the overeagerness of publishers in *Shogun's Ghost*, p. 13. Walter Feinberg has written a provocative essay on why the Japanese school system has drawn so much attention in the United States, *Japan and the Pursuit of a New Identity.*

6. In English, for example, see Amano, "The Bright and Dark Sides of Japanese Education"; Yamazumi, "Educational Democracy Versus State Control." Some of the most graphic descriptions of the "dark side" in either language can be found in Schooland, *Shogun's Ghost.*

7. See Wheeler, "The Postmodern Student Movement."

8. Inoguchi and Kabashima, "The Status Quo Student Elite."

9. Quoted in Beauchamp, "Report from Japan, 1976," p. 341; also see Schoppa, *Education Reform*, pp. 201–204. Ironically, Nagai himself did not personally favor the *shunin* system.

10. See the analysis by Schoppa, *Education Reform*, pp. 157–163.

11. See Schoppa's description of the "education subgovernment" in *Education Reform;* and "Zoku Power."

12. See Schoppa, "Zoku Power," p. 190.

13. As translated in Horio, *Educational Thought*, p. 203.

14. As quoted in Beer, *Freedom of Expression*, p. 268.

15. As quoted in Horio, *Educational Thought*, pp. 203, 206.

16. As quoted in ibid., p. 223.

17. For example, see Kitai, "Textbooks Versus Teaching."

18. For convenient translations from some of the opinion magazines, see *Japan Echo* 9, no. 4 (Winter 1982).

19. See Lee, "History and Politics," pp. 73–76; also Yayama, "The Newspapers Conduct a Mad Rhapsody over the Textbook Issue."

20. Matsuno Yasuki, as quoted in Lee, "History and Politics," p. 71; van Wolferen attributes this or a similar remark to Minister of Education Fujio Masayuki, who then was pressured into resigning (*The Enigma of Japanese Power*, p. 291). For a more general argument about the universality of such reshaping of history, see Satō Kōmei, *Kyōkasho kentei no genba kara*, pp. 401–438.

21. Lee, "History and Politics," p. 72.

22. Beer, *Freedom of Expression*, p. 273.

23. As translated in Lee, "History and Politics," p. 75.

24. Hata, "When the Ideologues Rewrite History"; Muramatsu, "In Search of National Identity," p. 317.

25. Suzuki, "Liberalizing Textbook Screening," p. 24.

26. Hata, "When the Ideologues Rewrite History."

27. As translated in Yamazumi, "Educational Democracy Versus State Control," p. 112.

28. In recent years the Education Ministry has made some modification in its screening procedures; see Takahashi, *Kyōkasho kentei*, pp. 98–99.

29. As translated in Yamazumi, "Educational Democracy Versus State Control," pp. 105–106, 111. Although Nakasone has been a professional politician most of his adult life, he also served as president of the conservative Takashoku University in the 1960s. For more on the context of Nakasone's educational policies, see van Wolferen, *The Enigma of Japanese Power*, pp. 291–292; and Pyle, *The Japanese Question*, pp. 95–101.

30. Hardacre points out that there is also a separate Tomb for Unidentified War Victims that "most nearly approximates Arlington National Cemetery" (*Shinto and the State*, pp. 140–142, 145–149). The distinction, however, is probably lost on most Japanese.

31. See, for example, Fukatsu, "A State Visit to Yasukuni Shrine." The criticism was not merely from the opposition parties. One of Nakasone's fellow Liberal Democratic Party members, a former aide to Prime Minister Tanaka Kakue, has been quoted as calling Nakasone "fundamentally a monarchist, a Bonapartist, and even more fundamentally a fascist" (*Far Eastern Economic Review*, September 3, 1992, p. 24).

32. van Wolferen, *The Enigma of Japanese Power*, p. 292.

33. Beauchamp, ed., *Learning to Be Modern*, p. 354.

34. Kitai, "Textbooks Versus Teaching."

35. Cummings, "Patterns of Academic Achievement," p. 123. On preschools, see Hendry, *Becoming Japanese;* Boocock, "Controlled Diversity"; Boocock, "The Japanese Preschool System"; Tobin et al., *Preschool in Three Cultures;* and the articles by DeCoker, Lewis, and Tobin in Shields, ed., *Japanese Schooling.*

36. Calculated from Dore and Sako, *How the Japanese Learn to Work*, table 1.1, p. 2.

37. Rohlen, "Education in Japanese Society," p. 25.

38. From Keizai Koho Center, *Japan*, p. 93.

39. Dore and Sako, *How the Japanese Learn to Work*, pp. 10–11.

40. For example, see Vogel, *Japan as Number 1*, p. 159.

41. Rohlen, "Education in Japanese Society," pp. 25–26.

42. Cummings, *Education and Equality in Japan*, p. 6.

43. Schoppa, "Zoku Power," p. 92n.

44. Kurimoto, *Meidai kyōju jishoku shimatsu*.

45. Tominaga, "The University in Contemporary Society," pp. 65, 66.

46. Bowman, *Educational Choice*, p. 158; for statistical data that challenge such generalizations see Ishida, *Social Mobility in Contemporary Japan*. Whatever the realities, the prevailing myth of egalitarian opportunity continues to dominate political discourse.

47. For some evidence on this, see Tominaga, "The University in Contemporary Society," pp. 64–65; and Cummings, *Education and Equality in Japan*. For the argument that Japan is more like the West in this respect, see Ishida, Goldthorpe, and Erikson, "Intergenerational Class Mobility in Postwar Japan."

48. Hellmann, "Review of Ezra Vogel's *Japan as Number One*," pp. 426–427.

49. For the pecking order in Kobe, see Rohlen, "Is Japanese Education Becoming Less Egalitarian?" The hierarchy of admissions test scores in Tokyo is described in Cummings et al., *Educational Policies in Crisis*, p. 130.

50. This and other material for and by Japanese youth are translated in Maki, ed., *We the Japanese*, pp. 88–98.

51. For example, Gotoda provides 1983 information on the educational backgrounds of 3,131 business executives in Kyoto Prefecture showing the domination of Ritsumeikan and Dōshisha universities (*The Local Politics of Kyoto*, table 10, p. 114).

52. Koh, *Japan's Administrative Elite*, tables 9 and 10, pp. 86–89. Enrollments for private colleges can be found in Japan Association of Private Colleges and Universities, *Japan's Private Colleges and Universities*, appendix, pp. 232–237.

53. Survey by *Tōyō Keizai* as reported in *Japan Times International Weekly Edition*, October 26–November 1, 1992. It should be noted that there are also important business firms run as family enterprises that are less impressed with such educational credentials; see, for example, Hamabata, *Crested Kimono*, especially p. 129.

54. James and Benjamin, in *Public Policy and Private Education*, summarize data on benefits of graduating from different echelons, pp. 69–83.

55. Rohlen, "Education in Japanese Society," p. 27.

56. James and Benjamin summarize data on minimum entrance exam scores needed to be accepted at various types of colleges in *Public Policy and Private Education*, pp. 84–86; data on applicants can found in table 2.3, p. 53.

57. See Cummings, *Education and Equality*; and Cummings, "Expansion, Examination Fever, and Equality"; for an economist's perspective, see Blumenthal, "Japan's *Juken* Industry." Robert August discusses the costs of *juku* in his article "*Yobiko*." For similar institutions in other parts of East Asia, see Thomas and Postlewaite, eds., *Schooling in East Asia*.

58. Kondō, "Off We Go to Our Lessons," p. 15.

59. See Tsukada's participant-observer study, "*Yobiko*" *Life*, which is summarized in part in his article "Institutionalized Supplementary Education."

60. *Japan Times International Edition*, June 8–14, 1992, p. 2; the 1943 figure is given in Tsukada, *"Yobiko" Life*, p. 6.

61. See Shimizu, "Entrance Examinations."

62. McKean, "Equality," table 1, p. 202. For more on this subject, see Verba et al., *Elites and the Idea of Equality*.

63. Rohlen, "Education in Japanese Society," p. 26.

64. Pharr, *Political Women in Japan*, p. 90; see also pp. 55–56, 64.

65. JTU Council on Educational Reform, "What Japan's Education Should Be," p. 353.

66. Baba, "A Study of Minority-Majority Relations"; Kōno and Bowles, "Ainu"; Sala, "Protest and the Ainu of Hokkaido"; and Wetherall, "Ethnic Ainu Seek Official Recognition." On Ainu schooling, see Peng, "Education: An Agent of Change in Ainu Community Life."

67. Umakoshi, "The Role of Education in Preserving the Ethnic Identity of Korean Residents in Japan."

68. A concise summary of these cases and others can be found in Lee, "Koreans in Japan."

69. For the Yata incident, see Upham, *Law and Social Change in Postwar Japan*, pp. 87–103. For the Yōka incident, see Rohlen, "Violence at Yoka High School"; and Pharr, *Losing Face*, chapters 5 and 7. All these observers stress that both sides in these clashes have ties with the left in Japanese politics: The league has ties with the Japan Socialist Party, and the unionized teachers and the National Liaison Council have ties with the Japan Communist Party.

70. Shimahara, *Burakumin*; Yoshino and Murakoshi, "Burakumin"; Cummings, *Education and Equality*, p. 186; Broadbent, "A Question of Academic Freedom."

71. Merry White provides a good starting place for descriptions of some of the more sensationalized aspects in *The Japanese Educational Challenge*, pp. 136–144. Schooland, *Shogun's Ghost*, repeats many of the horror stories that appeared in the media.

72. Kumajira, "Laying the Groundwork," p. 45.

73. Quoted in Schoppa, *Education Reform*, p. 125.

74. Sakaiya, "Supply-Side Competition for the School System," pp. 37–43.

75. See, for example, Kuroha, "School Dropouts and High School Education," p. 118; Fukushima, "Causes of Adolescent Violence."

76. Schooland reports some of the more appalling cases in *Shogun's Ghost*, pp. 50–87.

77. Kumajira, "Laying the Groundwork," p. 48; Merry White, *The Japanese Educational Challenge*, pp. 136–142.

78. Thorstein, "Education Mamas"; and White, *The Japanese Educational Challenge*, pp. 33–42, 142–144.

79. *New York Times*, April 27, 1973. See, for example, the English translation of the much earlier 1967 article by a young Tokyo University professor, Orihara Hiroshi, "'Test Hell' and Alienation."

80. See Mouer and Sugimoto, *Images of Japanese Society*, pp. 377–404.

81. Schoppa, *Education Reform*, pp. 214–215. Compare the 1984 proposals by the Kyoto Group for the Study of Global Issues reprinted in Beauchamp and Vardaman, eds., *Japanese Education Since 1945*, pp. 280–284.

82. An English translation is available in *Minerva* 8, no. 4 (October 1970): 581–593. A discussion of who served on this advisory body can be found in Kitamura and Cummings, "The 'Big Bang' Theory," pp. 309–310.

83. See Schoppa, *Education Reform*, pp. 192–194. James and Benjamin analyze the finances of private schools in *Public Policy and Private Education*, pp. 64–68, 166–174. Article 89 of the postwar constitution prohibits public monies being expended "for the use, benefit or maintenance of any religious institution or association, or for any charitable, educational or benevolent enterprises not under the control of public authority." From time to time Conservatives in favor of revising other parts of the constitution—particularly Article 9, which renounces the use of force in international disputes—will remind the public of such anomalies.

84. Excerpts are available in *Minerva* 11, no. 3 (July 1973): 387–414. For the views of business leaders, see Schoppa, *Education Reform;* and Beauchamp and Vardaman, eds., *Japanese Education Since 1945*, pp. 230–233.

85. Kitamura and Cummings, "The 'Big Bang' Theory," p. 304.

86. Ivan Hall, "Organizational Paralysis," p. 328.

87. Schoppa, *Education Reform*, pp. 194–199.

88. Tsukada, *"Yobiko Life,"* p. 9.

89. There are 3,440 municipalities in 43 prefectures and 4 equivalent units (Tokyo, Osaka, Kyoto, and Hokkaido). On the issue of centralized government as a whole, see Reed, *Japanese Prefectures and Policymaking.*

90. Nishikawa, "The Postwar Educational Reform in Japan," p. 269; Mouer and Sugimoto, *Images of Japanese Society*, p. 258.

91. See table 10.2 in Bingman, *Japanese Government Leadership and Management*, p. 111; also Ichikawa, "Finance of Higher Education"; and Cummings, "Patterns of Academic Achievement," pp. 123–124.

92. Bingman, *Japanese Government Leadership and Management*, p. 117.

93. See, for example, Victor N. Kobayashi, "Japanese and U.S. Curricula Compared," p. 69.

94. Cummings, "Patterns of Academic Achievement," pp. 123–124.

95. Morito, *Daisan no kyōiku kaikaku;* Beauchamp, "The Development of Japanese Educational Policy," p. 319; Cummings, "The Aftermath of the University Crisis," p. 350.

96. English translations are available in Beauchamp, ed., *Learning to Be Japanese*, pp. 372–396.

97. Beauchamp, "The Development of Japanese Educational Policy"; Kobayashi Tetsuya, *Society, Schools and Progress in Japan*, p. 77.

98. Compare, for example, the 1951 statement by Amano quoted above in Chapter 7.

99. Halliday, *A Political History of Japanese Capitalism*, pp. 259–261; JTU Council on Education Reform, "What Japan's Education Should Be," p. 356; Kobayashi Tetsuya, *Society, Schools and Progress*, p. 77.

100. Quoted in Schoppa, *Education Reform*, p. 224.

101. Quoted in ibid., p. 156.

102. JTU Council on Education Reform, "What Japan's Education Should Be," pp. 356–359; I have corrected some spelling errors in the English translation.

103. See the account in Schoppa, *Education Reform*, especially pp. 101–102, 179–181, 204–207.

104. Victor N. Kobayashi, "Japanese and U.S. Curricula Compared." For more on vocational programs, see Dore and Sako, *How Japan Learns to Work*, chapter 3.

105. Schoppa, *Education Reform*, pp. 155–156.

106. Pempel, *Patterns*, pp. 163–183; it is perhaps useful to recall that this same "differentiation of function" theme was sounded in the United States by the Carnegie Commission on Higher Education in its 1973 report.

107. Eighty-three percent in one 1977 poll; reported in Tominaga, "The University in Contemporary Society," p. 62.

108. For example, see summaries of 1977–1978 articles in "Too Much Emphasis on Education."

109. Takane, "How Much Education Is Right?" p. 73.

110. Ibid, p. 73–75, 81.

111. Miyahara et al., eds., *Shiryō Nihon gendai kyōikushi*, 3:214.

112. Murakami, "The Debt Comes Due for Mass Education." For an excellent description of the organization of Tokyo University, see Ivan Hall, "Organizational Paralysis."

113. Mouer and Sugimoto, *Images of Japanese Society*, p. 260.

114. Quoted from the April 1985 report of the Ad Hoc Council on Education, Schoppa, *Education Reform*, p. 226.

Notes to Chapter 9

1. Gluck, "The Idea of Shōwa," p. 1. For other reflections on the Shōwa era by U.S. and Japanese scholars, see the Summer 1990 issue of *Daedalus* or the versions reprinted in Gluck and Graubard, eds., *Showa*.

2. Shimahara, "Japanese Educational Reforms," p. 217.

3. Gluck, "The Idea of Shōwa," p. 4.

4. Schooland, *Shogun's Ghost*, p. 174; van Wolferen, *The Enigma*, p. 292.

5. Reported in *Japan Times Weekly International Edition*, January 25–31, 1993, p. 5.

6. Todd, "Educational and Social Reform."

7. As reported in *Asahi Access* 3, no. 48 (December 14, 1992): 17.

8. Kawamura Gakuen Women's University survey, as reported in ibid.

9. *Japan Times Weekly International Edition*, February 3–9, 1992.

10. Ishida, "Stratification and Mobility," p. 541.

11. Beauchamp, "The Development of Japanese Educational Policy," p. 307.

12. Organization of Economic Cooperation and Development, *Reviews of National Policies for Education—Japan*, p. 27.

13. There is a growing literature analyzing *Nihonjinron* discourse; especially good introductions can be found in Dale, *The Myth of Japanese Uniqueness;* and Yoshino, *Cultural Nationalism in Contemporary Japan*. The quotation is from the latter, p. 10. Somewhat more theoretical treatments can be found in Mouer and Sugimoto, *Images of Japanese Society*, but the authors sometimes misread U.S. scholarship on Japanese nationalism, as on p. 27 when they mistakenly characterize my own work as an example of Parsonian modernization theory. The book in question was actually critical of Parsonian views when applied to ideology. See also Bellah, "Japan's Cultural Identity."

14. On the issue of ascription versus achievement, see also Lebra, *Above the Clouds*, pp. 7–8.

15. *Japan Times International Edition*, November 8–14, 1993, p. 8.

16. Miura, "So What if the Textbooks Are Biased?"

17. Reported in Kitai, "Textbooks Versus Teaching," pp. 84–85.

18. Kitamura and Cummings, "The 'Big Bang' Theory," p. 303.

Bibliography

The following list includes only those works actually cited in the text. The best starting place for further reading in English–language materials is *Education in Japan: A Source Book*, compiled by two of the most productive U.S. scholars in this field, Edward R. Beauchamp and Richard Rubinger. They provide both an annotated bibliography and excellent introductory notes as well as lists of other bibliographies, the best for materials published before the 1960s being Herbert Passin, *Japanese Education: A Bibliography of Materials in the English Language.* "An Annotated Bibliography of English Language Works on the Social History of Modern Japanese Science," compiled by James Bartholomew, can be found in Nakayama Shigeru et al., eds., *Science and Society in Modern Japan.* The annual *Bibliography of Asian Studies*, published by the Association for Asian Studies, provides easy access to both books and articles in a number of Western languages but is unannotated. Japanese bibliographies on the history of education are far too numerous to mention, but there is a very useful if somewhat dated introduction available in Shinichi Watanabe, compiler, *A Select List of Books on the History of Education in Japan and a Select List of Periodicals on Education.*

There are several collections of documents available in English translation. Herbert Passin's *Society and Education in Japan* includes a selection of prewar materials whereas the postwar is more fully sampled in Edward R. Beauchamp and James M. Vardaman, Jr., eds., *Japanese Education Since 1945: A Documentary Study.* There are numerous translations of Ministry of Education publications available. See, for example, the list in James J. Shields, Jr., ed., *Japanese Schooling.* There are also relevant materials translated in David Lu, ed., *Sources of Japanese History;* W. W. McLaren, ed., *Japanese Government Documents; Meiroku Zasshi: Journal of the Japanese Enlightenment,* translated by William R. Braisted; and *The Meiji Japan Through Contemporary Sources,* edited by the Centre for East Asian Cultural Studies.

Beginning in the 1960s there have been three valuable periodicals published in Japan that have regularly carried translations from Japanese opinion magazines: *Journal of Social and Political Ideas in Japan,* its successor *Japan Interpreter,* and *Japan Echo.* Unfortunately, only the latter is still being published. The Asia Foundation also has a useful Japanese Translation Series entitled "Japan Views."

There are, of course, a large number of English-language scholarly periodicals specializing in education that occasionally carry articles on Japan, including *Comparative Education Review, History of Education Quarterly,* and *International Review of Education,* but the only English-language periodical that focused tightly on this field is *Education in Japan: Journal for Overseas*, the official journal of the International Research Institute, Hiroshima University. Conversely, among the best of those periodicals on East Asia that occasionally publish articles on Japanese education are *Journal of Asian Studies, Journal of Japanese Studies, Modern Asian Studies*, and *Monumenta Nipponica*.

Works Cited

Abe, Hakaru. "Education of the Legal Profession in Japan." In *Law in Japan: The Legal Order in a Changing Society*, 153–187, edited by Arthur Taylor von Mehren. Cambridge: Harvard University Press, 1963.

Abosch, David. "Katō Hiroyuki and the Introduction of German Political Thought in Modern Japan, 1868–1883." Doctoral dissertation, University of California, Berkeley, 1964.

Adachi Kenji. "An Interpretation of Article X of the Fundamental Law of Education." *Journal of Social and Political Ideas in Japan* 1, no. 3 (December 1963): 58–62.

Ahn, Choong-sik. "The Japanese Cabinet Ministers: Change and Continuity, 1885 Through 1965." Doctoral dissertation, Columbia University, 1973.

Amano, Ikuo. "The Bright and Dark Sides of Japanese Education." *Japan Foundation Newsletter* 19, nos. 5–6 (May 1992).

———. "Continuity and Change in the Structure of Japanese Higher Education." In *Changes in the Japanese University: A Comparative Perspective*, 10–39, edited by William K. Cummings, Ikuo Amano, and Kazuyuki Kitamura. New York: Praeger, 1979.

———. "The Dilemma of Japanese Education Today." *Japan Foundation Newsletter* 13, no. 5 (March 1986). Reprinted in James J. Shields, Jr., *Japanese Schooling: Patterns of Socialization, Equality and Political Control*. University Park: Pennsylvania University Press, 1989.

———. "Educational Crisis in Japan." In *Educational Policies in Crisis: Japanese and American Perspectives*, 23–58, edited by William K. Cummings, Edward R. Beauchamp, Shogo Ichikawa, Victory N. Kobayashi, and Morikazu Ushiogi. New York: Praeger, 1986.

———. *Education and Examination in Modern Japan*. Translation by William K. Cummings and Fumiko Cummings. Tokyo: University of Tokyo Press, 1990.

———. "'Popular Higher Education' in Japan." *Daigaku ronshū* 21 (1991): 211–221.

Anderson, Ronald S. *Japan: Three Epochs of Modern Education*. Bulletin 1959, No. 11. Washington, D.C.: U.S. Office of Education, 1959.

Aonuma Yoshimatsu. *Nihon no keieisō: sono shusshin to seikaku* (The Managerial Class in Japan: Its Background and Character). Tokyo: Nihon Keizai Shinbunsha, 1965.

Arisawa Hiromi. *Gakumon to shisō to ningen: wasureenu hitobito o omoide* (Scholarship, Thought, and Human Beings: Remembering Unforgettable People). Tokyo: Mainichi Shinbunsha, 1957.

August, Robert L. "*Yobiko*: Prep Schools for College Entrance in Japan." In *Japanese Educational Productivity*, edited by Robert Leestma and Herbert J. Walberg. Ann Arbor: Michigan Papers on Japan, 1992.

Azumi, Koya. *Higher Education and Business Recruitment in Japan*. New York: Teachers' College, Columbia University, 1969.

Baba Yūko. "A Study of Minority-Majority Relations: The Ainu and Japanese in Hokkaido." *Japan Interpreter* 13, no. 1 (Summer 1980): 60–92.

Barshay, Andrew E. *State and the Intellectual in Imperial Japan: The Public Man in Crisis.* Berkeley: University of California Press, 1988.

Bartholomew, James R. *The Formation of Science in Japan: Building a Research Tradition.* New Haven: Yale University Press, 1989.

Baxter, James C. "Local Government." *Kodansha Encyclopedia of Japan*, 5: 62–65. Tokyo and New York: Kodansha, 1983.

Beauchamp, Edward R. "The Development of Japanese Educational Policy, 1945–1985." *History of Education Quarterly* 27, no. 3 (Fall 1987): 299–324. Reprinted in Edward R. Beauchamp, ed., *Windows on Japanese Education*, 27–50. New York: Greenwood Press, 1991.

———. "Reform Traditions in the United States and Japan." In *Educational Policies in Crisis: Japanese and American Perspectives*, 3–22, edited by William K. Cummings, Edward R. Beauchamp, Shogo Ichikawa, Victory N. Kobayashi, and Morikazu Ushiogi. New York: Praeger, 1986.

———. "Report from Japan 1976." In *Learning to Be Japanese*, 338–346, edited by Edward R. Beauchamp. Hampden, CT: Linnet Books, 1978.

———, ed. *Learning to Be Japanese: Selected Readings on Japanese Society and Education.* Hampden, CT: Linnet Books, 1978.

———, ed. *Windows on Japanese Education.* New York: Greenwood Press, 1991.

Beauchamp, Edward R., and Richard Rubinger. *Education in Japan: A Source Book.* New York: Garland Publishing, 1989.

Beauchamp, Edward R., and James M. Vardaman, Jr., eds. *Japanese Education Since 1945: A Documentary Study.* Armonk, NY: M. E. Sharpe, 1994.

Beckmann, George M., and Okubo Genji. *The Japanese Communist Party, 1922–1945.* Stanford: Stanford University Press, 1969.

Beer, Lawrence Ward. *Freedom of Expression in Japan: A Study in Comparative Law, Politics, and Society.* Tokyo: Kodansha International, 1984.

Bellah, Robert N. "Japan's Cultural Identity: Some Reflections on the Work Of Watsuji Tetsuro." *Journal of Asian Studies* 24, no. 4 (August 1965): 573–594.

Berger, Gordon Mark. *Parties Out of Power in Japan, 1931–1941.* Princeton: Princeton University Press, 1977.

Bernstein, Gail Lee. *Japanese Marxist: A Portrait of Kawakami Hajime, 1879–1946.* Cambridge: Harvard University Press, 1976.

———, ed. *Recreating Japanese Women, 1600–1945.* Berkeley: University of California Press, 1991.

Bingman, Charles. *Japanese Government Leadership and Management.* New York: St. Martin's Press, 1989.

Blacker, Carmen. *The Japanese Enlightenment: A Study of the Writings of Fukuzawa Yukichi.* Cambridge: Cambridge University Press, 1964.

Blumenthal, Tuvia. "Japan's *Juken* Industry." *Asian Survey* 32, no. 5 (May 1992), 448–460.

Boocock, Sarane Spence. "Controlled Diversity: An Overview of the Japanese Preschool System." *Journal of Japanese Studies* 15, no. 1 (Winter 1989): 41–65.

———. "The Japanese Preschool System." In *Windows on Japanese Education*, 97–126, edited by Edward R. Beauchamp. New York: Greenwood Press, 1991.

Bowman, Mary Jean. *Educational Choice and Labor Markets in Japan,* with the collaboration of Hideo Ikeda and Yasumasa Tomoda. Chicago: University of Chicago Press, 1981.

Braisted, William R., trans. *Meiroku Zasshi: Journal of the Japanese Enlightenment.* Cambridge: Harvard University Press, 1976.

Broadbent, Jeffrey. "A Question of Academic Freedom in Japan." *American Sociological Association Footnotes* (April 1991): 5.

Brown, Sidney D. "Kido Takayoshi (1833–1877): Meiji Japan's Cautious Revolutionary." *Pacific Historical Review* 25, no. 2 (May 1956): 151–162.

Burkman, Thomas W., ed. *The Occupation of Japan: Educational and Social Reforms.* Norfolk, VA: MacArthur Memorial Foundation, 1982.

Caiger, John. "The Aims and Content of School Courses in Japanese History, 1872–1945." In *Japan's Modern Century*, edited by Edmund Skrzupckak. Tokyo: Sophia University Press, 1968.

———. "Ienaga Saburo and the First Postwar Japanese History Textbook." *Modern Asian Studies* 3, no. 1 (1969): 1–16.

Centre for East Asian Cultural Studies, ed. *The Meiji Japan Through Contemporary Sources.* Tokyo: Centre for East Asian Cultural Studies, 3 vols., 1969–1972.

Colbert, Evelyn S. *The Left Wing in Japanese Politics.* New York: Institute of Pacific Relations, 1952.

Collcutt, Martin. "Buddhism: The Threat of Eradication." In *Japan in Transition: From Tokugawa to Meiji*, 143–167, edited by Marius B. Jansen and Gilbert Rozman. Princeton: Princeton University Press, 1986.

Conte, James Thomas. "Overseas Study in the Meiji Period: Japanese Students in America, 1867–1902." Doctoral dissertation, Princeton University, 1977.

Craig, Albert M. *Chōshū in the Meiji Restoration.* Cambridge: Harvard University Press, 1961.

———. "Kido Koin and Okubo Toshimichi: A Pyschohistorical Analysis." In *Personality in Japanese History*, 264–334, edited by Albert M. Craig and Donald Shively. Berkeley: University of California Press, 1970.

Craig, Albert M., and Donald H. Shively, eds. *Personality in Japanese History.* Berkeley: University of California Press, 1970.

Cummings, William K. "The Aftermath of the University Crisis." *Japan Interpreter* 10, nos. 3–4 (Winter 1976): 350–360.

———. "The Conservatives Reform Higher Education." *Japan Interpreter* 8, no. 4 (Winter 1974): 421–431. Reprinted in Edward R. Beauchamp, ed., *Learning to Be Japanese: Selected Readings on Japanese Society and Education*, 316–328. Hampden, CT: Linnet Books, 1978.

———. *Education and Equality in Japan.* Princeton: Princeton University Press, 1980.

———. "Expansion, Examination Fever, and Equality." In *Changes in the Japanese University: A Comparative Perspective*, 83–106, edited by William K. Cummings et al. New York: Praeger, 1979.

———. "Japan's Science and Engineering Pipeline: Structure, Politics, and Trends." In *Windows on Japanese Education*, 175–208, edited by Edward R. Beauchamp. New York: Greenwood Press, 1991.

———. "Patterns of Academic Achievement in Japan and the United States." In *Educational Policies in Crisis: Japanese and American Perspectives*, edited by William K. Cummings, Edward R. Beauchamp, Shogo Ichikawa, Victor N. Kobayashi, and Morikazu Ushiogi. New York: Praeger, 1986.

Cummings, William K., Edward R. Beauchamp, Shogo Ichikawa, Victor N. Kobayashi, Morikazu Ushiogi, eds. *Educational Policies in Crisis: Japanese and American Perspectives*. New York: Praeger, 1986.

Cummings, William K., Ikuo Amano, and Kazuyuki Kitamura, eds. *Changes in the Japanese University: A Comparative Perspective*. New York: Praeger, 1979.

"Daigaku oyobi seifu no kokkakan ni tsuite" (On the Nationalist View of the Government and the University). *Kaizō* (July 1923): 1.

Dale, Peter N. *The Myth of Japanese Uniqueness*. New York: St. Martin's Press, 1986.

Daniels, Gordon. "Social Reform in Postwar Japan: British Perspectives on Education and Land Reform." In *The Occupation of Japan: Educational and Social Reforms*, 457–469, edited by Thomas W. Burkman. Norfolk, VA: MacArthur Memorial Foundation, 1982.

Dore, Ronald P. *City Life in Japan: A Study of a Tokyo Ward*. Berkeley: University of California Press, 1958.

———. *The Diploma Disease: Education, Qualification, and Development*. Berkeley: University of California Press, 1976.

———. *Education in Tokugawa Japan*. Berkeley: University of California Press, 1965.

———. "The Ethics of New Japan." *Pacific Affairs* 25, no. 2 (June 1952): 147–159.

Dore, Ronald P., and Mari Sako. *How the Japanese Learn to Work*. London and New York: Routledge, 1989.

Dower, John. *Empire and Aftermath: Yoshida Shigeru and the Japanese Experience, 1878–1954*. Cambridge: Harvard Council on East Asian Studies, 1979.

Duke, Benjamin C. *Japan's Militant Teachers: A History of the Left Wing Teachers' Movement*. Honolulu: University of Hawaii Press, 1973.

———. "The Textbook Controversy." *Japan Quarterly* 19, no. 3 (July–September 1972): 337–352. Reprinted in Edward R. Beauchamp, ed., *Learning to Be Japanese: Selected Readings on Japanese Society and Education*, 240–264. Hampden, CT: Linnet Books, 1978.

———, ed. *Ten Great Educators of Modern Japan: A Japanese Perspective*. Tokyo: University of Tokyo Press, 1989.

Eppstein, Ury. "Musical Instruction in Meiji Education." *Monumenta Nipponica* 40, no. 1 (1985): 1–37.

Evans, David Christian. "The Satsuma Faction and Professionalism in the Japanese Naval Officer Corps of the Meiji Period, 1868–1912." Doctoral dissertation, Stanford University, 1978.

Evans, Robert, Jr. "The Contribution of Education to Japan's Economic Growth." In *Windows on Japanese Education*, 209–228, edited by Edward R. Beauchamp. New York: Greenwood Press, 1991.

Feinberg, Walter. *Japan and the Pursuit of a New American Identity: Work and Education in a Multicultural Age*. London: Routledge, 1989.

Friedman, Neil Kassel. "Education as a Political Issue in Japan." Doctoral dissertation, Stanford University, 1977.

Frost, Peter. "Examination Hell: The Reform of Entrance Examinations in Occupied Japan." In *The Occupation of Japan: Educational and Social Reforms in Japan, 1945–1952*, 211–218, edited by Thomas W. Burkman. Norfolk, VA: MacArthur Memorial Foundation, 1982.

Fujimura-Faneslow, Kumiko, and Anne E. Imamura. "The Education of Women in Japan." In *Windows on Japanese Education,* 229–258, edited by Edward R. Beauchamp. New York: Greenwood Press, 1991.

Fujita, Wakao. "Yanaihara Tadao: Disciple of Uchimura Kanzō and Nitobe Inazō." In *Pacifism in Japan,* 199–219, edited by Nobuya Bamba and John F. Howes. Vancouver: University of British Columbia Press, 1978.

Fujitani, Takashi. "Japan's Modern National Ceremonies, 1868–1912." Doctoral dissertation, University of California, Berkeley, 1986.

Fukatsu Masumi, "A State Visit to Yasukuni Shrine." *Japan Quarterly* 33, no. 1 (January–April 1986): 19–24.

Fukushima, Akira. "Causes of Adolescent Violence." *Japan Echo* 9, Special Issue (Winter 1982).

Fukuzawa Yukichi. *The Autobiography of Yukichi Fukuzawa.* Translated by Eiichi Kiyooka. New York: Columbia University Press, 1966.

———. *Fukuzawa Yukichi on Japanese Women.* Translated and edited by Eiichi Kiyooka. Tokyo: University of Tokyo Press, 1988.

———. *Fukuzawa Yukichi zenshō.* Edited by Keiō Gijuku. Vol. 5. Tokyo: Iwanami Shoten, 1959.

———. *An Outline of a Theory of Civilization.* Translated by David A. Dilworth and G. Cameron Hurst. Tokyo: Sophia University, 1973.

Gluck, Carol. "The Idea of Shōwa—The Idea in Present Perspective." *IHJ Bulletin* 9, no. 4 (Autumn 1989): 8–13.

———. *Japan's Modern Myths: Ideology in the Late Meiji Period.* Princeton: Princeton University Press, 1985.

———. "The Past in the Present." In *Postwar Japan as History,* 64–95, edited by Andrew Gordon. Berkeley: University of California Press, 1993.

Gluck, Carol, and Stephen R. Graubard, eds. *Showa: The Japan of Hirohito.* New York: W. W. Norton, 1992.

Gotoda, Teruo. *The Local Politics of Kyoto.* Berkeley: Institute of East Asian Studies, University of California, 1985.

Griesy, Paul Val. "The Dōshisha, 1875–1919: The Indigenization of an Institution." Doctoral dissertation, Columbia University, 2 vols., 1973.

Griffis, William E. *The Mikado's Empire.* New York: Harper and Brothers, 2 vols., 1877.

Hackett, Roger. *Yamagata Aritomo and the Rise of Modern Japan, 1838–1922.* Cambridge: Harvard University Press, 1971.

Hall, Ivan P. *Mori Arinori.* Cambridge: Harvard University Press, 1973.

———. "Organizational Paralysis: The Case of Todai." In *Modern Japanese Organization and Decision-Making,* 304–330, edited by Ezra F. Vogel. Berkeley: University of California Press, 1975.

Hall, John W. "Education and Modern National Development." In *Twelve Doors to Japan,* 384–426, edited by John W. Hall and Richard K. Beardsley. New York: McGraw-Hill, 1965.

Hall, Robert King. "The Battle of the Mind: American Educational Policy in Germany and Japan." *Columbia Journal of International Affairs* 2 (Winter 1948): 59–70.

———. "Education in the Development of Postwar Japan." In *The Occupation of Japan: The Proceedings of a Seminar on the Occupation of Japan and Its Legacy to the Postwar World.* Norfolk, VA: MacArthur Memorial, 1976.

———. *Shūshin: Ethics of a Defeated Nation.* New York: Columbia University Press, 1949.

Hall, Robert King, editor, and John O. Gauntlett, translator. *Kokutai no hongi: Cardinal Principles of the National Entity of Japan.* Cambridge: Harvard University Press, 1949.

Halliday, Jon. *A Political History of Japanese Capitalism.* New York: Pantheon Books, 1975.

Hamabata, Matthew Masayuki. *Crested Kimono: Power and Love in the Japanese Business Family.* Ithaca: Cornell University Press, 1990.

Hane, Mikiso, ed. *Reflections on the Way to the Gallows: Voices of Japanese Rebel Women.* Berkeley: University of California Press, 1988.

Hani Makoto. "Stories of My Life," abridged and translated by Chieko Irie Mulhern. In *Heroic with Grace: Legendary Women of Japan,* 236–264, edited by Chieko Irie Mulhern. Armonk, NY: M. E. Sharpe, 1991.

Hara Kei. *Hara Kei nikki* (The Diary of Hara Kei). Edited by Hara Kei'ichirō. 9 vols. Tokyo: Gengensha, 1950–1951.

Hardacre, Helen. "Creating State Shintō: The Great Promulgation Campaign and the New Religions." *Journal of Japanese Studies* 12, no. 1 (Winter 1986): 29–63.

———. "The Economic Rehabilitation of the Samurai in the Early Meiji Period." *Journal of Asian Studies* 19, no. 4 (August 1960): 433–444.

———. *Shintō and the State, 1868–1988.* Princeton: Princeton University Press, 1989.

Harootunian, Harry D. "The Economic Rehabilitation of the Samurai in the Early Meiji Period." *Journal of Asian Studies* 19, 4 (August 1960): 433–444.

———. "The Progress of Japan and the Samurai Class." *Pacific Historical Review* 3 (1959): 255–266.

———. "The Samurai Class During the Early Years of the Meiji Period in Japan, 1868–1882." Doctoral dissertation, University of Michigan, 1956.

———. *Toward Restoration: The Growth of Political Consciousness in Tokugawa Japan.* Berkeley: University of California Press, 1970.

Hastings, Sally A. "Plotting Escape from the Slums: Private and Public Policy Toward Children of the Poor, 1900–1919." Unpublished paper delivered at the 1986 annual meeting of the Association for Asian Studies.

———. "Women Educators of the Meiji Era and the Making of Modern Japan." *International Journal of Social Education* 6, no. 1 (Spring 1991): 83–94.

Hata Ikuhiko. "When the Ideologues Rewrite History" [abridged translation of "Kyōkasho sōdō no seiji rigaku," *Chūō Kōron* (October 1986): 238–250]. *Japan Echo* 13, no. 4 (Winter 1986): 73–78.

Havens, Thomas R. H. *Fire Across the Sea: The Vietnam War and Japan, 1965–1975.* Princeton: Princeton University Press, 1987.

———. "Japan's Enigmatic Election of 1928." *Modern Asian Studies* 11, no. 4 (1977): 143–173.

———. *Nishi Amane and Modern Japanese Thought.* Princeton: Princeton University Press, 1970.

———. *Valley of Darkness: The Japanese People and World War Two.* New York: W. W. Norton, 1978.

Hellmann, Donald. "Review of Ezra Vogel's *Japan as Number One.*" *Journal of Japanese Studies* 6, no. 2 (Summer 1980): 426–427.

Hendry, Joyce. *Becoming Japanese: The World of the Pre-School Child.* Honolulu: University of Hawaii Press, 1987.

Hidaka Rokurō. "The Role and Aims of Social Studies Education." *Journal of Social and Political Ideas in Japan* 1, no. 3 (December 1963): 77–81.

Higuchi, Keiko. "The PTA—A Channel for Political Activism." *Japan Interpreter* 10, no. 2 (Autumn 1975): 133–140.

Hirai, Atsuko. *Individualism and Socialism: Kawai Eijirō's Life and Thought (1891–1944)*. Cambridge: Council on East Asian Studies, Harvard University, 1986.

Hiratsuka Masunori. "World Education and Japan." *Journal of Social and Political Ideas in Japan* 1, no. 3 (December 1963): 12–15.

Honda Akira. "The Barren Social Climate of Postwar Japan." *Journal of Political and Social Ideas in Japan* 1, no. 3 (December 1963): 64–67.

Horio Teruhisa. *Educational Thought and Ideology in Modern Japan: State Authority and Intellectual Freedom*. Edited and translated by Steven Platzer. Tokyo: University of Tokyo Press, 1988.

Hōsei Daigaku. *Hōsei Daigaku 80 nenshi*. Tokyo: Hōsei Daigaku, 1961.

Howes, John F. "Japanese Christians and American Missionaries." In *Changing Japanese Attitudes Toward Modernization*, 337–368, edited by Marius B. Jansen. Princeton: Princeton University Press, 1965.

Huffman, James L. *Politics of the Meiji Press: The Life of Fukuchi Gen'ichiro*. Honolulu: University of Hawaii Press, 1980.

Hunter, Janet. "Women's Labour Force Participation in Interwar Japan." *Japan Forum* 2, no. 1 (April 1990): 105–125.

Ichikawa Shogo. "Finance of Higher Education." In *Changes in the Japanese University: A Comparative Perspective*, 40–63, edited by William K. Cummings et al. New York: Praeger, 1979.

Ienaga Saburō. *Daigaku no jiyū no rekishi* (The History of Freedom in the University). Tokyo: Hanawa Shobō, 1962.

———. "The Glorification of War in Japanese Education." Translated by Frank Baldwin. *International Security* 18, no. 3 (Winter 1993–94): 113–133.

———. "The Historical Significance of the Japanese Textbook Lawsuit." *Bulletin of the Committee of Concerned Asian Scholars* 2 (1970): 3–12.

———. *The Pacific War, 1931–1945: A Critical Perspective on Japan's Role in World War II*. Translated by Frank Baldwin. New York: Pantheon Books, 1978.

Inoguchi Takashi and Kabashima Ikuo. "The Status Quo Student Elite." *Japan Echo* 11, no. 1 (Spring 1984): 27–34.

Inoue, Kyoko. *MacArthur's Japanese Constitution: A Linguistic and Cultural Study of Its Making*. Chicago: University of Chicago Press, 1991.

Irokawa Daikichi. *The Culture of the Meiji Period*, translation edited by Marius Jansen. Princeton: Princeton University Press, 1985.

Ishida, Hiroshi. *Social Mobility in Contemporary Japan: Educational Credentials, Class, and the Labour Market in a Cross-National Perspective*. Stanford: Stanford University Press, 1992.

———. "Stratification and Mobility: The Case of Japan." In *Asia: Case Studies in the Social Sciences*, 526–547, edited by Myron L. Cohen. Armonk, NY: M. E. Sharpe, 1992.

Ishida, Hiroshi, John Goldthorpe, and Robert Erikson. "Intergenerational Class Mobility in Postwar Japan." *American Journal of Sociology* (January 1991): 954–992.

Itō Mikiharu. *Kazoku kokkan no jinruigaku* (The Anthropology of the Nation-as-Family). Tokyo: Mineruva, 1982.

James, Estelle, and Gail Benjamin. *Public Policy and Private Education in Japan.* New York: St. Martin's Press, 1988.

Jansen, Marius B. *Sakamoto Ryōma and the Meiji Restoration.* Princeton: Princeton University Press, 1961.

Japan Association of Private Colleges and Universities. *Japan's Private Colleges and Universities: Yesterday, Today and Tomorrow.* Tokyo: Japan Association of Private Colleges and Universitites, 1987.

Japan, Ministry of Education Research Bureau. *Japan's Growth and Education: Educational Development in Relation to Socio-economic Growth—The 1962 White Paper on Education.* Tokyo: Ministry of Education, Government of Japan, 1963.

Johnson, Chalmers. *Conspiracy at Matsukawa.* Berkeley: University of California Press, 1972.

Jones, Hazel J. "The Meiji Government and Foreign Employees, 1868–1900." Doctoral dissertation, University of Michigan, 1967.

JTU Council on Educational Reform. "What Japan's Education Should Be." An excerpt from "How to Reform Japan." In *Learning to Be Japanese: Selected Readings on Japanese Society and Education,* 349–370, edited by Edward R. Beauchamp. Hampden, CT: Linnet Books, 1978.

Kaigo Tokiomi. *Japanese Education: Its Past and Present,* 2d ed. Tokyo: Kokusai Bunka Shinkokai, 1968.

———, ed. *Rinji Kyōiku Kaigi no kenkyū* (Research on the Special Conference on Education). Tokyo: Tōkyō Daigaku Shuppankai, 1960.

Karasawa Tomitarō. "Changes in Japanese Education as Revealed in Textbooks." *Japan Quarterly* (July–September 1955): 365–383.

———. "A History of Japanese Teachers." In *Kyōshi no rekishi* (History of Teachers), 4th ed., 15–34, by Karasawa Tomitarō. Tokyo: Sōbunsha, 1968.

———. *Kyōkasho no rekishi* (A History of Textbooks). Tokyo: Sōbunsha, 1956.

———. *Kyōshi no rekishi* (A History of Teachers), 4th ed. Tokyo: Sōbunsha, 1968.

Kasza, Gregory J. *The State and Mass Media in Japan, 1918–1945.* Berkeley: University of California Press, 1988.

Kawai Eijirō. "Minobe mondai no hihan" (A Critique of the Minobe Question). *Teikoku Daigaku shinbun* (April 15, 1935). Reprinted in *Kawai zenshū* 12: 11–17.

———. "Daigaku no jiū to wa nani ka" (What Is Academic Freedom?). Reprinted in *Kawai Eijirō zenshū* 15: 114–141. Tokyo: Shakai shisō, 1969–1970.

Kawai Eijirō and Rōyama Masamichi. *Gakusei shisō mondai* (The Student Thought Problem). Tokyo: Iwanami Shoten, 1932.

Kawakami Hajime. *Jijoden* (Autobiography). Tokyo: Iwanami Shoten, 1962.

Keene, Donald. "The Sino-Japanese War of 1894–95 and Its Cultural Effects on Japan." In *Tradition and Modernization in Japanese Culture,* 121–175, edited by Donald H. Shively. Princeton: Princeton University Press, 1971.

Keiō Gijuku, ed. *Keiō Gijuku 100 nenshi* (One Hundred Years of Keiō Gijuku). 6 vols. Tokyo: Keiō Gijuku, 1969.

Keizai Koho Center. *Japan 1990: An International Comparison.* Tokyo: Keizai Koho Center, 1989.

Kerlinger, Fred N. "The Development of Democratic Control in Japanese Education: A Study of Attitude Change in Shikoku, 1948–1949." Doctoral dissertation, University of Michigan, 1953.

———. "Educational Affairs Boards: Precursors of Modern Japanese Boards of Education." *History of Education Journal* 5 (1954): 90–96.

Ketelaar, James Edward. *Of Heretics and Martyrs in Meiji Japan: Buddhism and Its Persecution.* Princeton: Princeton University Press, 1990.

Kinmonth, Earl H. *The Self-Made Man in Meiji Japanese Thought: From Samurai to Salary Man.* Berkeley: University of California Press, 1981.

Kitai Yoshihiko. "Textbooks Versus Teaching." *Japan Echo* 9, no. 1 (Spring 1982): 83–92.

Kitamura Kazuyuki and William Cummings. "The 'Big Bang' Theory and Japanese University Reform." *Comparative Education Review* 16, no. 2 (1972): 303–324.

Kiyama Terumichi. "Meeting at Yasukuni Shrine." In *Japan at War: An Oral History*, 447–453, edited by Haruko Taya Cook and Theodore F. Cook. New York: New Press, 1992.

Kobayashi Tetsuya. *Society, Schools and Progress in Japan.* Oxford: Pergamon Press, 1976.

Kobayashi, Victor N. "Japanese and U.S. Curricula Compared." In *Educational Policies in Crisis: Japanese and American Perspectives*, 23–58, edited by William K. Cummings, Edward R. Beauchamp, Shogo Ichikawa, Victor N. Kobayashi, and Morikazu Ushiogi. New York: Praeger, 1986.

Kodansha Encyclopedia of Japan. 9 vols. Tokyo and New York: Kodansha, 1983.

Koh, B. C. *Japan's Administrative Elite.* Berkeley: University of California Press, 1989.

Kokuritsu Kyōiku Kenkyūjo, ed. *Nihon kindai kyōiku 100 nenshi* (A Hundred Years of Modern Japanese Education). 10 vols. Tokyo: Kyōiku Kenkyūjo Shinkōkai, 1974.

Kondō Sumio. "'Off We Go to Our Lessons.'" *Japan Interpreter* 9, no. 1 (Spring 1974): 155–224.

Kōno Motomichi and Gordon T. Bowles. "Ainu." In *Kodansha Encyclopedia of Japan*, vol. 1: 34–36. Tokyo and New York: Kodansha, 1983.

Koschmann, J. Victor. "Intellectuals and Politics." In *Postwar Japan as History*, 395–423, edited by Andrew Gordon. Berkeley: University of California Press, 1993.

Krauss, Ellis. *Japanese Radicals Revisited: Student Protest in Postwar Japan.* Berkeley: University of California Press, 1974.

Krauss, Ellis S., Thomas P. Rohlen, and Patricia Steinhoff, eds. *Conflict in Japan.* Honolulu: University of Hawaii Press, 1984.

Kubota, Akira. *Higher Civil Servants in Postwar Japan: Their Social Origins, Educational Backgrounds, and Career Patterns.* Princeton: Princeton University Press, 1969.

Kumajira Hajime. "Laying the Groundwork for School Reform." *Japan Echo* 11, no. 2 (Summer 1984): 45–51.

Kuno Akiko. *Unexpected Destinations: The Poignant Story of Japan's First Vassar Graduate.* Translated by Kirsten McIvor. New York: Kodansha, 1993.

Kurimoto Shin'ichirō. *Meidai kyōju jishoku shimatsu* (The End of Professors' Resigning at Meiji University). Tokyo: Kōdansha, 1992.

Kuroha, Ryōichi. "School Dropouts and High School Education." *Japan Echo* 5, no. 2 (Summer 1978): 115–124.

Lande, Aasulv. *Meiji Protestantism in History and Historiography.* Uppsala: Uppsala University, 1988.

Langer, Paul F. *Communsm in Japan: A Case of Political Naturalization.* Stanford: Hoover Institution Press, Stanford University, 1972.

Larson, Phyllis. "Yosano Akiko." Doctoral dissertation, University of Minnesota, 1985.

Lebra, Takie Sugiyama. *Above the Clouds: Status Culture of the Modern Japanese Nobility.* Berkeley: University of California Press, 1993.

Lee, Changsoo. "Koreans in Japan." *Kodansha Encyclopedia of Japan,* vol. 4: 291–292. Tokyo and New York: Kodansha, 1983.

Lee, Chong-sik. "History and Politics in Japanese-Korean Relations: The Textbook Controversy and Beyond." *Journal of Northeast Asian Studies* 2, no. 4 (December 1983): 60–93.

Leestma, Robert, and Herbert J. Walberg, eds. *Japanese Educational Productivity.* Ann Arbor: Michigan Papers on Japan, 1992.

Levenson, Joseph R. "'History' and 'Value': The Tensions of Intellectual Choice in Modern China." In *Studies in Chinese Thought,* 146–194, edited by Arthur Wright. Chicago: University of Chicago Press, 1953.

Levine, Solomon B., and Hiroshi Kawada. *Human Resources in Japanese Industrial Development.* Princeton University Press, Princeton, 1980.

Lu, David, ed. *Sources of Japanese History.* 2 vols. New York: McGraw-Hill, 1973–1974.

Lynn, Richard. *Educational Achievement in Japan: Lessons for the West.* Armonk, NY: M. E. Sharpe, 1988.

Maki, John M., ed. *We the Japanese: Voices from Japan.* New York: Praeger Publishers, 1972.

Malm, William P. "The Modern Music of Meiji Japan." In *Tradition and Modernization in Japanese Culture,* 257–300, edited by Donald H. Shively. Princeton: Princeton University Press, 1971.

Maloney, Kathleen S. "Feminist Ideology in Prewar Japan." In *Proceedings of the Tokyo Symposium on Women,* 13–24, edited by Merry I. White and Kathleen S. Maloney. Tokyo: International Group for the Study of Women, 1978.

Marshall, Byron K. *Academic Freedom and the Japanese Imperial University, 1886–1939.* Berkeley: University of California Press, 1992.

Mason, R.H.P. *Japan's First General Election, 1890.* Cambridge: Cambridge University Press, 1969.

Matsumoto, Sannosuke. "Nakae Chōmin and Confucianism." In *Confucianism and Tokugawa Culture,* 251–266, edited by Peter Nosco. Princeton: Princeton University Press, 1984.

Maynes, Mary Jo. *Schooling for the People: Comparative Local Studies of Schooling History in France and Germany, 1750–1850.* New York: Holmes and Meier, 1985.

———. *Schooling in Western Europe: A Social History.* Albany: State University of New York, 1985.

Mayo, Marlene. "Psychological Disarmament: Planning for Education and Re-education of Defeated Japan, 1943–1945." In *The Occupation of Japan: Educational and Social Reforms,* 21–128, edited by Thomas W. Burkman. Norfolk, VA: MacArthur Memorial Foundation, 1982.

McKean, Margaret A. "Equality." In *Democracy in Japan,* 201–224, edited by Ishida Takeshi and Ellis S. Krauss. Pittsburgh: University of Pittsburgh Press, 1989.

McLaren, W. W., ed. *Japanese Government Documents.* 2 vols. Tokyo: Asiatic Society of Japan, 1914. Reprint edition, Washington, DC: University Publications of America, 1979.

Miller, Frank O. *Minobe Tatsukichi: Interpreter of Constitutionalism in Japan.* Berkeley: University of California Press, 1965.

Minear, Richard C. *Japanese Tradition and Western Law: Emperor, State and Law in the Thought of Hozumi Yatsuka.* Cambridge: Harvard University Press, 1970.

————. *Victor's Justice: The Tokyo War Crimes Trial.* Princeton: Princeton University Press, 1971.

Mitchell, Richard H. *Censorship in Imperial Japan.* Princeton: Princeton University Press, 1983.

————. *Thought Control in Prewar Japan.* Ithaca: Cornell University Press, 1976.

Miura Shumon. "So What If the Textbooks Are Biased?" *Japan Echo* 9, no. 1 (Spring 1982): 93–100.

Miwa, Keiko. "Analysis of the Effect of Major American Ideas upon the Organization of Japanese Higher Education from 1946 to 1967." Doctoral dissertation, Washington State University, 1969.

Miyahara Seiichi, Maruki Seihin, Ikazaki Akio, Fujioka Tadahiko, eds. *Shiryō Nihon gendai kyōikushi* (Documentary History of Contemporary Japanese Education). 4 vols. Tokyo: Sanseidō, 1974.

Miyaji Masato. "Morito jiken: gakumon no jiyū no hajime no shiren" (The Morito Case: The First Test of Academic Freedom). In *Nihon seiji saiban shiroku: Taishō* (Historical Record of Political Trials in Japan), 228–272, edited by Wagatsuma Sakae et al. 5 vols. Tokyo: Daiichi Hōki Kaisha, 1969–1970.

Mizuuchi, Hiroshi. "Sawayanagi Masataro." In *Ten Great Educators of Modern Japan: A Japanese Perspective,* 149–165, edited by Benjamin Duke. Tokyo: University of Tokyo Press, 1989.

Mochizuki, Muneaki. "Munakata Seiya (1908–1970)." In *Ten Great Educators of Modern Japan: A Japanese Perspective,* 215–232, edited by Benjamin Duke. Tokyo: University of Tokyo Press, 1989.

Monbushō. *Gakusei 80 nenshi* (The School System over the Past Eighty Years). Tokyo: Monbushō, 1954.

————. *Gakusei 90 nenshi* (The School System over the Past Ninety Years). Tokyo: Ōokurashō Insatsu Kyoku, 1964.

————. *Gakusei 100 nenshi* (The School System over the Past One Hundred Years). 2 vols. Tokyo: Monbushō, 1972.

Monbushō, Kyōiku Hensankai, ed. *Meiji ikō kyōiku seido hattatsushi* (The History of the Development of the Educational System Since the Beginning of the Meiji). Rev. ed. 12 vols. Tokyo: Ryūginsha, 1964–1965.

Monbushō, Meiji ikō. See Monbushō, Kyōiku Hensankai, ed. *Meiji ikō kyōiku seido hattatsushi.*

Morikawa Terumichi. "Mori Arinori." In *Ten Great Educators of Modern Japan: A Japanese Perspective,* 39–65, edited by Benjamin Duke. Tokyo: University of Tokyo Press, 1989.

Morito Tatsuo. *Daisan no kyōiku kaikaku: Chūkyōshin tōshin to kyōiku kaikaku* (The Third Education Revolution). Tokyo: Daiichi Hōki, 1973.

Moriya Katsuhisa. "Urban Networks and Information Networks." In *Tokugawa Japan: The Social and Economic Antecedents of Modern Japan,* 97–123, edited by Nakane Chie, translated by Conrad Totman. Tokyo: University of Tokyo Press, 1990.

Morris, Ivan I. *Nationalism and the Right Wing in Postwar Japan: A Study of Postwar Trends.* London: Oxford University Press, 1960.

Mouer, Elizabeth. "Women in Teaching." In *Women in Changing Japan,* 157–190, edited by Joyce Lebra, Joy Paulson, and Elizabeth Mouer. Stanford: Stanford University Press, 1976.

Mouer, Ross, and Yoshio Sugimoto. *Images of Japanese Society: A Study in the Social Construction of Reality.* London: Kegan Paul, 1986.

Mulhern, Chieko Irie. "Hani Motoko: The Journalist-Educator." In *Heroic with Grace: Legendary Women of Japan,* 208–235, edited by Chieko Irie Mulhern. Armonk, NY: M. E. Sharpe, 1991.

———, ed. *Heroic with Grace: Legendary Women of Japan.* Armonk, NY: M. E. Sharpe, 1991.

Munakata Seiya. "The Fundamental Law of Education." *Journal of Social and Political Ideas in Japan* 1, no. 3 (December 1963): 54–58.

Murakami Yasusuke. "The Debt Comes Due for Mass Education." *Japan Echo* 15, no. 3 (Autumn 1988): 71–80.

Muramatsu Michio. "In Search of National Identity: The Politics and Policies of the Nakasone Administration." *Journal of Japanese Studies* 13, no. 2 (Summer 1987): 307–342.

Murata, Suzuko. "A Study of the Impact of the American Educational System on Higher Education in Japan." Doctoral dissertation, Indiana University, 1969.

Nagai Michio. "Westernization and Japanization: The Early Meiji Transformation of Education." In *Tradition and Modernization in Japanese Culture,* 35–76, edited by Donald H. Shively.

Nagao Ryuichi. "Did the Kokutai Change? Problems of Legitimacy in Postwar Japan." In *Creating a Single-Party Democracy: Japan's Postwar Political System,* 133–150, edited by Kataoka Tetsuya. Stanford: Hoover Institution, 1992.

Nagy, Margit. "Middle-Class Working Women During the Interwar Years." In *Recreating Japanese Women, 1600–1945,* 199–216, edited by Gail Lee Bernstein. Berkeley: University of California Press, 1991.

Naikaku Tokei Kyoku. *Nihon teikoku tokei nenkan* (Annual statistics of the Japanese Empire). Tokyo: Naikaku Tokei Kyoku, annual.

Najita, Tetsuo. *Visions of Virtue in Tokugawa Japan: The Kaitokudō Merchant Academy of Osaka.* Chicago: University of Chicago Press, 1987.

Nakajima Kuni. "Naruse Jinzo." In *Ten Great Educators of Modern Japan: A Japanese Perspective,* 67–85, edited by Benjamin Duke. Tokyo: University of Tokyo Press, 1989.

Nakamura Kikuji. *Kyōkasho no shakaishi: Meiji ishin kara sengo made* (A Social History of Textbooks: From the Meiji Restoration to Postwar). Tokyo: Iwanami, 1992.

Nakamura Masanori. *The Japanese Monarchy: Ambassador Joseph Grew and the Making of the 'Symbol Emperor System,' 1931–1991.* Translated by Herbert P. Bix, Jonanthan Baker-Bates, and Derek Bowen. Armonk, NY: M. E. Sharpe, 1992.

Nakane Chie and Shinsaburō Ōishi, eds. *Tokugawa Japan: The Social and Economic Antecedents of Modern Japan.* Translation edited by Conrad Totman. Tokyo: University of Tokyo Press, 1990.

Nakano, Akira. "Shimonaka Yasaburo (1875–1961)." In *Ten Great Educators of Modern Japan: A Japanese Perspective,* 166–189, edited by Benjamin Duke. Tokyo: University of Tokyo Press, 1989.

Nakayama Shigeru et al., eds. *Science and Society in Modern Japan.* Tokyo: University of Tokyo Press, 1974.

Nanbara Shigeru, Rōyama Masamichi, and Yabe Teiji. *Onozuka Kiheiji.* Tokyo: Iwanami Shoten, 1963.

Nishi, Toshio. *Unconditional Democracy: Education and Politics in Occupied Japan, 1945–1952.* Stanford: Hoover Institution Press, 1982.

Nishikawa Toshiyuki. "The Postwar Educational Reform in Japan: Thirty Years After the Allied Occupation." In *The Occupation of Japan: Educational and Social Reforms,* 259–282, edited by Thomas W. Burkman. Norfolk, VA: MacArthur Memorial Foundation, 1982.

Nitobe, Inazo. *Japan: Some Phases of Her Problems and Development.* New York: Charles Scribner's Sons, 1931.

Nitobe, Inazo, and others. *Western Influences in Modern Japan: A Series of Papers on Cultural Relations.* Chicago: University of Chicago Press, 1931.

Nolte, Sharon. "National Morality and Universal Ethics: Onishi Hajime and the Imperial Rescript on Education." *Monumenta Nipponica* 13 (1983): 283–294.

Nolte, Sharon H., and Sally Ann Hastings. "The Meiji State's Policy Toward Women, 1890–1910." In *Recreating Japanese Women, 1600–1945,* 151–174, edited by Gail Lee Bernstein. Berkeley: University of California Press, 1991.

Notehelfer, F. G. *American Samurai: Captain L. L. Janes and Japan.* Princeton: Princeton University Press, 1985.

Oda, R. "Mikadoism: A Resume of Professor Uyesugi's *Shinsei Nippon no Kensetsu.*" In *What Japan Thinks,* 49–62, edited by K. K. Kawakami. New York: Macmillan, 1921.

Ogawa Tarō. "Reflections on Postwar Education." *Journal of Political and Social Ideas in Japan* 1, no. 3 (December 1963): 24–30.

Ōkubo Toshiaki. "Meiji shonen no gakushinmatsuri ni tsuite" (Concerning Academic Rituals in the Early Years of Meiji). *Kokugakuin zasshi* 45, no. 1 (January 1939): 60–65; 45, no. 2 (February 1939): 33–48.

Olson, Lawrence. "Hara Kei, a Political Biography." Doctoral dissertation, Harvard University, 1954.

Organization of Economic Cooperation and Development (OECD). *Reviews of National Policies for Education—Japan.* Paris: OECD, 1971.

Orihara Hiroshi. "'Test Hell' and Alienation. A Study of Tokyo University Freshmen." *Journal of Political and Social Ideas in Japan* 5, nos. 2–3 (December 1967): 225–245.

Osada Arata. "Problems Involved in Providing Ethical Foundation." *Journal of Political and Social Ideas in Japan* 1, no. 3 (December 1963): 67–69.

Ōshima Kiyoshi. *Takano Iwasaburō den* (The Biography of Takano Iwasaburō). Tokyo: Iwanami Shoten, 1968.

Ōshima Yasumasa. "Japan's Defeat and Ethical Education." *Journal of Political and Social Ideas in Japan* 1, no. 3 (December 1963): 70–72.

Ōsugi Sakae. *The Autobiography of Ōsugi Sakae.* Translated by Byron K. Marshall. Berkeley: University of California Press, 1992.

Ota Haruo. "Political Unionism in Japan." In *Japanese Schooling: Patterns of Socialization, Equality and Political Control,* 242–259, edited by James J. Shields, Jr.

Packard, George R., III. *Protest in Tokyo: The Security Treaty Crisis of 1960.* Princeton: Princeton University Press, 1966.

Passin, Herbert. *Japanese Education: A Bibliography of Materials in the English Language.* New York: Teachers College, Columbia University, 1970.

————. *Society and Education in Japan.* New York: Teachers College, Columbia University, 1965.

Pempel, T. J. *Patterns of Japanese Policymaking: Experiences in Higher Education.* Boulder: Westview Press, 1978.

————. "Patterns of Policymaking: Higher Education." In *Policymaking in Contemporary Japan,* 268–323, edited by T. J. Pempel. Ithaca: Cornell University Press, 1977.

————. "The Politics of Enrollment Expansion in Japanese Universities." *Journal of Asian Studies* 33, no. 1 (November 1973): 67–86.

Pempel, T. J., ed. *Policymaking in Contemporary Japan.* Ithaca: Cornell University Press, 1977.

Peng, Fred C. C. "Education: An Agent of Change in Ainu Community Life." In *Learning to Be Japanese: Selected Readings on Japanese Society and Education,* 265–288, edited by Edward R. Beauchamp. Hampden, CT: Linnet Books, 1978.

Pharr, Susan J. *Losing Face: Status Politics in Japan.* Berkeley: University of California Press, 1990.

————. *Political Women in Japan: The Search for a Place in Political Life.* Berkeley: University of California Press, 1981.

————. "Soldiers as Feminists: Debate Within the U.S. Occupation Ranks over Women's Rights Policy in Japan." In *Proceedings of the Tokyo Symposium on Women,* 25–35, edited by Merry I. White and Kathleen S. Maloney. Tokyo: International Group for the Study of Women, 1978.

Pierson, John D. *Tokutomi Sohō, 1863–1957: A Journalist for Modern Japan.* Princeton: Princeton University Press, 1980.

Pittau, Joseph. "Inoue Kowashi (1843–1895) and the Formation of Modern Japan." In Edward Beauchamp, ed., *Learning to Be Japanese: Selected Readings on Japanese Society and Education,* 80–119. Reprinted from *Monumental Nipponica* 20, nos. 3–4 (1965): 253–282.

Powell, Irdena. "Through the Writer's Prism: The Waseda Revolt of 1917 in the Life and Fiction of Ozaki Shirō (1898–1964)." *Japan Forum* 5, no. 1 (April 1993): 75–93.

Pritchard, R. John, and Sonia Magbanua Zaide, eds. *The Tokyo War Crimes Trials: The Complete Transcripts of the Proceedings of the International Military Tribunal for the Far East.* 22 vols. New York: Garland Publishing, 1981.

Pyle, Kenneth B. *The Japanese Question: Power and Purpose in a New Era.* Washington, DC: AEI Press, 1992.

————. *The New Generation in Meiji Japan: Problems of Cultural Identity, 1885–1895.* Stanford: Stanford University Press, 1969.

Quigley, Harold S. *Japanese Government and Politics: An Introductory Study.* New York: Century Co., 1932.

Quigley, Harold S., and John E. Turner. *The New Japan: Government and Politics.* Minneapolis: University of Minnesota Press, 1956.

Ramsdell, Daniel B. *The Japanese Diet: Stability and Change in the Japanese House of Representatives, 1890–1990.* Lanham, MD: University Press of America, 1992.

Reed, Steven R. *Japan Election Data: The House of Representatives, 1947–1990.* Ann Arbor: Center for Japanese Studies, University of Michigan, 1992.

————. *Japanese Prefectures and Policymaking.* Pittsburgh: University of Pittsburgh Press, 1986.

Robertson, Jennifer. "The Shingaku Woman: Straight from the Heart." In *Recreating Japanese Women, 1600–1945*, 88–107, edited by Gail Lee Bernstein. Berkeley: University of California Press, 1991.

Robins-Mowry, Dorothy. *The Hidden Sun: Women of Modern Japan*. Boulder: Westview Press, 1983.

Roden, Donald T. *Schooldays in Imperial Japan: A Study in the Culture of a Student Elite*. Berkeley: University of California Press, 1980.

Rohlen, Thomas P. "Conflict in Institutional Environments: Politics in Education." In *Conflict in Japan*, 136–173, edited by Ellis S. Krauss, Thomas S. Rohlen, and Patricia G. Steinhoff. Honolulu: University of Hawaii Press, 1984.

———. "Education in Japanese Society." In *Inside the Japanese System*, 25–30, edited by Daniel Okimoto and Thomas P. Rohlen. Stanford: Stanford University Press, 1988.

———. "Is Japanese Education Becoming Less Egalitarian?" *Journal of Japanese Studies*, 3, no. 1 (Winter 1977): 37–70.

———. *Japan's High Schools*. Berkeley: University of California Press, 1984.

———. "Violence at Yoka High School: The Implications for Japanese Coalition Politics of the Confrontation Between the Communist Party and the Buraku Liberation League." *Asian Survey* 16, no. 7 (July 1976): 682–699.

Rose, Barbara. *Tsuda Umeko and Women's Education in Japan*. New Haven: Yale University Press, 1993.

Rōyama Masamichi. "Kyōdai gakusei ni atauru no gaki" (A Letter to the Students of Kyoto University). *Chūōkōron* 48, no. 10 (October 1933): 43–52.

Rubin, Jay. "From Wholesomeness to Decadence: The Censorship of Literature Under the Allied Occupation." *Journal of Japanese Studies* 11, no. 1 (Winter 1985): 71–103.

Rubinger, Richard. "Education: From One Room to One System." In *Japan in Transition*, 195–230, edited by Marius B. Jansen and Gilbert Rozman. Princeton: Princeton University Press, 1986.

———. *Private Academies of Tokugawa Japan*. Princeton: Princeton University Press, 1982.

Sakaiya Taichi. "Supply-Side Competition for the School System." *Japan Echo* 11, no. 2 (November 1984): 38–44.

Sakisaka Itsurō. *Arashi no naka no hyakunen: gakumon dan'atsu shoshi* (A Century Amidst the Storm: A Short History of the Suppression of Scholarship). Tokyo: Keisō Shobō, 1952.

Sakurai Jōji. *Omoide kazukazu: Danshaku Sakurai Jōji ikō* (Memories of Many Things: The Unpublished Writings of Baron Sakurai Jōji). Tokyo: Herado, 1940.

Sala, Gary Clark. "Protest and the Ainu of Hokkaido." *Japan Interpreter* 10, no. 1 (Summer 1975): 44–65.

Sansom, George B. *The Western World and Japan*. New York: Alfred A. Knopf, 1965.

Sasaki Sōichi. "Daigaku kyōju no kenkyū no genkai" (Limitations on the Research of University Professors). *Hōgaku Ronsō* 3, no. 3 (1920): 18–41.

Satō Kōmei. *Kyōkasho kentei no genba kara: 17 nen no insaido repōto* (The Scene of Textbook Screening: A Report from a 17 Year Insider). Tokyo: Waseda Shuppan, 1987.

Satō, Mamoru. "The Development of Vocational Continuation Schools." In *Vocational Education in the Industrialization of Japan*, 46–69, edited by Toyoda Toshio. Tokyo: United Nations University Press, 1987.

Schaller, Michael. *The American Occupation of Japan: The Origins of the Cold War in Asia*. New York: Oxford University Press, 1985.

Schooland, Ken. *Shogun's Ghost: The Dark Side of Japanese Education*. New York: Bergin and Garvey, 1990.

Schoppa, Leonard James. *Education Reform in Japan: A Case of Immobilist Politics*. London: Routledge, Nissan Institute, 1991.

————. "*Zoku* Power and LDP Power: A Case Study of the *Zoku* Role in Education Policy." *Journal of Japanese Studies* 17, no. 1 (Winter 1991): 79–106.

Shields, James J., Jr., ed. *Japanese Schooling: Patterns of Socialization, Equality and Political Control*. University Park: Pennsylvania University Press, 1989.

Shillony, Ben-ami. "Universities and Students in Wartime Japan." *Journal of Asian Studies* 45, no. 4 (August 1986): 769–787.

Shimahara, Nobuo K. *Burakumin: A Japanese Minority and Education*. The Hague: Martinus Nijhoff, 1971.

————. "Japanese Education Reforms in the 1980s: A Political Commitment." Reprinted in James J. Shields, Jr., ed., *Japanese Schooling: Patterns of Socialization, Equality and Political Control*, 270–281. University Park: Pennsylvania University Press, 1989.

Shimbori Michiya. "The Sociology of a Student Movement—A Japanese Case Study." *Daedalus* 97, no. 1 (Winter 1968). Reprinted in Edward R. Beauchamp, ed., *Learning to Be Japanese: Selected Readings on Japanese Society and Education*, 289–315. Hampden, CT: Linnet Books, 1978.

Shimizu Hideo. *Tōkyō Daigaku Hōgakubu: Nihon eriito no manmosu kichi* (The Tokyo University Law Department: The Mammoth Base of Japan's Elite). Tokyo: Kōdansha, 1965.

Shimizu Yoshihiro. "Entrance Examinations: A Challenge to Equal Opportunity in Education." Excerpted from *Shiken* (Examinations) (Tokyo: Iwanami Shoten, 1957) in "Education in Japan, 1945–1963." Special issue of *Journal of Social and Political Ideas in Japan* 1, no. 3 (December 1963): 88–93.

Shively, Donald H. "The Japanization of the Middle Meiji." In *Tradition and Modernization in Japanese Culture*, 77–119, edited by Donald H. Shively.

————. "Motoda Eifu: Confucian Lecturer to the Meiji Emperor." In *Confucianism in Action*, 302–333, edited by David S. Nivison and Arthur F. Wright. Stanford: Stanford University Press, 1959.

————. "Nishimura Shigeki: A Confucian View of Modernization." In *Changing Japanese Attitudes Toward Modernization*, 193–241, edited by Marius B. Jansen. Princeton: Princeton University Press, 1965.

Silverberg, Miriam. "Constructing a New Cultural History of Prewar Japan." In *Japan in the World*, edited by Masao Miyoshi and Harry D. Harootunian. Durham: Duke University Press, 1993.

————. "The Modern Girl as Militant." In *Recreating Japanese Women, 1600–1945*, 239–266, edited by Gail Lee Bernstein. Berkeley: University of California Press, 1991.

Simmons, Cyril. *Growing Up and Going to School in Japan: Tradition and Trends*. Philadelphia: Open University Press, 1990.

Singleton, John. *Nichu: A Japanese School*. New York: Holt, Rinehart and Winston, 1967.

Smethurst, Richard J. "The Military Reserve Association and the Minobe Crisis of 1935." In *Crisis Politics in Prewar Japan: Institutional and Ideological Problems of the 1930s*, 1–23, edited by George M. Wilson. Tokyo: Sophia University Press, 1970.

Smith, Henry D., II. *Japan's First Student Radicals*. Cambridge: Harvard University Press, 1972.

Smith, Robert J., and Ella Lury Wiswell. *The Women of Suye Mura*. Chicago: University of Chicago Press, 1982.

Smith, Thomas C. "'Merit' as Ideology in the Tokugawa Period." In *Aspects of Social Change in Modern Japan*, 71–90, edited by Ronald P. Dore. Princeton: Princeton University Press, 1967.

———. "Ogura Nagatsune and the Technologists." In *Personality in Japanese History*, 127–154, edited by Albert M. Craig and Donald H. Shively. Berkeley: University of California Press, 1970.

Smith, Warren W., Jr. *Confucianism in Modern Japan: A Study of Conservatism in Japanese Intellectual History*. Tokyo: Hokuseido Press, 1959.

Spaulding, Robert M., Jr. *Imperial Japan's Higher Civil Service Examinations*. Princeton: Princeton University Press, 1967.

———. "The Intent of the Charter Oath." In *Studies in Japanese History and Politics*, 3–36, edited by Richard K. Beardsley. Ann Arbor: University of Michigan, Center for Japanese Studies Occasional Papers No. 10, 1967.

———. "Japan's 'New Bureaucrats,' 1932–1945." In *Crisis Politics in Prewar Japan: Institutional and Ideological Problems of the 1930s*, 51–70, edited by George M. Wilson. Tokyo: Sophia University Press, 1970.

Staubitz, Richard Louis. "The Establishment of the System of Local Government in Meiji Japan (1888–1890): Yamagata Aritomo and the Meaning of 'Jichi' (Self-Government)." Doctoral dissertation, Yale University, 1973.

Stead, Alfred, ed. *Japan by the Japanese: A Survey by Its Highest Authorities*. London: William Heinemann, 1904. Reprint edition, 2 vols. Washington, DC: University Publications of America, 1979.

Steiner, Kurt. *Local Government in Japan*. Stanford: Stanford University Press, 1965.

Steinhoff, Patricia G. "Student Conflict." In *Conflict in Japan*, 174–213, edited by Ellis S. Krauss, Thomas P. Rohlen, and Patricia Steinhoff. Honolulu: University of Hawaii Press, 1984.

———. "Tenkō: Ideology and Societal Integration in Prewar Japan." Doctoral dissertation, Harvard University, 1969.

Sugihara, Shirō. "In the Schools of Law: Hōsei, Meiji and Chūō." In *Enlightenment and Beyond: Political Economy Comes to Japan*, 139–149, edited by Chūhei Sugiyama and Hiroshi Mizuta. Tokyo: University of Tokyo Press, 1988.

Sugimoto, Yoshio. "Quantitative Characteristics of Popular Disturbances in Post-Occupation Japan (1952–1960)." *Journal of Asian Studies* 37, no. 2 (February 1978): 273–291.

Suh, Doo Soo. "The Struggle for Academic Freedom in Japanese Universities Before 1945." Doctoral dissertation, Columbia University, 1953.

Supreme Commander for the Allied Powers. *Education in a New Japan*. 2 vols. Tokyo: General Headquarters, Supreme Commander for the Allied Powers, Civil Information and Education Section, Education Division, 1948.

———. *Political Reorientation of Japan: September 1945 to September 1948*. 2 vols. Washington, DC: Government Printing Office, 1948.

Supreme Commander for the Allied Powers, Civil Information and Education Section. *Postwar Developments in Japanese Education*. 2 vols. Tokyo: General Headquarters,

Supreme Commander for the Allied Powers, Civil Information and Education Section, Education Division, 1952.

Suzuki Hiroo. "Liberalizing Textbook Screening." *Japan Echo* 9, no. 4 (Winter 1982): 21–28.

Swearingen, Rodger, and Paul Langer. *Red Flag in Japan: International Communism in Action*. Cambridge: Harvard University Press, 1952.

Takahashi Shirō. *Kyōkasho kentei* (Textbook Screening). Tokyo: Chūōkōronsha, 1988.

Takane Masa'aki. "Factors Influencing the Mobility of the Japanese Political Elite: 1860–1920." Doctoral dissertation, University of California, Berkeley, 1972.

———. "How Much Education Is Right? The Coming of Overeducated Society." *Japan Echo* 5, no 1 (Spring 1978): 73–82.

Tamaki, Norio. "The American Professors' Regime: Political Economy at Keiō University, 1890–1912." In *Enlightenment and Beyond*, 75–95, edited by Chūhei Sugiyama and Hiroshi Mizuta. Tokyo: University of Tokyo Press, 1988.

Tanaka Kōtarō, Suekawa Hiroshi, Wagatsuma Sakae, Ōuchi Hyōe, and Miyazawa Toshiyoshi. *Daigaku no jiji* (University Self-Government). Tokyo: Asahi Shinbunsha, 1963.

Taueber, Irene. *The Population of Japan*. Princeton: Princeton University Press, 1958.

Thakur, Yoko H. "Textbook Reform in Allied Occupied Japan, 1945–1952." Doctoral dissertation, University of Maryland, 1990.

Thomas, R. Murray, and T. Neville Postlethwaite, eds. *Schooling in East Asia*. New York: Pergamon, 1983.

Thorstein, Marie. "Education Mamas: The Social Creation of Monsters." *Kyoto Journal* 15 (Summer 1990): 4–11.

Thurston, Donald R. *Teachers and Politics in Japan*. Princeton: Princeton University Press, 1973.

Tipton, Elise K. *The Japanese Police State: The Tokkō in Interwar Japan*. Honolulu: University of Hawaii Press, 1990.

Tobin, Joseph J., David Y. H. Wu, and Dana H. Davidson. *Preschool in Three Cultures: Japan, China and the United States*. New Haven: Yale University Press, 1989.

Tōdai. *Gakujutsu taikan*. See Tōkyō Teikoku Daigaku. *Tōkyō Teikoku Daigaku gakujutsu taikan*.

Tōdai. *50 nenshi*. See Tōkyō Teikoku Daigaku. *Tōkyō Teikoku Daigaku 50 nenshi*.

Todd, Vivian Edmiston. "Educational and Social Reform Through Enlightened Curriculum Development." In *The Occupation of Japan: Educational and Social Reforms*, 243–259, edited by Thomas W. Burkman. Norfolk, Virginia: The MacArthur Memorial Foundation, 1982.

Tōkyō Teikoku Daigaku. *Tōkyō Teikoku Daigaku 50 nenshi* (Fifty Years of Tokyo Imperial University). 5 vols. Tokyo: Tōkyō Teikoku Daigaku, 1932.

Tōkyō Teikoku Daigaku. *Tōkyō Teikoku Daigaku gakujutsu taikan* (An Overview of Scholarship at Tokyo Imperial University). Tokyo: Tōkyō Teikoku Daigaku, 1942–1944.

Tominaga Ken'ichi. "The University in Contemporary Society—A View of the Education-Conscious Society." *Japan Echo* 5, no. 1 (Spring 1978): 62–72.

"Too Much Emphasis on Education?" *Japan Echo* 5, no. 1 (Spring 1978): 60–82.

Toyoda, Toshio, ed. *Vocational Education in the Industrialization of Japan*. Tokyo: United Nations University Press, 1987.

Trainor, Joseph C. *Educational Reform in Occupied Japan: Trainor's Memoir.* Tokyo: Meisei University Press, 1983.

Tsuji Kiyoaki. "Toward Understanding the Teachers' Efficiency Rating." *Journal of Political and Social Ideas in Japan* 1, no. 3 (December 1963): 51–54.

Tsukada Mamoru. "Institutionalized Supplementary Education in Japan: The *Yobiko* and *Ronin* Student Adaptations." *Comparative Education* 24, no. 3 (1988): 285–303.

————. *"Yobiko" Life: A Study of the Legitimation Process of the Social Stratification in Japan.* Berkeley: Institute of East Asian Studies, University of California, 1992.

Tsunoda, Ryusaku, Wm. Theodore de Bary, Donald Keene, compilers. *Sources of Japanese Tradition.* New York: Columbia University Press, 1958.

Tsurumi, E. Patricia. *Factory Girls: Women in the Thread Mills of Meiji Japan.* Princeton: Princeton University Press, 1990.

————. *Japanese Colonial Education in Taiwan, 1895–1945.* Cambridge: Harvard University Press, 1977.

————. "Meiji Primary School Language and Ethics Textbooks: Old Values for a New Society?" *Modern Asian Studies* 8, no. 2 (1974): 247–261.

————. "Toward a Case Study of the Overseas Educator: The Mystery of William Griffis in Early Meiji Japan." *History of Education Quarterly* 20, no. 4 (Winter 1980): 487–492.

Tsurumi, Shunsuke. *An Intellectual History of Wartime Japan, 1931–1945.* London: KPI Limited, 1986.

Twine, Nanette. "Toward Simplicity: Script Reform Movements in the Meiji Period." *Monumenta Nipponica* 38, no.2 (Summer 1983): 116–132.

Umakoshi Toru. "The Role of Education in Preserving the Ethnic Identity of Korea Residents." In *Windows on Japanese Education,* 281–305, edited by Edward R. Beauchamp. New York: Greenwood Press, 1991.

"University and Society." Special issue of *Journal of Social and Political Ideas in Japan* 5, nos. 2–3 (December 1967).

Uno, Kathleen S. "Death of 'Good Wife, Wise Mother'?" In *Postwar Japan as History,* 293–322, edited by Andrew Gordon. Berkeley: University of California Press, 1993.

Upham, Frank K. *Law and Social Change in Postwar Japan.* Cambridge: Harvard University Press, 1987.

Usami Shō. "Zengakuren." *Japan Quarterly* 15, no. 2 (April–June, 1968).

U.S. Department of State. *Foreign Relations of the United States: Japan, 1931–1941.* 2 vols. Washington, DC: Department of State, 1943.

————. *Report of the United States Education Mission to Japan.* Tokyo: SCAP, 1946.

Verba, Sidney, Steven Kelman, Gary R. Orren, Ichiro Miyake, Joji Watanuki, Ikuo Kabashima, and G. Donald Ferree, Jr. *Elites and the Idea of Equality: A Comparison of Japan, Sweden, and the United States.* Cambridge: Harvard University Press, 1987.

Vogel, Ezra. *Japan as Number 1: Lessons for America.* New York: Harper, 1980.

Walthall, Anne. "The Life Cycle of Farm Women in Tokugawa Japan" In *Recreating Japanese Women, 1600–1945,* 42–70, edited by Gail Lee Bernstein. Berkeley: University of California Press, 1991.

Waseda Daigaku. *Hanseiki no Waseda* (A Half Century of Waseda). Tokyo: Waseda Daigaku Shuppanbu, 1932.

Waseda Daigaku Daigakushi Shiryō Shitsu, ed. *Waseda Daigaku 80 nenshi* (A History of Waseda University Over Eighty Years). Tokyo: Waseda Daigaku, 1962.

Waswo, Ann. *Japanese Landlords: The Decline of a Rural Elite.* Berkeley: University of California Press, 1977.

Watanabe, Shinichi, compiler. *A Select List of Books on the History of Education in Japan and a Select List of Periodicals on Education.* Ann Arbor: University of Michigan, The Asia Library, 1976.

Waters, Neil L. *Japan's Local Pragmatists: The Transition from Bakumatsu in the Kawasaki Region.* Cambridge: Council on East Asian Studies, Harvard University, 1983.

———. "Local Leadership in the Kawasaki Region from Bakumatsu to Meiji." *Journal of Japanese Studies* 7, no. 1 (Winter 1981): 53–83.

———. "The Second Transition: Early to Mid-Meiji in Kanagawa Prefecture." *Journal of Asian Studies* 49, no. 2 (May 1990): 305–322.

Webb, Herschel. *The Japanese Imperial Institution in the Tokugawa Period.* New York: Columbia University Press, 1968.

Wetherall, William. "Ethnic Ainu Seek Official Recognition." *Japan Times Weekly International Edition,* January 25–31, 1993: 1, 10–11.

Wheeler, Donald F. "Japan's Postmodern Student Movement." In *Changes in the Japanese University: A Comparative Perspective,* 202–216, edited by William K. Cummings et al. New York: Praeger, 1979.

White, James. "State Growth and Popular Protest in Tokugawa Japan." *Journal of Japanese Studies* 14, no. 1 (Winter 1988): 1–25.

White, Merry. *The Japanese Educational Challenge: A Commitment to Children.* New York: Free Press, 1987.

Wilson, George M. *Crisis Politics in Prewar Japan: Institutional and Ideological Problems of the 1930s.* Tokyo: Sophia University Press, 1970.

———. *Radical Nationalist in Japan: Kita Ikki, 1883–1937.* Cambridge: Harvard University Press, 1969.

———. "Ultranationalism." In *Kodansha Encyclopedia of Japan,* vol. 8: 144–146. Tokyo and New York: Kodansha, 1983.

Wolferen, Karel van. *The Enigma of Japanese Power: People and Politics in a Stateless Nation.* New York: Alfred A. Knopf, 1989.

Wray, Harry. "A Study in Contrasts: Japanese School Textbooks of 1903 and 1941–1945." *Monumenta Nipponica* 28, no. 1 (Spring 1973): 69–86.

Wray, William D. *Mitsubishi and the N.Y.K., 1870–1914: Business Strategy in the Japanese Shipping Industry.* Cambridge: Harvard University Press, 1984.

Yabe Teiji. *Yabe Teiji nikki* (The Diary of Yabe Teiji). Tokyo: Yomiuru Shinbun, 1974.

Yamamoto Nobuyoshi and Konno Toshihiko. *Kindai kyōiku no tennōsei ideorogi* (Emperor-ism Ideology in Modern Education). Tokyo: Shinsensha, 1973.

Yamazaki Takako. "Tsuda Ume." In *Ten Great Educators of Modern Japan: A Japanese Perspective,* 125–148, edited by Benjamin Duke. Tokyo: University of Tokyo Press, 1989.

Yamazumi, Masami. "Educational Democracy Versus State Control." In *Democracy in Contemporary Japan,* 90–113, edited by Gavan McCormack and Yoshio Sugimoto. Armonk, NY: M. E. Sharpe, 1986.

Yanaga, Chitoshi. *Big Business in Japanese Politics.* New Haven: Yale University Press, 1968.

Yanaihara Tadao. *Watakushi no ayunde kita michi* (The Road by Which I Have Come). Tokyo: Tōkyō Daigaku Shuppankai, 1958.

Yayama Tarō. "The Newspapers Conduct a Mad Rhapsody over the Textbook Issue."
    Journal of Asian Studies 9, no. 2 (Summer 1983): 297–318.
Yoshino, I. Roger, and Murakoshi Sueo. "Burakumin." *Kodansha Encyclopedia of Japan*,
    vol. 1: 216–217. Tokyo and New York: Kodansha, 1983.
————. *The Invisible Visible Minority—Japan's Burakumin*. Osaka: Buraku Kaiho
    Kenkyusho, 1977.
Yoshino Kosaku. *Cultural Nationalism in Contemporary Japan: A Sociological Inquiry*.
    New York: Routledge, 1992.

About the Book and Author

In the increasingly global economy, commentators often cite education as a key source of competitive advantage for nations locked in economic contention on the world stage. Byron Marshall examines the evolution of Japanese schools over the past 120 years. Emphasizing the political discourse and conflict that have surrounded Japanese education, the author focuses on the three main issues of central versus local control, elitism versus equality, and nationalism versus universalism. The prewar education system in Japan was formulated in the 1870s and modeled after the Western system of public education. After World War II, the American Occupation authorities attempted to reform this system further, but how much discontinuity with the past was produced by the postwar reforms is still an open question.

Of course, the dilemmas facing Japanese schools are endemic to all modern school systems, and Marshall's broad historical survey provides a valuable case study of Japanese attempts to strike a balance between equality and excellence, individual creativity and team cooperation, standardization and innovation, and internationalism and cultural identity. The book thus provides a valuable historical perspective on contemporary American issues of "political correctness" such as gender and ethnicity.

As we head toward the "Pacific Century," this book gives readers the background and insight necessary to make informed judgments about the relative strength of Japanese education and the merits of school reforms.

Byron K. Marshall is professor of history at the University of Minnesota. He is the author of several books and articles on Japan and Asia, including *Academic Freedom and the Japanese Imperial University*.

Index